REFUGEES FROM ARMED CONFLICT

REFUGEES FROM ARMED CONFLICT

The 1951 Refugee Convention and International Humanitarian Law

Vanessa Holzer

intersentia
Cambridge – Antwerp – Portland

Intersentia Ltd
Sheraton House | Castle Park
Cambridge | CB3 0AX | United Kingdom
Tel.: +44 1223 370 170 | Email: mail@intersentia.co.uk

Distribution for the UK:
NBN International
Airport Business Centre, 10 Thornbury Road
Plymouth, PL6 7 PP
United Kingdom
Tel.: +44 1752 202 301 | Fax: +44 1752 202 331
Email: orders@nbninternational.com

Distribution for the USA and Canada:
International Specialized Book Services
920 NE 58th Ave. Suite 300
Portland, OR 97213
USA
Tel.: +1 800 944 6190 (toll free)
Email: info@isbs.com

Distribution for Austria:
Neuer Wissenschaftlicher Verlag
Argentinierstraße 42/6
1040 Wien
Austria
Tel.: +43 1 535 61 03 24
Email: office@nwv.at

Distribution for other countries:
Intersentia Publishing nv
Groenstraat 31
2640 Mortsel
Belgium
Tel.: +32 3 680 15 50
Email: mail@intersentia.be

Refugees from Armed Conflict. The 1951 Refugee Convention and International Humanitarian Law
Vanessa Holzer

ISBN 978-1-83970-234-1
D/2015/7849/100
NUR 828

GPRC
Guaranteed
Peer Reviewed
Content

British Library Cataloguing in Publication Data. A catalogue record for this book is available from the British Library.

To my mother Hildegard

ACKNOWLEDGEMENTS

This book is based on my doctoral thesis which was accepted by the Law Faculty of Goethe University in Frankfurt in 2014. I am very grateful to my supervisor Professor Dr Dr Rainer Hofmann for his support. I also wish to thank Professor Dr Stefan Kadelbach for acting as my examiner.

This book would not have been possible without the support from a number of people. While in Heidelberg I learned a great deal from Professor Dr Ulrich Beyerlin, and Dr Christine Fuchs provided encouragement. When conducting a study for UNHCR, Dr Alice Edwards, Dr Cornelis Wouters and many others lent assistance. Dr Nina Burri, Dr Anthony Cullen, Dr Sarah Nouwen and Dr Ruvi Ziegler offered helpful comments on draft chapters. Michael Meyer OBE provided invaluable support and inspiration during my time at the British Red Cross. The German National Academic Foundation funded my doctoral research. I am grateful to them all. Any errors are of course my own.

Last but not least I thank my husband Wes for being there for me during each and every step of this journey. I am grateful to my mother Hildegard for her support and encouragement. This book is dedicated to her.

CONTENTS

ABBREVIATIONS

AIT	Asylum and Immigration Tribunal
BGBl.	*Bundesgesetzblatt* (Federal Law Gazette)
BVerwG	*Bundesverwaltungsgericht* (Federal Administrative Court)
BIA	Board of Immigration Appeals
CAT	Convention against Torture and Other Cruel, Inhuman or Degrading Treatment or Punishment
CLR	Commonwealth Law Reports
CNDA	*Cour nationale du droit d'asille* (National Asylum Court)
CRC	Convention on the Rights of the Child
DRC	Democratic Republic of the Congo
CanLII	Canadian Legal Information Institute
CEDAW	Convention on the Elimination of All Forms of Discrimination against Women
CERD	Convention on the Elimination of All Forms of Racial Discrimination
Cir.	Circuit
ECHR	European Convention for the Protection of Human Rights and Fundamental Freedoms
ECOSOC	United Nations Economic and Social Council
e.g.	*exempli gratia*
ER	English Reports
EU	European Union
ELN	*Ejército de Liberación Nacional* (National Liberation Army)
EWCA	England and Wales Court of Appeal
EXCOM	Executive Committee
FARC	*Fuerzas Armadas Revolucionarias de Colombia* (Revolutionary Armed Forces of Colombia)
FC	Federal Court
FCA	Federal Court of Appeal
ICC	International Criminal Court
ICESCR	International Covenant on Economic, Social and Cultural Rights
ICCPR	International Covenant on Civil and Political Rights
ICJ	International Court of Justice
ICRC	International Committee of the Red Cross

ICTR	International Criminal Tribunal for Rwanda
ICTY	International Criminal Tribunal for the former Yugoslavia
IFOR	Implementation Force
IHL	international humanitarian law
Imm AR	Immigration Appeal Reports
INLR	Immigration and Nationality Law Reports
INS	Immigration and Naturalization Service
IPA	internal protection alternative
IRB	Immigration and Refugee Board
i.e.	*id est*
LNTS	League of Nations Treaty Series
LTTE	Liberation Tigers of Tamil Eelam
mn	margin number
NVwZ	*Neue Zeitschrift für Verwaltungsrecht* (New Journal for Administrative Law)
NZRSAA	New Zealand Refugee Status Appeals Authority
MIMA	Minister for Immigration and Multicultural Affairs
OJ	Official Journal
para.	paragraph
QB	Queen's Bench
RRTA	Refugee Review Tribunal of Australia
SCR	Supreme Court Reports
SSHD	Secretary of State for the Home Department
UDHR	Universal Declaration of Human Rights
UK	United Kingdom of Great Britain and Northern Ireland
UKAIT	United Kingdom Asylum and Immigration Tribunal
UKHL	United Kingdom House of Lords
US	United States of America
UN	United Nations
UNTS	United Nations Treaty Series
UNHCR	Office of the United Nations High Commissioner for Refugees
VCLT	Vienna Convention on the Law of Treaties
VG	*Verwaltungsgericht* (Administrative Court)
VGH	*Verwaltungsgerichtshof* (Higher Administrative Court)
WL	Westlaw Transcripts
WLR	Weekly Law Reports

CHAPTER 1
INTRODUCTION

1. OVERVIEW OF THE TOPIC

Hailed as the "*magna charta* of refugees"[1] and the "foundation of the international refugee protection regime",[2] the 1951 Convention relating to the Status of Refugees (Refugee Convention),[3] together with its 1967 Protocol relating to the Status of Refugees (Protocol),[4] is the key international instrument for the protection of refugees. International refugee protection today faces challenges, including forced displacement caused by armed conflicts, as the UN High Commissioner for Refugees noted: "Wars are driving more and more people to seek asylum … [T]his makes upholding the international system of asylum more critical than ever."[5] Since 1945, the world has seen numerous, mostly non-international armed conflicts.[6] In 2013, there were 33 active armed conflicts worldwide, while 32 armed conflicts persisted in 2012.[7] The number

1 Andreas Zimmermann, "Preface", in *The 1951 Convention relating to the Status of Refugees and its 1967 Protocol*, edited by Andreas Zimmermann (editor), Jonas Dörschner, and Felix Machts (assistant editors) (Oxford: Oxford University Press, 2011), p. v.

2 Ministerial Communiqué adopted at the intergovernmental event at the ministerial level of United Nations (UN) Member States on the occasion of the 60th anniversary of the Refugee Convention, UN Doc. HCR/MINCOMMS/2001/6, 8 December 2011, para. 2.

3 189 UNTS 137, adopted 25 July 1951, entered into force 22 April 1954.

4 606 UNTS 267, adopted 16 December 1966, entered into force 4 October 1967. Throughout this book, references to the Refugee Convention relate to the Refugee Convention as altered by its Protocol. By implication, they also refer to the Protocol with respect to those States who ratified this Protocol but not the Refugee Convention.

5 The UN High Commissioner for Refugees is quoted in: UNHCR, "Syria Conflict Contributing to Rising Asylum Claims in Industrialized Countries" (2013), available at www.unhcr.org/5149c6f46.html, accessed 10.03.2015.

6 See Lotta Harbom and Peter Wallensteen, "Armed Conflicts, 1946–2009", *Journal of Peace Research* 47, no. 4 (2010): 501–509, 503.

7 These numbers were recorded by the Uppsala Conflict Data Program, which defines armed conflict as "a contested incompatibility that concerns government or territory or both, where the use of armed force between two parties results in at least 25 battle-related deaths in a year. Of these two parties, at least one has to be the government of a State". See Lotta Themnér and Peter Wallensteen, "Armed Conflicts, 1946–2012", *Journal of Peace Research* 50, no. 4 (2013): 509–521, 509 and 520 and Lotta Themnér and Peter Wallensteen, "Armed Conflicts, 1946–2013", *Journal of Peace Research* 51, no. 4 (2014): 541–554.

of forcefully displaced people has grown in recent years, with armed conflicts constituting a major cause.[8]

Since 2000, Afghanistan, Colombia, the Democratic Republic of Congo (DRC), Iraq, Somalia, Sri Lanka, and Syria – countries which have experienced armed conflict[9] – have been amongst the main countries of origin of asylum-seekers in industrialised States.[10]

While forced displacement is often a side-effect of armed conflict, it can also be prompted by systematic human rights abuses and by violations of international humanitarian law (IHL).[11] The 31st International Conference of the Red Cross and Red Crescent emphasised that:

---

8 See UNHCR, "Syria Conflict". Similarly: UNHCR, "Number of Forcibly Displaced Rises to 43.3 Million Last Year, The Highest Level Since Mid-1990s" (2010), available at www.unhcr.org/4c176c969.html, accessed 10.03.2015. Many people displaced by armed conflict remain within their countries of origin or flee to neighbouring (developing) countries. Thus, only a relatively small portion of those displaced by armed conflict seeks refugee protection in industrialised countries. See UNHCR, "Global Report 2012" (2012), available at www.unhcr.org/gr12/index.xml, accessed 10.03.2015, 84; Internal Displacement Monitoring Centre, "Global Overview 2011. People Internally Displaced by Conflict and Violence" (2012), available at www.unhcr.org/50f95f7a9.html, accessed 10.03.2015, 8.

9 The ICRC stated publicly that there have been armed conflicts in these countries. Regarding Afghanistan, Colombia, the DRC, Somalia, and Sri Lanka (noting that these armed conflicts have been going on for decades and that the armed conflict in Sri Lanka ended), see ICRC, "International Humanitarian Law and the Challenges of Contemporary Armed Conflicts", *31st International Conference of the Red Cross and Red Crescent, Geneva, 28 November – 1 December 2011* (2011), available at www.icrc.org/eng/assets/files/red-cross-crescent-movement/31st-international-conference/31-int-conference-ihl-challenges-report-11-5-1-2-en.pdf, accessed 10.03.2015, 6. Regarding Iraq, see ICRC, "Annual Report" (2011), available at www.icrc.org/eng/resources/documents/annual-report/icrc-annual-report-2011.htm, accessed 10.03.2015, 382. On Syria, see ICRC, "Syria: ICRC and Syrian Arab Crescent Maintain Aid Effort Amid Increased Fighting" (2012), available at www.icrc.org/eng/resources/documents/update/2012/syria-update-2012–07–17.htm, accessed 10.03.2015.

10 See UNHCR, "Asylum Trends, First half of 2014. Levels and Trends in Industrialized Countries", available at www.unhcr.org/5423f9699.html, accessed 10.03.2015, 13; UNHCR; "Asylum Trends 2013. Levels and Trends in Industrialized Countries" (2014), available at www.unhcr.org/5329b15a9.html, accessed 10.03.2015, 17; UNHCR, "Asylum Levels and Trends in Industrialized Countries" (2010), available at www.unhcr.org/4d8c5b109.html, accessed 10.03.2015, 13; UNHCR, "Trends in Asylum Applications Lodged in Europe, North-America, Australia and New Zealand, 2001: Updated Tables" (2002), available at www.unhcr.org/3c887b9d4.html, accessed 10.03.2015.

11 See Mélanie Jaques, *Armed Conflict and Displacement. The Protection of Refugees and Displaced Persons under International Humanitarian Law* (Cambridge: Cambridge University Press, 2012), 19. Similarly: Ryszard Piotrowicz, "Displacement and Displaced Persons", in *Perspectives on the ICRC Study on Customary International Humanitarian Law*, edited by Elizabeth Wilmshurst and Susan Breau (Cambridge: Cambridge University Press, 2007), 337. People flee from the indirect effects of armed conflict such as poverty or famine and the direct effects such as bodily harm. See Theo Farrell and Olivier Schmitt, "The Causes, Character and Conduct of Armed Conflict, and the Effects of on Civilian Populations, 1990–2010" (2012), available at www.unhcr.org/4f8d606d9.html, accessed 10.03.2015, 12.

> "armed conflicts continue to cause enormous suffering, including violations of IHL, such as murder, forced disappearance, the taking of hostages, torture, cruel or inhumane treatment, rape and other forms of sexual violence."[12]

Civilians frequently bear the brunt of hostilities in today's armed conflicts.[13] In contravention of IHL, the civilian population is often directly targeted.[14] Recent armed conflicts have seen civilians forced to flee because of *inter alia* mass killings, sexual violence and mutilations,[15] and thus due to IHL violations. Regarding Somalia, for example, UNHCR noted that the armed conflict in the country has been a major cause of forced displacement and has been characterised by consistent failure of the parties to the conflict to respect fundamental principles of IHL.[16] Armed conflicts today have numerous, often inter-related causes. Some are economic in nature, such as control over national resources,[17] while others concern identity politics, i.e. claims for power based on a certain ethnic, religious or other identity.[18]

---

12 International Conference of the Red Cross and Red Crescent, "Resolution 1. Strengthening Legal Protection for Victims of Armed Conflict" (2011), available at www.icrc.org/eng/resources/documents/resolution/31-international-conference-resolution-1–2011.htm, accessed 10.03.2015, first preambular recital.

13 See ICRC, "International Humanitarian Law and the Challenges of Contemporary Armed Conflict", *30th International Conference of the Red Cross and Red Crescent, Geneva, 26–30 November 2007* (2007), available at www.icrc.org/eng/assets/files/other/ihl-challenges-30th-international-conference-eng.pdf, accessed 10.03.2015, 3.

14 See ICRC, "International Humanitarian Law", 3; Monika Heupel and Bernhard Zangl, "Von 'alten' und 'neuen' Kriegen – Zum Gegenstand kriegerischer Gewalt", *Politische Vierteljahresschrift* 45, no. 3 (2004): 346–369, 354; UN Secretary-General, *Report of the Secretary-General on the Protection of Civilians in Armed Conflict,* UN Doc. S/2009/277 (29 May 2009), paras. 6 and 9; UN Secretary-General, *Report of the Secretary-General on the Protection of Civilians in Armed Conflict,* UN Doc. S/2005/740 (28 November 2005), para. 3; UN Secretary-General, *Report of the Secretary-General on the Protection of Civilians in Armed Conflict,* UN Doc. S/1999/957 (8 September 1999), paras. 2 and 8.

15 See Mary Kaldor, *New & Old Wars*, 2nd ed. (Cambridge: Polity Press, 2006), 9; UN Secretary-General, *Report of the Secretary-General on the Protection of Civilians in Armed Conflict (2005)*, para. 4; UN Secretary-General, *Report on the Protection of Civilians in Armed Conflict (1999)*, para. 12.

16 See UNHCR, "Eligibility Guidelines for Assessing the International Protection Needs of Asylum-Seekers from Somalia" (2010), available at www.refworld.org/docid/4be3b9142.html, accessed 10.03.2015, 2.

17 As argued by, e.g., David Keen, *The Economic Functions of Violence in Civil Wars* (Oxford: Oxford University Press, 1998).

18 As contended by, e.g., Kaldor, *New & Old Wars*, 7. Farrell and Schmitt provide an overview of the two main schools of thought, known as the "greed v. grievance debate", on the causes of armed conflict. While one school of thought concentrates on the political economy of armed conflict, the other stresses the role of ethnic and religious identity. See Farrell and Schmitt, "The Causes, Character and Conduct of Armed Conflict, and the Effects of on Civilian Populations, 1990–2010", 3–5. Markard comprehensively analyses the debate about "old wars" and "new wars": Nora Markard, *Kriegsflüchtlinge. Gewalt gegen Zivilpersonen in bewaffneten Konflikten als Herausforderung für das Flüchtlingsrecht und den subsidiären Schutz* (Tübingen: Mohr Siebeck, 2012), 57–89.

The mere fact of having fled from an armed conflict does not in and of itself suffice to fulfil the criteria for refugee status under the Refugee Convention. Article 1A(2) Refugee Convention defines a refugee as a person who:

> "owing to well-founded fear of being persecuted for reasons of race, religion, nationality, membership of a particular social group or political opinion, is outside the country of his nationality, and is unable, or owing to such fear, is unwilling to avail himself of the protection of that country; or who, not having a nationality and being outside the country of his former habitual residence as a result of such events, is unable or, owing to such fear, is unwilling to return to it."[19]

Individuals who fled from an armed conflict in their country of origin may have a well-founded fear of being persecuted for a Refugee Convention ground, as UNHCR's Executive Committee (EXCOM) acknowledged:

> "Persons displaced by war or conflict can legitimately fear persecution. War may well be the very instrument of persecution, the method chosen by the persecutors – whether part of the State apparatus or not – to repress or eliminate entire groups of people because of their ethnicity or other affiliations."[20]

A number of States parties to the Refugee Convention or its Protocol have expressly accepted that people fleeing armed conflict may qualify as refugees under the Refugee Convention.[21] In addition, some States which in the past considered that situations of armed conflict and other situations of violence did not at all or only exceptionally give rise to legitimate claims to refugee protection

---

19 Article 1A(2) Refugee Convention continues: "In the case of a person who has more than one nationality, the term 'the country of his nationality' shall mean each of the countries of which he is a national, and a person shall not be deemed to be lacking the protection of the country of his nationality if, without any valid reason based on well-founded fear, he has not availed himself of the protection of one of the countries of which he is a national." Article 1A(2) Refugee Convention is hereafter referred to as "refugee definition".

20 UNHCR Executive Committee, *Conclusion No. 85 (XLIX)* (1998), para. 4.

21 See, e.g., Immigration and Refugee Board of Canada, "Civilian Non-Combatants Fearing Persecution in Civil War Situations. Guidelines Issued by the Chairperson Pursuant to Section s65(3) of the Immigration Act" (1996), available at www.irb-cisr.gc.ca/Eng/BoaCom/references/pol/GuiDir/Pages/GuideDir01.aspx, accessed 10.03.2015 (Canada); UK Border Agency, *Considering the Protection (Asylum) Claim and Assessing Credibility* (2011), 25 (UK); *Minister for Immigration and Multicultural Affairs v. Haji Ibrahim* [2000] HCA 55, para. 141 per Gummow J (Australia); BVerwG 1 C 21.04 (1 November 2005), para. 24 (Germany); *Refugee Appeal No. 76551* [2010] NZRSAA 103 (21 September 2010), para. 66 (New Zealand); *Mohamed v. Ashcroft*, 396 F.3d 999, 1006 (8th Cir. 2005) (US); Federal Department of Foreign Affairs, "Protecting the Civilian Population in Armed Conflict" (2011), available at www.eda.admin.ch/eda/en/home/topics/human/hum/proci.html, accessed 10.03.2015 (Switzerland). See also Vanessa Holzer, "The 1951 Refugee Convention and the Protection of People Fleeing Armed Conflict and Other Situations of Violence", Legal and Protection Policy Research Series (2012), available at www.unhcr.org/refworld/docid/50474f062.html, accessed 10.03.2015; Markard, *Kriegsflüchtlinge*, 125–302.

under the Refugee Convention have recently adopted more inclusive approaches. For example, past jurisprudence in France, Canada and the United States of America (US) exhibited a more restrictive approach to refugee claimants fleeing armed conflict than more current jurisprudence.[22]

UNHCR's position on protecting people fleeing armed conflict under the Refugee Convention has also developed towards a more inclusive understanding. UNHCR's Handbook on Procedures and Criteria for Determining Refugee Status under the 1951 Convention and the 1967 Protocol relating to the Status of Refugees (UNHCR Handbook) states:

> "Persons compelled to leave their country of origin as a result of international or national armed conflicts are *not normally* considered refugees under the 1951 [Refugee] Convention or Protocol."[23]

This statement could indicate that UNHCR only considers people fleeing from armed conflict as refugees in exceptional circumstances.[24] Yet, as UNHCR subsequently made clear, it considers that persons fleeing armed conflict may have a well-founded fear of persecution for a Refugee Convention ground.[25]

---

22 The French *Conseil d'État* (Council of State) held an armed conflict may prompt a well-founded fear of persecution in the sense of the Refugee Convention (*Conseil d'État, no. 154321, Mlle STRBO*, 12 May 1997 (France)). In 2009, the Council of State held that as soon as a persecution ground exists and the other conditions for qualifying for refugee status are fulfilled, refugee protection must be granted rather than subsidiary protection, including in a context of generalised violence. *Conseil d'État, no. 292564, Mlle K*, 15 May 2009 (France). This decision ended previous jurisprudence by the *Commission des recours des réfugiés* (Refugee Appeals Board), which had held the dangers resulting from conflict do not constitute a risk of persecution in the sense of the refugee definition (*Commission des recours des réfugiés, Zein El Abiddine*, 13 June 1985 (France); *Taha*, 30 October 1989 (France)). See Vanessa Holzer, "The 1951 Refugee Convention". On the US and Canada, see Markard, *Kriegsflüchtlinge*, 130 referring to *Salibian v. Canada (Minister of Employment and Immigration)* 1990 3 FC 250, 258 (Canada) and *Zavala Bonilla v. INS*, 730 F.2d 562 (9th Cir. 1984) (US). Both judgments ended the previously more restrictive approaches that required particularised evidence (Canada) or being singled out for persecution (US). With *In re H-*, 21 I. & N. Dec. 337, Interim Decision 3276, 1996 WL 291910 (Board of Immigration Appeals, BIA), the jurisprudence in the US began to reject the view that persons having fled from clan warfare or civil strife cannot qualify as refugees under the Protocol (noted by Mark R. von Sternberg, *The Grounds of Refugee Protection in the Context of International Human Rights and Humanitarian Law. Canadian and United States Case Law Compared* (The Hague/London/New York: Martinus Nijhoff, 2002), 107.

23 UNHCR, *Handbook on Procedures and Criteria for Determining Refugee Status under the 1951 Convention and the 1967 Protocol relating to the Status of Refugees*, UN Doc. HCR/IP/4/Eng/REV.1 (1992), paras. 164–165 (emphasis added).

24 Storey and Wallace call this approach the "exceptionality approach": Hugo Storey and Rebecca Wallace, "War and Peace in Refugee Law Jurisprudence", *American Journal of International Law* 95 (2001): 349–366, 350.

25 See UNHCR, *Note on International Protection*, UN Doc. A/AC.96/850 (1 September 1995), para. 11.

However, the interpretation and application of the refugee definition with regard to claims to refugee status based on situations of armed conflict in the country of origin have long been marred with difficulties. Decision-makers have often understood the existence of an armed conflict in the country of origin as precluding the possibility of persecution.[26] The general tenet has frequently been that victims of armed conflict are not normally refugees in the sense of Article 1A(2) Refugee Convention because they fled from generalised or indiscriminate violence without being targeted for a Refugee Convention ground.[27] An expert meeting convened by UNHCR and the International Criminal Tribunal for Rwanda (ICTR) concluded in 2011:

> "It is ... often wrongly assumed that 'war refugees' or those fleeing armed conflict fall outside the scope of the 1951 [Refugee] Convention. In fact, many modern conflicts are characterized by targeted violence against particular ethnic, racial or religious groups."[28]

Contexts of armed conflict have in some States given rise to more restrictive interpretations of the refugee definition than adopted in peacetime situations,[29]

26 See Joachim Henkel, "Who Is a Refugee? Refugees from Civil War and Other Internal Armed Conflicts" (paper presented at the First International Judicial Conference, Inner Temple, London, 1–2 December 1995), 18; Guy S. Goodwin-Gill and Jane McAdam, *The Refugee in International Law*, 3rd ed. (Oxford: Oxford University Press, 2007), 128. UNHCR's Director of International Protection noted: "Although the majority of persons of concern to UNHCR are fleeing violence and conflict, they are not always recognized as refugees under the 1951 [Refugee] Convention." Volker Türk, "Introductory Statement at the 54th Meeting of the Standing Committee of the Executive Committee of the High Commissioner's Programme" (2012), available at www.unhcr.org/4fedc0609.html, accessed 10.03.2015. Binder states that while refugee claimants from communist States were recognised as refugees in the US almost automatically, recognition rates for people fleeing from the civil wars in Guatemala and El Salvador were relatively low. See Andrea Binder, *Frauenspezifische Verfolgung vor dem Hintergrund einer menschenrechtlichen Auslegung des Flüchtlingsbegriffs unter besonderer Berücksichtigung der schweizerischen, deutschen, kanadischen und amerikanischen Flüchtlings- und Asylpraxis* (Basel et al.: Helbing & Lichtenhahn, 2001), 885.

27 As noted by Cornelis Wouters, "Protecting People fleeing Conflict and Generalized Violence. UNHCR's Perspective" (paper presented at the Joint Council of Europe/UNHCR Colloquium of Regional Human Rights Courts in Interpreting and Enforcing Legal Standards for the Protection of Forcibly Displaced Persons, Strasbourg, 15–16 June 2011), 1 (on file with author); Henkel, "Who Is a Refugee? Refugees from Civil War and Other Internal Armed Conflicts", 17–18; Binder, *Frauenspezifische Verfolgung*, 169–179.

28 Expert Meeting on Complementarities between International Refugee Law, International Criminal Law and International Human Rights Law, Arusha, 11–13 April 2011, "Summary Conclusions" (2011), available at www.refworld.org/docid/4e1729d52.html, accessed 10.03.2015, para. 25.

29 The judgment of the UK House of Lords in *Adan* epitomises such a restrictive approach: See e.g. *Adan v. Secretary of State for the Home Department* [1998] 2 WLR 702, per Lord Slynn of Hadley (UK). Similarly: *Mohamed v. Ashcroft*, 396 F.3d 999, 1006 (8th Cir. 2005) (US). Kälin contrasts restrictive and liberal interpretative approaches to the refugee definition in contexts of civil war: Walter Kälin, "Refugees and Civil Wars: Only a Matter of Interpretation?", *International Journal of Refugee Law* 3, no. 3 (1991): 435–451.

though decision-makers in other States have rejected such restrictive approaches.[30] This problem has recently received increasing attention from UNHCR[31] and researchers,[32] with Nora Markard providing the first in-depth analysis of the protection of "war refugees" under the Refugee Convention.[33]

The refugee definition must be interpreted with reference to objective standards rather than by way of subjective assessment.[34] For reasons of

30 See *Minister for Immigration and Multicultural Affairs v. Haji Ibrahim* [2000] HCA 55, para. 70 per McHugh J and para. 147 per Gummow J (Australia); *Minister for Immigration and Multicultural Affairs v. Abdi* (1999) 162 ALR 105 (FC:FC), para. 66 per O'Connor, Tamberlin & Mansfield JJ (Australia); *Refugee Appeal No. 71462* [1999] NZRSAA (27 September 1999), para. 77 (New Zealand); *Refugee Appeal No 76551* [2010] NZRSAA 103 (21 September 2010) (New Zealand). For a brief jurisprudence survey, see Eric Fripp, "Inclusion of Refugees from Armed Conflict. Combatants and Ex-combatants", in *Refuge from Inhumanity? War Refugees and International Humanitarian Law*, edited by David James Cantor and Jean-François Durieux (Leiden: Koninklijke Brill, 2014), 137–140. Türk and Dowd also note that States' application of the Refugee Convention to persons fleeing armed conflict and generalised violence differ considerably: Volker Türk and Rebecca Dowd, "Protection Gaps", in *The Oxford Handbook of Refugee and Forced Migration Studies*, edited by Elena Fiddian-Qasmiyeh, Gil Loescher, Katy Long and Nando Sigona (2014), 250. See also Vincent Chetail, "Armed Conflict and Forced Migration. A Systematic Approach to International Humanitarian Law, Refugee Law, and International Human Rights Law", in *The Oxford Handbook of International Law in Armed Conflict*, edited by Andrew Clapham, Paola Gaeta (editors), Tom Haeck and Alice Pritty (assistant editors) (Oxford: Oxford University Press, 2014), 723–724.

31 UNHCR convened two expert roundtables on this topic. See the aforementioned Expert Meeting on Complementarities between International Refugee Law, International Criminal Law and International Refugee Law, "Arusha Summary Conclusions" and Cape Town Roundtable on International Protection of Persons Fleeing Armed Conflict and Other Situations of Violence, 13–14 September 2012, "Summary Conclusions" (2012), available at www.refworld.org/docid/50d32e5e2.html, accessed 10.03.2015. UNHCR is also developing guidelines on international protection that focus on refugee claims arising out situations of conflict and violence. See Türk, "Introductory Statement".

32 See, e.g., Michael Kagan and William P. Johnson, "Persecution in the Fog of War: The House of Lords' Decision in Adan", *Michigan Journal of International Law* 23 (2001–2002): 247–264; Ulrike Brandl, "Die Anwendbarkeit des Flüchtlingsbegriffs der Genfer Flüchtlingskonvention auf Bürgerkriegsflüchtlinge", in *Temporary Protection für Flüchtlinge in Europa. Analysen und Schlussfolgerungen*, edited by Hannes Tretter (Vienna: Verlag Österreich, 2005); Hugo Storey, "Armed Conflict in Asylum Law: The 'War-Flaw'", *Refugee Survey Quarterly* 31, no. 2 (2012): 1–32; Jean-Francois Durieux, "Of War, Flows, Laws and Flaws: A Reply to Hugo Storey", *Refugee Survey Quarterly* 31, no. 3 (2012): 161–176; David James Cantor and Jean-François Durieux (editors), *Refuge from Inhumanity? War Refugees and International Humanitarian Law* (Leiden: Koninklijke Brill, 2014).

33 See Markard, *Kriegsflüchtlinge*.

34 See Elihu Lauterpacht and Daniel Bethlehem, "The Scope and Content of the Principle of *Non-Refoulement*: Opinion", in *Refugee Protection in International Law. UNHCR's Global Consultations on International Protection*, edited by Erika Feller, Volker Türk, and Francis Nicholson (Cambridge: Cambridge University Press, 2001), 38; Storey, "Armed Conflict in Asylum Law", 2; Michelle Foster, *International Refugee Law and Socio-Economic Rights. Refuge from Deprivation* (Cambridge: Cambridge University Press, 2007), 36–37, Hugo Storey, "The 'War Flaw' and Why it Matters", in *Refuge from Inhumanity? War Refugees and International Humanitarian Law*, edited by David James Cantor and Jean-François Durieux (Leiden: Koninklijke Brill, 2014), 41.

transparency and fairness, its interpretation should be as consistent and uniform as possible within and across jurisdictions. This ensures that refugee claimants receive the same level of protection irrespective of where they lodge their claim.[35] However, some European States have seen stark variations in refugee recognition rates at first instance for Afghan, Somali and Iraqi claimants, suggesting significant divergences in the interpretation of the refugee definition in contexts of armed conflict.[36] International law provides objective standards for the interpretation of the refugee definition that can enhance the consistency of refugee status decision-making.[37] Drawing on other branches of international law in the interpretation of the refugee definition may also ensure that protection pursuant to the Refugee Convention does not fall short of universally agreed standards of protection. It is well established in times of peace that the refugee definition is to be interpreted in light of international human rights law. In times of armed conflict, the international legal framework for the protection of the individual includes not only international human rights law, but also IHL and international criminal law. UNHCR,[38] a few States parties to

---

35 See Foster, *International Refugee Law*, 36. Similarly: Storey, "The 'War Flaw' and Why it Matters", 41. UNHCR's acknowledgement of the need for consistency across jurisdictions is reflected in the UNHCR Handbook, Guidelines on International Protection, and Eligibility Guidelines. On the status of this Handbook in the interpretation of the refugee definition, see Chapter 4.

36 See UNHCR, "Safe at Last? Law and Practice in Selected EU Member States with Respect to Asylum-Seekers Fleeing Indiscriminate Violence" (2011), available at www.unhcr.org/refworld/docid/4e2ee0022.html, accessed 10.03.2015, 17. Similarly stark variations have been identified regarding Syrian refugee status applications: European Legal Network on Asylum, "Information Note on Syrian Asylum Seekers and Refugees in Europe" (2013), available at www.ecre.org/component/content/article/70-weekly-bulletin-articles/506-ecreelena-publishes-information-note-on-syrians-seeking-protection-in-europe.html, accessed 10.03.2015, 6.

37 Foster makes this argument with regard to international human rights law: Foster, *International Refugee Law*, 36. Jastram, however, notes that other factors also contribute to a lack of consistency in refugee status decision-making, including decentralised domestic refugee status determination systems, the lack of a single authoritative arbiter at the international level, and insufficient resources limiting training and professional development of decision-makers. See Kate Jastram, "Economic Harm as a Basis for Refugee Status and the Application of Human Rights Law to the Interpretation of Economic Persecution", in *Critical Issues in International Refugee Law. Strategies toward Interpretative Harmony*, edited by James C. Simeon (Cambridge: Cambridge University Press, 2010), 164. Further on discrepancies in asylum recognition rates: Jaya Ramji-Nogales, Andrew I. Schoenholtz, and Philip G. Schrag, *Refugee Roulette: Disparities in Asylum Adjudication and Proposals for Reform* (New York: New York University Press, 2009). On harmonising the interpretation of the refugee definition see also Brian Gorlick, "Common Burdens and Standards: Legal Elements in Assessing Claims to Refugee Status", *International Journal of Refugee Law* 15, no. 3 (2003): 357–376, 358.

38 As indicated by UNHCR's convening of expert roundtables on this topic. See Alice Edwards and Agnes Hurwitz, "Introductory Note to the Arusha Summary Conclusions on Complementarities between International Refugee Law, International Human Rights Law", *International Journal of Refugee Law* 23, no. 4 (2011): 856–85; Expert Meeting on Complementarities between International Refugee Law, International Criminal Law and International Refugee Law, "Arusha Summary Conclusions"; Roundtable on International

the Refugee Convention,[39] and a small number of refugee law experts[40] have begun to ponder the implications of this legal framework for the interpretation of the refugee definition in contexts of armed conflict without, however, offering a comprehensive analysis.

Therefore, this book examines the interpretation of the refugee definition regarding refugee protection claims of individuals who had to flee from their country of origin due to armed conflict in light of international human rights law, IHL and international criminal law. The book shows that customary IHL and international criminal law, though not providing comprehensive interpretative guidance, can complement the human rights-based interpretation of the refugee definition and strengthen protection under the Refugee Convention for individuals forcefully displaced by armed conflict, in particular as regards two elements of the refugee definition: the notion of persecution and the requirement that a refugee claimant's predicament be causally linked to a Refugee Convention ground.

2. STRUCTURE OF THE BOOK

2.1. RESEARCH QUESTIONS AND OBJECTIVES

This book investigates what role international human rights law, customary IHL and international criminal law should play in the interpretation of the refugee

Protection of Persons Fleeing Armed Conflict and Other Situations of Violence, "Cape Town Summary Conclusions".

39 Refugee status decision makers have drawn on IHL in interpreting the refugee definition in the US, the UK and Canada. See US Immigration and Naturalization Service, *The Basic Law Manual: U.S. Law and INS Refugee/Asylum Adjudications* 22 (1995) (US), cited by Sternberg, *The Grounds of Refugee Protection*, 37. See also *Montecino v. Immigration and Naturalization Service*, 915 F.2d 518 (9th Cir. 1990), 520 (US); *In re S-P-*, 21 I. & N. Dec. 486, Interim Decision 3287, 1996 WL 422990 (BIA), 493–494 (US); *AM & AM v. Secretary of State for the Home Department* (armed conflict: risk categories) Somalia CG [2008] UKAIT 00091, para. 76 (UK); Immigration and Refugee Board of Canada, "Civilian Non-Combatants Fearing Persecution in Civil War Situations".

40 Mark von Sternberg pioneered this analysis, focussing on the Refugee Convention grounds (race, religion, nationality, etc.): Sternberg, *The Grounds of Refugee Protection.* Strong advocates of a coalescence between the Refugee Convention and IHL are Storey, "Armed Conflict in Asylum Law; Storey and Wallace, "War and Peace" and Stéphane Jaquemet, "The Cross-Fertilization of International Humanitarian Law and International Refugee Law", *International Review of the Red Cross* 83, no. 843 (2001): 651–674. Acceptance of recourse to IHL in the interpretation of the refugee definition is indicated, though rather cursorily, by various scholars, e.g. Markard, *Kriegsflüchtlinge*, 158–172; Brandl, "Die Anwendbarkeit des Flüchtlingsbegriffs"; Binder, *Frauenspezifische Verfolgung.* More sceptical: Durieux, "Of War, Flows, Laws and Flaws"; Andreas Zimmermann and Claudia Mahler, "Article 1A, para. 2", in *The 1951 Convention relating to the Status of Refugees and its 1967 Protocol*, edited by Andreas Zimmermann (editor), Jonas Dörschner, and Felix Machts (assistant editors) (Oxford: Oxford University Press, 2011).

definition as regards claims to refugee protection of individuals who had to leave their country of origin due to armed conflict or who fear return to their country of origin because of armed conflict. In particular, the book seeks to calibrate the extent to and the way in which customary IHL and international criminal law should provide interpretative guidance regarding the meaning and scope of the refugee definition in a context of armed conflict. It focusses on customary IHL and draws on international criminal law where it clarifies matters pertaining to IHL that are relevant for the interpretation of the refugee definition. In so doing, the book endeavours to provide guidance for refugee status decision-makers as to the interpretation of the refugee definition in light of international human rights law, customary IHL and international criminal law with regard to refugee protection claims of individuals forced to flee from their country of origin due to armed conflict.

2.2. METHODOLOGY AND SOURCES

2.2.1. *General Observations*

This book is a legal analysis whose objective is to find the "international meaning"[41] of the refugee definition in Article 1A(2) Refugee Convention as regards refugee protection claims related to situations of armed conflict in the country of origin. The book therefore primarily draws on international sources, including judgments and advisory opinions of the International Court of Justice (ICJ), pronouncements of international human rights treaty monitoring bodies, the views of the International Committee of the Red Cross (ICRC), whose mandate includes the supervision and promotion of IHL,[42] and the views of

---

41 The Court of Appeal for England and Wales emphasised the "importance now placed … on the international meaning of the [Refugee] Convention": Court of Appeal for England and Wales (Civil Division), *R v. Secretary of State for the Home Department, ex parte Osungo*, Buxton LJ, 21 August 2000, unreported (UK), quoted pursuant to Foster, *International Refugee Law*, 29.

42 The mandate of the ICRC set out in the Statutes of the International Red Cross and Red Crescent Movement, as adopted by the 25th International Conference of the Red Cross in 1986 and as amended in 1995 and 2006, entails: "to work for the faithful application of international humanitarian law applicable in armed conflicts and to take cognizance of any complaints based on alleged breaches of that law" (Article 5(c) of these Statutes) and "to work for the understanding and dissemination of knowledge of international humanitarian law applicable in armed conflicts and to prepare any development thereof" (Article 5(g) of these Statutes). These Statutes are available at www.icrc.org/eng/assets/files/other/statutes-en-a5.pdf, accessed 10.03.2015. Further: Hans-Peter Gasser, "International Committee of the Red Cross (ICRC)", in *Max Planck Encyclopedia of Public International Law*, edited by Rüdiger Wolfrum (Oxford: Oxford University Press, 2009), available at www.mpepil.com, accessed 10.03.2015, para. 14; Rüdiger Wolfrum and Dieter Fleck, "Enforcement of International Humanitarian Law", in *The Handbook of International Humanitarian Law*, edited by Dieter Fleck (Oxford: Oxford University Press, 2008), mn. 1422, 713–715; François Bugnion,

UNHCR and its EXCOM, as well as international legal scholarship. With respect to international criminal law, the book concentrates on war crimes and the most recent and most comprehensive codification of war crimes in Article 8 of the Rome Statute of the International Criminal Court (ICC).[43] It draws on the ICC's jurisprudence. Since this jurisprudence is as yet incomplete, it also considers decisions and judgments of the International Criminal Tribunal for the Former Yugoslavia (ICTY) and the ICTR. Because of the book's focus on armed conflict, crimes against humanity and genocide, which can also be committed outside of armed conflict, are not analysed. The notion of international criminal law as used in this book is limited to international criminal law as it relates to war crimes.

The book also draws on practice from a variety of States on the interpretation and application of the refugee definition to individuals forced to flee from armed conflict – Australia, Belgium, Canada, France, Germany, New Zealand, the United Kingdom of Great Britain and Northern Ireland (UK), and the US – in order to illustrate or strengthen certain arguments. The countries were selected in order to reflect both civil and common law traditions and to ensure a degree of geographic and linguistic diversity. The practice of States in Latin America and Africa is not included due to the operation of wider regional protection mechanisms.[44] Because of its focus on the meaning of the refugee definition in light of international human rights law, customary IHL and international criminal law, the book does not conduct a comparative analysis of the interpretation of the refugee definition by States parties to the Refugee Convention as regards refugee protection claims related to armed conflicts in countries of origin.[45] It must be acknowledged that this book will therefore not result in a definite interpretation of the refugee definition as regards refugee protection claims concerning situations of armed conflict in the country or origin. However, its conclusions will indicate an interpretation in accordance with the international legal framework of the Refugee Convention in armed conflict, based on authoritative international sources, and will thus provide

The International Committee of the Red Cross and the Protection of War Victims (Oxford: Macmillan, 2003).

43 2187 UNTS 90, adopted 17 July 1998, entered into force 1 July 2002.

44 Article 1(II) of the Convention Governing the Specific Aspects of Refugee Problems in Africa (1001 UNTS 45, adopted 10 September 1969, entered into force 20 June 1974 (OAU Convention)) is one such broader refugee definition, stating: "The term 'refugee' shall also apply to every person who, owing to external aggression, occupation, foreign domination or events seriously disturbing public order in either part or the whole of his country of origin or nationality, is compelled to leave his place of habitual residence in order to seek refuge in another place outside his country of origin or nationality." A similar but not identical definition is included in para. 3 of the Cartagena Declaration on Refugees adopted at the Colloquium on the International Protection of Refugees in Central America, Mexico and Panama, 22 November 1984, available at www.refworld.org/docid/3ae6b36ec.html, accessed 10.03.2015 (Cartagena Declaration).

45 For such an analysis, see Markard, *Kriegsflüchtlinge*.

guidelines for the interpretation and application of the refugee definition as regards refugee protection claims of individuals forcefully displaced by armed conflict.[46]

2.2.2. *The Views of UNHCR and its Executive Committee*

Although the Refugee Convention, in contrast to international human rights treaties, does not establish a treaty monitoring body, UNHCR and its EXCOM play a special role in supervising and guiding the interpretation of the refugee definition by States parties. UNHCR's positions carry weight in the interpretation and application of the refugee definition because UNHCR exerts a supervisory role with respect to the application of the Refugee Convention.[47] The basis for this supervisory role lies in Article 8(a) of UNHCR's Statute, which states:

> "The High Commissioner shall provide for the protection of refugees falling under the competence of his Office by:
> (a) Promoting the conclusion and ratification of international conventions for the protection of refugees, *supervising their application* and proposing amendments thereto."[48]

Moreover, Article 35(1) Refugee Convention provides that States parties shall co-operate with UNHCR in the exercise of its function, in particular by facilitating "its duty of supervising the application of the provisions of this Convention".[49] In exercising its supervisory mandate, UNHCR published a number of documents on the interpretation of the refugee definition, including: the aforementioned UNCHR Handbook, Guidelines on International

---

46 Wouters employed a similar methodology in his comparative study of the prohibition on *refoulement* in various international treaties. See Cornelis Wolfram Wouters, *International Legal Standards for the Protection from Refoulement* (Antwerp: Intersentia, 2009), 4.

47 On UNHCR's supervisory role, see e.g. Volker Türk, "UNHCR's Supervisory Responsibility", *Revue Québécoise de Droit International* 14, no. 1 (2001): 135–158; Walter Kälin, "Supervising the 1951 Convention Relating to the Status of Refugees: Article 35 and beyond", in *Refugee Protection in International Law*, edited by Erika Feller, Volker Türk, and Frances Nicholson (Cambridge: Cambridge University Press, 2003); Corinne Lewis, *UNHCR and International Refugee Law* (2012); Roundtable on the Future of Refugee Convention Supervision, "Summary Conclusions", *Journal of Refugee Studies* 26, no. 3 (2013): 327–330.

48 Statute of the UN High Commissioner for Refugees, adopted by UN General Assembly, *Resolution 428 (V)* (14 December 1959) (UNHCR Statute) (emphasis added).

49 See also Article II(1) Protocol. Moreover, the sixth preambular recital of the Refugee Convention states that "the United Nations High Commissioner for Refugees is charged with the task of supervising international conventions providing for the protection of refugees". Chapter 4 examines the status of UNHCR's views and EXCOM conclusions for the purposes of interpreting the refugee definition.

Protection which update the UNHCR Handbook,[50] and Eligibility Guidelines concerning the interpretation and application of the Refugee Convention with regard to asylum-seekers from specific countries of origin,[51] as well as other official documents.[52] This book focusses on Eligibility Guidelines that concern countries of origin which in the past were in armed conflict or which still are experiencing armed conflict, namely: Afghanistan, Colombia, the DRC, Iraq, Somalia, and Sri Lanka. That they were or still are in armed conflict is confirmed by the ICRC.[53]

Established pursuant to UN General Assembly Resolution E/RES/672 (XXV) of 30 April 1958,[54] the EXCOM *inter alia* advises the UN High Commissioner for Refugees in the exercise of his or her functions.[55] In addition, the EXCOM exerts governing functions with respect to certain UNHCR organisational

---

50 See, e.g., UNHCR, *Guidelines on International Protection No. 1: Gender-Related Persecution within the Context of Article 1A(2) of the 1951 Refugee Convention and/or its 1967 Protocol relating to the Status of Refugees,* UN Doc. HCR/GIP/02/01 (7 May 2002); UNHCR, *Guidelines on International Protection No. 2: "Membership of a Particular Social Group" within the Context of Article 1A(2) of the 1951 Refugee Convention and/or its 1967 Protocol relating to the Status of Refugees,* UN Doc. HRC/GIP/02/02 (7 May 2002). Note, however, Goodwin-Gill's sceptical assessment of UNHCR Guidelines: Guy S. Goodwin-Gill, "The Dynamic of International Refugee Law", *International Journal of Refugee Law* 25, no. 4, 659–661.

51 See, e.g., UNHCR, "Eligibility Guidelines for Assessing the International Protection Needs of Afghan Asylum-Seekers" (2007), available at www.refworld.org/docid/477ce70a2.html, accessed 10.03.2015. See also UNHCR, "Position on Returns to North Kivu, South Kivu and Adjacent Areas in the Democratic Republic of Congo Affected by On-going Conflict and Violence in the Region" (2012), available at www.refworld.org/docid/50a369022.html, accessed 10.03.2015, which does not constitute fully-fledged Eligibility Guidelines, but fulfils the same purpose albeit with a narrower scope.

52 Such as: UNHCR, "Information Note on Article 1 of the 1951 Convention" (1995), available at www.refworld.org/docid/3ae6b32c8.html, accessed 10.03.2015; UNHCR, *UNHCR Observations on the Commission's Proposal for a Joint Action Concerning Temporary Protection of Displaced Persons* (24 June 2009 1997); UNHCR, "Annotated Comments on the EC Council Directive 2004/83/EC of 29 April 2004 on Minimum Standards for the Qualification and Status of Third Country Nationals or Stateless Persons as Refugees or as Persons Who Otherwise Need International Protection and the Content of the Protection Granted (OJ L 204/12 of 20.9.2004)" (2005), available at www.refworld.org/docid/4200d8354.html, accessed 10.03.2015, and the annual Reports of the UN High Commissioner for Refugees titled "Notes on International Protection" (e.g. UNHCR, *Note on International Protection,* UN Doc. A/AC.96/1098 (2011)).

53 See *supra*, note 9.

54 Türk analyses the predecessors of the EXCOM and the EXCOM's establishment in detail: Volker Türk, *Das Flüchtlingshochkommissariat der Vereinten Nationen (UNHCR)* (Berlin: Duncker & Humblot, 1992), 98–101.

55 The terms of reference of the UNHCR EXCOM, set out in UN General Assembly, *Resolution 1166(XII)* (26 November 1957), para. 5(b), include advising the High Commissioner for Refugees on the exercise of his or her functions. See Türk, *Flüchtlingshochkommissariat,* 101. UNHCR notes that the EXCOM advices UNHCR on international protection issues: UNHCR, "Executive Committee of the High Commissioner's Programme (ExCom)", available at www.unhcr.org/pages/49c3646c83.html, accessed 10.03.2015.

matters, including the approval of UNHCR's programme and budget.[56] A subsequent General Assembly resolution requested the High Commissioner "to abide by directions which that Committee might give him in regard to situations concerning refugees".[57] Membership of the EXCOM has been gradually increasing from 25 States in 1958 to 94 States in 2014.[58] In its conclusions, the EXCOM makes statements that are pertinent for the meaning and scope of the refugee definition. EXCOM conclusions are adopted by consensus.[59]

2.2.3. *Customary International Humanitarian Law*

For various reasons, this book focusses on customary IHL as opposed to international humanitarian treaty law.[60] Customary IHL binds all parties to an international or non-international armed conflict around the world. In non-international armed conflict, customary IHL contains considerably more rules than the applicable IHL treaties.[61] This book does not and cannot itself examine which rules of IHL are customary in nature. Such an endeavour would exceed its scope and distract from its main focus. Rather, the book draws on the seminal research on customary IHL by the ICRC which identified 161 rules of customary IHL, most of which apply in international and non-international armed

56 See Türk, *Flüchtlingshochkommissariat*, 102–104, who notes that the resolutions adopted by EXCOM in the exercise of its governing functions are binding on UNHCR. See also: UNHCR, "The Executive Committee's Origins and Mandate", available at www.unhcr.org/pages/49c3646c86.html, accessed 10.03.2015.

57 UN General Assembly, *Resolution 1672 (XVI)* (18 December 1961), para. 1. This request was repeated by UN General Assembly, *Resolution 1783 (XVII)* (7 December 1962), para. 2. Both resolutions identified by Jerzy Sztucki, "The Conclusions on the International Protection of Refugees Adopted by the Executive Committee of the UNHCR Programme", *International Journal of Refugee Law* 1, no. 3 (1989): 285–318, 288.

58 See UNHCR, "ExCom Members and How to Apply" (2012), available at www.unhcr.org/pages/49c3646c89.html, accessed 10.03.2015.

59 See Bryan Deschamp and Rebecca Dowd, "Review of the Use of UNHCR Executive Committee Conclusions on International Protection" (2008), available at www.unhcr.org/483d701f2.html, accessed 10.03.2015, 6–7. On the EXCOM and its conclusions, see also Türk, *Flüchtlingshochkommissariat*, 98–111. Chapter 4 examines in more detail the role and status of EXCOM conclusions in the interpretation of the refugee definition.

60 According to Article 38(1)(b) ICJ Statute (annexed to the Charter of the UN, 1 UNTS XVI, adopted 26 June 1945, entered into force 24 October 1945), international custom is "a general practice accepted as law". See further, e.g., Wolfgang Graf Vitzthum, "Begriff, Geschichte und Rechtsquellen des Völkerrechts", in *Völkerrecht*, edited by Wolfgang Graf Vitzthum (Berlin: De Gruyter, 2010), 60–64.

61 The ICRC Study on Customary IHL identified 148 rules of customary IHL applicable in non-international armed conflict: Jean-Marie Henckaerts, "Study on Customary International Humanitarian Law: A Contribution to the Understanding and Respect for the Rule of Law in Armed Conflict", *International Review of the Red Cross* 87, no. 857 (2005): 175–212, 198–212. The number of international humanitarian treaty provisions applicable in non-international armed conflicts pales in comparison to this large number of customary rules.

conflict.[62] Methodologically, the ICRC study is premised on the understanding that:

> "the existence of a rule of customary international law requires the presence of two elements, namely State practice (*usus*) and a belief that such practice is required, prohibited or allowed, depending on the nature of the rule, as a matter of law (*opinio juris sive necessitatis*)."[63]

The ICRC study adopted a classic approach to determine whether a rule of customary international law exists as set out by the ICJ in several cases, in particular the *North Sea Continental Shelf cases*.[64]

It must be acknowledged that the ICRC study has not been without criticism.[65] A major point of criticism concerned the relevance of physical and verbal acts of States in the formation of customary IHL. The ICRC study considered that both physical acts of States, for example battlefield behaviour, and verbal acts of States, for instance military manuals or national legislation, constitute State practice that contributes to the creation of customary IHL.[66] Some commentators have argued that the study relies too much on verbal State practice to the detriment of physical practice.[67] Indeed, physical acts such as military operations are a significant type of State practice. If available, official reports on battlefield practice were examined for the ICRC study.[68] However, for an accurate analysis of customary IHL, the description of physical acts must be

---

62 See Jean-Marie Henckaerts and Louise Doswald-Beck, *Customary International Humanitarian Law*, vol. I: Rules (Cambridge: Cambridge University Press, 2005); Jean-Marie Henckaerts and Louise Doswald-Beck, *Customary International Humanitarian Law*, vol. II: Practice (Cambridge, Cambridge University Press, 2005).

63 Jean-Marie Henckaerts and Louise Doswald-Beck, *Customary International Humanitarian Law*, vol. I: Rules (Cambridge: Cambridge University Press, 2005), xxxviii.

64 See Henckaerts and Doswald-Beck, *Customary International Humanitarian Law*, xxxviii, and ICJ, *North Sea Continental Shelf cases (Federal Republic of Germany v. Denmark; Federal Republic of Germany v. the Netherlands)*, Judgment of 20 February 1969, ICJ Reports 1969, 3.

65 The scope of this book does not allow a discussion of every single point of criticism of the ICRC Study. Therefore, two major points of criticisms have been selected.

66 See Henckaerts and Doswald-Beck, *Customary International Humanitarian Law*, xxxviii.

67 See, e.g., John B. II Bellinger and William J. II Haynes, "A US Government Response to the International Committee of the Red Cross study Customary International Humanitarian Law", *International Review of the Red Cross* 89, no. 866 (2007): 443–471, 445; W. Hays Parks, "The ICRC Study on Customary IHL: A Preliminary Assessment", *American Society of International Law Proceedings* 99 (2005): 208–212, 201; Eloisa Newalsing, "Jean-Marie Henckaerts and Louise Doswald-Beck (editors), Customary International Humanitarian Law, Geneva and Cambridge, International Committee of the Red Cross and Cambridge University Press (2005)", *Leiden Journal of International Law* 21, no. 1 (2008): 255–279, 266–267. Wilmshurst also notes that this criticism has been raised: Elizabeth Wilmshurst, "Conclusions", in *Perspectives on the ICRC Study on Customary International Humanitarian Law*, edited by Elizabeth Wilmshurst and Susan Breau (Cambridge: Cambridge University Press, 2007), 403–404.

68 See Jean-Marie Henckaerts, "Customary International Humanitarian Law: A Response to US Comments", *International Review of the Red Cross* 89, no. 866 (2007): 473–488, 477.

complemented with their legal assessment, which can only be found in the verbal acts of States. For example, if a practice is generally considered to breach existing rules (such as the targeting of civilians), it does not modify existing rules but merely constitutes a violation of existing rules.[69]

Another major point of criticism concerns the weighing of State practice. Some commentators have argued that the ICRC study should have given more weight to the practice of specially affected States, i.e. States that have had more experience with armed conflict, as opposed to the practice of States that have rarely or never seen armed conflict.[70] There are certainly States which have contributed a larger volume of practice than others since they have been involved more often in armed conflict. Yet this does not necessarily mean that their practice must be given more weight in the formation of customary IHL. For the coming into existence of a rule of customary international law, State practice must be extensive and representative.[71] True, the ICJ did state that the practice considered "must include that of States whose interests are specially affected".[72] However, this statement was made in the context of the law of the sea which concerns situations based on inherent, geographic facts that objectively make certain States specially affected. It is questionable whether the same considerations can apply to IHL which regulates situations of armed conflict that can potentially affect any State.[73] Therefore, all States have a legitimate and equal interest in the development of IHL. Thus, there is no place for a rule on specially affected States in customary IHL.[74]

---

69 See Henckaerts, "Customary International Humanitarian Law: A Response to US Comments", 477. Supporting the Study's approach to physical and verbal practice: Michael Bothe, "Customary International Humanitarian Law: Some Reflections on the ICRC Study", *Yearbook of International Humanitarian Law* 8 (2005): 143–178, 156. In *The Prosecutor v. Anto Furundžija*, Judgment, Trial Chamber II, 10 December 1998, Case No. IT-95-17/1-T, para. 138, the ICTY Trial Chamber noted that despite the occurrence of torture in State practice, States' manifested belief that such practice is unlawful confirms the prohibition of torture under customary international law. See also Tullio Treves, "Customary International Law", in *Max Planck Encyclopedia of Public International Law*, edited by Rüdiger Wolfrum (Oxford: Oxford University Press, 2009), available at www.mpepil.com, accessed 10.03.2015, para. 13.

70 See Bellinger and Haynes, "A US Government Response", 445; Leah M. Nicholls, "The Humanitarian Monarchy Legislates: The International Committee of the Red Cross and the Rules of Customary International Humanitarian Law", *Duke Journal of Comparative and International Law* 17 (2006): 223–252, 240.

71 See Henckaerts and Doswald-Beck, *Customary International Humanitarian Law*, xliv.

72 ICJ, *North Sea Continental Shelf cases (Federal Republic of Germany v. Denmark; Federal Republic of Germany v. the Netherlands)*, Judgment of 20 February 1969, ICJ Reports 1969, para. 74, 43.

73 See Henckaerts, "Customary International Humanitarian Law", 481–482.

74 See Dieter Fleck, "Die IKRK-Gewohnheitsstudie: polarisierend oder konsensbildend?", *Humanitäres Völkerrecht Informationsschriften* 22, no. 3 (2009): 120–124. More tentative: Henckaerts, "Customary International Humanitarian Law", 481–482. Henckaerts notes that some States may have contributed more practice and more detailed practice than others in fields in which they are "specially affected".

Hence, the main methodological challenges to the ICRC study are rebuttable and therefore do not pre-empt drawing on the study for the purposes of this book. Moreover, a growing number States[75] and international courts and tribunals[76] have drawn on the ICRC study's findings, thereby confirming that the study is useful in identifying customary IHL. There is also a more pragmatic reason for drawing on the ICRC study: the 161 rules which the study identified as being customary in nature, the commentary on these rules and the underpinning national and international practice are now available on an online database.[77] The database's practice section is being continuously updated which ensures its topicality.[78] For refugee status decision-makers, this database constitutes a user-friendly and easily accessible resource on customary IHL which they could use to identify rules of customary IHL that may inform their

---

75 See, e.g., Memorial of the United Kingdom of Belgium, *Case concerning Questions relating to the Obligation to Prosecute or Extradite (Belgium v. Senegal)*, 1 July 2010, available at www.icj-cij.org/docket/files/144/16933.pdf, accessed 10.03.2015, mn. 100, 67 (Belgium); The Supreme Court sitting as the High Court of Justice, *The Public Committee against Torture in Israel and others v. The Government of Israel and others*; 13 December 2006, HCJ 769/02, paras. 23, 29–30 and 41–42 (Israel); *Bundesgeneralanwalt beim Bundesgerichtshof* (Federal Prosecutor General at the Federal Court of Justice), *Ermittlungsverfahren gegen Oberst Klein und Hauptfeldwebel Wilhelm wegen des Verdachts einer Strafbarkeit nach dem VStGB und anderer Delikte* (Investigation proceedings against Colonel Klein and Company Seargent Major Wilhem because of suspected offences under the International Crimes Code and other offences), *Einstellung des Verfahrens gemäß §170 Abs. 2 Satz 1 StPO* (Termination of proceedings pursuant to §170 para. 2 sentence 1 of the Penal Procedure Code), 3 BJs 6/10–4, 16 April 2010, 65–67 (Germany); Opening Address by the Minister for Foreign Affairs at a Workshop on International Humanitarian Law and the Protection of Civilians, Jakarta, 8 November 2010, available at www.regjeringen.no/en/dep/ud/Whats-new/Speeches-and-articles/speeches_foreign/2010/jakarta_workshop.html?id=624746, accessed 10.03.2015 (Norway); Ministry of Defence, Closing Submissions to the Baha Mousa Public Inquiry on Modules 1–3, 25 June 2010, available at www.bahamousainquiry.org/linkedfiles/baha_mousa/hearings/oral_submission/sub000947.pdf, 28–33, accessed 10.03.2015 (UK).

76 See, e.g., ICTY, *The Prosecutor v. Enver Hadžihasanović and Amir Kubura*, Decision on Joint Defence Interlocutory Appeal of Trial Chamber Decision on Rule 98 bis Motions for Acquittal, Appeals Chamber, 11 March 2005, Case No. IT-01-47-AR73.3, paras. 29–30, 38 and 45–46 (wanton destruction of cities, plunder of public or private property, attacks against cultural property and attacks on civilian objects more generally); Eritrea-Ethiopia Claims Commission, Partial Award, *Prisoners of War, Eritrea's Claim 17*, 1 July 2003, para. 41 (finding a number of the provisions of the (Protocol Additional to the Geneva Conventions of 12 August 1949, and Relating to the Protection of Victims of International Armed Conflicts, 1125 UNTS 3, adopted 8 June 1977, entered into force 7 December 1978 (Additional Protocol I) on the conduct of hostilities to be customary in nature); Special Court of Sierra Leone, *The Prosecutor v. Issa Hassan Sesay also known as Issa Sesay, Morris Kallon also known as Bilai Karim, and Augustine Gbao also known as Augustine Bao*, Judgment, Trial Chamber I, 2 March 2009, Case No. SCSL-04-15-T, para. 216 (attacks against peacekeeping personnel).

77 See ICRC Database on Customary IHL, available at www.icrc.org/customary-ihl, accessed 10.03.2015.

78 On the updating of the practice underpinning the ICRC Study on Customary IHL, see Iris Müller, "Follow-up der IKRK-Gewohnheitsrechtsstudie", *Humanitäres Völkerrecht Informationsschriften* 22, no. 3 (2009): 131–136, 136.

interpretation of the refugee definition. For these reasons, this book considers the ICRC study as correctly identifying customary IHL.

2.3. SCOPE OF THE BOOK

This book concentrates on refugee protection claims of individuals who were forced to leave their country of origin due to armed conflict. Its findings are also pertinent for *sur place* refugee protection claims of individuals whose well-founded fear of persecution has arisen after their departure from the country of origin because of the outbreak of an armed conflict in this country.

2.3.1. Delimitations

While all elements of the refugee definition are addressed, emphasis is placed on those elements which promise most insights if analysed in light of international human rights law, customary IHL and international criminal law. These elements are: the notion of persecution and the causal link between a well-founded fear of being persecuted and a Refugee Convention ground. The book focusses on acts of violence during armed conflict and thus on the *ius in bello*; it neither considers matters pertaining to the *ius ad bellum* nor addresses genocide and crimes against humanity.

To ensure worldwide validity, emphasis is placed on universal rather than regional international treaties and other instruments. As a result, regional refugee protection instruments and regional international human rights treaties are not examined in any detail.[79] For the same reason, this book does not focus on the so-called Qualification Directive[80] and Recast Qualification Directive.[81] The book does not address the concurrent application of international refugee law and IHL concerning refugees caught up in an armed conflict.[82] Neither does it examine exclusion from or cessation

---

79 Such regional instruments comprise the OAU Convention, and the Cartagena Declaration as well as regional human rights treaties and declarations.

80 The full title of this directive is: Council Directive 2004/83/EC of 29 April 2004 on minimum standards for the qualification and status of third country nationals or stateless persons as refugees or as persons who otherwise need international protection and the content of the protection granted.

81 The full title of this directive is: Directive 2011/95/EU of the European Parliament and of the Council of 13 December 2011 on standards for the qualification of third-country nationals or stateless persons as beneficiaries of international protection, for a uniform status for refugees or for persons eligible for subsidiary protection, and for the content of the protection granted (recast). Pursuant to Article 40 of the Recast Qualification Directive, the Qualification Directive is repealed for Member States bound by the Recast Qualification Directive with effect from 21 December 2013. For an analysis of the protection of "war refugees" under the Qualification Directive and Recast Qualification Directive, see Markard, *Kriegsflüchtlinge*.

82 See the detailed analysis by Jaques, *Armed Conflict and Displacement*.

of refugee status,[83] complementary or subsidiary protection[84] or the protection of internally displaced people.

2.3.2. *Definition of Armed Conflict*

This book explores the meaning and scope of the refugee definition with regard to refugee protection claims arising out of situations of armed conflict in the country of origin. It is therefore necessary to define "armed conflict". There is no universally agreed definition of armed conflict in international treaty law.[85] The Appeals Chamber of the ICTY, in the *Tadić Jurisdiction Decision,* adopted the following definition of armed conflict:

> "[A]n armed conflict exists whenever there is a resort to armed force between states or protracted armed violence between government authorities and organized armed groups or between such groups within a state."[86]

The Appeals Chamber understood international armed conflicts as a resort to armed force between States. An international armed conflict can exist between two or more States.[87] Regarding the definition of international armed conflict, the term "whenever" indicates that the threshold for this type of armed conflict is very low, without there being a required minimum duration or a minimum number of victims.[88] A non-international armed conflict can occur between

---

83 Pursuant to Articles 1C and 1F Refugee Convention.

84 As provided for in, e.g., Article 15 Qualification Directive and Article 15 Recast Qualification Directive. Articles 15(c) of these instruments specifically addresses subsidiary protection in international and internal armed conflicts. On subsidiary protection in contexts of armed conflict, see e.g. Markard, *Kriegsflüchtlinge*, 303–355; Hélène Lambert and Theo Farrell, "The Changing Character of Armed Conflict and the Implications for Refugee Protection Jurisprudence", *International Journal of Refugee Law* 22, no. 2 (2010): 237–273; and Céline Bauloz, "The (Mis)Use of International Humanitarian Law under Article 15(c) of the EU Qualification Directive", in *Refuge from Inhumanity? War Refugees and International Humanitarian Law*, edited by David James Cantor and Jean-François Durieux (Leiden: Koninklijke Brill, 2014), 247–569.

85 See International Law Association, "Final Report on the Meaning of Armed Conflict in International Law" (2010), available at www.ila-hq.org/en/committees/index.cfm/cid/1022, accessed 10.03.2015, 1.

86 ICTY, *The Prosecutor v. Dusko Tadić*, Decision on the Defence Motion for Interlocutory Appeal on Jurisdiction, IT-94-1-A, 2 October 1995, para. 70.

87 See ICRC, "How is the Term 'Armed Conflict' Defined in International Humanitarian Law? Opinion Paper" (2008), available at www.icrc.org/eng/resources/documents/article/other/armed-conflict-article-170308.htm, accessed 10.03.2015, 5.

88 The International Law Association argues that a certain intensity of the fighting between States is necessary for the existence of an international armed conflict: International Law Association, "Final Report", 32. However, numerous authors and the ICRC find that no such minimum threshold is required for international armed conflict: Sylvain Vité, "Typology of Armed Conflicts in International Humanitarian Law: Legal Concepts and Actual Situations", *International Review of the Red Cross* 91, no. 873 (2009): 69–94, 72; Dapo Akande, "Classification of Armed Conflicts: Relevant Legal Concepts", in *International Law and*

government authorities, involving a State's armed forces,[89] and one or more armed groups, or solely between armed groups. The phrase "protracted armed violence" would suggest that violence needs to extend over a certain period of time. But it has become accepted that the key criterion is the intensity of the violence, with timing and duration constituting factors for assessing intensity.[90]

Central criteria for determining the existence of a non-international armed conflict are that the armed violence must reach "a minimum level of intensity and the parties involved in the conflict must show a minimum level of organization."[91] Factors which indicate the degree of organisation of an armed group include:

> "the existence of a command structure and disciplinary rules and mechanisms within the armed group, the group's ability to plan, coordinate and carry out military

---

the Classification of Conflicts, edited by Elizabeth Wilmshurst (Oxford: Oxford University Press, 2012), 41; ICRC, "International Humanitarian Law", 7. Commenting on the notion of international armed conflict in Common Article 2 of the Geneva Conventions, Jean Pictet stated: "It makes no difference how long the conflict lasts, or how much slaughter takes place." Jean Pictet, *Commentary on the Third Geneva Convention Relative to the Treatment of Prisoners of War* (Geneva: International Committee of the Red Cross, 1960), 23. Geneva Convention for the Amelioration of the Condition of the Wounded and Sick in Armed Forces in the Field, 75 UNTS 31, adopted 12 August 1949, entered into force 21 October 1950 (Geneva Convention I); Geneva Convention for the Amelioration of the Condition of Wounded, Sick and Shipwrecked Members of Armed Forces at Sea, 75 UNTS 85, adopted 12 August 1949, entered into force 21 October 1950 (Geneva Convention II); Geneva Convention relative to the Treatment of Prisoners of War, 75 UNTS 135, adopted 12 August 1949, entered into force 21 October 1950 (Geneva Convention III); Geneva Convention relative to the Protection of Civilian Persons in Time of War, 75 UNTS 287, adopted 12 August 1949, entered into force 21 October 1950 (Geneva Convention IV).

89 See ICRC, "How is the Term 'Armed Conflict' Defined", 5.

90 See ICTY, *The Prosecutor v. Ramush Haradinaj, Idriz Balaj and Lahi Brahimaj*, Third Amended Indictment, 7 September 2007, Case No. IT-04-84-T, para. 49. In more detail: ICTY, *The Prosecutor v. Ljube Boškoski and Johan Tarčulovski*, Amended Indictment, 2 November 2005, Case No. IT-04-82-PT, paras. 177–193. Further: Akande, "Classification of Armed Conflicts", 52; Marco Sassòli, "The Role of Human Rights and International Humanitarian Law in New Types of Armed Conflicts", in *International Humanitarian Law and International Human Rights Law*, edited by Orna Ben-Naftali (Oxford: Oxford University Press, 2011), 54. Kathleen Lawand of the ICRC identifies the duration of violence as one of various indicators in assessing the level of intensity of the violence: Kathleen Lawand, "Internal Conflicts or other Situations of Violence – What is the Difference for Victims?" (2012), available at www.icrc.org/eng/resources/documents/interview/2012/12-10-niac-non-international-armed-conflict.htm, accessed 10.03.2015.

91 ICRC, "How is the Term 'Armed Conflict' Defined", 5. Similarly: *The Prosecutor v. Duško Tadić aka "Dule"*, Judgment, Trial Chamber II, 7 May 1997, Case No. IT-94-1-T, para. 562. Further: Anthony Cullen, *The Concept of Non-International Armed Conflict in International Humanitarian Law* (Cambridge: Cambridge University Press, 2010), 122–123. The ICRC's definition of non-international armed conflict differs in some respects from the definition used by the ICTY Appeals Chamber in the *Tadić Jurisdiction Decision*.

> operations, including troop movements and logistics, its ability to negotiate and conclude agreements such as cease-fire or peace accords, etc."[92]

Regarding the intensity of the violence, the following factors are indicative:

> "the number, duration and intensity of individual confrontations, the type of weapons and other military equipment used, the number and calibre of munitions fired, the number of persons and types of forces partaking in the fighting, the number of casualties, the extent of material destruction, and the number of civilians fleeing combat zones."[93]

The motivation or objectives of the parties involved, such as criminal or political motives, do not constitute criteria that determine the existence of an armed conflict.[94]

The definition of armed conflict by the ICTY Appeals Chamber in the *Tadić Jurisdiction Decision* has been widely accepted by international criminal courts and tribunals[95] and has been used in State practice.[96] This definition was

---

92 ICRC, "International Humanitarian Law", 8. The ICTY Trial Chamber identified these factors in *The Prosecutor v. Ramush Haradinaj, Idriz Balaj and Lahi Brahimaj*, Judgment, Trial Chamber, 3 April 2008, Case No. IT-04-84-T, para. 60. See also Akande, "Classification of Armed Conflicts", 51–52.

93 ICRC, "International Humanitarian Law", 8–9. The ICTY Trial Chamber identified these factors in *The Prosecutor v. Ramush Haradinaj, Idriz Balaj and Lahi Brahimaj*, Judgment, Trial Chamber, 3 April 2008, Case No. IT-04-84-T, para. 49. See also Akande, "Classification of Armed Conflicts", 53.

94 See ICRC, "International Humanitarian Law", 11; Akande, "Classification of Armed Conflicts", 52; Elizabeth Wilmshurst, "Conclusions", in *International Law and the Classification of Conflicts*, edited by Elizabeth Wilmshurst (Oxford: Oxford University Press, 2012), 481.

95 As noted by Cullen, *The Concept of Non-International Armed Conflict in International Humanitarian Law*, 120–121. See, e.g., ICTY, *The Prosecutor v. Fatmir Limaj, Haradin Bala and Isak Musliu*, Judgment, Trial Chamber II, 30 November 2005, Case No. IT-03-66-T, para. 84 (noting that the case law of the ICTY consistently applies this definition of armed conflict); ICTR, *The Prosecutor v. Jean Paul Akayesu*, Judgment, 2 September 1998, Case No. ICTR-96-4-T, para. 619; ICTR, *The Prosecutor v. Georges Anderson Nderubumwe Rutaganda*, Judgment, 6 December 1999, Case No. ICTR-96-3-T, para. 621.

96 See, e.g., The Manual of the Law of Armed Conflict, Australian Defence Doctrine Publication 06.4, Australian Defence Headquarters, 11 May 2006, para. 3.4 (Australia); Court of Bosnia and Herzegovina, Panel, Section I for War Crimes, Case No. X-KR-06/290, Judgment of 28 November 2007, 29–30 (Bosnia and Herzegovina) and Constitutional Court, *Constitutional Case No. C-291/07*, Judgment of 25 April 2007, 49–52 (Colombia); The Manual of the Law of Armed Conflict, Ministry of Defence, 1 July 2004, 39 (UK). See also Cullen, *The Concept of Non-International Armed Conflict in International Humanitarian Law*, 121. However, Graham argues that "it remains to be seen whether future State practice will, in fact, sanction the validity of this approach [of the ICTY]." David E. Graham, "Defining Non-International Armed Conflict: A Historically Difficult Task", in *Non-International Armed Conflict in the Twenty-first Century*, edited by Kenneth Watkin and Andrew J. Norris, *International Law Studies* (Newport, RI: US Naval War College, 2012), 49.

incorporated into the second sentence of Article 8(2)(f) of the Rome Statute,[97] which indicates its customary status.[98] An expert meeting on complementarities between international refugee law, international criminal law and international human rights law, convened by UNHCR and the ICTR, observed that there is broad agreement on the definition of armed conflict as set out in the *Tadić Jurisdiction Decision*.[99] For these reasons, this book employs the definition of armed conflict developed in the *Tadić Jurisdiction Decision*.

The book analyses refugee protection claims of individuals forced to leave their country of origin because of armed conflict or who fear return due to armed conflict. It does not examine all potential constellations of parties to an armed conflict, but solely those that bear relevance for the refugee definition. Thus, the book considers the following types of armed conflict: (1) international armed conflicts to which the country of origin is a party and which are taking place on the territory of the country of origin, and (2) non-international armed conflicts occurring on the territory of the country of origin, irrespective of whether this country is a party to such conflicts. The book concentrates on cases in which the persecutor is the country of origin, its agents or non-State actors. It does not consider situations of belligerent occupation and situations in which harm is feared at the hand of a State which is not the country of origin.[100]

2.4. OUTLINE OF THE BOOK

The analysis of the refugee definition in light of international human rights law, customary IHL and international criminal law proceeds in eight chapters. Chapter 2 situates the Refugee Convention in its historical context by examining the evolution of international refugee law against the backdrop of conflict-induced forced displacement. The chapter considers refugee protection instruments adopted in the inter-war period, showing that the crucial criterion

97 For a thorough analysis, see Cullen, *The Concept of Non-International Armed Conflict in International Humanitarian Law*, 159–185.

98 See Michael Bothe, "War Crimes", in *The Rome Statute of the International Criminal Court: A Commentary*, edited by Antonio Cassese, Paola Gaeta, and John R.W.D. Jones (Oxford: Oxford University Press, 2002), 423; Cullen, *The Concept of Non-International Armed Conflict in International Humanitarian Law*, 122.

99 Expert Meeting on Complementarities between International Refugee Law, International Criminal Law and International Refugee Law, "Arusha Summary Conclusions", para. 22.

100 It must be noted that if a State intervenes in a non-international armed conflict on the side of the government or at its invitation and against the armed group which is a party to the conflict, the armed conflict retains its non-international character. This study is not, however, ceased with the question of whether this State could be a persecutor for the purposes of the refugee definition. On this type of armed conflict, see Dieter Fleck, "The Law of Non-International Armed Conflicts", in *The Handbook of International Humanitarian Law*, edited by Dieter Fleck (Cambridge: Cambridge University Press, 2008), mn. 1201, 605; Akande, "Classification of Armed Conflicts", 62–63; ICRC, "International Humanitarian Law", 10.

for defining a refugee was lack of protection by the country of origin, which applied irrespective of whether the person had fled from an armed conflict in the country of origin. The chapter also scrutinises refugee protection measures adopted after the Second World War, in particular the International Refugee Organisation and its successor, UNHCR. It examines the Refugee Convention's *travaux préparatoires* which reveal the drafters' understanding that armed conflicts may give rise to a well-founded fear of persecution for a Refugee Convention ground. Chapter 2 demonstrates that international refugee protection was historically designed to encompass persons compelled to leave their country of origin due to armed conflict if they fulfilled the criteria for refugee status.

International refugee protection is surrogate protection for individuals who lack the protection of their country of origin, including in situations of armed conflict, with Article 1A(2) Refugee Convention further defining the individuals who lack protection by the country of origin. In order to comprehend such lack of protection during armed conflict in light of international human rights law, IHL and international criminal law, Chapter 3 analyses the protection of the individual in the country of origin during armed conflict under these branches of international law. It shows that international human rights law continues to provide protection to the individual in armed conflict *vis-à-vis* the country of nationality or, in the case of stateless persons, the country of habitual residence, although such protection may be more limited than in times of peace due to derogations. It further demonstrates that IHL and international criminal law also play a protective role in armed conflict. Chapter 3 also provides this book's analytical framework by identifying and conceptualising the numerous interfaces between the Refugee Convention, international human rights law, IHL and international criminal law.

The analysis then turns to the interpretation of the refugee definition with respect to refugee protection claims of individuals compelled to leave their country of origin due to armed conflict or who fear return to their country of origin because of armed conflict. Noting that customary IHL and international criminal law can only provide interpretative guidance with respect to refugee protection claims related to an armed conflict in the country of origin, Chapter 4 shows that refugee status decision-makers can determine whether there was, is or is likely to be an armed conflict in the country of origin. It addresses the role of UNHCR and its EXCOM as particularly relevant international actors in the interpretation of the refugee definition. Chapter 4 demonstrates that an interpretation of the refugee definition in light of these branches of international law is in accordance with the rules on treaty interpretation set out in the 1969 Vienna Convention on the Law of Treaties (VCLT).[101] In particular, it argues that the refugee definition must be interpreted in an inclusive and dynamic

101 1155 UNTS 331, adopted 23 May 1969, entered into force 27 January 1980.

way, which means that recourse to customary IHL and international criminal law in the interpretation of the refugee definition is only possible if it serves to strengthen rather than undermine refugee protection. With this in mind, Chapters 5 to 7 then examine the different elements of the refugee definition in light of international human rights law, customary IHL and international criminal law, focussing on those definitional elements with regard to which these branches of international law offer most insights.

Chapter 5 addresses the requirement of a well-founded fear of being persecuted. With respect to "well-founded fear", it establishes that the burden of proof in refugee status determination procedures should be shared between the refugee claimant and the receiving country, with the standard of proof being that of reasonable possibility. It explores the subjective-objective and objective approaches to understanding "well-founded fear", supporting the objective approach pursuant to which a risk appraisal must be carried out that takes into account the objective situation in the country of origin, including compliance with IHL in case of a previous armed conflict, and the individual circumstances. Chapter 5 also demonstrates that a refugee claimant need not show that they would be singled out for persecution during armed conflict or that they would be more at risk than other individuals or groups in the country of origin. Persecution is one of the refugee definition's elements with regard to which international human rights law, customary IHL and international criminal law offer considerable interpretative guidance. Therefore, persecution is the main focus of the analysis in Chapter 5 which juxtaposes the hierarchical and two-tiered approach to a human rights-based interpretation of persecution before discussing the material scope of persecution in times of peace and armed conflict, the potential persecutors and victims of persecution. Chapter 5 examines whether violations of customary IHL can constitute persecution and whether war crimes can function as yardsticks for assessing whether a violation of customary IHL is serious enough to amount to persecution. The chapter develops a complementary approach to persecution in armed conflict that draws on international human rights law, customary IHL and international criminal law and applies this approach to selected forms of persecution which are frequent in armed conflict.

Chapter 6 considers the definitional requirement that a refugee must lack the protection of their country of origin. It examines the textual and conceptual bases of the lack-of-national-protection requirement, analyses which entities can provide protection and how the effectiveness of protection is to be assessed. It notes that an armed conflict may result in the country of origin's inability to provide protection. This chapter also scrutinises the concept of internal protection alternative with respect to cases in which the fear of persecution is geographically confined, noting that the proposed area of relocation must be accessible and provide protection in the narrow sense (including protection from experiencing IHL violations and war crimes) as well as protection in the broader sense, with all these requirements being possibly infringed upon by an armed conflict.

Chapter 7 examines the requirement that a refugee must have a well-founded fear *for reasons of* race, religion, nationality, membership of a particular social group or political opinion. It focusses on the causal link between the refugee claimant's predicament and a Refugee Convention ground which is another element of the refugee definition with regard to which customary IHL and international criminal law offer instructive interpretative guidance. The chapter analyses which inferences can be drawn from the IHL principles of military necessity, distinction and proportionality for the interpretation of the refugee definition's nexus requirement. It shows that patterns of IHL violations in the country of origin indicate that the victims' predicament cannot be justified by military necessity, pointing to other causes that may relate to a Refugee Convention ground. Chapter 7 also briefly examines these grounds.

Chapter 8 provides general concluding observations and offers an outlook on refugee protection for individuals forcefully displaced by armed conflict.

CHAPTER 2
THE HISTORICAL EVOLUTION OF INTERNATIONAL REFUGEE LAW IN LIGHT OF ARMED CONFLICT

1. INTRODUCTION

This chapter situates the Refugee Convention in its historical context. It examines the development of international refugee law in the inter-war period and after the Second World War at the universal level, focussing on the extent to which the refugee definitions in the different instruments adopted during this period encompassed individuals forced to leave their country of origin due to armed conflict.[102]

2. THE INTER-WAR PERIOD

The early efforts of the international community to devise legal instruments for the protection of refugees stem from several mass exoduses during and after the First World War. The first group of refugees whose protection was addressed under the auspices of the League of Nations were from Russia, with subsequent arrangements concerning Armenian refugees. Towards the end of the inter-war period, some measures were also adopted with respect to German refugees fleeing the Third Reich.

2.1. ARRANGEMENTS FOR RUSSIAN AND ARMENIAN REFUGEES

The causes of the refugee movement from Russia between 1918 and 1922 were multi-faceted and often inter-related; they include the Russian Revolution

---

102 On the historical evolution of international refugee law against the backdrop of conflict and violence, see also: Vanessa Holzer, "The 1951 Refugee Convention", 7–11.

of 1917 and pursuant Civil War as well as the 1921 famine.[103] The group of Russian refugees was of mixed composition including, for example, members of defeated "White" armies or resistance groups, civilians affected by the hostilities, prisoners of war who refused to return to Russia, political opponents of the Bolsheviks and famine victims.[104] Armed conflict was thus one of several reasons that prompted the Russian refugees to leave their country of origin.

What put all Russian refugees in a difficult situation was their loss of protection by their country of origin. Most of them were formally denationalised in 1921 by the new Soviet government.[105] As a result, the Russian refugees were in a legally anomalous situation. They lacked a secure identity and were unable to travel freely between States.[106] It was hence not the reason for their flight, for example an armed conflict, that prompted the need for international protection, but their lack of State protection and identity documents. The measures adopted under the aegis of the League of Nations for the protection of the Russian refugees were designed to mitigate this legally anomalous situation. Following an initiative by the ICRC, the Council of the League of Nations undertook the first measure of refugee protection in 1921 by establishing the High Commissioner for Russian Refugees as an independent organ of the League of Nations.[107] In 1922,

103 For a detailed analysis of the Russian refugees see John Hope Simpson, *The Refugee Problem. Report of a Survey* (London/New York/Toronto: Oxford University Press, 1939), 62–63; Louise W. Holborn, *The International Refugee Organization. A Specialized Agency of the United Nations. Its History and Work 1946–1952* (London et al.: Oxford University Press, 1956), 3.

104 See Simpson, *The Refugee Problem*, 6; Holborn, *International Refugee Organization*; Ivor C. Jackson, *The Refugee Concept in Group Situations* (The Hague et al.: Martinus Nijhoff, 1999), 12–13. Similarly: Terje Einarsen, "Drafting History of the 1951 Convention and the 1967 Protocol", in *The 1951 Convention relating to the Status of Refugees and its 1967 Protocol*, edited by Andreas Zimmermann (editor), Jonas Dörschner, and Felix Machts (assistant editors) (Oxford: Oxford University Press, 2011), mn. 8, 43.

105 See James C. Hathaway, "The Evolution of Refugee Status in International Law: 1920–1950", *International and Comparative Law Quarterly* 33 (1984): 348–380, 351. Similarly: Claudena M. Skran, "Historical Development of International Refugee Law", in *The 1951 Convention relating to the Status of Refugees and its 1967 Protocol*, edited by Andreas Zimmermann (editor), Jonas Dörschner, and Felix Machts (assistant editors) (Oxford: Oxford University Press, 2011), mn. 4–5, 7; Jane McAdam, "Rethinking the Origins of 'Persecution' in Refugee Law", in *International Journal of Refugee Law* 25, no. 4 (2014): 675.

106 On the whole, see James C. Hathaway, *The Rights of Refugees Under International Law* (Cambridge: Cambridge University Press, 2005), 84; Louise W. Holborn, "The Legal Status of Political Refugees, 1920–1938", *American Journal of International Law* 32 (1938): 680–703; Skran, "Historical Development", mn. 5, 7.

107 See *Procès Verbal de la Quatorzième Session du Conseil de la Société des Nations*, August-September 1921, Annex 245, 64. The mandate of the High Commissioner for Russian Refugees was subsequently extended to cover other groups of refugees that became the concern of the League of Nations until the Second World War. See Jackson, *The Refugee Concept*, 11; Holborn, *International Refugee Organization*, 1–27; Hathaway, *The Rights of Refugees*, 83–91; Waltraud von Glahn, *Der Kompetenzwandel internationaler Flüchtlingsorganisationen – vom Völkerbund bis zu den Vereinten Nationen* (Baden-Baden: Nomos, 1992), 12–13 and Goodwin-Gill and McAdam, *The Refugee in International Law*, 16–20.

Russian refugees were the first group of refugees whose status was regularised by a legally non-binding arrangement adopted under the aegis of the League of Nations.[108] Pursuant to this arrangement, governments would issue and renew identity documents to refugees present within their territories. These identity documents, known as "Nansen passports" after the first High Commissioner for Russian Refugees, enabled governments to monitor the refugee population and to issue visas.[109]

The 1922 arrangement did not define Russian refugees. It was extended in 1924 to cover Armenian refugees without, however, adding a refugee definition.[110] The Armenian refugees had fled from the genocide in Asia Minor which had occurred partly in the context of the First World War.[111] There was little need for these arrangements to define refugees because the Russian and Armenian refugees had already been granted *en masse* the protection of the League of Nations.[112]

Identity certificates for Russian or Armenian refugees, respectively, were only issued to persons who met certain criteria. An applicant had to demonstrate that he or she was of Russian territorial origin and outside the boundaries of the Soviet Union or that he or she was of Armenian ethnic origin and outside Turkish territory.[113] The reasons for flight were irrelevant for refugee status under the arrangements adopted between 1922 and 1924. Those who had fled from armed conflict in their country of origin benefited from refugee protection if they met the aforementioned criteria.

In 1926 and 1928, the arrangements for these two refugee groups were further specified.[114] These definitions included two criteria such that refugees

108 See Arrangement with regard to the Issue of Certificates of Identity to Russian Refugees, adopted 5 July 1922, 355 LNTS 238. See also Hathaway, "Evolution of Refugee Status", 350–352; Glahn, *Kompetenzwandel*, 16–17.

109 See Skran, "Historical Development", mn. 5, 7–8, who also notes that the Nansen passport was widely recognised in the 1920s.

110 See Plan for the Issue of a Certificate of Identity to Armenian Refugees, adopted 31 May 1924, printed in *League of Nations Official Journal* 7–10 (1924): 969–970.

111 For detailed information on the genocide against the Armenians, see Vahakn N. Dadrian, "The Historical and Legal Interconnections Between the Armenian Genocide and the Jewish Holocaust: From Impunity to Retributive Justice", *Yale Journal of International Law* 23 (1998): 503–559, 507–517.

112 See Skran, "Historical Development", mn. 12, 9. McAdam's recent historical research reveals that the notion of persecution, though not explicitly mentioned in the inter-war instruments, was understood at the time as being implied in the refugee concept. See Jane McAdam, "Rethinking the Origins of 'Persecution' in Refugee Law", in *International Journal of Refugee Law* 25, no. 4 (2014): 673.

113 See Holborn, *International Refugee Organization*, 3–4; Hathaway, "Evolution of Refugee Status", 352; Jackson, *The Refugee Concept*, 13–15. Skran notes that the identity certificates for Armenian refugees were not as widely accepted as those for Russian refugees: Skran, "Historical Development", mn. 8, 8.

114 See Arrangement relating to the Issue of Identity Certificates to Russian and Armenian Refugees, Supplementing and Amending the Previous Arrangements of 5 July 1922 and 31 May 1924, adopted 12 May 1926, 2004 LNTS 249, and Arrangement relating to the Legal

must: lack protection from the country of origin and be of a specified ethnic or territorial origin.[115] While having fled from a situation of armed conflict was not a legally relevant criterion for refugee status, it did not preclude a finding of refugee status either. On 10 December 1926, the League of Nations Council requested the High Commissioner for Refugees to examine how the existing arrangements for refugee protection could be extended to refugees in analogous situations resulting from the First World War or events directly related to the War.[116] These additional groups were identified according to the following three criteria: (1) *de jure* lack of protection by the country of origin; (2) this lack of protection resulted from events connected to the First World War; and (3) territorial or ethnic origin.[117] Hence, the expansion of refugee protection encompassed persons who escaped events related to the First World War.

In 1933, the Twelfth Assembly of the League of Nations undertook to transform these arrangements for refugee protection into a legally binding treaty.[118] The Convention relating to the International Status of Refugees was adopted on 28 October 1933 (1933 Convention).[119] It did not include a refugee definition of its own but stipulated in Article 1 that it applied to Russian, Armenian and assimilated refugees as defined in the arrangements of 1926 and 1928 and as modified by the States parties to the 1933 Convention upon signature or accession. The 1933 Convention for the first time endeavoured to accord specific rights to refugees.[120] However, its relevance was limited because it was only ratified by eight States, some of which entered significant reservations.[121]

In sum, the fact of having fled from armed conflict or other situations of violence did not pre-empt a finding of refugee status in the inter-war period.

Status of Russian and Armenian Refugees, adopted 30 June 1928, 2005 LNTS 55. See also Hathaway, "Evolution of Refugee Status", 353–354.

115 The origin requirements were designed so as to restrict eligibility for refugee protection to those persons who *de jure* lacked protection by their country of origin. Since the Russian refugees comprised persons from several ethnic, religious and social groups, the broad criterion of territorial origin was necessary. Only certain Turks lacked legal protection by their country of origin (namely those of Armenian ethnic origin), hence the more narrow ethnic criterion. See Hathaway, "Evolution of Refugee Status", 360.

116 A record of the decision of the League of Nation's Council can be found in *League of Nations Official Journal* 2 (1927) 155 and *League of Nations Official Journal* 10 (1927) 1336. See also Jackson, *The Refugee Concept*, 15–18 and Hathaway, *The Rights of Refugees*, 87–88.

117 See *League of Nations Official Journal* 10 (1927), 1138; Arrangement concerning the Extension to Other Categories of Refugees of Certain Measures Taken in Favour of Russian and Armenian Refugees, adopted 30 June 1928, 2006 LNTS 64. See also Hathaway, "Evolution of Refugee Status", 360–361.

118 See Hathaway, *The Rights of Refugees*, 87. See also Skran, "Historical Development", mn. 34, 16, who points out that despite the temporal coincidence, the drafting of this convention was not triggered by concern for people fleeing from Germany.

119 Entered into force 13 June 1935, 159 LNTS 266.

120 See Hathaway, *The Rights of Refugees*, 87.

121 See Skran, "Historical Development", mn. 63–64, 24–25; Hathaway, *The Rights of Refugees*, 87–88.

In some cases it was even decisive in bringing groups of people within the mandate of the League of Nations. The crucial legal criterion – lack of protection by the country of origin – applied irrespective of whether a country was experiencing an armed conflict.

2.2. ARRANGEMENTS FOR REFUGEES FROM GERMANY

Approximately 400,000 people fled from the Third Reich between 1933 and the outbreak of the Second World War in 1939. Rather than extending existing instruments to them, a separate legal regime was created largely because States were unwilling to grant them full protection.[122] A High Commissioner for Refugees coming from Germany was established in 1933.[123] Arrangements were made under the aegis of the League of Nations for German refugees from the *Saarland* after the 1935 plebiscite[124] and in 1936 with the adoption of the Provisional Arrangement concerning the Status of Refugees coming from Germany (1936 Provisional Arrangement).[125] The 1936 Provisional Arrangement defined refugees coming from Germany as persons settled in Germany whose sole nationality was German and who did not, in law or in fact, enjoy the protection of the Government of the Reich.[126] In this definition, the *de jure* or *de facto* lack of protection by the country of origin was a crucial criterion. Nevertheless, the concept of persecution for political or religious reasons was implied in the understanding of the German refugee at the time.[127] As its title indicates, the 1936 Provisional Arrangement was meant to be temporary.[128]

The Convention concerning the Status of Refugees coming from Germany was concluded in 1938 and identifies the following criteria for eligibility for refugee protection:

> "(a) Persons possessing or having possessed German nationality and not possessing any other nationality who are proved not to enjoy, in law or in fact, the protection of the German Government.

---

122 See Skran, "Historical Development", mn. 69, 26.

123 James G. McDonald took up this position but resigned in 1935 in protest of the lack of support he had received from States and to draw attention to the current and impending crisis. See Skran, "Historical Development", mn. 70, 26.

124 As noted in: *League of Nations Official Journal* 6(1935) 634 and *League of Nations Official Journal* 12 (1935), 1681–1682. See further Skran, "Historical Development", mn. 69–71, 26–27.

125 Adopted 4 July 1936, 3952 LNTS 77.

126 See Article I of the 1936 Provisional Arrangement.

127 As shown by McAdam's recent research: Jane McAdam, "Rethinking the Origins of 'Persecution' in Refugee Law", in *International Journal of Refugee Law* 25, no. 4 (2014): 679.

128 See Skran, "Historical Development", mn. 70, 26.

(b) Stateless persons not covered by previous Conventions or Agreements who have left German territory after being established therein and who are proved not to enjoy, in law or in fact, the protection of the German Government."[129]

Since only two States ratified this Convention, its impact was negligible.[130]

In view of the forcefully displaced people from the Sudeten region of Czechoslovakia, the Council of the League of Nations extended the mandate of the High Commissioner in January 1939.[131] Yet the 1938 Convention was never amended to account for the needs of the Sudeten refugees. In March 1938, the Council of the League of Nations broadened the mandate of the High Commissioner to encompass refugees coming from Austria. In September 1939, the Council also opened for signature a protocol to the 1938 Convention.[132] Taken together, the refugee definitions in these instruments confirm the importance of the *de jure* or *de facto* lack of protection by the country of origin as the crucial criterion for refugee status.[133] Since the Third Reich was not yet at war during this period, these measures do not directly relate to flight from armed conflict.

3. THE AFTERMATH OF THE SECOND WORLD WAR AND BEYOND

The forced displacement of at least 40 million people as a result of the Second World War[134] and subsequent further displacement prompted the creation of

129 Article I(1) of the Convention concerning the Status of Refugees coming from Germany, adopted 10 February 1938, entered into force 26 October 1938, 4461 LNTS 59.

130 See Skran, "Historical Development", mn. 94, 34. Moreover, an Inter-Governmental Conference for Refugees was convened by US President Roosevelt at Evian in July 1938 but had limited success. See Naomi S. Stern, "Evian's Legacy: The Holocaust, the United Nations Refugee Convention, and Post-War Refugee Legislation in the United States", *Georgetown Immigration Law Journal* 19 (2004–2005): 313–331.

131 See Hathaway, "Evolution of Refugee Status", 366 quoting *League of Nations Official Journal* 20 (1939), vol. 2, 73.

132 See Hathaway, "Evolution of Refugee Status", 366–367, referring to the Additional Protocol Concerning the Status of Refugees Coming from Germany, adopted 14 September 1939, 4634 LNTS 142.

133 McAdam argues that these instruments can be conceived as implying an understanding of a refugee as a person persecuted for reasons of race, religion or political opinion See Jane McAdam, "Rethinking the Origins of 'Persecution' in Refugee Law", in *International Journal of Refugee Law* 25, no. 4 (2014): 681.

134 See Einarsen, "Drafting History", mn. 12, 45, acknowledging that others have estimated different numbers. For example, Zolberg et al. speak of approximately eleven million forcibly displaced persons. See Aristide R. Zolberg, Astri Suhrke, and Sergio Aguayo, *Escape from Violence. Conflict and the Refugee Crisis in the Developing World* (Oxford/New York: Oxford University Press, 1989), 21.

the International Refugee Organisation (IRO) and later UNHCR as well as the adoption of the Refugee Convention.

3.1. THE ESTABLISHMENT OF THE INTERNATIONAL REFUGEE ORGANISATION

Created in 1946 as a temporary international organisation,[135] the IRO was tasked with achieving a solution of the refugee problem through repatriation, resettlement or temporary establishment of the refugees and displaced persons within its mandate.[136] Its Constitution included definitions of the terms "refugees" and "displaced persons" which were delimitations of the IRO's mandate *ratione personae*.[137]

In continuation of the instruments for refugee protection adopted in the inter-war period, the IRO Constitution defined particular categories of refugees such as the victims of Nazi or fascist regimes,[138] Spanish Republicans or other victims of the Falangist regime in Spain,[139] and "persons who were considered refugees before the outbreak of the Second World War for reasons of race, religion, nationality or political opinion".[140] Furthermore, persons of Jewish origin who had resided in Germany or Austria and had become victims of Nazi persecution were also of concern to the IRO if they fulfilled certain conditions.[141] So were unaccompanied children who were war orphans or the whereabouts of whose parents were unknown and who were outside their country of origin.[142]

135 See second preambular recital of the Constitution of the International Refugee Organisation (18 UNTS 3, adopted 15 December 1946, entered into force 20 August 1948) (IRO Constitution). The IRO was created as a special organisation of the UN pursuant to Articles 57 and 63 of the UN Charter. See Louise W. Holborn, *Refugees: A Problem of Our Time. The Work of the United Nations High Commissioner for Refugees, 1951–1972*, vol. I (Metuchen NJ: The Scarecrow Press, 1975), 47.

136 See second preambular recital of the IRO Constitution. Temporary establishment in a State other than the home State was envisaged for Spanish Republicans who would only be able to return to Spain when the Falangist regime which existed at the time would have been superseded by a democratic government. See also Holborn, *International Refugee Organization*, 47. The IRO's functions are listed in Article 2 of its Constitution.

137 Other delimitations of the scope of IRO's competence *ratione personae* are: Section C of Annex 1 which stipulates the conditions under which refugees and displaced persons would become the concern of the IRO and section D of Annex 1 which determines the circumstances in which refugees and displaced persons would cease to be the concern of the IRO. Part II of Annex 1 to the IRO Constitution determines the persons who would not be the concern of the IRO, such as war criminals, quislings and traitors.

138 See Part I, section A I (1) (a) of Annex 1 to the IRO Constitution.

139 See Part I, section A I (1) (b) of Annex 1 to the IRO Constitution.

140 Part I, section A I (1) (c) of Annex 1 to the IRO Constitution.

141 See Part I, section A (3) of Annex 1 to the IRO Constitution.

142 See Part I, section A (4) of Annex 1 to the IRO Constitution.

The IRO Constitution also struck a new path in defining refugees by including a more abstract definition according to which a refugee was a person other than a displaced person

> "who, as a result of events subsequent to the outbreak of the second world war, is unable or unwilling to avail himself of the protection of the Government of his country of nationality or former nationality."[143]

According to the IRO Constitution a displaced person was someone who, as a result of the actions of the Nazi or fascist authorities or of regimes which took part on their side in the Second World War or assisted them in the Second World War, "has been deported from, or has been obliged to leave, his country of nationality or of former habitual residence".[144] Thus, in defining several, but not all, categories of refugees and displaced persons, the IRO Constitution alluded to the Second World War as the central event that defined political allegiances and thus people who merited international protection.

With the exception of Jews in Germany or Austria, refugees and displaced persons had to be outside their countries of origin. The aforementioned definitions of refugees and displaced persons were subject to certain conditions under which the thus defined persons would become the concern of the IRO.[145] One such condition was that the persons in question had to express valid objections to returning to their states of origin. "Persecution, or fear, based on reasonable grounds of persecution because of race, religion, nationality or political opinions"[146] was a valid objection. The IRO Constitution was the first legally binding international instrument to use the term "persecution" in the context of a refugee definition.[147]

3.2. THE CREATION OF UNHCR AND THE EVOLUTION OF ITS MANDATE

After the dissolution of the IRO,[148] UNHCR was initially set up in 1950 as a temporary organisation "with the sole responsibility of addressing the needs

---

143 Part I, section A (2) of Annex 1 to the IRO Constitution.

144 Part I, section B of Annex 1 to the IRO Constitution.

145 See Part I, section C of Annex 1 to the IRO Constitution.

146 Part I, section C (1) (a) (i) of Annex 1 to the IRO Constitution.

147 McAdam argues that the IRO Constitution with its reference to persecution did not constitute a dramatic shift in emphasis as regards the definition of a refugee but represented a natural evolution of earlier implicit references to persecution for political or religious reasons. See McAdam, "Rethinking the Origins", 668.

148 On the dissolution of the IRO, see Türk, *Flüchtlingshochkommissariat*, 20 and Hathaway, *The Rights of Refugees*, 91.

of refugees in Europe who had been displaced by the Second World War."[149] According to paragraph 6(ii) of the UNHCR Statute, persons considered refugees under several inter-war refugee instruments and persons with a well-founded fear of persecution on account of several proscribed grounds fall within UNHCR's competence.[150]

UNHCR's competence is not only determined by its Statute, but also by subsequent resolutions of the UN General Assembly and the UN Economic and Social Council (ECOSOC).[151] Conclusions of UNHCR's EXCOM have also influenced the exercise of UNHCR's functions.[152] Consequently, UNHCR's competence *ratione personae* has considerably evolved over time. Early expansions of UNHCR's mandate *ratione personae* date back to the 1950s. The General Assembly adopted resolutions so that UNHCR was able to take measures for several refugee groups. UNHCR's mandate was widened on an *ad hoc*, reactive basis with regard to specific refugee groups. One such group comprised Algerian refugees in Morocco and Tunisia. Many, if not all, Algerians had left their country of origin for reasons related to the armed conflict that was taking place in Algeria in the late 1950s and early 1960s.[153] UNHCR extended its good offices to this refugee group.[154] The case of the Algerian refugees illustrates that already in the late 1950s UNHCR's mandate covered refugees who, at least in part, had to leave their country of origin for reasons related to an armed conflict.

---

149 Gil Loescher, Alexander Betts, and James Milner, *The United Nations High Commissioner for Refugees (UNHCR). The politics and practice of refugee protection into the twenty-first century* (London/New York: Routledge, 2008), 1, who at 10–22 note that UNHCR's establishment must also be seen in the context of the Cold War. See also Holborn, *Refugees*, 37 and 57. UNHCR was established as a specialised organ of the General Assembly pursuant to the aforementioned UN General Assembly, *Resolution 428 (V)*.

150 Para. 6A(i) and (ii) of the UNHCR Statute refers to "any person who, as a result of events occurring before 1 January 1951 and owing to well-founded fear of being persecuted for reasons of race, religion, nationality or political opinion, is outside the country of his nationality and is unable or, owing to such fear or for reasons other than personal convenience, is unwilling to avail himself of the protection of that country".

151 According to para. 3 of the UNHCR Statute, UNHCR "shall follow policy directives given him by the general Assembly or the Economic and Social Council." See also para. 9 of the UNHCR Statute.

152 It is still unclear from a theoretical perspective whether conclusions by UNHCR's EXCOM are legally binding for UNHCR if they have not been subsequently endorsed by the General Assembly. In practice, however, UNHCR treats these resolutions as binding by consistently acting upon the advice rendered by the EXCOM. See Corinne Lewis, "UNHCR's Contribution to the Development of International Refugee Law: Its Foundations and Evolution", *International Journal of Refugee Law* 17 (2005): 76–90, 79–80. See also Sztucki, "The Conclusions on International Protection".

153 See Jackson, *The Refugee Concept*, 122–126. See also Loescher, Betts, and Milner, *The United Nations High Commissioner for Refugees*, 19 and T. Alexander Aleinikoff, "The Mandate of the Office of the United Nations High Commissioner for Refugees", in *Research Handbook on International Law and Migration*, edited by Vincent Chetail and Céline Bauloz (Cheltenham/Northampton: Edward Elgar, 2014), 395–397.

154 On the good offices concept, see Jackson, *The Refugee Concept*, 90–110.

Moreover, UNHCR's competence *ratione personae* has been expanded by General Assembly resolutions to include individuals falling within the expanded refugee definitions of the OAU Convention and the Cartagena Declaration.[155] Thus, insofar as these refugee definitions cover individuals compelled to leave their country of origin due to armed conflict, these persons also fall within UNHCR's competence *ratione personae*. Indeed, UNHCR's mandate has evolved to cover

> "a variety of situations of forced displacement resulting from conflict, indiscriminate violence or public disorder. ... [S]erious (including indiscriminate) threats to life, physical integrity or freedom resulting from generalized violence or events seriously disturbing public order are valid reasons for international protection under its mandate."[156]

3.3. THE ADOPTION OF THE REFUGEE CONVENTION AND ITS PROTOCOL

The Refugee Convention was adopted in order to solve the remaining problems of refugees in Europe whose flight had been caused by the Second World War and related events as well as to address the refugee situations that had since come into being.[157] The drafters of the Refugee Convention generally understood the substance of the refugee definition to be broad and applicable to almost all known categories or groups of refugees.[158] Rather than being substantially influenced by the Cold War, they developed the refugee definition against the backdrop of thirty years of experience with refugees.[159]

Originally, the refugee definition was temporarily and geographically limited because the negotiating States hesitated to commit to protecting an unforeseeable population of future refugees, with the US representative arguing, for example, that "[t]oo vague a definition, which would amount ... to a blank check,

155 See the preamble (last recital) and para. 1 of General Assembly Resolution 2594 of 16 December 1969 for the OAU Convention and the preamble (third recital) of General Assembly Resolution 42/110 of 7 December 1987 for the Cartagena Declaration.

156 UNHCR, "Statement on Subsidiary Protection under the EC Qualification Directive for People Threatened by Indiscriminate Violence" (2008), available at www.refworld.org/docid/479df7472.html, accessed 10.03.2015, 2. See also UNHCR, "Eligibility Guidelines for Assessing the International Protection Needs of Asylum-Seekers from Afghanistan" (2013), available at http://www.refworld.org/docid/51ffdca34.html, accessed 10.03.2015, 6.

157 See Türk, *Flüchtlingshochkommissariat*, 274. Article 1A(1) Refugee Convention includes persons whose status of refugees was acknowledged by the inter-war instruments and the IRO Constitution.

158 See Einarsen, "Drafting History", mn. 64, 66.

159 See Einarsen, "Drafting History", mn. 64, 67.

would not be sufficient."[160] The drafters were thus concerned with limiting the personal scope of the Refugee Convention. During the drafting of the Refugee Convention, the Israeli representative observed that the refugee definition

> "obviously did not refer to refugees from natural disasters, for it was difficult to imagine that fires, floods, earthquakes or volcanic eruptions, for instance, differentiated between their victims on the grounds of race, religion, or political opinion. Nor did the text cover all man-made events. There was no provision, for example, for refugees fleeing from hostilities unless they were otherwise covered by article 1 of the Convention."[161]

The pivotal aspect of this statement is the differentiation required for victims of hostilities to be considered refugees. It recognises that if situations of violence in some way distinguish between victims, the victims may fall within the refugee definition. This statement illustrates the understanding that persons who escape armed conflict can be refugees in the sense of Article 1A(2) of the Refugee Convention if they fulfil the criteria therein. The drafters were aware that persecution during armed conflict had given rise to numerous *bona fide* refugees in the past.[162]

The statement of the Israeli delegate suggests that it was not the intention of the Refugee Convention's drafters that the refugee definition should cover persons who "merely" fled from general dangers arising from events such as armed conflicts. This proposition is also supported by the drafters' rejection of an ICRC proposal. The ICRC had suggested that "[e]very person forced by grave events to seek refuge outside his country of ordinary residence is entitled to be received".[163] Presumably such grave events would have included armed conflicts.

With the adoption of the 1967 Protocol relating to the Status of Refugees, the temporal and geographic limitations of the Refugee Convention's refugee definition were removed. There are two main reasons for the adoption of the Protocol. First, in the years following the adoption of the Refugee Convention, decolonisation considerably altered the community of States. New groups of forcefully displaced persons emerged, particularly in Africa and Asia, uprooted

---

160 Statement by the representative of the US in the Ad Hoc Committee on Statelessness and Related Problems, Summary Record of the Third Meeting, 26 January 1950, UN Doc. E/AC.32/SR.3, para. 37. See also Paul Weis, "Legal Aspects of the Convention of 21 July 1951 Relating to the Status of Refugees", *British Yearbook of International Law* 30 (1953): 478–488, 479.

161 Statement by the representative of Israel at the Conference of the Plenipotentiaries on the Status of Refugees and Stateless Persons, Summary Record of the Twenty-Second Meeting, 26 November 1951, UN Doc. A/CONF.2/SR.22, 6. Fripp cautions against attaching too much interpretative weight to this statement. See Fripp, "International Humanitarian Law", 391.

162 See Einarsen, "Drafting History", mn. 65, 67. See also Edwards and Hurwitz, "Introductory Note", 858.

163 Aide Memoire on the Refugee Question, Statement submitted by the International Committee of the Red Cross to the Conference of Plenipotentiaries on the Status of Refugees and Stateless Persons, 4 July 1951, UN Doc. A/CONF./NGO.2, 1.

largely because of armed conflicts fought during decolonisation, widespread human rights violations or political upheaval. The refugee problem in Europe paled in comparison, given that the situation of the post-Second World War refugees was mostly resolved by the 1960s.[164] Second, it was considered desirable to overcome the discrepancy which had developed between the refugee definition in the Refugee Convention and UNHCR's competence *ratione personae*. The latter did not include any temporal or geographical limitations.[165]

4. CONCLUSION

Forced displacement caused by armed conflict or other situations of violence underpins much of the historical evolution of international refugee law. International refugee protection was traditionally designed to be available to individuals forced to flee from their country of origin due to armed conflict if they fell within the respective refugee definitions.

Mass exoduses during and after the First World War prompted the League of Nations to adopt measures for refugee protection. The first group of refugees with which the League of Nations was concerned were from Russia and had fled for various reasons, including the Russian civil war. Loss of protection of the country of origin prompted the need for international refugee protection and was the central criterion in the refugee definitions adopted during this period. Having fled from armed conflict did not rule out a finding of refugee status. The measures taken with respect to German refugees in the inter-war period, whose flight was not prompted by armed conflict, affirm the criterion of *de facto* or *de jure* lack of protection by the country of origin as central for the definition of a refugee.

After the Second World War, which had caused large-scale forced displacement, the IRO was established in 1946 to tackle the refugee problem. Pursuant to the IRO Constitution, which pioneered the definition of a refugee with reference to a fear of persecution on account of stipulated grounds, an armed conflict in the country of origin did not preclude a person from coming within the IRO's mandate. UNHCR succeeded the IRO in 1950 to address the situation of the refugees who had been displaced by the Second World War and subsequent events. Its mandate has since evolved to encompass forcefully

164 See Sara E. Davies, "Redundant or Essential? How Politics Shaped the Outcome of the 1967 Protocol", *International Journal of Refugee Law* 19, no. 4 (2007): 703–727, 706 and 715; Kazimierz Bem, "The Coming of a 'Blank Cheque' – Europe, the 1951 Convention, and the 1967 Protocol", *International Journal of Refugee Law* 16, no. 4 (2004): 609–627, 623 and Jackson, *The Refugee Concept*, 85–176.

165 See Paul Weis, "The 1967 Protocol relating to the Status of Refugees and Some Questions of the Law of Treaties", *British Yearbook of International Law* 42 (1967): 39–70, 40. On UNHCR, see also Jackson, *The Refugee Concept*, 85–176.

displaced individuals who face serious threats to life, physical integrity or freedom due to generalised violence or events seriously disturbing public order, including individuals who fled from armed conflict. Having adopted the Refugee Convention against the backdrop of the forced displacement caused by the Second World War, the drafters understood that armed conflicts can give rise to a well-founded fear of being persecuted for one of the proscribed grounds. The original temporal and geographic limitations on the Refugee Convention's refugee definition were removed by the 1967 Protocol.

CHAPTER 3
THE INTERNATIONAL LEGAL FRAMEWORK FOR THE PROTECTION OF THE INDIVIDUAL IN ARMED CONFLICT

1. INTRODUCTION

The Refugee Convention is part and parcel of the international legal framework for the protection of the individual in armed conflict, with international human rights law, IHL and international criminal law constituting the other main components of this framework.[166] The Refugee Convention does not address protection in armed conflict as such, but rather some of the specific consequences of armed conflict.[167] The Refugee Convention provides surrogate protection for individuals who lack the protection of their country of origin,[168] including in situations in which there is an armed conflict in the country of

166 It is conceivable that the international legal framework for the protection of the individual in armed conflict comprises further branches of international law, such as international environmental law. However, for the purposes of this analysis, the branches of international law with the strongest focus on the human person and armed conflict were selected.

167 See Michael Bothe, "The Historical Evolution of International Humanitarian Law, International Human Rights Law, Refugee Law and International Criminal Law", in *Krisensicherung und Humanitärer Schutz – Crisis Management and Humanitarian Protection. Festschrift für Dieter Fleck*, edited by Horst Fischer et al. (Berlin: Berliner Wissenschaftsverlag, 2004), 43.

168 Article 1A(2) Refugee Convention refers to the refugee as a person who "is outside the country of his nationality, and is unable, or owing to such fear, is unwilling to avail himself of the protection of that country; or who, not having a nationality and being outside the country of his former habitual residence as a result of such events, is unable or, owing to such fear, is unwilling to return to it". Grahl-Madsen stated that in the case of a refugee, "the normal mutual bond of trust, loyalty, protection, and assistance between an individual and the government of his home country has been broken". Atle Grahl-Madsen, *The Status of Refugees in International Law*, vol. I (Leiden: A.W. Sijthoff, 1966), 79. See also James C. Hathaway, "Is Refugee Status Really Elitist? An Answer to the Ethical Challenge", in *Europe and Refugees: A Challenge? L'Europe et les Refugiés: Un Défi?*, edited by Jean-Yves Carlier and Dirk Vanheule (The Hague et al.: Kluwer Law International, 1997), 86.

origin. To recall, Article 1A(2) Refugee Convention defines a refugee as a person who:

> "owing to well-founded fear of being persecuted for reasons of race, religion, nationality, membership of a particular social group or political opinion, is outside the country of his nationality, and is unable, or owing to such fear, is unwilling to avail himself of the protection of that country; or who, not having a nationality and being outside the country of his former habitual residence as a result of such events, is unable or, owing to such fear, is unwilling to return to it."[169]

In order to analyse the refugee definition in light of international human rights law, IHL and international criminal law with respect to refugee protection claims arising out of situations of armed conflict, it is first necessary to examine protection in the country of origin under international human rights law, IHL and international criminal law. This analysis will form the backdrop against which subsequent chapters will scrutinise the different elements of the refugee definition in light of international human rights law, IHL and international criminal law.

2. THE PROTECTION OF THE INDIVIDUAL IN ARMED CONFLICT

The refugee definition addresses both individuals who lack the protection of their country of nationality and stateless persons who lack the protection of their country of habitual residence. Therefore, this analysis considers the protection of individuals from acts by their country of nationality and the protection of stateless persons from acts by their country of habitual residence, as well as protection from non-State actors on the territory of the country of origin during armed conflict. Such protection is usually framed in terms of international human rights law and has rarely been conceived in light of IHL in armed conflict.[170] This is why the subsequent analysis places more emphasis on IHL than on international human rights law.

---

169 Article 1A(2) Refugee Convention continues: "In the case of a person who has more than one nationality, the term 'the country of his nationality' shall mean each of the countries of which he is a national, and a person shall not be deemed to be lacking the protection of the country of his nationality if, without any valid reason based on well-founded fear, he has not availed himself of the protection of one of the countries of which he is a national."

170 On the conceptualisation of protection in the country of origin as human rights protection, see, e.g., James C. Hathaway, "New Directions to Avoid Hard Problems: The Distortion of the Palliative Role of Refugee Protection", *Journal of Refugee Studies* 8, no. 3 (1995): 288–294, 293. See also Deborah E. Anker, "Refugee Law, Gender, and the Human Rights Paradigm", *Harvard Human Rights Journal* 15 (2002): 133–154, 135; Niraj Nathwani, *Rethinking Refugee Law* (The Hague et al.: Martinus Nijhoff, 2003), 364.

2.1. INTERNATIONAL HUMAN RIGHTS LAW

International human rights law comprises norms that grant rights to individuals, limiting the authority which States yield over them,[171] including in times of armed conflict.[172] International human rights treaties such as the International Covenant on Civil and Political Rights (ICCPR),[173] the Convention against Torture and Other Cruel, Inhuman or Degrading Treatment or Punishment (CAT),[174] the International Convention on the Elimination of all Forms of Racial Discrimination (CERD),[175] the Convention on the Elimination of all Forms of

171 International human rights law can be defined as "those entitlements, opposable in principle to states on the international plane, which public international law, be it custom or treaty, vests in individuals and certain groups as an avowed function of their humanity." Roger O'Keefe, "State Immunity and Human Rights: Heads and Walls, Hearts and Minds", *Vanderbilt Journal of Transnational Law* 44 (2011): 999–1045, 1004.

172 See ICJ, *Legality of the Threat or Use of Nuclear Weapons*, Advisory Opinion of 8 July 1996, ICJ Reports 1996, 240, para. 25 (regarding the International Covenant on Civil and Political Rights (ICCPR), 99 UNTS 171, adopted 16 December 1966, entered into force 23 March 1967); ICJ, *Legal Consequences of the Construction of a Wall in the Occupied Palestinian Territory*, Advisory Opinion, ICJ Reports 2004, 178, para. 106 (referring to "human rights conventions"). This book is not concerned with the prohibition of *refoulement* under international human rights law.

173 999 UNTS 171, adopted 16 December 1966, entered into force 23 March 1976. On the ICCPR's applicability in armed conflict, see Human Rights Committee, *General Comment 31: Nature of the General Legal Obligation on States Parties to the Covenant,* UN Doc. CCPR/C/21/Rev. 1/Add. 13 (26 May 2004), para. 11 and Human Rights Committee, *Concluding Observations,* UN Doc. CCPR/C/USA/CO/3 (15 September 2006), para. 10 (observing that the US should acknowledge the ICCPR's "applicability in times of war"); Human Rights Committee, *Concluding Observations,* UN Doc. CCPR/C/USA/CO/3 (15 September 2006), para. 13 (recommending that the DRC "should take all necessary steps to strengthen its capacity to protect civilians in the zones of armed conflict, especially women and children"); Human Rights Committee, *Concluding Observations,* UN Doc. CCPR/C/79/Add.93 (18 August 1998), para. 10 and Human Rights Committee, *Concluding Observations,* UN Doc. CCPR/CO/78/ISR (5 August 2003), para. 11 (noting with regard to Israel that the applicability of IHL does not per se preclude the application of the ICCPR).

174 1465 UNTS 85, adopted 10 December 1984, entered into force 26 June 1987. Article 2(2) CAT states: "No exceptional circumstances whatsoever, whether a state of war or a threat of war, internal political instability or any other public emergency, may be invoked as a justification of torture." The Committee against Torture stated that the CAT applies in armed conflict: Committee Against Torture, *Conclusions and Recommendations on the Second Periodic Report of the United States of America,* UN Doc. CAT/C/USA/CO/2 (25 July 2006), para. 14. The CAT is listed here as a human rights treaty even though its provisions are phrased as State parties' obligations rather than as individual rights.

175 660 UNTS 195, adopted 7 March 1966, entered into force 4 January 1969. The Committee on the Elimination of Racial Discrimination affirmed the CERD's applicability in armed conflict, noting that certain forms of racial discrimination directed at women because of their gender include sexual violence against women members of ethnic groups in armed conflict. See Committee on the Elimination of Racial Discrimination, *General Recommendation 25. Gender Related Dimensions of Racial Discrimination,* UN Doc. A/55/18 (20 March 2003), para. 2.

Discrimination against Women (CEDAW),[176] the Convention on the Rights of the Child (CRC)[177] and its Optional Protocol on the Involvement of Children in Armed Conflict (Optional Protocol)[178] as well as the International Covenant on Economic, Social and Cultural Rights (ICESCR)[179] apply in armed conflict within the territory of a State party.[180]

The material scope of protection under some international human rights treaties may be more limited in times of armed conflict than in peacetime because States may derogate from certain obligations in situations of emergency, as which armed conflicts may qualify.[181] For example, the Human Rights Committee stated regarding the ICCPR:

> "During armed conflict, whether international or non-international, rules of IHL become applicable and help, in addition to the provisions in article 4 and article 5, paragraph 1, of the Covenant, to prevent the abuse of a State's emergency powers. The Covenant requires that even during an armed conflict measures derogating from the Covenant are allowed only if, and to the extent that, the situation constitutes a threat to the life of the nation."[182]

---

176 1249 UNTS 13, adopted 18 December 1979, entered into force 3 September 1981. The Committee on the Elimination of Discrimination against Women emphasised: "The obligations of States parties [under the CEDAW] do not cease in periods of armed conflict." Committee on the Elimination of Discrimination against Women, *General Recommendation No. 28 on the Core Obligations of States Parties under Article 2 of the Convention on the Elimination of All Forms of Discrimination against Women*, UN Doc. CEDAW/C/GC/28 (16 December 2010), para. 11.

177 1577 UNTS 3, adopted 20 November 1989, entered into force 2 September 1990. Several provisions of the CRC refer to IHL or armed conflict, thereby confirming that the CRC applies in armed conflict. See tenth preambular recital and Articles 38 and 39 CRC.

178 2173 UNTS 222, adopted 25 May 2000, entered into force 12 February 2002. The title of this Protocol confirms its applicability in armed conflict.

179 993 UNTS 3, adopted 16 December 1966, entered into force 3 January 1976. On the ICESCR's applicability in armed conflict, see ICJ, *Legal Consequences of the Construction of a Wall in the Occupied Palestinian Territory*, Advisory Opinion, ICJ Reports 2004, 180, para. 112. See also Committee on Economic, Social and Cultural Rights, *General Comment No. 7. The Right to Adequate Housing (Art. 11.1 of the Covenant): Forced Evictions*, UN Doc. E/1998/22 (20 May 1997), para. 5; Committee on Economic, Social and Cultural Rights, *General Comment No. 15*, UN Doc. E/C.12/2002/11 (20 January 2002), paras. 21–22. Further: Amrei Müller, *The Relationship between Economic, Social and Cultural Rights and International Humanitarian Law. An Analysis of Health-Related Issues in Non-International Armed Conflicts* (Leiden/Boston: Martinus Nijhoff, 2013); Elizabeth Mottershaw, "Economic, Social and Cultural Rights in Armed Conflict: International Human Rights Law and International Humanitarian Law", *The International Journal of Human Rights* 12, no. 3 (2008): 449–470, 452 and Eibe Riedel, "Economic, Social, and Cultural Rights in Armed Conflict", in *The Oxford Handbook of International Law in Armed Conflict*, edited by Andrew Clapham, Paola Gaeta (editors), Tom Haeck and Alice Priddy (assistant editors) (Oxford: Oxford University Press: 2014), 441–468.

180 The extra-territorial applicability of international human rights treaties falls outside the scope of the present book.

181 Article 4 ICCPR, for example, contains such a derogation clause.

182 Human Rights Committee, *General Comment 29: States of Emergency (Article 4)*, UN Doc. CCPR/C/21/Rev.1/Add.11 (2001), para. 3.

However, certain human rights are non-derogable and thus apply during armed conflict, for example the right not to be subjected to torture, inhuman or degrading treatment or punishment[183] and the right not to be arbitrarily deprived of one's life.[184] Moreover, the ICESCR does not provide for derogations. Article 4 ICESCR, however, states:

> "The States Parties to the present Covenant recognise that, in the enjoyment of those rights provided by the State in conformity with the present Covenant, the State may subject such rights only to such limitations as are determined by law only in so far as this may be compatible with the nature of these rights and solely for the purpose of promoting the general welfare in a democratic society."

States parties to the ICESCR are obliged to progressively realise the stipulated rights, but are directly bound – including in situations of armed conflict – by a "minimum core obligation to ensure the satisfaction of, at the very least, minimum essential levels of each of the rights".[185]

Notwithstanding the rise of non-State actors and their influence, the majority view remains that States are the sole duty bearers under international human rights law.[186] However, States are obliged to exercise due diligence in order to prevent non-State actors and individuals from abusing human rights within their territory.[187] International human rights law addresses people within a State's jurisdiction, granting rights to nationals *vis-à-vis* their State of

183 See Article 7 ICCPR and Article 1 CAT. Torture is examined in more detail in Chapter 5.

184 See Article 6(1) ICCPR. The interpretation of the right not to be arbitrarily deprived of one's life in times of armed conflict is discussed in Chapter 5.

185 Committee on Economic, Social and Cultural Rights, *General Comment 3*, UN Doc. E/1991/23 (14 December 1990), para. 10. See also Mottershaw, "Economic, Social and Cultural Rights in Armed Conflict", 457.

186 See Robert McCorquodale, "Non-State Actors and International Human Rights Law", in *Research Handbook on International Human Rights Law*, edited by Sarah Joseph and Adam McBeth (Cheltenham/Northampton, MA: Edward Elgar, 2010), 97. Sassòli, though acknowledging that a growing body of soft law considers non-State actors or at least armed groups as being bound by human rights law, cautions that international human rights law "needs much more practical translation and adjustment to the special problems raised by armed groups involved in armed conflicts than do the rules of behaviour mandated under IHL". Sassòli, "The Role of Human Rights", 56–57. However, Clapham argues that "the existing general rules of international human rights law, created and acknowledged by States, now fix on non-state actors so that they may be held accountable for violations of this law." Andrew Clapham, *Human Rights Obligations of Non-State Actors* (Oxford: Oxford University Press, 2006), 28. Matas and Zegveld also argue that armed opposition groups are bound by international human rights law: David Matas, "Armed Opposition Groups", *Manitoba Law Journal* 24 (1996–1997): 621–664, 630–634; Liesbeth Zegveld, *Accountability of Armed Opposition Groups in International Law* (Cambridge: Cambridge University Press, 2002), 38–55.

187 See McCorquodale, "Non-State Actors", 104–109; Erik Bjorge, "Human Rights, Treaties, Third-Party Effect" in *Max Planck Encyclopedia of Public International Law*, edited by Rüdiger Wolfrum (Oxford: Oxford University Press, 2011), available at www.mpepil.com, accessed 10.03.2015.

nationality and to stateless persons *vis-à-vis* their State of habitual residence.[188] For example, Article 6(1) ICCPR provides: "*Every human being* has the inherent right to life."[189] Article 6(1) IESCR states that States Parties "recognize the right of *everyone* to the opportunity to gain his living by work which he freely chooses or accepts".[190] Yet the passive personal scope of a few rights is limited to the nationals of a State party, as the example of the right to vote (Article 25 ICCPR) illustrates.[191]

2.2. INTERNATIONAL HUMANITARIAN LAW

The protective role of IHL, in particular with respect to protection of individuals within their country of nationality or, in case of stateless persons, within their country of habitual residence, must be clarified because it is precisely this role which makes IHL relevant for the interpretation of the refugee definition.

2.2.1. Material Scope of Protection

IHL does not protect from armed conflict as such but places constraints on how armed conflict is fought.[192] IHL limits the use of violence by sparing those who do not or no longer participate in hostilities and by restricting the means and methods of warfare.[193] IHL balances the humanitarian imperative to "mitigate

188 On the rights of stateless persons, see generally David Weissbrodt and Clay Collins, "The Human Rights of Stateless Persons", *Human Rights Quarterly* 28 (2006): 245–276.

189 Emphasis added.

190 Emphasis added.

191 The terms "citizens" and "nationals" are used interchangeably in this book.

192 See Frits Karlshoven and Liesbeth Zegveld, *Constraints on the Waging of War. An Introduction to International Humanitarian Law*, 4th ed. (Cambridge: Cambridge University Press, 2011), 1.

193 See Marco Sassòli, Anotine A. Bouvier, and Anne Quintin, *How does Law Protect in War? Cases, Documents and Teaching Materials on Contemporary Practice in International Humanitarian Law*, vol. I (2011), available at www.icrc.org/eng/assets/files/publications/icrc-0739-part-i.pdf, accessed 10.03.2015, 1–2; ICRC, "What is International Humanitarian Law?" (2004), available at www.icrc.org/eng/resources/documents/legal-fact-sheet/humanitarian-law-factsheet.htm, accessed 10.03.2015. Jochnik and Normand, however, argued that IHL favours military necessity over humanitarian values and consequently facilitates rather than restrains violence. See Chris af Jochnick and Roger Normand, "The Legitimation of Violence: A Critical History of the Laws of War", *Harvard International Law Journal* 35, no. 1 (1994): 49–95, 53. True, rules of IHL entail a compromise between humanitarian considerations and military necessity, a compromise which may mean that little protection is granted to victims of armed conflict. But: "Although the results are often disappointing, every little helps." A.P.V. Rogers, *Law on the Battlefield*, 3rd ed. (Manchester: Manchester University Press, 2012), 7.

the human suffering caused by war"[194] against military necessity.[195] Therefore, protection granted under IHL is qualified. IHL does not protect from all violence during armed conflict. The aim of IHL is merely "to prevent wanton cruelty and ruthlessness and to provide essential protection to those most directly affected by the conflict."[196]

Traditionally, the law of armed conflict had two strands: the law of The Hague[197] on the conduct of hostilities and the law of Geneva[198] which is concerned with the protection of the victims of armed conflict. Today, these two strands, whilst retaining their distinct identities, form an inseparable part of IHL.[199] The system of protection under the law of Geneva is status-based

194 Frits Karlshoven and Liesbeth Zegveld, *Constraints on Waging War. An Introduction to International Humanitarian Law*, 3rd ed. (Geneva: International Committee of the Red Cross, 2001), 12. Thürer notes that IHL assigns the highest value to the human person: Daniel Thürer, *International Humanitarian Law: Theory, Practice, Context*, edited by The Hague Academy of International Law, vol. 338, Recueil des Cours (Leiden: Martinus Nijhoff, 2011), 51.

195 See Rogers, *Law on the Battlefield*, 3; Yoram Dinstein, "Military Necessity", in *Max Planck Encyclopedia of Public International Law*, edited by Rüdiger Wolfrum (Oxford: Oxford University Press, 2009), available at http://mpepil.com, accessed 10.03.2015, para. 2. Thürer notes that three kinds of motives underpin the development of IHL, namely self-interest premised on reciprocity, combatants' codes of honours, and ideals of humanity: Thürer, *International Humanitarian Law*, 50.

196 Karlshoven and Zegveld, *Constraints (2011)*, 2. Dinstein notes that the law of international armed conflict does not eliminate the calamities of war completely but merely strives to attenuate them. As long as hostilities are conducted in accordance with the law, they may be fought fiercely and relentlessly. See Yoram Dinstein, *The Conduct of Hostilities under the Law of International Armed Conflict*, 2nd ed. (Cambridge: Cambridge University Press, 2010), 2 and 5.

197 Named after the 1899 First Hague Peace Conference at which the Convention (II) with Respect to the Laws and Customs of War on Land and its annex: Regulations concerning the Laws and Customs of War on Land was adopted. This annex is hereinafter referred to as the Hague Regulations. The 1907 Second Hague Peace Conference adopted further instruments regulating certain aspects of warfare. The origins of this branch of IHL, however, go back to the Lieber Code adopted in 1863 during the American Civil War, and the 1868 St Petersburg Declaration Renouncing the Use, in Time of War, of Explosive Projectiles Under 400 Grammes Weight. All aforementioned instruments are available at www.icrc.org/ihl, accessed 10.03.2015. See further Karlshoven and Zegveld, *Constraints (2011)*, 8–15.

198 This branch of IHL dates back to the efforts of the Genevan businessman Henry Dunant in the aftermath of the 1859 battle of Solferino to care for the wounded and sick, which eventually led to the adoption of the first Geneva Conventions and the establishment of the International Committee of the Red Cross. See Karlshoven and Zegveld, *Constraints (2011)*, 16–20. Karlshoven and Zegveld identify a third current of IHL, the "New York current", in which the United Nations becomes involved in the development of IHL under the heading "human rights in armed conflict". Karlshoven and Zegveld, *Constraints (2011)*, 20–24.

199 As manifested by the 1977 Additional Protocols. See François Bugnion, "Droit de Genève et Droit de La Haye", *International Review of the Red Cross* 83, no. 844 (2001): 901–922, 921. Thürer argues that since the adoption of the Additional Protocols, a clear-cut distinction between Geneva law and The Hague law has become infeasible because the Additional Protocols integrated the two strands: Thürer, *International Humanitarian Law*, 50.

and revolves around the concept of protected persons and protected objects.[200] Protected persons include civilians[201] and persons *hors de combat*.[202] Protected objects are civilian objects.[203] At the core of this system of protection lies the obligation of parties to the conflict to respect and protect protected persons in all circumstances and to treat them humanely without adverse distinction based on race, colour, sex, language, religion or belief, political or other opinion, national or social origin, wealth, birth or other status, or on any other similar criteria.[204] Numerous IHL rules further specify these central tenets.[205]

It is not only the law of Geneva which protects individuals in armed conflict. By placing restraints on the means and methods that can lawfully be used in the conduct of hostilities, the law of The Hague also has a protective function. This is reflected, for example, in the principles underpinning the restrictions on the methods and means of warfare, namely that the right of the parties to a conflict to choose means of injuring the enemy is not unlimited,[206] and the rule prohibiting the use of weapons of a nature to cause superfluous injury or unnecessary suffering.[207]

---

200 See generally Susan Breau, "Protected Persons and Objects", in *Perspectives on the ICRC Study on Customary International Humanitarian Law*, edited by Elizabeth Wilmshurst and Susan Breau (Cambridge: Cambridge University Press, 2007).

201 The fundamental principle of IHL is that parties to a conflict must distinguish between civilians and combatants, with attacks against civilians being prohibited. See Henckaerts and Doswald-Beck, *Customary International Humanitarian Law*, 3 on customary IHL and, for example, Article 4 Geneva Convention IV which defines persons protected under Geneva Convention IV.

202 See Henckaerts and Doswald-Beck, *Customary International Humanitarian Law*, 164. Also: Article 41(1) Additional Protocol I and Article 85(3)(2) Additional Protocol II.

203 See Henckaerts and Doswald-Beck, *Customary International Humanitarian Law*, 25 and 32. Also: Articles 48 and 52(1) Additional Protocol I. Special protection is granted to cultural property. For the position under customary IHL, see Henckaerts and Doswald-Beck, *Customary International Humanitarian Law*, 127–138. Also: 1954 Hague Convention on Cultural Property (249 UNTS 240, adopted 14 May 1954, entered into force 7 August 1957) and its two Protocols (Protocol for the Protection of Cultural Property in the Event of Armed Conflict, 249 UNTS 358, adopted 14 May 1954, entered into force 7 August 1956 and Second Protocol to the Hague Convention for the Protection of Cultural Property in the Event of Armed Conflict, 38 ILM (1999) at 769, adopted 26 March 1999, entered into force 9 March 2004); Articles 53 and 85(4)(d) Additional Protocol I; Article 16 Additional Protocol II.

204 See Karlshoven and Zegveld, *Constraints (2011)*, 48.

205 Karlshoven and Zegveld note this with regard to the Geneva Conventions. See Karlshoven and Zegveld, *Constraints (2011)*, 48. This observation is also correct for customary IHL. For example, the prohibition of attacks against civilians flows from the obligation to respect civilians. The obligation to spare the civilian population in the conduct of hostilities fleshes out the obligation to protect civilians. The obligation to provide persons deprived of their liberty with adequate food, water, clothing, shelter and medical education specifies the obligation of humane treatment. On these obligations under customary IHL, see Henckaerts and Doswald-Beck, *Customary International Humanitarian Law*, 3, 51 and 428.

206 This principle is *inter alia* laid down in Article 22 of the 1907 Hague Regulations and Article 35(1) Additional Protocol I. See Karlshoven and Zegveld, *Constraints (2011)*, 24.

207 This principle is laid down in Article 35(2) Additional Protocol I. See also Article 22 of the 1907 Hague Regulations.

In any armed conflict, the material scope of protection depends on the status (for example as a person *hors de combat*) and conduct of the individuals concerned (such as participation in hostilities), which is further examined in the next section and in Chapter 5. In international armed conflict, the material scope of protection under IHL may also differ depending on the status of the territory.[208] This is illustrated by the customary IHL prohibition on attacking, destroying, removing or rendering useless objects indispensable to the survival of the civilian population, which entails an exception concerning the defence against invasion of the own territory of a State party to an international armed conflict.[209] This exception allows for "scorched earth" policies to prevent or slow down the advance of enemy forces.[210] While the destruction of objects indispensable to the survival of the civilian population may be permissible in international armed conflict on a State's own territory, it is prohibited outside such territory.[211]

2.2.2. Protection of Nationals and Stateless Persons

As previously noted, this book considers two main types of armed conflict: (1) international armed conflicts to which the country of origin is a party and which are taking place on the territory of the country of origin, and (2) non-international armed conflicts occurring on the territory of the country of origin, irrespective of whether this country is a party to such conflicts.[212] It focusses on the country of origin and non-State actors as persecutors. In view of this, it must be examined to what extent the country of origin as a party to the conflict is obliged under IHL to protect its nationals and stateless persons on its territory and to what extent armed groups which are parties to the conflict are obliged to provide protection on the country of origin's territory.

Traditionally, IHL has developed to regulate international, i.e. inter-State, armed conflicts, focussing on providing protection to nationals of the adversary.[213] It is therefore necessary to examine to what extent IHL provides

---

208 See Marco Sassòli and Laura M. Olson, "The Judgment of the ICTY Appeals Chamber on the Merits in the Tadic Case", *International Review of the Red Cross* 82, no. 839 (2000): 733–769, 745.

209 See Henckaerts and Doswald-Beck, *Customary International Humanitarian Law*, 189–193.

210 See Yves Sandoz, Christophe Swinarski, and Bruno Zimmermann (editors), *Commentary on the Additional Protocols of 8 June 1977 to the Geneva Conventions of 12 August 1949* (Geneva: Martinus Nijhoff, 1987), mn. 2116, 658, commenting on Article 54(5) Additional Protocol I.

211 See Yves Sandoz, Christophe Swinarski, and Bruno Zimmermann (editors), *Commentary on the Additional Protocols of 8 June 1977 to the Geneva Conventions of 12 August 1949* (Geneva: Martinus Nijhoff, 1987), mn. 2122, 659, commenting on Article 54(5) Additional Protocol I.

212 As set forth in the Introduction of this book.

213 See Jean Pictet, *Development and Principles of International Humanitarian Law* (Dordrecht: Martinus Nijhoff, 1985), 3; Christopher Greenwood, "Historical Development and Legal Basis", in *The Handbook of International Humanitarian Law*, edited by Dieter Fleck (Oxford: Oxford University Press, 2008), mn. 102, 12; Theodor Meron, "The Humanization of

for the protection of the nationals of a party to an international armed conflict. Such protection is particularly relevant for the interpretation of the refugee definition, as the following example clarifies: State A and State B are parties to an international armed conflict. Ethnic group X forms the majority of the population in State A, while ethnic group Y is the main ethnic group in State B. State A also has amongst its nationals a minority with ethnicity Y. Hostilities take place in the border region of State A and State B, including on the territory of State A. In an armed conflict fuelled by ethnic resentment, the armed forces of State A commit atrocities against members of the ethnic group Y who are State A's nationals and located on its territory. These members of ethnic group Y could claim refugee protection in a State party to the Refugee Convention. It is hence pertinent to scrutinise the protection under IHL of the nationals of a State party to an international armed conflict or of stateless persons. This analysis includes treaties such as the 1949 Geneva Conventions[214] despite the book's focus on customary law. Such treaties regulate their respective passive personal scope in more detail than rules of customary IHL, offering insights into the structure of IHL as regards the protection of a State's own nationals and stateless persons on the territory of the State party to the conflict.

The 1949 Geneva Convention I addresses the protection of the wounded and sick in armed forces in the field. Its keystone provision, Article 12, sets out the principle of the inviolability of the wounded and sick in armed forces in the field. Article 12(1) Geneva Convention I provides: "Members of the armed forces …, who are wounded or sick, shall be respected and protected in all circumstances."

A similar provision can be found in Article 12(1) Geneva Convention II which addresses the wounded, sick and shipwrecked members of the armed forces at sea. The wording ("in all circumstances") and the humanitarian purpose of Article 12(1) Geneva Convention I and Article 12(1) Geneva Convention II (care for the wounded and sick) indicate that these provisions apply to wounded, sick or shipwrecked combatants irrespective of whether they find themselves with their own armed forces or in the hands of another party to the conflict.[215] Indeed, the initial Geneva Convention of 1864 provided that

Humanitarian Law", *American Journal of International Law* 94 (2000): 239–278, 256; Sassòli, Bouvier, and Quintin, *How does Law Protect in War?*, 32.

214 The four Geneva Conventions are widely considered to have customary character. See: Theodor Meron, "The Geneva Conventions as Customary Law", *American Journal of International Law* 81, no. 2 (1987): 348–370; Waldemar A. Solf, "Protection of Civilians Against the Effects of Hostilities Under Customary International Law and Under Protocol I", *American University International Law Review* 1, no. 1 (1986): 117–135, 124; Jean-Marie Henckaerts, "The Grave Breaches as Customary International Law", *Journal of International Criminal Justice* 7, no. 4 (2009): 683–701, xxxvi.

215 See Jean Pictet (editor), *Commentary on the Geneva Convention for the Amelioration of the Condition of the Wounded and Sick in Armed Forces in the Field* (Geneva International Committee of the Red Cross, 1952), 134–135 and 138; Jean Pictet (editor), *Commentary on the Second Geneva Convention for the Amelioration of the Condition of the Wounded, Sick and Shipwrecked Members of Armed Forces at Sea of 12 August, 1949* (Geneva: International

"[w]ounded or sick combatants, to whatever nation they may belong, shall be collected and cared for".[216] The 1864 Geneva Convention supports the view that the Geneva Conventions I and II provide for the protection of nationals of a State party to the armed conflict *vis-à-vis* this State and to stateless persons *vis-à-vis* their State of habitual residence. The military manuals of various States further strengthen this view because they note that the wounded and sick must be cared for regardless of whether they are friend or foe.[217] While "foe" refers to the wounded and sick affiliated with the adversary, "friend" can allude to both the wounded and sick of an allied party to the conflict or of the same nationality.[218]

The Geneva Convention III, which concerns the treatment of prisoners of war, does not in principle address the treatment of the nationals of a State party to the conflict. Prisoners of war are typically in the hands of a State of which they are not nationals.[219] Stateless persons are thus protected under the Geneva Convention III. Situations may occasionally arise, however, in which combatants who fall into the hands of an adversary State have the latter's nationality. Normally, nationals of the detaining power who were captured as members of the adverse armed forces are not entitled to prisoner-of-war status.[220] Yet it is

---

Committee of the Red Cross, 1960), 91. Rogers notes that the definition of the wounded and sick is very wide: Rogers, *Law on the Battlefield*, 76. Article 31(1) VCLT provides: "A treaty shall be interpreted in good faith in accordance with the ordinary meaning to be given to the terms of the treaty in their context and in the light of its object and purpose." The full title of the Geneva Convention IV, which refers to the protection of the civilian population, shows that the purpose of this convention is a humanitarian one. On treaty interpretation, see Chapter 4.

216 Article 6(1) of the Convention for the Amelioration of the Wounded in Armies in the Field, Geneva, 22 August 1864 (printed in Dietrich Schindler and Jiri Toman, *The Laws of Armed Conflicts* (The Hague: Martinus Nijhoff, 1988, 280–281), as noted by Sassòli, Bouvier, and Quintin, *How does Law Protect in War?*, 31.

217 See Code of Conduct for CF Personnel, Office of the Judge Advocate General, 2005, Rule 7, para. 1 (Canada); *IFOR Instructiekaart, geweldsinstructie* (IFOR Instruction Card), 1st ed., 18 December 1995, para. 6 (Netherlands); *Droit international humanitaire, Manuel de l'instructeur en vigueur dans les forces armées et de sécurité* (International Humanitarian Law, Instructors' Manual in force in the security forces), Ministère de la Défense, Présidence de la République, Etat-major des Armées (Ministry of Defence, Presidency of the Republic, Chief of staff), 2006 edition, 26 and 47, (Chad); *Cartilla de Derecho Internacional Humanitario* (International Humanitarian Law Guidelines), Ministry of National Defence, 2009, para. 14(p) (Mexico); Law of Armed Conflict, Military Basic Course (ORS), 4 Précis, The School of Military Police (Kenya), Précis No. 3, 14; Soldier's Rules, in Handbook on Discipline, Annex C(I), General Headquarters, Armed Forces of the Philippines, Camp General Emilio Aguinaldo, Quezon City, 1989 (Philippines), para. 5; *Lois et coutumes de la guerre (Extrait et commentaire)* (Law and Customs of War (Extract and Commentary), Règlement 51.7/II f, Armée Suisse (Regulation 51.7/II f, Swiss Army) 1987 (Switzerland), Article 71.

218 Rogers implicitly supports this view, noting that "there is a general duty on the parties to the conflict in relation to people in their area of military control who are in need of medical treatment." Rogers, *Law on the Battlefield*, 76.

219 See Article 4A Geneva Convention III.

220 See Sassòli, Bouvier, and Quintin, *How does Law Protect in War?*, 52, footnote 32; Rogers, *Law on the Battlefield*, 36. Rogers points to the Privy Council case *Public Prosecutor v. Koi*, 1968 All ER 419, in which a Malaysian national who was a member of the Indonesian armed forces

conceivable that such persons would be entitled to prisoner-of-war status at least where their nationality has been forced upon them.[221] Hence, the Geneva Convention III confers to a very limited extent obligations upon its parties as regards the treatment of their own nationals.

The Geneva Convention IV addresses the protection of civilians. Article 4(1) Geneva Convention IV states:

> "Persons protected by the Convention are those who, at a given moment and in any manner whatsoever, find themselves, in case of a conflict or occupation, in the hands of a Party to the conflict or Occupying Power of which they are not nationals."

The requirement that the protected persons be in the hands of a party to the armed conflict is to be understood broadly as being within the territory that is under the control of a party to the armed conflict.[222] Pursuant to the plain wording, protected persons must be located within the territory of a State of which they are *not* nationals. Stateless persons thus fall within this definition of protected persons. The ICRC commentary emphasises that the Geneva Convention IV honours the principle that international law "does not interfere in a State's relations with its own nationals".[223]

However, international law has developed since the mid-twentieth century and now addresses a State's relations with its nationals in certain circumstances.[224] The ICTY Appeals Chamber has interpreted the nationality requirement broadly, which fits within this development of international law. The ICTY Appeals Chamber found in the *Tadić case* that Article 4 Geneva Convention IV

> "does not make its applicability dependent on formal bonds and purely legal relations. Its primary purpose is to ensure the safeguards afforded by the Convention to those civilians who do not enjoy the diplomatic protection, and correlatively are not subject to the allegiance and control, of the State in whose hands they may find

---

operating in Malaysia was captured and denied prisoner-of-war-status because he owed allegiance to the detaining power.

221 See Greenwood, "Historical Development and Legal Basis", mn. 103, 14.

222 See Jean Pictet (editor), *Commentary on the Fourth Geneva Convention Relative to the Protection of Civilian Persons in Times of Armed Conflict* (Geneva: International Committee of the Red Cross, 1958), 47; Gerhard Werle, *Völkerstrafrecht* (Tübingen: Mohr Siebeck, 2012), mn. 1113, 493; Guénaël Mettraux, *International Crimes and the Ad Hoc Tribunals* (Oxford: Oxford University Press, 2006) and ICTY, *The Prosecutor v. Zejnil Delalić, Zdravko Mucić, aka "Pavo", Hazim Delić, Esad Landžo, aka "Zenga"*, Judgment, Appeals Chamber, 20 February 2001, Case No. IT-96-21-A, para. 246.

223 Pictet (editor), *Commentary on the Fourth Geneva Convention Relative to the Protection of Civilian Persons in Times of Armed Conflict*, 46.

224 As evidenced, for example, by the development of international human rights law.

themselves. In granting its protection, Article 4 intends to look to the substance of relations, not to their legal characterisation."[225]

The Appeals Chamber held that more weight is placed in the Geneva Convention IV on substantial relations rather than formal bonds, rejecting a literal interpretation of Article 4(1) Geneva Convention IV. It stressed that in current armed conflicts, ethnicity often determines national allegiance.[226] Similarly, the ICTY Trial Chamber in the *Blaškić case* found:

> "In an inter-ethnic armed conflict, a person's ethnic background may be regarded as a decisive factor in determining to which nation he owed his allegiance and may thus serve to establish the status of the victims as protected persons."[227]

Further ICTY judgments support this view.[228] The International Criminal Court also appears to accept it.[229] This understanding is in line with the humanitarian object and purpose of Article 4(1) Geneva Convention IV, the protection of civilians, and reflects the realities of many armed conflicts where allegiance is defined by substantive bonds including ethnicity rather than formal links such as nationality. For these reasons, it is adopted by this book.[230] Thus, the

---

225 ICTY, *The Prosecutor v. Duško Tadić aka "Dule"*, Judgment, Appeals Chamber, 15 July 1999, Case No. IT-94-1-A, para. 168.

226 See ICTY, *The Prosecutor v. Duško Tadić aka "Dule"*, Judgment, Appeals Chamber, 15 July 1999, Case No. IT-94-1-A, Appeals Chamber, Judgment, 15 July 1999, para. 166.

227 ICTY, *The Prosecutor v. Tihomir Blaškić*, Judgment, Trial Chamber I, 3 March 2000, Case No. IT-95-14-T, para. 127.

228 See ICTY, *The Prosecutor v. Zlatko Aleksovski*, Judgment, Appeals Chamber, 24 March 2000, Case No. IT-95-14/1-A, paras. 149–152; ICTY, *The Prosecutor v. Zejnil Delalić, Zdravko Mucić, aka "Pavo", Hazim Delić, Esad Landžo, aka "Zenga"*, Judgment, Appeals Chamber, 20 February 2001, Case No. IT-96-21-A, paras. 144–146; and ICTY, *The Prosecutor v. Tihomir Blaškić*, Judgment, Appeals Chamber, 29 July 2004, Case No. IT-95-14-A, paras. 167–182.

229 See ICC, *The Prosecutor v. Germain Katanga and Mathieu Ngudjolo Chui*, Decision on the confirmation of charges, Pre-Trial Chamber I, 30 September 2008, Case No. ICC-01/04-01/07, paras 289–293.

230 Also supporting this understanding of protected person under the Geneva Convention IV: Werle, *Völkerstrafrecht*, mn. 118, 495; Cátia Lopes and Noëlle Quénivet, "Individuals as Subjects of Humanitarian Law and Human Rights Law", in *International Humanitarian Law and Human Rights Law. Towards a Merger in International Law*, edited by Roberta Arnold and Noëlle Quénivet (Leiden/Boston: Martinus Nijhoff, 2008), 213; apparently also M. Cherif Bassiouni, *International Criminal Law*, Vol. III International Enforcement (Leiden: Martinus Nijhoff, 2008), 79–80. Quéginer finds that this interpretation of "protected persons" warrants respect, but cautions whether it is pertinent for all types of international armed conflict and wonders whether the determination of allegiance to a party to the conflict is too nebulous. See Jean-François Quéguiner, "Dix ans après la création du Tribunal pénal international pour l'ex-Yougoslavie: évaluation de l'apport de sa jurisprudence au droit international humanitaire", *International Review of the Red Cross* 85, no. 850 (2003): 271–311, 302–303. Sassòli and Olson raise similar concerns: Sassòli and Olson, "The Judgment of the ICTY", 744. For an the judicial development of the nation of "protected person" by the ICTY, see also Darcy, *Judges, War and Law*, 114–112.

Geneva Convention IV can be understood as placing in certain circumstances obligations on States parties regarding their own nationals if their allegiance lies with the adverse party to the conflict. Article 27 Geneva Convention IV sets out obligations owed to protected persons, *inter alia* stating:

> "Protected persons are entitled, in all circumstances, to respect for their persons, their honour, their family rights, their religious convictions and practices, and their manners and customs. They shall at all times be humanely treated, and shall be protected especially against all acts of violence or threats thereof and against insults and public curiosity."

Irrespective of the interpretation of Article 4 Geneva Convention IV, Part II of the Geneva Convention IV on "General Protection of Populations Against Certain Consequences of War" is concerned with both nationals and non-nationals of a State party to an international armed conflict. Article 13 Geneva Convention IV states that the provisions of Part II of this Convention

> "cover the whole of the populations of the countries in conflict, without any adverse distinction based, in particular, on race, nationality, religion or political opinion, and are intended to alleviate the sufferings caused by war."

Thus, States are bound by these provisions *vis-à-vis* their own nationals.[231] Part II of the Geneva Convention IV focusses on medical care and special protection of certain groups. It *inter alia* contains provisions on the establishment of hospital and safety zones and localities (Article 14), neutralised zones (Article 15), the particular protection of the wounded, sick, infirm and expectant mothers as well as the dead, shipwrecked and other persons exposed to grave danger (Article 16).[232]

Thus, the Geneva Conventions confer some obligations in certain circumstances on their States parties as regards the protection of their nationals and stateless persons on their territory during international armed conflict. These obligations include humane treatment and protection from all acts of violence as well as care for the wounded and sick.

We now turn to the other major IHL treaty applicable in international armed conflict, the Additional Protocol I, which *inter alia* develops the rules on the wounded, sick and shipwrecked of the Geneva Conventions and addresses the conduct of hostilities. Article 1(4) Additional Protocol I extends the scope of

---

231 See also Pictet (editor), *Commentary on the Fourth Geneva Convention Relative to the Protection of Civilian Persons in Times of Armed Conflict*, 350.

232 These rules reflect customary IHL. See Henckaerts and Doswald-Beck, *Customary International Humanitarian Law*, 119–126, 400, 403, 406, 475, 479, and 489. Article 70(2) Geneva Convention IV addresses the nationals of the occupying Power who, before the outbreak of hostilities, have sought refuge in the territory of the occupied State. Since this book does not examine belligerent occupation, this provision is not further analysed here.

application of this treaty to wars of national liberation. In such armed conflicts, members of the parties to the armed conflict typically have the same nationality. The special character of the situations covered by Article 1(4) Additional Protocol I must be acknowledged. As the ICRC commentary explains, in such situations, the question of whether or not the obligations set out by the Additional Protocol I apply does not depend on the nationality of the addressees or beneficiaries because international law overrides this criterion. Members of the adversary party to such an armed conflict do not owe allegiance to the State whose nationality they have.[233] Hence, the Additional Protocol I is premised on an understanding that actual bonds of allegiance may override formal ties of nationality.

In contrast to the Geneva Conventions I and II, Additional Protocol I defines the wounded, sick and shipwrecked. The definitions of the wounded, sick (Article 8(a) Additional Protocol I) and shipwrecked (Article 8(b)) do not contain any reference to nationality.[234] What is more, Article 10(1) Additional Protocol I expressly provides that "[a]ll the wounded, sick and shipwrecked, to whichever Party they belong, shall be respected and protected." This provision stipulates that the States parties to the Additional Protocol I are obliged to respect and protect the wounded, sick and shipwrecked irrespective of their affiliation to a party to the armed conflict. The obligations regarding the wounded, sick and shipwrecked thus encompass the treatment of a State party to the conflict's own nationals[235] and stateless persons. Parties to an international armed conflict have a general obligation with respect to the people in their area of military control who require medical care.[236]

Part III of the Additional Protocol I *inter alia* addresses means and methods of warfare. Article 35(2) Additional Protocol I prohibits the use of weapons,

---

233 See Sandoz, Swinarski, and Zimmermann (editors), *Commentary on the Additional Protocols of 8 June 1977 to the Geneva Conventions of 12 August 1949*, mn. 3013, 867.

234 Article 8(a) Additional Protocol I states: "'wounded' and 'sick' mean persons, whether military or civilian, who, because of trauma, disease or other physical or mental disorder or disability, are in need of medical assistance or care and who refrain from any act of hostility. These terms also cover maternity cases, new-born babies and other persons who may be in need of immediate medical assistance or care, such as the infirm or expectant mothers, and who refrain from any act of hostility". Article 8(b) Additional Protocol I provides: "'shipwrecked' means persons, whether military or civilian, who are in peril at sea or in other waters as a result of misfortune affecting them or the vessel or aircraft carrying them and who refrain from any act of hostility. These persons, provided that they continue to refrain from any act of hostility, shall continue to be considered shipwrecked during their rescue until they acquire another status under the Conventions or this Protocol".

235 See Sandoz, Swinarski, and Zimmermann (editors), *Commentary on the Additional Protocols of 8 June 1977 to the Geneva Conventions of 12 August 1949*, para. 320. The obligation to search for, collect and evacuate the wounded, sick and shipwrecked and to provide them with medical care to the fullest extent possible and with the least possible delay reflects customary IHL. See Henckaerts and Doswald-Beck, *Customary International Humanitarian Law*, 396–405.

236 See Rogers, *Law on the Battlefield*, 76.

projectiles and material and methods of warfare of a nature which cause superfluous injury or unnecessary suffering.[237] During the drafting process, this provision was initially limited to enemy combatants and their relationship with one another, but was subsequently broadened so as to include the wider impact of means and methods of warfare on the population.[238] This indicates that a State is bound by Article 35(2) *vis-à-vis* its own nationals and stateless persons, a view which is corroborated by the context of this provision. Article 35(1) Additional Protocol I stipulates that the right of the parties to the armed conflict to choose methods or means of warfare is not unlimited. This provision does not contain a qualification as regards the treatment of a State's own nationals or stateless persons. Moreover, the object and purpose of Article 35(2) Additional Protocol I, protection from superfluous injury or unnecessary suffering, would be undermined if certain means or methods of warfare were unlawful if they affect the adversary's nationals but lawful *vis-à-vis* the State party's own nationals or stateless persons. It can therefore be argued that Article 35(1) and (2) Additional Protocol I confer obligations on States parties that include the effects of means and methods of warfare upon their own nationals and stateless persons.

Part IV of the Additional Protocol I deals with the civilian population. It comprises *inter alia* the principle of distinction (Article 48).[239] Article 49(2) Additional Protocol I states:

> "The provisions of this Protocol with respect to attacks apply to all attacks in whatever territory conducted, including the national territory belonging to a Party to the conflict but under the control of an adverse Party."

The provisions of the Additional Protocol I regarding attacks thus apply in the territory of a State party to an armed conflict that is under the control of an adversary. The notion of "in whatever territory" indicates that the own territory of a Party to the armed conflict is covered irrespective of whether it is controlled by an adversary Party to the conflict.[240] The context of Article 49(2) Additional Protocol I supports this view. The prohibition in Article 54 Additional Protocol I of attacking, destroying, removing or rendering useless objects indispensable to the survival of the civilian population includes an exception in cases where a State's own territory needs to be defended against invasion.[241] The fact that

---

237 This prohibition reflects customary IHL. See Henckaerts and Doswald-Beck, *Customary International Humanitarian Law*, 237.

238 As noted by Michael Bothe, Karl Josef Partsch, and Waldemar A. Solf, *New Rules for Victims of Armed Conflicts: Commentary on the two 1977 Protocols Additional to the Geneva Conventions of 1949* (The Hague/Boston: Martinus Nijhoff, 1982), 193.

239 The principle of distinction is customary in nature. See Henckaerts and Doswald-Beck, *Customary International Humanitarian Law*, 3 and 25.

240 See Sassòli, Bouvier, and Quintin, *How does Law Protect in War?*, Chapter 9, 3.

241 See Article 54(2) and (5) Additional Protocol I. This prohibition, which is customary in nature, is discussed further in Chapter 5.

Article 54(5) Additional Protocol I makes an exception to the prohibition in Article 54(2) regarding a party's own territory under its control means that without such an exception, the prohibition in Article 54(2) would apply to such territory and thus to the population within such territory. The scope of application of Article 54 is determined by the aforementioned Article 49(2). It can therefore be concluded that the scope of application of the provisions on attacks in Additional Protocol I, as set out by Article 49(2), includes a State party's own territory and by implication the population on such territory.

Article 50 Additional Protocol I defines civilians as persons who are not members of the armed forces or similar groups,[242] with the civilian population comprising all persons who are civilians.[243] Article 50 is situated in Chapter II of Part IV of the Additional Protocol I. This Chapter specifies which attacks are unlawful, for example indiscriminate attacks (Article 51(4)), whose scope of application is also determined by Article 49(2), thus encompassing a State's own territory. The State party's own civilian population hence benefits from the provisions on targeting in Part IV of the Additional Protocol I. Indeed, the ICRC commentary notes:

> "In protecting civilians against the dangers of war, the important aspect is not so much their nationality as the inoffensive character of the person to be spared and the situation in which they find themselves."[244]

Setting out fundamental guarantees in relation to persons in the power of a party to the conflict, Article 75 Additional Protocol I is designed to fill the gaps in treaty law faced by those who are not protected persons under the Geneva Conventions or this Protocol. Article 75(1) Additional Protocol I states:

> "In so far as they are affected by a situation referred to in Article 1 of this Protocol, persons who are in the power of a Party to the conflict and who do not benefit from more favourable treatment under the Conventions or under this Protocol shall be treated humanely in all circumstances and shall enjoy, as a minimum, the protection

---

242 A civilian is defined in Article 50(1) Additional Protocol I as "any person who does not belong to one of the categories of persons referred to in Article 4A(1), (2), (3) and (6) of the Third Convention and in Article 43 of this Protocol. In case of doubt whether a person is a civilian, that person shall be considered to be a civilian." Sassóli et al. identify Articles 49 and 50 Additional Protocol I as applicable in the relationship between a State party to an international armed conflict and its own nationals. See Sassòli, Bouvier, and Quintin, *How does Law Protect in War?*, 32, footnote 54. For the purpose of applying the principle of distinction, customary IHL defines a civilian as "persons who are not members of the armed forces." Henckaerts and Doswald-Beck, *Customary International Humanitarian Law*, 17.

243 See Article 50(2) Additional Protocol I. This definition reflects customary IHL. See Henckaerts and Doswald-Beck, *Customary International Humanitarian Law*, 17.

244 Sandoz, Swinarski, and Zimmermann (editors), *Commentary on the Additional Protocols of 8 June 1977 to the Geneva Conventions of 12 August 1949*, para. 1909.

> provided by this Article without any adverse distinction based upon race, colour, sex, language, religion or belief, political or other opinion, national or social origin, wealth, birth or other status, or any other similar criteria."[245]

The ICRC's original draft of this provision contained an express reference to nationals of parties to the armed conflict, but this reference was deleted during the negotiations. This might indicate the drafters' intention to exclude nationals. On the other hand, it can also be argued that since it is apparent from the wording of Article 75 that nationals are included, there was no need for an express reference to them.[246] The same can be said for stateless persons.

In order to benefit from the fundamental guarantees set out in Article 75 Additional Protocol I, an individual must (1) be in the power of a party to the armed conflict; (2) be affected by an armed conflict or an occupation as referred to in Article 1 Additional Protocol I; and (3) not benefit from more favourable treatment under the Geneva Conventions or the Additional Protocol I.[247] As is apparent from the wording of Article 75(1) Additional Protocol I, the first requirement does not specify whether or not the party to the conflict in question is the country of which the affected individuals are nationals. Additional Protocol I employs the terms "party to the conflict" and "adverse party" frequently without differentiating between the categories of persons being covered.[248]

The second requirement could also indicate that own nationals and stateless persons are covered. Article 72 Additional Protocol I sets out the field of application of Section III in which Article 75 is located. Article 72 Additional Protocol I stipulates that the provisions in Section III are additional to the rules in Parts I and III of the Geneva Convention IV on the protection of civilians and civilian objects in the power of a party to the conflict. A particular focus of Section III Additional Protocol I lies on "enemy" civilians. However, Article 72 Additional Protocol I also stipulates that the provisions of Section III Additional Protocol I are additional to "other applicable rules of international law relating to the protection of fundamental human rights during international armed conflict." Clearly, human rights regulate the relationship between a State and its nationals and also apply to stateless persons. It can therefore be argued that some

---

245 These provisions reflect customary IHL. See Henckaerts and Doswald-Beck, *Customary International Humanitarian Law*, 306 and 308.

246 See Sandoz, Swinarski, and Zimmermann (editors), *Commentary on the Additional Protocols of 8 June 1977 to the Geneva Conventions of 12 August 1949*, para. 3018.

247 See Sandoz, Swinarski, and Zimmermann (editors), *Commentary on the Additional Protocols of 8 June 1977 to the Geneva Conventions of 12 August 1949*, para. 3009.

248 See Sandoz, Swinarski, and Zimmermann (editors), *Commentary on the Additional Protocols of 8 June 1977 to the Geneva Conventions of 12 August 1949*, para. 3021.

provisions of Section III Additional Protocol I, in particular Article 75, address such individuals as well.[249]

Furthermore, the purpose of Article 75 Additional Protocol I is to fill gaps in the Geneva Conventions and the Additional Protocol I by providing protection to persons who do not fall within any category of protected persons. To the extent that the Geneva Conventions and the Additional Protocol I do not address a State's own nationals or stateless persons, such individuals fall within the scope of Article 75 Additional Protocol I. Thus, Article 75 Additional Protocol I can be construed so as to encompass a State's own nationals and stateless persons to the extent that they are involved in actions related to an armed conflict in the sense of Article 1 Additional Protocol I.[250]

Hence, there are provisions in the Additional Protocol I which confer protection obligations upon its States parties in relation to their own nationals and stateless persons on their territory in international armed conflict. They include the obligation to respect and protect the wounded, sick and shipwrecked and certain obligations regarding the civilian population. They also comprise the fundamental guarantees set out in Article 75 and obligations concerning the conduct of hostilities.

There are several treaties which could contain obligations of States parties *vis-à-vis* their nationals and stateless persons during international armed conflict. Since a comprehensive analysis of all such treaty provisions is beyond this book's scope, suffice it to point to treaties on the conduct of hostilities which, in phrasing the respective prohibitions, use the phrase "never under any circumstances", for example:

- Article 1 of the 1971 Convention on the Prohibition of the Development, Production and Stockpiling of Bacteriological (Biological) and Toxic Weapons and on their Destruction (Biological Weapons Convention);[251] and
- Article 1(1) 1993 Paris Convention on the Prohibition of the Development, Production, Stockpiling and Use of Chemical Weapons and on their Destruction (Chemical Weapons Convention).[252]

---

249 See Sandoz, Swinarski, and Zimmermann (editors), *Commentary on the Additional Protocols of 8 June 1977 to the Geneva Conventions of 12 August 1949*, para 2926. The commentary points to the declaration of Finland upon ratifying the Additional Protocol I. According to this declaration, the field of application of Article 75 Additional Protocol I includes *inter alia* nationals of contracting States. See Sandoz, Swinarski, and Zimmermann (editors), *Commentary on the Additional Protocols of 8 June 1977 to the Geneva Conventions of 12 August 1949*, para 2913.

250 See Bothe, Partsch, and Solf, *New Rules for Victims of Armed Conflicts*, 444. See also Meron, "The Humanization of Humanitarian Law", 256–257 and footnote 99.

251 1015 UNTS 163, adopted 10 April 1972, entered into force 25 March 1975. The use of biological weapons is prohibited under customary IHL. See Henckaerts and Doswald-Beck, *Customary International Humanitarian Law*, 256.

252 1974 UNTS 45, adopted 3 September 1992, entered into force 29 April 1997. Customary IHL prohibits the use of chemical weapons. See Henckaerts and Doswald-Beck, *Customary*

The phrase "never under any circumstances" can be interpreted as meaning that the respective international treaty applies at all times, including when actions affect own nationals or stateless persons. It applies not only to actions of contracting States within the territory of an adversary and *vis-à-vis* the latter's nationals, but also within their own territory and in relation to their own nationals and stateless persons.

Many of the treaty provisions outlined above are also part of customary international law in international armed conflicts.[253] To the extent that they confer obligations on States regarding their own nationals or stateless persons, the same is true for the corresponding rules of customary IHL. Moreover, there are rules of customary international law whose wording shows that they confer obligations on a State party to an international armed conflict *vis-à-vis* its own nationals or stateless persons. For example, customary IHL provides:

> "Attacking persons who are recognized as *hors de combat* is prohibited. A person *hors de combat* is:
> (a) anyone who is in the power of an adverse party;
> (b) anyone who is defenceless because of unconsciousness, shipwreck, wounds or sickness; or
> (c) anyone who clearly expresses an intention to surrender; provided he or she abstains from any hostile act and does not attempt to escape."[254]

Persons *hors de combat* are defined as persons in the power of the adverse party, without reference to nationality. The State practice underpinning this rule of customary IHL refers to adversaries who are *hors de combat*, but refrains from further specifying a nationality requirement.[255] The omission of a nationality requirement means that the obligation to refrain from attacking persons *hors de combat* applies to own nationals and stateless persons.

Prohibitions on certain weapons under customary IHL are cast in absolute terms, as the rule of customary IHL on indiscriminate weapons in international

---

International Humanitarian Law, 259.

253 As noted in the above analysis of international humanitarian treaty law.

254 Henckaerts and Doswald-Beck, *Customary International Humanitarian Law*, 306.

255 See, e.g., the following military manuals: *Droit de la Guerre, Manuel d'Instruction pour Officiers, Etat-Major Général, Division Opérations* (Law of War, Instruction Manual for Officers, Chief of Staff, Operational Division), 1994, Part I, Title II, 34 (Belgium); *Le Droit de la Guerre*, III fascicules, Forces Armées du Bénin, Ministère de la Défense nationale (The Law of War, III volumes, Armed Forces of Benin, Ministry of National Defence), 1995, Fascicule II, 4 (Benin); *Transcripción Normas Fundamentales del Derecho Humanitario Aplicables en los Conflictos Armados*, Circular No. 033/DIPL-SERPO-526, Policía Nacional, Dirección General (Transcript of Fundamental Norms of Humanitarian Law Applicable in Armed Conflcits, Cicular No.033/DIPL-SERPO-526, National Police, Directorate General), Santafé de Bogotá, 14 May 1992, para. 2 (Colombia); *Humanitair Oorlogsrecht: Handleiding*, Voorschift No. 27–412, Koninklijke Landmacht, Militair Juridische Dienst (Humanitarian Law Manual, Regulations No. 27–412, Royal Netherlands Army, Military Legal Services), 2005, para. 1042 (Netherlands).

and non-international armed conflict exemplifies: "The use of weapons which are by nature indiscriminate is prohibited."[256] The absolute nature of this prohibition means that it applies in all circumstances, including when a State's actions affect its own nationals or stateless persons during international armed conflict. This is also the case, for instance, for the absolute prohibition of using human shields.[257]

As regards other rules of customary IHL, the fact that they confer obligations on a State party to an armed conflict *vis-à-vis* its own nationals and stateless persons is more apparent in the wording of the rule, as the following example illustrates:

> "The wounded, sick and shipwrecked must receive, to the fullest extent practicable and with the least possible delay, the medical care and attention required by their condition. No distinction may be made among them founded on any grounds other than medical ones."[258]

The prohibition of distinction amongst the wounded, sick and shipwrecked on any grounds other than medical ones means that distinction based on nationality or on the lack of a nationality is not permitted. A State's own nationals and stateless persons are thus covered by this rule.

Customary IHL also provides that "[c]hildren must not be recruited into armed forces or armed groups."[259] With respect to the armed forces, this rule confers obligations on States regarding their child nationals. The same is true for the rule of customary IHL that "[c]hildren must not be allowed to take part in hostilities".[260]

Turning to non-international armed conflicts which typically take place within a State's territory, the applicable IHL necessarily imposes obligations on the State *vis-à-vis* its own nationals.[261] Usually, members of an armed group which is a party to a non-international armed conflict will have the nationality of the State on whose territory they are fighting. Article 3 common to the Geneva Conventions, the "convention in miniature",[262] applies in non-international armed conflict. Common Article 3(1) contains a non-discrimination clause, providing that "[p]ersons taking no active part in the hostilities ... shall in all circumstances be treated humanely, without any adverse distinction founded

---

256 Henckaerts and Doswald-Beck, *Customary International Humanitarian Law*, 244.
257 See Henckaerts and Doswald-Beck, *Customary International Humanitarian Law*, 337.
258 Henckaerts and Doswald-Beck, *Customary International Humanitarian Law*, 400.
259 Henckaerts and Doswald-Beck, *Customary International Humanitarian Law*, 482.
260 Henckaerts and Doswald-Beck, *Customary International Humanitarian Law*, 485.
261 As set out in the Introduction, the book does not analyse the intervention of third States on the side of a party to a non-international armed conflict taking place outside the intervening State's territory.
262 Pictet (editor), *Commentary on the Fourth Geneva Convention Relative to the Protection of Civilian Persons in Times of Armed Conflict*, 33.

on race, colour, religion or faith, sex, birth or wealth, or any other similar criteria." Nationality was omitted as a prohibited criterion. However, the ICRC commentary notes that it is nonetheless prohibited to treat people of a certain nationality in an arbitrary way and that a State's own nationals are covered by Common Article 3.[263] Arguably, this principle also applies to stateless persons. Common Article 3 thus confers obligations on States parties *vis-à-vis* their own nationals and stateless persons.

The 1977 Additional Protocol II also applies in non-international armed conflict, though its threshold of application is higher than that of Common Article 3.[264] Article 2(1) Additional Protocol II defines the Protocol's personal field of application:

> "This Protocol shall be applied without any adverse distinction founded on race, colour, sex, language, religion or belief, political or other opinion, national or social origin, wealth, birth or other status, or on any other similar criteria ..."

The ground of national origin can be interpreted as including nationality, as confirmed by the ICRC commentary, which notes: "The Protocol applies to all residents of the country engaged in a conflict, irrespective of their nationality".[265] Hence, the Additional Protocol II contains obligations of States regarding their own nationals and stateless persons, for example the fundamental guarantees (prohibition of violence to life, collective punishments, hostage taking, etc.) set out in Article 4 Additional Protocol II to which persons who are not or no longer participating in hostilities are entitled.

There are also customary international humanitarian rules that apply in non-international armed conflict. Examples include the rule quoted above prohibiting attacks against persons *hors de combat*, the prohibition on using human shields, the obligation not to recruit children into the armed forces or armed groups and the obligation not to use children for participation in hostilities.[266] For the same

263 See Pictet (editor), *Commentary on the Fourth Geneva Convention Relative to the Protection of Civilian Persons in Times of Armed Conflict*, 40.

264 Protocol Additional to the Geneva Conventions of 12 August 1949, and relating to the Protection of Victims of Non-International Armed Conflicts (Additional Protocol II), 1125 UNTS 609, adopted 8 June 1977, entered into force 7 December 1978. Article 1(1) Additional Protocol II states: "This Protocol ... shall apply to all armed conflicts which are not covered by Article 1 of the ... [Additional Protocol I] and which take place in the territory of a High Contracting Party between its armed forces and dissident armed forces or other organized armed groups which, under responsible command, exercise such control over a part of its territory as to enable them to carry out sustained and concerted military operations and to implement this Protocol."

265 Sandoz, Swinarski, and Zimmermann (editors), *Commentary on the Additional Protocols of 8 June 1977 to the Geneva Conventions of 12 August 1949*, para. 448, 1359.

266 See Henckaerts and Doswald-Beck, *Customary International Humanitarian Law*, 306, 337, 482 and 485.

reasons as set out above, these rules confer obligations on States *vis-à-vis* their own nationals and stateless persons.

2.3. INTERNATIONAL CRIMINAL LAW

International criminal law is concerned with violations of IHL that entail individual criminal responsibility. It is a branch of international law that is accessory to IHL.[267] International criminal law protects the individual during armed conflict by criminalising and thus prohibiting certain acts and omissions. It thereby strives to prevent the occurrence of such conduct.[268] War crimes protect individual *Rechtsgüter* (legally protected goods).[269] For example, by criminalising wilful killing, torture or inhuman treatment and other conduct, the grave breaches provisions of the Geneva Conventions and Additional Protocol I protect the most elementary *Rechtsgüter* of dignity, life and physical integrity.[270] Regarding the war crimes premised on The Hague law, it is less apparent that they protect individual *Rechtsgüter*. This is nonetheless the case because the prohibition of certain means and methods of warfare aims at the prevention of unnecessary and superfluous suffering.[271]

In principle, war crimes can be committed in any armed conflict by members of the armed forces or, in non-international armed conflict, by members of armed opposition groups (irrespective of rank) or by civilians.[272] Moreover, the perpetrator's nationality is irrelevant to their individual criminal responsibility. An individual can commit a war crime against a co-national or a stateless

267 See Werle, *Völkerstrafrecht*, mn. 1052, 466 and Bothe, "The Historical Evolution", 44.

268 For example, States parties to the Rome Statute established the ICC "to contribute to the prevention of such crimes", including war crimes, as stated in the fifth preambular recital of the Rome Statute. See generally Otto Triffterer, "The Preventive and the Repressive Function of the International Criminal Court", in *The Rome Statute of the International Criminal Court. A Challenge to Immunity*, edited by Mauro Politi and Giuseppe Nesi (Dartmouth: Ashgate, 2001).

269 Whether and if so, to what extent, international criminal law protects individual *Rechtsgüter* remains unsettled amongst legal scholars. See Werle, *Völkerstrafrecht*, mn. 1065–1066, 472–473.

270 See Article 50 Geneva Convention I, Article 51 Geneva Convention II, Article 130 Geneva Convention III, Article 147 Geneva Convention IV, and Article 11 Additional Protocol I.

271 See Werle, *Völkerstrafrecht*, mn. 1065, 476 and more generally Theodor Meron, "The Martens Clause, Principles of Humanity, and Dictates of Public Conscience", *American Journal of International Law* 94 (2000): 239–278.

272 See Henckaerts and Doswald-Beck, *Customary International Humanitarian Law*, 573 concerning customary IHL, who identify supporting State practice. Further: Antonio Cassese, *International Criminal Law*, 2nd ed. (Oxford: Oxford University Press, 2008), 82; Mettraux, *International Crimes*, 272 and ICTR, *The Prosecutor v. Jean de Dieu Kamuhanda*, Judgment, Trial Chamber II, 22 January 2004, Case No. ICTR-99-54A-T, paras. 725–728.

person.[273] Traditionally, the grave breaches regime constituted an exception to this rule as it required that victim and perpetrator have different nationalities.[274] However, as shown above, allegiance to a party to a conflict is no longer exclusively understood in terms of nationality but, as explained above, may also be demonstrated by ethnicity. Furthermore, the perpetrator of a war crime need not be linked to a party to the armed conflict.[275]

Because of their link to IHL, the passive personal scope of international criminal law is identical to that of the underlying IHL rules in international and non-international armed conflict which was discussed above. Consequently, international criminal law addresses acts against co-nationals and stateless persons to the same extent as the corresponding rules of IHL.[276]

2.4. RESULT

The Refugee Convention, international human rights law and IHL share a concern for the protection of human dignity and well-being.[277] International human rights law sets forth a broad array of rights which States must guarantee to nationals and, to a somewhat lesser extent, stateless persons within their territory, although the material scope of protection in armed conflict under some treaties can be limited to non-derogable human rights. While

---

273 In its 1952 judgment in the *Enigster case* in 1952, Israel's District Court of Tel Aviv stated that "it is possible to find a man guilty of a war crime even though he is of the population of occupied territory and possesses the same national character as his victims, if his actions show that he identified himself with the Occupant." District Court of Tel Aviv, *Attorney-General v. Yehezkel Ben Alish Enigster*, Judgment of 4 January 1952 (Israel), summarised in *Annual Digest and Reports of Public International Law Cases*, Vol. 18, 1951, 540. In the *Cantos case* before the Philippine Supreme Court in 1946, the court held that it was well settled that war crimes can be committed not only by lawful belligerents. The case concerned a Filipino national of Japanese descent who associated himself with Japan in the Second World War and committed atrocities against Filipino civilians. The Court concluded that the accused was a war criminal subject to the jurisdiction of a military commission. Supreme Court, *Teodoro Cantos (Teodoro Tatishi) v. Lt. General Wilhelm D. Steyer*, G.R. No. L-492, Judgment of 28 June 1946 (Phillippines). See also Mettraux, *International Crimes*, 275.

274 Noted by Mettraux, *International Crimes*, 275. On grave breaches of the Geneva Conventions, see: Article 49 Geneva Convention I, Article 50 Geneva Convention II, Article 129 Geneva Convention III and Article 146 Geneva Convention IV.

275 See ICTR, *The Prosecutor v. Jean Paul Akayesu*, Judgment, Appeals Chamber, 1 June 2001, Case No. ICTR-96-4, para. 640. See also: ICTR, *The Prosecutor v. Jean de Dieu Kamuhanda*, Judgment, Trial Chamber II, 22 January 2004, Case No. ICTR-99-54A-T, para. 728.

276 There are also war crimes in international armed conflict whose definition refers to the nationals of the hostile party, as illustrated by the example of "[c]ompelling the nationals of the hostile party to take part in the operations of war directed against their own country, even if they were in the belligerent's service before the commencement of the war": Article 8(2)(b)(xv) Rome Statute.

277 Similarly: Jaques, *Armed Conflict and Displacement*, 7.

international human rights law applies in times of peace and armed conflict, IHL only applies in armed conflict. IHL protects individuals by limiting the violence, sparing those who do not or no longer directly participate in hostilities and restricting the means and methods of warfare to what is necessary to overcome the enemy. Protection under IHL depends to some extent on the status and conduct of an individual and, in international armed conflict, also on the status of the territory. The material scope of protection of international criminal law is premised on that of IHL. IHL has evolved to impose certain obligations on States *vis-à-vis* their own nationals and stateless persons during international armed conflict. In non-international armed conflict, IHL also protects individuals irrespective of what nationality they have or whether they are stateless.

3. INTERACTIONS

Having considered the Refugee Convention, international human rights law, IHL, and international criminal law separately, this section explores their interactions.

3.1. THE REFUGEE CONVENTION AND OTHER BRANCHES OF INTERNATIONAL LAW

In order to interpret the refugee definition in light of international human rights law, IHL and international criminal law, it is first necessary to understand the relationship between the Refugee Convention and international human rights law, IHL and international criminal law.

3.1.1. International Human Rights Law

Although the preamble of the Refugee Convention refers to the Universal Declaration of Human Rights (UDHR),[278] there are clear differences between the Refugee Convention and international human rights law. The Refugee Convention stipulates a number of obligations which States parties owe to all refugees. Additional obligations ensue as the attachment to the asylum State increases.[279] A fundamental set of obligations applies once a refugee is

278 See first preambular recital of the Refugee Convention. The UDHR was adopted by UN General Assembly, *Resolution 271A (III)* (10 December 1948).

279 See Hathaway, *The Rights of Refugees*, 154–156, who points out that the structure of entitlements under the Refugee Convention was influenced by its historic predecessor, international aliens law. Edwards also notes that the rights stipulated by the Refugee Convention are limited guarantees. See Alice Edwards, "Crossing Legal Borders: The

within the jurisdiction of a State party.[280] Another set of obligations becomes additionally pertinent once a refugee is physically on a State's territory,[281] with further obligations applying incrementally and cumulatively once a refugee is lawfully within the State's territory,[282] lawfully staying there,[283] and has become a durable resident.[284] Moreover, the standard of treatment which States parties to the Refugee Convention must grant to refugees depends on the treatment afforded to other groups under the laws and practices of the asylum countries such as aliens generally in the same circumstances,[285] although a few rights must be guaranteed absolutely.[286] In contrast, international human rights law is guided by the principles of equality and non-discrimination. Hence, the Refugee Convention would appear not to constitute a human rights treaty in the strict sense.[287]

However, the growth of international human rights law since 1951 has influenced the conceptualisation and interpretation of international refugee law. States parties to the Refugee Convention have recognised the close connection between this Convention and international human rights law. Adopted on the occasion of the fiftieth anniversary of the Refugee Convention in 2001, the Declaration of States Parties acknowledged that the Refugee Convention "sets out rights, including human rights, and minimum

Interface Between Refugee Law, Human Rights Law and Humanitarian Law in the 'International Protection' of Refugees", in *International Humanitarian Law and Human Rights Law. Towards a New Merger in International Law*, edited by Roberta Arnold and Noëlle Quénivet (Boston et al.: Martinus Nijhoff Publishers, 2008), 427–428.

280 See, e.g., Article 3 Refugee Convention (obligation not to discriminate between and among refugees) and Article 33 Refugee Convention (prohibition of *refoulement*).

281 See, e.g., Article 4 Refugee Convention (freedom of religion), Article 27 Refugee Convention (obligation to issue identity papers) and Article 31(2) (movements of refugees unlawfully on the territory).

282 See, e.g., Article 18 Refugee Convention (self-employment) and Article 26 Refugee Convention (freedom of movement).

283 See, e.g., Article 17 Refugee Convention (wage-earning employment), Article 21 Refugee Convention (housing) and Article 28 Refugee Convention (travel documents).

284 See, e.g., Article 16(2) Refugee Convention (legal aid) and Article 7(2) Refugee Convention (exemption from legislative reciprocity).

285 See, e.g., Article 26 Refugee Convention (freedom of movement).

286 See, e.g., Article 33 Refugee Convention (prohibition of *refoulement*).

287 As argued by Vincent Chetail, "Are Refugee Rights Human Rights? An Unorthodox Questioning of the Relations between Refugee Law and Human Rights Law" (2012), available at http://papers.ssrn.com/sol3/papers.cfm?abstract_id=2147763, accessed 10.03.2015, 4. Goodwin-Gill also emphasises the differences between the Refugee Convention and most other human rights treaties: Guy S. Goodwin-Gill, "The International Law of Refugee Protection", in *The Oxford Handbook of Refugee and Forced Migration Studies*, edited by Elena Fiddian-Qasmiyeh, Gil Loescher, Katy Long and Nando Sigona (Oxford: Oxford University Press, 2014), 41. Bothe, however, considers the Refugee Convention as a "specialised human rights treaty concerning the relationship between a state and specific aliens". Bothe, "The Historical Evolution", 42–43. A definition of international human rights law is given above in note 170, drawing on O'Keefe, "State Immunity", 1004.

standards of treatment".[288] Having initially adopted a cautious approach to international human rights law,[289] UNHCR now acknowledges that "[h]uman rights law is a prime source of existing refugee protection principles and structures, at the same time, it works to complement them."[290] The UNHCR's EXCOM encourages States to adopt a comprehensive approach to particular problems of displacement that entails "the protection of all human rights".[291] It acknowledged "the multifaceted linkages between refugee issues and human rights" and noted "that the refugee experience, in all its stages, is affected by the degree of respect by States for human rights and fundamental freedoms".[292] It also emphasised "the complementary nature of international refugee and human rights law".[293]

Refugee protection under the Refugee Convention has come to be conceived as palliative or remedial human rights protection, i.e. protection for persons compelled to leave their country of origin because of serious human rights violations.[294] Retrospectively, the references to fundamental rights and the UDHR in the Refugee Convention's preamble have been interpreted as firmly placing the Convention within the human rights paradigm.[295]

---

288 Declaration of States Parties to the 1951 Convention and or its 1967 Protocol relating to the Status of Refugees (Declaration of States Parties), adopted on 13 December 2001 at the Ministerial Meeting of States Parties to the 1951 Convention and/or its 1967 Protocol relating to the Status of Refugees, available at www.unhcr.org/refworld/docid/3d60f5557.html, accessed 10.03.2015, second preambular recital.

289 See UNHCR, "UNHCR and Human Rights. A Policy Paper Resulting from Deliberations in the Policy Committee on the Basis of a Paper Prepared by the Division of International Protection" (1997), available at www.unhcr.org/refworld/docid/3ae6b332c.html, accessed 10.03.2015, 1.

290 UNHCR, *Note on International Protection,* UN Doc. A/AC.96/898 (3 July 1998), para. 1. In 2001, the then Director of UNHCR's Department of International Protection stated that "[t]he refugee protection regime … has its origins in general principles of human rights." Erika Feller, "Refugee Protection 50 Years On", *International Review of the Red Cross* 843 (2001): 581–606, 582. In 2008, UNHCR stressed the complementary nature of international human rights law and international refugee law. It also noted that the right to seek and enjoy asylum (Article 14 UDHR) is given clear expression in the Refugee Convention. See UNHCR, *Note on International Protection,* UN Doc. A/AC.96/1053 (30 June 2008), paras. 2–3.

291 See UNHCR Executive Committee, *Conclusion No. 80 (XLVII). Comprehensive and Regional Approaches Within a Protection Framework* (1996), para. e. See also UNHCR Executive Committee, *Conclusion No. 81 (XLCIII)* (1997).

292 UNHCR Executive Committee, *Conclusion No. 95 (LIV)* (2003), para. k.

293 UNHCR Executive Committee, *Conclusion No. 95 (LIV)* (2003), para. l. The EXCOM further emphasised this complementary relationship with regard to detention (UNHCR Executive Committee, *Conclusion No. 93 (LIII). Conclusion on reception of asylum-seekers in the context of individual asylum systems* (8 October 2002), third preambular recital) and child and adolescent refugees (UNHCR Executive Committee, *Conclusion No. 84 (XLVIII) on Refugee Children and Adolescents* (1997)).

294 Hathaway emphasises "the palliative, the protective, the stop-gap role of refugee law": Hathaway, "New Directions", 293. See also Anker, "Refugee Law", 135; Nathwani, *Rethinking Refugee Law,* 364.

295 See Chetail, "Are Refugee Rights Human Rights?", 7–12. See also first and second preambular recitals of the Refugee Convention.

3.1.2. *International Humanitarian Law*

The Refugee Convention and IHL are distinct bodies of international law. They have different purposes: while the Refugee Convention seeks to provide protection for those who no longer enjoy the protection of their country of origin, IHL regulates the means and methods of warfare and strives to protect those who do not or no longer participate in hostilities.[296] Despite these differences, IHL and the Refugee Convention share the humanitarian purpose of protecting human dignity. They regulate exceptional circumstances: lack of protection by the country of origin in the case of the Refugee Convention and armed conflict as regards IHL. Both seek to provide transitory forms of protection in such circumstances.[297] There has been a tentative and gradual coalescence of IHL and an international refugee law in recent years in the views of States parties to the Refugee Convention, UNHCR and its EXCOM.

A few States parties to the Refugee Convention have drawn on IHL in the interpretation of the refugee definition.[298] In the 2001 Declaration of States Parties to the Refugee Convention, States noted the

---

296 In a case concerning subsidiary protection, the Court of Justice of the European Union emphasised that while IHL is *inter alia* designed to protect civilians in conflict zones, the purpose of Article 15(c) of the Qualification Directive is to provide protection to civilians outside conflict zones and outside the territory of the parties to the conflict. See Case C-285/12 *Aboubacar Diakité v. Commissaire général aux réfugiés et aux apatrides* [2014] OJ 235/11, para. 24. Arguably the difference to the Refugee Convention, which does not expressly address civilians and armed conflict, is even starker. Fripp also notes the different purposes between the Refugee Convention and IHL: Eric Fripp, "International Humanitarian law and the Interpretation of 'Persecution' in Article 1A(2) CSR51", *International Journal of Refugee Law* 26, no. 3 (2014): 398.

297 See Jean-François Durieux and David James Cantor, "Refuge from Inhumanity? Canvassing the Issues", in *Refuge from Inhumanity? War Refugees and International Humanitarian Law*, edited by David James Cantor and Jean-François Durieux (Leiden: Koninklijke Brill, 2014), 9–10. In addition, Chetail shows that Article 8 of the Refugee Convention contains an implicit reference to IHL because it reproduces in substance Article 44 of Geneva Convention IV, although the respective scopes of these provisions differ. See Chetail, "Armed Conflict and Forced Migration", 712.

298 The US Basic Law Manual acknowledges that violations of the 1949 Geneva Conventions may constitute the basis for an asylum claim. See US Immigration and Naturalization Service, *The Basic Law Manual: U.S. Law and INS Refugee/Asylum Adjudications* 22 (1995), cited by Sternberg, *The Grounds of Refugee Protection*. The US Board of Immigration Appeals noted that "the evidence must [*inter alia*] be evaluated in the context of the ongoing civil conflict [in Sri Lanka] to determine whether the motive for the abuse in the particular case ... was part of the violence inherent in an armed conflict (i.e. lawful acts of war)." *In re S-P*, 21 I. & N. Dec. 486, Interim Decision 3287, 1996 WL 422990 (BIA), 493–494. See also *Montecino v. Immigration and Naturalization Service*, 915 F.2d 518, 520 (9th Cir.1990) (US). In the UK, when discussing what "distinguishes persecution from the ordinary incidents of civil war", Lord Lloyd rejected the proposition that a reference to IHL would be helpful. See *Adan v. Secretary of State for the Home Department* [1998] 2 WLR 702, per Lord Lloyd of Berwick (UK). However, the UK Asylum and Immigration Tribunal found that subsequent legal developments warranted a renewed look at the guidance in *Adan*, stating that ordinary incidents of civil war are to be determined according to whether or not they comply with IHL.

> "complex features of the evolving environment in which refugee protection has to be provided, including the nature of armed conflict, ongoing violations of human rights and IHL, current patterns of displacement."[299]

This statement indicates a recognition that IHL is part of the international legal framework for the protection of individuals forcefully displaced by armed conflict. Marking the twentieth anniversary of the Cartagena Declaration, the representatives of several Latin American States affirmed in 2004:

> "the complementary nature of international refugee law, international human rights law, and international humanitarian law and, hence, the importance of using, according to the principle of *pro homine*, the norms and principles of these three bodies of international law to strengthen the protection of refugees and other persons entitled to international protection."[300]

These States understood the relationship between international refugee law and IHL as complementary in nature without, however, specifying the implications of this understanding.

UNHCR emphasised that parties to non-international armed conflicts are obliged to *inter alia* refrain from indiscriminate attacks, torture or arbitrary

---

See *AM & AM v. Secretary of State for the Home Department* (armed conflict: risk categories) Somalia CG [2008] UKAIT 00091, para. 76 (UK). In *Zolfagharkhani v. Canada* [1993] 3 FC 540, a case concerning the refusal of an Iranian member of the armed forces to participate in chemical warfare against the Kurds, MacGuigan J upheld the claim to refugee status, noting the prohibition of chemical warfare in international law (Canada). The 1996 guidelines by the Canadian IRB provide that in addition to international human rights law, the Geneva Convention IV, in particular Common Article 3, and the Additional Protocol II may assist in determining what constitutes permissible conduct. See Immigration and Refugee Board of Canada, "Civilian Non-Combatants Fearing Persecution in Civil War Situations". But since September 2001, the few references that do exist in jurisprudence regarding the guidelines have omitted to specifically refer to their provisions on IHL. See, e.g., *Sheriff v. Canada (Minister of Citizenship and Immigration)* 2002 FCT 8. The 1996 Joint Position of the Council of the European Union (EU) suggested that conduct is not persecution by a State's armed forces if it complies with IHL: "[T]he use of the armed forces does not constitute persecution where it is in accordance with international rules of war". Council of the European Union, "Joint Position Defined by the Council on the basis of Article K.3 of the Treaty on European Union on the Harmonized Application of the Definition of the Term 'Refugee' in Article 1 of the Geneva Convention of 28 July 1951 Relating to the Status of Refugees (Annex 1)" (1996), available at www.refworld.org/docid/3ae6b37f44.html, accessed 10.03.2015. This section focusses on the Refugee Convention and is therefore not concerned with the interpretation of Article 15(c) Qualification Directive and Article 15(c) Recast Qualification Directive in light of IHL.

299 Declaration of States Parties, sixth preambular recital.

300 See *Declaración y Plan de Acción de México Para Fortalecer la Protección Internacional de los Refugiados en América Latina* (Declaration and Plan of Action to Strengthen the International Protection of Refugees in Latin America) (Mexico Declaration), adopted 16 November 2004, available at www.acnur.org/t3/fileadmin/scripts/doc.php?file=biblioteca/pdf/3016, accessed 10.03.2015, sixth preambular recital (unofficial English translation).

punishment and that such acts may give rise to refugee status.[301] UNHCR further noted:

> "If someone is forced to flee armed conflict in their country because of human rights violations and breaches of humanitarian law, these factors will be part of what determines that person's refugee status."[302]

UNHCR thereby acknowledged that IHL violations cause forced displacement and influence the determination of whether a person is a refugee. In a few Eligibility Guidelines, UNHCR considered the situation in the country of origin as an armed conflict and referred to violations of human rights and IHL in the context of inclusion within refugee protection. For example, UNHCR stated that *inter alia* because of the massive and widespread violations of human rights and IHL during the armed conflict, many Colombian asylum-seekers fall within the Refugee Convention's definition of a refugee.[303] UNHCR also stressed that the Refugee Convention is complemented by international human rights law and IHL.[304]

UNHCR's EXCOM noted that "blatant disregard of international humanitarian law"[305] is a root cause of forced displacement. In particular, it considered that sexual violence during armed conflict is a grave breach of IHL and constitutes persecution.[306] It stressed the role of IHL in preventing forced displacement.[307] The EXCOM also emphasised that States must respect IHL.[308] Recalling the relevant provisions of international refugee law, human rights law and humanitarian law,[309] the EXCOM acknowledged that these bodies of international law form part of the international legal framework for the protection of forcefully displaced persons during armed conflict.

---

301 UNHCR, *Note on International Protection,* UN Doc. A/AC.96/975 (2 July 2003), para. 53.

302 UNHCR, *Note on International Protection (2003),* para. 53.

303 See UNHCR, "International Protection Considerations regarding Colombian Asylum-Seekers and Refugees" (2002), available at www.unhcr.org/refworld/docid/3d92d4204.html, accessed 10.03.2015, para. 83. Similarly: UNHCR, "UNHCR Eligibility Guidelines for Assessing the International Protection Needs of Asylum-Seekers from Somalia (2010)", 39–40 (attacks on civilians).

304 See UNHCR, *Note on International Protection,* UN Doc. A/AC.86/930 (7 July 2000), para. 32.

305 UNHCR Executive Committee, *Conclusion No. 87 (L)* (1999), para. a.

306 See UNHCR Executive Committee, *Conclusion No. 73 (XLIV) Refugee Protection and Sexual Violence* (1993), para. a.

307 See UNHCR Executive Committee, *Conclusion No. 71 (XLIV)* (1993), para. u.

308 See UNHCR Executive Committee, *Conclusion No. 83 (XLVIII)* (1997); UNHCR Executive Committee, *Conclusion No. 84 (XLVIII) on Refugee Children and Adolescents* (1997); UNHCR Executive Committee, *Conclusion No. 94 (LIII) on the Civilian and Humanitarian Character of Asylum* (2002); UNHCR Executive Committee, *Conclusion No. 98 (XIV)* (2003); and UNHCR Executive Committee, *Conclusion No. 48 (XXXXVIII) Military or Armed Attacks on Refugee Camps and Settlements* (1987), para. a.

309 See UNHCR Executive Committee, *Conclusion No. 94 (LIII) on the Civilian and Humanitarian Character of Asylum* (2002), second preambular recital; and UNHCR Executive Committee, *Conclusion No. 98 (XIV)* (2003), para. c.

The relationship of the Refugee Convention and IHL can be conceived as one of subsequent application in the sense of a qualified protection continuum.[310] Having been subjected to violations of IHL or fearing being subjected to such violations is remedied by protection based on the Refugee Convention for those individuals who fulfil the refugee definition in Article 1A(2) Refugee Convention. For various reasons, including the limited scope of the refugee definition, this continuum of protection is qualified.

3.1.3. International Criminal Law

There are clear differences between the Refugee Convention and international criminal law. While the latter is concerned with determining individual criminal responsibility for serious violations of IHL, the former addresses the protection of individuals who fled from their country of origin. International refugee law does not attribute responsibility for persecutory acts.[311] The interpretation and application of treaties or statutes in the field of international criminal law is guided by criminal law principles such as the principle of specificity, which often means that the material and personal scope of crimes are interpreted narrowly.[312] In contrast, treaty interpretation in the area of international refugee law is inspired by the humanitarian nature of this body of law and is thus inclusive.[313]

Notwithstanding these differences, the Refugee Convention and international criminal law are connected in various ways. War crimes may constitute root causes of forced displacement. Depending on the individual circumstances, the Refugee Convention and international criminal law may apply consecutively, forming a qualified continuum of protection. The fear or experience of being subjected to war crimes may constitute the reason why an individual flees from their country of origin.[314] Rutinwa argues that since war crimes are considered by the international community to be of such gravity as to warrant universal condemnation, it is logical that victims of such acts are entitled to international protection.[315] Similarly, Jaquemet contends that if individuals are compelled

310 Similarly: Jaquemet, "Cross-Fertilization", 625.

311 Similarly: Foster, *International Refugee Law*, 58. Indeed, States parties to the Refugee Convention, in the Convention's fifth preambular recital, expressed "the wish that all States, recognizing the social and humanitarian nature of the problem of refugees, will do everything within their power to prevent this problem from becoming a cause of tension between States". Price, however, argues that asylum expresses political values by condemning States for mistreating refugees: Matthew E. Price, *Rethinking Asylum. History, Purpose, and Limits* (Cambridge: Cambridge University Press, 2009), 14.

312 On the requirement that prohibitions in international criminal law be as clear, detailed and specific as possible: Cassese, *International Criminal Law*, 8.

313 On the interpretation of the refugee definition, see Chapter 4.

314 As noted by Jaquemet regarding grave breaches of IHL: Jaquemet, "Cross-Fertilization", 652.

315 See Bonaventure Rutinwa, "Refugee Claims Based On Violation of International Humanitarian Law: The 'Victim's' Perspective", *Georgetown Immigration Law Journal* 15

to leave their country of origin because of grave breaches of IHL, "those grave breaches constitute a substantial part of the refugee definition and become the determining factor triggering refugee protection."[316] True, war crimes epitomise universally condemned acts that entail grave consequences for the victims. However, the determining factor triggering refugee protection under the Refugee Convention is an individual's well-founded fear of being persecuted for a Refugee Convention ground. That the individual experienced or fears to experience grave breaches of IHL or other war crimes may contribute or lead to a finding that the individual fulfils the refugee definition, but it does not in and of itself suffice to qualify for refugee status.[317]

International criminal law and the Refugee Convention also intersect as regards exclusion from refugee protection.[318] Article 1F(a) Refugee Convention excludes a person from refugee status

> "with respect to whom there are serious reasons for considering that: (a) he has committed a crime against peace, a war crime, or a crime against humanity, as defined in the international instruments drawn up to make provision in respect of such crimes."

In determining whether this exclusion clause is applicable, national decision-makers frequently draw on international criminal law regarding the types of conduct that fall within Article 1F(a) and concerning individual criminal responsibility.[319]

3.1.4. Result

The Refugee Convention, though distinct, is related to international human rights law, IHL and international criminal law in various ways.[320] The

---

(2000–2001), 497. Similarly regarding war crimes and refugee status: Jaquemet, "Cross-Fertilization", 667.

316 Jaquemet, "Cross-Fertilization", 652.

317 Jaquemet appears to acknowledge this, noting: "The key question is whether the victim or the potential victim of a war crime who has fled his/her country of origin and has sought asylum in another country is a refugee meeting the rather strict definition of Article 1A(2) of the 1951 [Refugee] Convention." Jaquemet, "Cross-Fertilization", 665.

318 See Expert Meeting on Complementarities between International Refugee Law, International Criminal Law and International Refugee Law, "Arusha Summary Conclusions", para. 35; UNHCR, *Guidelines on International Protection No. 5: Application of the Exclusion Clauses: Article 1F of the 1951 Convention relating to the Status of Refugees*, UN Doc. HRC/GIP/03/05 (4 September 2003), paras. 10 and 12–13.

319 See Expert Meeting on Complementarities between International Refugee Law, International Criminal Law and International Refugee Law, "Arusha Summary Conclusions", para. 36.

320 Canefe and Edwards note that international refugee law is related but distinct from international human rights law and IHL. See Nergis Canefe, "The Fragmented Nature of the International Refugee Regime and Its Consequences: A Comparative Analysis of the Applications of the 1951 Convention", in *Critical Issues in International Refugee Law:*

complementary character of the Refugee Convention and international human rights law has long been recognised, and the interfaces between the Refugee Convention and IHL are increasingly acknowledged. Violations of IHL and war crimes constitute root causes of cross-border forced displacement. IHL and international criminal law on the one hand and the Refugee Convention on the other may apply consecutively. Such successive protection is not, however, co-extensive in the sense that conduct unlawful under IHL or constitutes a war crime does not necessarily fall within the refugee definition in Article 1A(2).

3.2. INTERNATIONAL HUMANITARIAN LAW AND INTERNATIONAL HUMAN RIGHTS LAW

Historically, IHL and international human rights law developed discretely. For example, the drafters of the 1948 UDHR and the 1949 Geneva Conventions barely took note of one another.[321] Subsequent decades saw an increase in the number of non-international armed conflicts around the world.[322] However, the development of IHL treaties all but stalled after the 19th International Conference of the Red Cross and Red Crescent in 1957.[323] This International Conference adopted without further pursuing the ICRC's Draft Rules for the Limitation of Dangers Incurred by the Civilian Population in Times of War, which were envisaged as being applicable in non-international armed conflict.[324] At the same time, the application of international human rights law in armed conflict received more and more attention within the UN. The UN General Assembly referred to human rights law with regard to the 1953 Korea War,[325] while the UN Security Council emphasised human rights with respect to the 1967 Six Day War.[326] The adoption of Resolution XXIII on Human Rights in Armed Conflict at the Teheran Conference in 1968 marked a milestone in the

Strategies toward Interpretative Harmony, edited by James C. Simeon (Cambridge: Cambridge University Press, 2010), 175 and Edwards, "Crossing Legal Borders", 421.

321 See Robert Kolb, "Human Rights and Humanitarian Law", in *Max Planck Encyclopedia of Public International Law*, edited by Rüdiger Wolfrum (Oxford: Oxford University Press, 2009), available at www.mpepil.com, accessed 10.03.2015, para. 5; and Cordula Droege, "Elective affinities? Human Rights and Humanitarian Law", *International Review of the Red Cross* 90, no. 871 (2003): 501–548, 504.

322 See Harbom and Wallensteen, "Armed Conflicts", 503.

323 See Droege, "Elective affinities?", 504.

324 See Article 2(b) of the Draft Rules for the Limitation of Dangers incurred by the Civilian Population in Times of War, available at www.icrc.org/ihl.nsf/FULL/420?OpenDocument, accessed 10.03.2015.

325 See UN General Assembly, *Questions of Atrocities Committed by the North Korean and Chinese Communist Forces against United Nations Prisoners of War in Korea. Resolution 804 (VII)*, UN Doc. A/804/VIII (3 December 1953) (emphasised by Droege, "Elective affinities?", 504).

326 See UN Security Council, *Resolution 237*, UN Doc. A/237/1967 (1967), preambular para. 1(b), as noted by Droege, "Elective affinities?", 504. Also: Nancie Prud'homme, "*Lex Specialis*:

rapprochement of IHL and international human rights law.[327] By then, the respect for human rights in armed conflict had become a constant concern of the UN and other international bodies.[328] Partly in reaction to this development, the Diplomatic Conference on the Reaffirmation and Development of International Humanitarian Law developed the two Additional Protocols to the Geneva Conventions between 1974 and 1977,[329] both of which recognise the application of human rights in armed conflict.[330] Since then, IHL and international human rights law have seen an ever increasing confluence. For example, recent international human rights treaties expressly refer to IHL.[331] Conversely, the 2008 Convention on Cluster Munitions incorporates a provision on human rights.[332] The ICJ and various human rights bodies and courts have addressed the relationship of IHL and international human rights law.[333]

IHL and international human rights law share a common concern for the protection of the individual, as the ICTY noted:

Oversimplifying a More Complex and Multifaceted Relationship", *Israel Law Review* 40 (2007): 356–395, 362.

327 See Final Act of the International Conference on Human Rights, Teheran, UN Doc. A/CONF.32/41, Resolution XXIII, Human Rights in Armed Conflict, 12 May 1968. Reaffirmed by UN General Assembly, *Resolution 2444* (19 December 1968). The UN General Assembly has since adopted various resolutions on human rights in armed conflict and has included this topic on its agenda every year since the Teheran Conference. See also Bothe, "The Historical Evolution", 41 and Prud'homme, "*Lex Specialis*", 264.

328 See Kolb, "Human Rights and Humanitarian Law", para. 20 and Droege, "Elective affinities?", 504–505.

329 See Droege, "Elective affinities?", 506.

330 See Article 72 Additional Protocol I and second preambular recital of the 1977 Additional Protocol II.

331 See, e.g., Article 38 CRC; Article 5 Optional Protocol; Article 11 Convention on the Rights of Persons with Disabilities (2515 UNTS 3, adopted 13 December 2006, entered into force 3 May 2008); Articles 16(2) and 43 International Convention on Enforced Disappearances (adopted by UN General Assembly, *Resolution 61/177,* UN Doc. A/61/488 (20 December 2008), entered into force 23 December 2010.

332 See Article 5 Cluster Munitions Convention (BGBl. 2009 II p. 504, adopted 30 March 2008, entered into force 1 August 2010).

333 See, e.g., ICJ, *Legality of the Threat or Use of Nuclear Weapons*, Advisory Opinion of 8 July 1996, ICJ Reports 1996; ICJ, *Legal Consequences of the Construction of a Wall in the Occupied Palestinian Territory*, Advisory Opinion (2004) ICJ Reports 136; *Case concerning Armed Activities on the Territory of the Congo (Democratic Republic of the Congo v. Uganda)* (2005) ICJ Reports 1. In the Latin American context, see, e.g., *Juan Carlos Abella v. Argentina*, Inter-American Commission on Human Rights, Case 11.137, Report No. 55/97, OAE/Ser.L/V/II.95 Doc. 7 rev. at 271 (18 November 1997); *Bámaca Velásquez Case*, Inter-American Court of Human Rights, Judgment of 25 November 2000, IACtHR Series C No. 70 (2002). In the European context, see e.g. *Banković and others v. Belgium and others* (Decision on Admissibility), Application No. 52207/99; *Isayeva, Yusupova and Bazeyeva v. Russia* (Applications Nos. 57947/00, 57948/00 and 57949/00), Judgment of 24 February 2005. In the African context, see, e.g., *Commission Nationale des Droit de l'Homme et des Libertés v. Chad*, African Commission on Human and Peoples' Rights, Communication No. 74/92 (October 1995).

> "The essence of the whole corpus of international humanitarian law as well as human rights law lies in the protection of the human dignity of every person, whatever his or her gender. The general principle of respect for human dignity is the basic underpinning and indeed the very raison d'être of international humanitarian law and human rights law ..."[334]

IHL and international human rights law overlap in various respects, for example in prohibiting torture, inhuman or degrading treatment, rape and other forms of sexual violence.[335] However, IHL and international human rights law also differ. In contrast to international human rights law, IHL balances humanitarian considerations with military necessity. While IHL binds State and non-State parties to non-international armed conflict, international human rights law is only binding on States. International human rights law grants rights to individuals and corresponding obligations to States. In contrast, IHL establishes States' obligations to accord standards of treatment to individuals.[336] This remains the case despite the influence of human rights on IHL as exemplified in Article 75 Additional Protocol I.[337]

In view of these overlaps, it is not surprising that IHL and international human rights law are no longer considered to be mutually exclusive.[338] It has

---

334 ICTY, *The Prosecutor v. Anto Furundžija*, Judgment, Trial Chamber II, 10 December 1998, Case No. IT-95-17/1-T, para. 189. Similarly: ICTY, *The Prosecutor v. Zlatko Aleksovski*, Judgment, Trial Chamber I, 25 June 1999, Case No. IT-95-14/1-T, para. 54. See also Thürer, *International Humanitarian Law*, 66 and Michael Bothe, "Humanitäres Völkerrecht und Menschenrechte", *Humanitäres Völkerrecht Informationsschriften* 1 (2008): 4–8, 4. In the views of the ICRC, IHL and international human rights law "share some of the same aims, that is to protect the lives, health and dignity of persons." ICRC, "International Humanitarian Law", 14.

335 Torture, rape and other forms of sexual violence are examined in detail in Chapter 5.

336 See Kate Parlett, *The Individual in the International Legal System. Continuity and Change in International Law* (Cambridge: Cambridge University Press, 2011), 195. On the difference between the duty bearers under international human rights law and IHL, see also Sandesh Sivakumaran, "Re-envisaging the International Law of Internal Armed Conflict", *European Journal of International Law* 22, no. 1 (2011): 219–254, 240–242 and Sassòli, "The Role of Human Rights", 56–59.

337 See Parlett, *The Individual in the International Legal System*, 196. The influence of human rights on IHL has been examined in detail by Theordor Meron, *The Humanization of International Law* (Leiden/Boston: Martinus Nijhoff, 2006).

338 This view was held in the past by e.g. Henri Meyrowitz, "Le droit de guerre et les droit de l'homme", *Revue de Droit Militaire et Droit de la Guerre* 88 (1972): 1095–1105, as noted by Kolb, "Human Rights and Humanitarian Law", para. 28. Ben-Naftali observes: "The idea that IHL and IHRL are complementary, rather than alternative regimes, has represented a paradigmatic shift in the international legal discourse, replacing the former convention which maintained that the two are mutually exclusive." Orna Ben-Naftali, *International Humanitarian Law and International Human Rights Law* (Oxford: Oxford University Press, 2011), 4. Yet she notes a recent publication that maintains that IHL and international human rights law ought to remain completely separate: Bill Bowring, "Fragmentation, *Lex Specialis* and the Tension in the Jurisprudence of the European Court of Human Rights", *Journal of Conflict & Security Law* 2009, no. 14 (2009): 3.

become generally accepted by the ICJ,[339] human rights treaty bodies,[340] in some State practice,[341] and in the literature[342] that international human rights law and IHL can apply in parallel during armed conflict within a State's territory.[343] Most scholars today consider that there is a large degree of complementarity between international human rights law and IHL that can be used for interpretative purposes.[344] However, opinions differ regarding the resolution of norm conflicts, in particular concerning the principle *lex specialis derogat legi generali.*[345] The implications of the complementarity between IHL and international

339 See ICJ, *Legality of the Threat or Use of Nuclear Weapons*, Advisory Opinion of 8 July 1996, ICJ Reports 1996, 75, para. 19; ICJ, *Legal Consequences of the Construction of a Wall in the Occupied Palestinian Territory*, Advisory Opinion, ICJ Reports 2004, 136, 136, para. 106.

340 See, e.g., Human Rights Committee, *General Comment 31: Nature of the General Legal Obligation on States Parties to the Covenant*, para. 11 referring to Human Rights Committee, *General Comment 29: States of Emergency (Article 4)*. See further: Droege, "Elective affinities?", 507–509.

341 For an overview of practice, see Droege, "Elective affinities?", 503–507. Kretzmer points out that this State practice remains inconsistent. See David Kretzmer, Rotem Giladi, and Yuval Shany, "International Humanitarian Law and International Human Rights Law: Exploring Parallel Application", *Israel Law Review* 40 (2007): 306–309, 306.

342 See, e.g., Michael Bothe, "Humanitäres Völkerrecht und Menschenrechte: Auf der Suche nach Synergien und Schutzlücken", in *Völkerrecht als Wertordnung. Common Values in International Law. Festschrift für? Essays in Honour of Christian Tomuschat*, edited by Pierre-Marie Dupuy, et al. (Kehl: N.P. Engel, 2006); Droege, "Elective affinities?"; Hans-Joachim Heintze, "On the Relationship between Human Rights Law Protection and International Humanitarian Law", *International Review of the Red Cross* 85, no. 856 (2004): 789–814; Hans-Peter Gasser, "International Humanitarian Law and Human Rights Law in Non-International Armed Conflicts: Joint Venture or Mutual Exclusion?", *German Yearbook of International Law* 45 (2002): 149–162; Nils Melzer, *Targeted Killing in International Law* (Oxford: Oxford University Press, 2008); Louise Doswald-Beck and Sylvain Vité, "International Humanitarian Law and Human Rights Law", *International Review of the Red Cross*, no. 293 (1993): 94–119 and René Provost, *International Human Rights and Humanitarian Law* (Cambridge: Cambridge University Press, 2002).

343 It is recalled that this book does not address extra-territorial application of international human rights treaties.

344 This trend in scholarly analysis is identified by Ben-Naftali, *International Humanitarian Law*, 5. A representative of this view is Alexander Orakhelashvili, "The Interaction between Human Rights and Humanitarian Law: Fragmentation, Conflict, Parallelism, or Convergence?", *European Journal of International Law* 19, no. 1 (2008): 161–182. The ICRC Study on Customary IHL also adopts this approach because it draws on international human rights law "in order to support, strengthen and clarify analogous principles of international humanitarian law" and acknowledges that "international humanitarian law contains concepts the interpretation of which needs to include a reference to human rights law". Henckaerts and Doswald-Beck, *Customary International Humanitarian Law*, xxxvii. The ICRC notes that "it is generally accepted that IHL and human rights law are complementary legal regimes, albeit with a different scope of application." ICRC, "International Humanitarian Law", 14.

345 As noted by Ben-Naftali, *International Humanitarian Law*, 5. See, e.g., Sassòli, "The Role of Human Rights", 70–93; Marco Milanović, *Norm Conflicts, International Humanitarian Law, and Human Rights Law*; Orna Ben-Naftali, *International Humanitarian Law and International Human Rights Law* (Oxford: Oxford University Press, 2011); ICRC, "International Humanitarian Law", 14; William A. Schabas, "*Lex Specialis*? Belt and Suspenders? The Parallel Operation of Human Rights Law and the Law of Armed Conflict, and the Conundrum of *Jus Ad Bellum*", *Israel Law Review* 40, no. 2 (2007): 592–613.

human rights law and the role of the *lex specialis* principle, which are difficult to determine in the abstract as much depends on the precise nature of State's obligations and other factors, shall be further explored in Chapter 5 with respect to persecution, including by drawing on concrete examples.

3.3. RESULT

The branches of international law forming the international legal framework for the protection of the individual in armed conflict, though distinct, overlap and interact in various ways. The Refugee Convention and international human rights law have long been closely intertwined. Recent years have seen a gradual coalescence of the Refugee Convention and IHL in the views of States parties to the Refugee Convention and UNHCR. There has also been a confluence between international human rights law and IHL over the last decades, with their complementarity being increasingly acknowledged.

4. CONCEPTUAL APPROACHES

Situated at opposite ends of a wide spectrum, the most relevant conceptualisations of the different branches of international law are "fragmentation" and "the international law for humankind".

4.1. FRAGMENTATION

Defined as "the emergence of specialized and (relatively) autonomous rules or rule-complexes, legal institutions and spheres of legal practice",[346] fragmentation

---

[346] Study Group of the International Law Commission, *Fragmentation of International Law: Difficulties Arising from the Diversification and Expansion of International Law. Report of the Study Group of the International Law Commission Finalized by Martti Koskenniemi,* UN Doc. A/CN.4/L.682 (13 April 2006), para. 8. However, the fragmentation of international law is not a new phenomenon, as noted by Joost Pauwelyn, "Fragmentation of International Law", in *Max Planck Encyclopedia of Public International Law,* edited by Rüdiger Wolfrum (Oxford: Oxford University Press, 2006), available at www.mpepil.com, accessed 10.03.2015, paras. 7–12. Martineau shows that since the mid-nineteenth century, international law has been described by lawyers as fragmented. Anne-Charlotte Martineau, "The Rhetoric of Fragmentation: Fear and Faith in International Law", *Leiden Journal of International Law* 22 (2009): 1–28. More generally, see Martti Koskenniemi and Päivi Leino, "Fragmentation of International Law? Postmodern Anxieties", *Leiden Journal of International Law* 15, no. 3 (2002): 553–579, and Nele Matz-Lück, "Harmonization, Systemic Integration, and 'Mutual Suportiveness' as Conflict-Solution Techniques: Different Modes of Interpretation as a Challenge to Negative Effects of Fragmentation?", *Finnish Yearbook of International Law* XVII (2006): 39–52, 39.

is a potential conceptualisation of the different branches of international law addressing the protection of the individual in armed conflict. International law is fragmented with regard to both its substantive and procedural norms.[347] Of particular relevance for the present analysis is substantive fragmentation, especially the compartmentalisation of international law along functional lines or issue areas as manifested in the emergence of international refugee law, international human rights law, IHL, and international criminal law. Some experts have framed these branches of international law as being fragmented, comprising different specialised regimes or systems.[348] The 2006 report of the Study Group of the International Law Commission (ILC) on fragmentation voiced concerns that the development of special regimes "does create the danger of conflicting and incompatible rules, principles, rule-systems and institutional practices."[349] The ILC Study Group identified the resulting risk of norm conflicts, divergences and the loss of unity of international law.[350] At the same time, the ILC Study Group acknowledged that due to the "spontaneous, decentralized and unhierarchical nature of international law-making",[351] coherence and plurality are constitutive virtues of the international legal system.[352]

4.2. THE INTERNATIONAL LAW FOR HUMANKIND

Advocated by Antônio Augusto Cançado Trindade,[353] the concept of humanisation of international law, culminating in the international law for humankind, offers another potential conceptualisation of the relationship between the previously examined branches of international law. Humanisation

347 See Pauwelyn, "Fragmentation of International Law", para. 7 and Study Group of the International Law Commission, *Fragmentation of International Law*, 10–14, paras. 5–12.

348 See Study Group of the International Law Commission, *Fragmentation of International Law*, para. 8; Expert Meeting on Complementarities between International Refugee Law, International Criminal Law and International Refugee Law, "Arusha Summary Conclusions", paras. 1–5.

349 Study Group of the International Law Commission, *Fragmentation of International Law*, para. 14.

350 See Study Group of the International Law Commission, *Fragmentation of International Law*, paras. 8, 129 and 158.

351 Study Group of the International Law Commission, *Fragmentation of International Law*, para. 486.

352 See Study Group of the International Law Commission, *Fragmentation of International Law*, para. 491.

353 See Antônio Augusto Cançado Trindade, *International Law for Humankind: Towards a New Jus Gentium (I). General Course on Public International Law*, The Hague Academy of International Law, Recueil des Cours/Collected Courses, Vol. 316 (Leiden/Boston: Martinus Nijhoff, 2005); Antônio Augusto Cançado Trindade, *International Law for Humankind: Towards a New Jus Gentium (II). General Course on Public International Law*, edited by The Hague Academy of International Law, Recueil des Cours/Collected Courses (Leiden/Boston: Martinus Nijhoff, 2005).

denotes a process of convergence of the different branches of international law for the protection of the individual towards an international law for humankind.[354] Cançado Trindade argues that a new *ius gentium* is emerging, "a *corpus juris* … increasingly oriented to the fulfillment of the needs and aspirations of human beings, of people and of humankind as a whole".[355] In his view, there is a trend in international law to replace the *raison d'État* with the *raison d'humanité*.[356] A similar opinion was expressed by the ICTY Appeals Chamber in the *Tadić case*:

> "A State-sovereignty-oriented approach has been gradually supplanted by a human-being-oriented approach. Gradually the maxim of Roman law *hominum causa omne jus constitutum est* (all law is created for the benefit of human beings) has gained a firm foothold in the international community as well …"[357]

This *pro homine* principle is also stressed in the aforementioned Mexico Declaration adopted by Latin American States on the occasion of the Cartagena Declaration's twentieth anniversary.[358] Cançado Trindade argues that the traditional compartmentalisation of the branches of international law concerned with the protection of the human person, namely international human rights law, humanitarian law and refugee law, has been overcome in light of their identical fundamental purpose. Based on basic considerations of humanity, there have been convergences between these bodies of international law at the normative, hermeneutic and operative level towards an international law "to the benefit of the protected human beings".[359] He states that the prohibition of *refoulement* and basic principles common to international human rights, humanitarian and refugee law such as the principle of equality and non-discrimination, the principle of inviolability of the human person, the principle of the inalienability

354 See Cançado Trindade, *International Law for Humankind*, 27 and 157–158. Meron, however, understands humanisation differently, namely as the influence of human rights law on other bodies of international law. See Meron, "The Humanization of Humanitarian Law".

355 Cançado Trindade, *International Law for Humankind*, 34.

356 See Cançado Trindade, *International Law for Humankind*, 171. In support: Thürer, *International Humanitarian Law*, 34–35 and 318–319.

357 ICTY, *Prosecutor v. Tadić*, Appeals Chamber, Case No. IT-94-1-AR72, Decision on the Defence Motion for Interlocutory Appeal on Jurisdiction, 2 October 1995, 35 ILM (1996) 32, at para. 97. See also ICTY, *The Prosecutor v. Anto Furundžija*, Judgment, Trial Chamber II, 10 December 1998, Case No. IT-95-17/1-T, para. 189. Ruti Teitel argues that the international legal order's normative foundations have shifted from a focus on State security to emphasising human security, with the law of humanity (comprising IHL, human rights and international criminal justice) reshaping the international relations discourse. See Ruti Teitel, *Humanity's Law* (Oxford: Oxford University Press, 2011), 4. Since Teitel does specifically not endorse a formal fusion of international rules, this concept is not further discussed here.

358 In its sixth preambular recital, the Mexico Declaration reaffirms the Refugee Convention and "the complementary nature of international refugee law, international human rights law, and IHL and, hence, the importance of using, according to the principle of *pro homine*, the norms and principles of these three bodies of international law to strengthen the protection of refugees and other persons entitled to international protection."

359 See Cançado Trindade, *International Law for Humankind*, 151.

and non-renounceability of the rights of the human person, and the principle of security of the human person illustrate this development.[360]

4.3. DISCUSSION

The concept of fragmentation emphasises the dissimilarities between international refugee law, international human rights law, IHL and international criminal law. It highlights their distinct nature and the differences in their normative purposes and structures and concerning the material scope of protection afforded. Fragmentation pinpoints the decentralised nature of international law-making.[361] Yet the notion of fragmentation also, and incorrectly, insinuates that what used to be a single body of law has fragmented over time. Although they originally evolved separately from one another, the development of these branches of international law has increasingly seen interaction and cross-fertilisation. Framing their relationship as fragmentation fails to adequately portray these interfaces.[362]

Contrastingly, the international law for humankind provides a comprehensive and progressive perspective *de lege ferenda*. While stressing the need to explore the interconnection between these branches of international law more closely, it downplays the differences between them and their discrete character. There has not been a merger of some or all of these branches of international law into a unified *corpus juris*. Because of the particular nature of the international law, absolute unity is hardly possible. Nevertheless, coherence is a desirable aspiration,[363] provided that it is not tantamount to achieving the "lowest common denominator" which undermines or reduces the existing substantive protection of the individual in armed conflict.

4.4. RESULT

The international legal framework for the protection of the individual during armed conflict is characterised by both unity in the sense that its component bodies of international law share a concern for the individual, for human dignity and integrity, and diversity in that they retain their distinct nature and

---

360 See Cançado Trindade, *International Law for Humankind*, 160–161.

361 See Bothe, "The Historical Evolution", 44.

362 Chetail notes that "a strict compartmentalization of the three branches of international law [IHL, international human rights law and international refugee law] is artificial and even counterproductive for the purpose of ensuring effective protection." Chetail, "Armed Conflict and Forced Migration", 703.

363 Similarly: Matz-Lück, "Harmonization, Systemic Integration, and 'Mutual Suportiveness' as Conflict-Solution Techniques: Different Modes of Interpretation as a Challenge to Negative Effects of Fragmentation?", 40.

unique characteristics.[364] Neither of the two diametrically opposed concepts of "fragmentation" or the "international law for humankind" offers an accurate conceptualisation. Adopting a middle way between them, this book understands the international legal framework for the protection of the individual during armed conflict as comprising various distinct but interrelated bodies of international law, namely international refugee law, international human rights law, IHL, and international criminal law.[365] It draws from and broadens Jean Pictet's vision of "humane law". Emphasising the distinct character of IHL and international human rights law as well as their complementarity, Pictet contended that together they form "humane law", namely "the totality of the international legal provisions which ensure for the human person respect and fulfilment".[366] The above analysis has shown that provisions which strive to ensure respect and protection for the individual in armed conflict cannot only be found in IHL and international human rights law, but also in international refugee law and in international criminal law.

5. CONCLUSION

Since international refugee protection is premised on the lack of protection by the country of origin, an understanding of such protection in armed conflict under international human rights law, IHL and international criminal law forms the backdrop of an analysis of the refugee definition in light of these branches of international law. Therefore, this chapter examined the protection of individuals from acts by their country of nationality and the protection of stateless persons from acts by their country of habitual residence, as well as protection from non-State actors on the territory of the country of origin during armed conflict under international human rights law, IHL and international criminal law.

International human rights law is applicable in armed conflict, although the material scope of some human rights treaties may be limited to non-derogable rights, depending on whether or not the State party concerned has actually made derogations. States parties are obliged to grant the rights stipulated in the respective treaty to their nationals and, with some exceptions, to stateless

364 On the unity and diversity of international law, see generally Andreas Zimmermann and Rainer Hofmann (editors), *Unity and Diversity in International Law. Proceedings of an International Symposium of the Kiel Walther Schücking Institute of International Law (November 4–7, 2004)* (Berlin: Duncker & Humblot, 2006).

365 Gillard, speaking for the ICRC, framed international human rights law, IHL and international refugee law as three pillars with the common goal of protecting the individual. See Emanuela-Chiara Gillard, "Humanitarian Law, Human Rights and Refugee Law – Three Pillars" *Statement at the International Association of Refugee Law Judges World Conference 21–23 April 2005* (2005), accessed 13 October 2013.

366 Pictet, *Development and Principles of International Humanitarian Law*, 3. In support: Sternberg, *The Grounds of Refugee Protection*, 313.

persons on their territory. Specifically designed for armed conflict, IHL balances humanitarian considerations with military necessity in restricting the use of violence in armed conflict. Even though IHL historically developed to protect the adversary's nationals in international armed conflict, pursuant to the Geneva Conventions, the Additional Protocol I, the Biological Weapons Convention and the Chemical Weapons Convention as well as customary IHL, States parties to an international armed conflict now incur certain protection obligations *vis-à-vis* their nationals and stateless persons on their territory. During a non-international armed conflict to which the country of origin is a party, it also incurs obligations with respect to its nationals or stateless persons on its territory under international humanitarian treaty law such as Article 3 common to the Geneva Conventions and Additional Protocol II, as well as under customary IHL. Armed groups which are parties to the conflict are also bound by IHL. Since international criminal law is intrinsically linked to IHL, these findings also apply to this branch of international law. International criminal law protects the individual by criminalising and thus prohibiting IHL violations.

Recent years have seen a gradual coalescence of the examined branches of international law. The Refugee Convention has come to be understood as providing surrogate human rights protection. Some States parties to the Refugee Convention and UNHCR (albeit somewhat tentatively) have also emphasised the complementarity between IHL and international refugee law and that IHL may play a role in interpreting the refugee definition. International human rights law and IHL are no longer considered mutually exclusive but have experienced a coalescence. Though remaining discrete, these branches of international law interact in various ways and share a common concern for the protection of the individual. The concept of fragmentation highlights the distinct nature of these branches of international law. Yet it fails to adequately reflect their commonalities and the cross-fertilisation between them. In contrast, the international law for humankind emphasises their complementarities, underscoring a development towards a new *ius gentium*. This concept provides an insightful perspective *de lege ferenda*, but does not entirely reflect the current state of the international legal framework for the protection of the individual in armed conflict because there has not been a merger between Refugee Convention, international human rights law, IHL and international criminal law. Therefore, the most suitable understanding is one that adopts a middle ground between "fragmentation" and "the international law for humankind", understanding the relevant branches of international law as distinct yet interrelated components of the international legal framework for the protection of the individual.

CHAPTER 4
THE INTERPRETATION OF THE REFUGEE DEFINITION

1. INTRODUCTION

This chapter addresses the interpretation of the refugee definition in Article 1A(2) Refugee Convention with respect to refugee protection claims of individuals forced to flee from their country of origin due to armed conflict.

2. ARMED CONFLICT AND REFUGEE STATUS DETERMINATION

Since IHL and international criminal law are specifically designed for armed conflict as opposed to situations of peace, they can only inform the interpretation of the refugee definition if an armed conflict in the country of origin existed, exists or is likely to arise and if the refugee protection claim is related to the armed conflict. The refugee definition cannot solely be interpreted in light of these bodies of international law in order to ensure that claims related to situations of violence which do not constitute armed conflicts are addressed.[367] However, in order to determine whether these branches of international law can complement and strengthen the interpretation of Article 1A(2) Refugee Convention, decision-makers ought to determine whether the situation in the country of origin was, is or is likely to constitute an armed conflict.[368]

In a number of instances, national refugee status decision-makers and UNHCR considered the fact that there is or was an armed conflict in the country of origin relevant for the interpretation and application of the refugee definition. For example, courts in the UK and New Zealand considered the situation in

[367] See Storey, "The 'War Flaw' and Why it Matters", 45.

[368] The arguments in this sections were first elaborated in Vanessa Holzer, "Persecution and the Nexus to a Refugee Convention Ground in Non-International Armed Conflict: Insights from Customary International Humanitarian Law", in *Refuge from Inhumanity? War Refugees and International Humanitarian Law*, edited by David James Cantor and Jean-François Durieux (Leiden: Brill, 2014), 101–127.

Somalia a "civil war".[369] Guidelines adopted by the Refugee and Immigration Board of Canada apply specifically to refugee claimants from "situations of civil war".[370] The US Board of Immigration Appeals stated that Sri Lanka was experiencing "civil unrest in the form of an armed conflict".[371] The Federal Court of Canada found that Sierra Leone was in "a tragic situation of war or armed conflict".[372] In its Eligibility Guidelines, UNHCR considered the situations in Sri Lanka,[373] Afghanistan,[374] Colombia,[375] Iraq,[376] and Somalia[377] as armed conflicts at different points in time. Yet national decision-makers and UNHCR do not necessarily intend to classify a situation as an armed conflict in the sense of IHL and may well base their assessments on varying definitions of armed conflict.

---

369 See *Adan v. Secretary of State for the Home Department* [1998] 2 WLR 702, per Lord Lloyd of Berwick (UK); *Refugee Appeal No 76551* [2010] NZRSAA 103 (21 September 2010), para. 62 (New Zealand). In the US, the Sixth Circuit Court of Appeal considered the fighting in the DRC a "civil war". See *Assy Diouf v. Holder*, 388 F. Appx. 525 (6th Cir. 2010) (US). A civil war is a form of non-international armed conflict. See Cullen, *The Concept of Non-International Armed Conflict in International Humanitarian Law*, 27.

370 Immigration and Refugee Board of Canada, "Civilian Non-Combatants Fearing Persecution in Civil War Situations".

371 *In re S-P-*, 21 I. & N. Dec. 486, Interim Decision 3287, 1996 WL 422990 (BIA), 493 (US).

372 *Sheriff v. Canada (Minister of Citizenship and Immigration)* 2002 FCT 8 (Canada).

373 See UNHCR, "Background Paper on Refugees and Asylum-Seekers from Sri Lanka" (2004), available at www.unhcr.org/refworld/docid/40d837f42.html, accessed 10.03.2015, para. 143; UNHCR, "Position on the International Protection Needs of Asylum-Seekers from Sri Lanka" (2006), available at www.refworld.org/docid/459a1fcb2.html, accessed 10.03.2015, 2 and UNHCR, "Eligibility Guidelines for Assessing the International Protection Needs of Asylum-Seekers from Sri Lanka" (2009), available at www.unhcr.org/refworld/docid/49de0b6b2.html, accessed 10.03.2015, 5.

374 See UNHCR, "Eligibility Guidelines for Asylum-Seekers from Afghanistan 2013", 5 (noting that Afghanistan continues to be affected by a non-international armed conflict). See also UNHCR, "Eligibility Guidelines for Afghan Asylum-Seekers 2007", 35; UNHCR, "Eligibility Guidelines for Assessing the International Protection Needs of Asylum-Seekers from Afghanistan" (2009), available at www.unhcr.org/refworld/docid/4a6477ef2.html, accessed 10.03.2015, 6.

375 See UNHCR, "International Protection Considerations regarding Colombian Asylum-seekers and Refugees 2002", para. 18; UNHCR, "International Protection Considerations Regarding Colombian Asylum-Seekers and Refugees" (2005), available at www.unhcr.org/refworld/docid/422c832e4.html, accessed 10.03.2015, para. 1 and UNHCR, "Eligibility Guidelines for Assessing the International Protection Needs of Asylum-Seekers from Colombia" (2010), available at www.refworld.org/docid/4bfe3d712.html, accessed 10.03.2015, 1.

376 See UNHCR, "Eligibility Guidelines for Assessing the International Protection Needs of Iraqi Asylum-Seekers" (August 2007), available at www.unhcr.org/refworld/docid/46deb05557.html, accessed 17 April 2013, 133; UNHCR, "Eligibility Guidelines for Assessing the International Protection Needs of Iraqi Asylum-Seekers" (2009), available at www.refworld.org/docid/49f569cf2.html accessed 10.03.2015, para. 19.

377 In 2014, UNHCR explicitly noted that the situation in Somalia qualifies as a non-international armed conflict under IHL: UNHCR, "International Protection Considerations with Regard to People Fleeing Southern and Central Somalia" (2014), 3, available at www.refworld.org/docid/52d7fc5f4.html, accessed 10.03.2015. See also UNHCR, "UNHCR Position on Returns to Southern and Central Somalia" (2014), para. 4, available at www.refworld.org/docid/53a04d044.html, accessed 10.03.2015. Note, however, that in a position on North Kivu, South Kivu and adjacent regions in the DRC, UNHCR chose to frame the situation as one of "conflict and violence": UNHCR, "Position on the Kivus", para. 1.

The classification of a situation in the country of origin as an armed conflict is not alien to Article 1 of the Refugee Convention. Article 1F(a) Refugee Convention *inter alia* provides for the exclusion from refugee protection of suspected war criminals. Since war crimes are intrinsically linked to armed conflict, the application of Article 1F(a) of the Refugee Convention requires an examination of whether the situation in question constituted an armed conflict.[378] However, classifying a situation in the country of origin as an armed conflict in the course of refugee status determination could be problematic for four reasons.

First, such classification often raises intricate factual challenges.[379] The existence of an armed conflict in an IHL sense is a question of fact at any given moment in time.[380] The factual challenges include the finding of objective and verifiable information. Participants in armed conflicts frequently fail themselves to clearly classify a situation as an armed conflict. States are often reluctant to acknowledge that there is an armed conflict and the opposing side is therefore an "equal" party to the conflict.[381] Conversely, however, other States classify situations as armed conflict although they should be considered as law enforcement operations.[382] Because situations of violence are often volatile and access to objectively verifiable information may be limited, the assessment of the intensity of violence and the degree of organisation of armed groups can be difficult.[383] Accurate, timely and comprehensive information on the country of origin is therefore a crucial evidentiary aspect of refugee status determination.[384]

378 Similarly: Expert Meeting on Complementarities between International Refugee Law, International Criminal Law and International Refugee Law, "Arusha Summary Conclusions", para. 23. But see Fripp, "International Humanitarian Law", 397.

379 See also Eric Fripp, "International Humanitarian law and the Interpretation of 'Persecution' in Article 1A(2) CSR51", *International Journal of Refugee* Law 26, no. 3 2014): 402.

380 See, e.g., Lawand, "Internal Conflicts". Yet McLaughlin argues that States and other traditionalists consider the facts on the ground when characterising a situation as an international armed conflict, while there is more latitude for legal-policy considerations when determining the existence of a non-international armed conflict: Robert McLaughlin, "Legal-Policy Considerations and Conflict Characterisation at the Threshold between Law Enforcement and Non-International Armed Conflict", *Melbourne Journal of International Law* 13, no. 1 (2012): 1–28.

381 See Sassòli, "The Role of Human Rights", 51–52 and Wilmshurst, "Conclusions", 479. The ICRC notes that "some governments continue to deny that there are NIACs [non-international armed conflicts] occurring within their territory and therefore that IHL applies". ICRC, "International Humanitarian Law", 5.

382 See Wilmshurst, "Conclusions", 479 and Sassòli, "The Role of Human Rights", 52.

383 These problems were identified by Elizabeth Wilmshurst who led a research project which examined whether various situations of violence around the world are and should be classified as international or non-international armed conflicts. See Wilmshurst, "Conclusions", 478–479. Farrell and Schmitt also highlight the volatility of today's armed conflicts, noting that armed conflicts usually persist for significant durations, with periods of lower levels of violence merely constituting intervals between cycles of more intense violence. See Farrell and Schmitt, "The Causes, Character and Conduct of Armed Conflict, and the Effects of on Civilian Populations, 1990–2010", 5.

384 As noted by Oosterveld concerning gender-related claims to refugee protection arising out of situations of armed conflict: Valerie Oosterveld, "Women and Girls Fleeing Conflict:

Second, classifying a situation of violence as an armed conflict also raises difficulties in applying the law,[385] in particular as regards non-international armed conflicts. To recall, a non-international armed conflict exists if armed violence reaches a minimum level of intensity and if the parties show a sufficient degree of organisation.[386] The distinction between violence that does reach the threshold of a non-international armed conflict and violence that does not is intricate. In particular, the minimum duration of violence and the degree of organisation of a non-State armed group can be contentious.[387] However, guidance which mitigates these challenges can be obtained from the jurisprudence of the ICTY, which has identified a number of factors that indicate whether the armed violence surpasses the intensity threshold, namely: the number, duration and intensity of individual confrontations; the type of weapons and other military equipment used; the number and calibre of munitions fired; the number of persons and type of forces partaking in the fighting; the number of casualties; the extent of material destruction; and the number of civilians fleeing combat zones.[388] Factors indicating whether the armed group exhibits a sufficient degree of organisation include: the existence of a command structure and disciplinary rules and mechanisms within the group; the existence of headquarters; control of a certain territory; the ability to gain access to weapons, other military equipment, recruits and military training; the ability to plan, coordinate and carry out military operations, including troop movements and logistics; the ability to define a unified military strategy and use military tactics; and the ability to speak with one voice and negotiate and conclude agreements such as cease-fire or peace accords.[389] The ICRC, which frequently carries out determinations of whether a situation of violence is an armed conflict,[390] uses similar indicia in assessing the intensity of violence and the level of organisation

---

Gender and the Interpretation and Application of the 1951 Refugee Convention" *UNHCR Legal and Protection Policy Research Series* (2012), available at www.unhcr.org/refworld/docid/504dcb172.html, accessed 10.03.2015, 41–43.

385 Pejić notes that in classifying a situation of violence as an armed conflict, the challenge is first to establish the facts on the ground and then to apply the law to the facts. See Jelena Pejić, "Status of Armed Conflicts", in *Perspectives on the ICRC Study on Customary International Humanitarian Law*, edited by Elizabeth Wilmshurst and Susan Breau (Cambridge: Cambridge University Press, 2007), 100.

386 The definition of armed conflict is examined in the Introduction.

387 See Wilmshurst, "Conclusions", 480.

388 See ICTY, *The Prosecutor v. Ramush Haradinaj, Idriz Balaj and Lahi Brahimaj*, Judgment, 3 April 2008, Case No. IT-04-84-T, para. 49. In more detail: ICTY, *The Prosecutor v. Ljube Boškoski and Johan Tarčulovski*, Judgment, 10 July 2008, Case No. IT-04-82-T, paras. 177–193.

389 See ICTY, *The Prosecutor v. Ramush Haradinaj, Idriz Balaj and Lahi Brahimaj*, Judgment, 3 April 2008, Case No. IT-04-84-T, para. 60. In more detail: ICTY, *The Prosecutor v. Ljube Boškoski and Johan Tarčulovski*, Judgment, 10 July 2008, Case No. IT-04-82-T, paras. 194–206.

390 The definition of armed conflict employed by the ICRC is very similar to the one given by the ICTY Appeals Chamber in the *Tadić Jurisdiction Decision*. On the definition of armed conflict, see the Introduction.

of armed groups.[391] These indicia can also facilitate the assessment of a situation in a country of origin by refugee status decision-makers.

A third challenge results from the forward-looking nature of refugee status determination which involves projections about the future.[392] For the purposes of applying the refugee definition, the question of whether there will be an armed conflict in the future could arise. Yet the challenges related to the determination of future risk are not unique to situations of armed conflict; any refugee status determination inevitably involves a degree of uncertainty. Armed conflicts usually persist for significant durations, with periods of lower levels of violence merely constituting intervals between cycles of more intense violence.[393] Thus, the past or present existence of an armed conflict in the country of origin may well indicate its future persistence or recurrence for the purposes of refugee status determination.

A fourth and final challenge is that classifying a situation of violence in the country of origin as an armed conflict in the course of refugee status determination could distract from the refugee claimant's predicament which should be the focus of refugee status determination.[394] The Refugee Convention applies irrespective of whether there is peace or armed conflict in the country of origin. Refugee protection does not depend on the existence of an armed conflict and the associated technical legal questions. In IHL, the qualification of a situation as an armed conflict has the purpose of determining the applicability of IHL. This purpose differs from an ascertainment of the objective circumstances in the country of origin during refugee status determination. This point is illustrated by the case of *Haji Ibrahim* before the High Court of Australia, in which Judge Gummow found that framing the "widespread disorder" in Somalia as a civil war risks "a blurring of the distinction between the persecutory acts which the asylum-seeker must show and the broader circumstances to those acts"[395] and distracting from the application of the

391 See Lawand, "Internal Conflicts" and ICRC, "International Humanitarian Law", 11.

392 On the forward-looking nature of refugee status determination, see Zimmermann and Mahler, "Article 1A, para. 2", mn. 199, 341.

393 See Farrell and Schmitt, "The Causes, Character and Conduct of Armed Conflict, and the Effects of on Civilian Populations, 1990–2010", 5.

394 Durieux argues that determining an individual's refugee status under the Refugee Convention is not a matter of armed conflict but of fear of persecution. See Durieux, "Of War, Flows, Laws and Flaws", 164 and 166. Participants of a UNHCR expert roundtable noted that although the classification of a situation as an armed conflict is relevant background information of a refugee protection claim, this often distorts the assessment of the basis of the claim. See Expert Roundtable, "Summary Conclusions on International Protection of Persons Fleeing Armed Conflict and Other Situations of Violence" (2012), available at www.unhcr.org/refworld/docid/50d32e5e2.html, accessed 10.03.2015 paras. 7 and 12.

395 *Minister for Immigration and Multicultural Affairs v. Haji Ibrahim* [2000] HCA 55, para. 145, per Gummow J (Australia).

refugee definition.[396] This risk may exist, but such a distraction need not arise. This worry concerns the quality of refugee status decision-making, rather than the point of principle as to whether refugee status decision-makers should consider whether there is an armed conflict. Refugee status decision-makers can determine whether there was, is or is likely to be an armed conflict in the home country and establish whether to draw on IHL and international criminal law in addition to international human rights law in interpreting Article 1A(2) Refugee Convention without being distracted from the determination of refugee status.[397]

To conclude, although refugee status decision-makers face a number of challenges in assessing whether there was, is or is likely to be an armed conflict in the country of origin, such an assessment is not alien to refugee status decision-making and can be undertaken in a way that is not disadvantageous to the individual claimant but rather facilitates the identification of the pertinent branches of international law that can lend interpretative guidance.

3. INTERPRETATIVE METHODS AND ACTORS

In order to analyse the refugee definition in light of international human rights law, customary IHL and international criminal law with respect to refugee protection claims of individuals compelled to flee from armed conflicts, it is first necessary to consider the rules on treaty interpretation set out in the VCLT.

3.1. OVERVIEW

The refugee definition in Article 1A(2) Refugee Convention contains a number of ambiguous terms such as "well-founded fear" or "persecution" and therefore needs to be interpreted. Interpreting a treaty means to "assign meaning to the words contained therein."[398] Article 31 of the VCLT sets out the general rule of interpretation:

> "1. A treaty shall be interpreted in good faith in accordance with the ordinary meaning to be given to the terms of the treaty in their context and in the light of its object and purpose.

---

396 See *Minister for Immigration and Multicultural Affairs v. Haji Ibrahim* [2000] HCA 55, para. 147, per Gummow J (Australia).

397 See also Holzer, "Persecution", 101–127.

398 Mark E. Villiger, "The Rules on Interpretation: Misgivings, Misunderstandings, Miscarriage? The 'Crucible' Intended by the International Law Commission", in *The Law of Treaties Beyond the Vienna Convention*, edited by Enzo Canniyyaro (Oxford: Oxford University Press, 2011), 106.

2. The context for the purpose of the interpretation of a treaty shall comprise, in addition to the text, including its preamble and annexes:
   (a) any agreement relating to the treaty which was made between all the parties in connection with the conclusion of the treaty;
   (b) any instrument which was made by one or more parties in connection with the conclusion of the treaty and accepted by the other parties as an instrument related to the treaty.
3. There shall be taken into account, together with the context:
   (a) any subsequent agreement between the parties regarding the interpretation of the treaty or the application of its provisions;
   (b) any subsequent practice in the application of the treaty which establishes the agreement of the parties regarding its interpretation;
   (c) any relevant rules of international law applicable in the relations between the parties.
4. A special meaning shall be given to a term if it is established that the parties so intended."

Article 31 VCLT codifies pre-existing customary international law and therefore applies to the Refugee Convention even though the latter was adopted before the VCLT.[399] There is no hierarchy between the various interpretative methods included in Article 31(1). The different methods are to be used in a single combined operation.[400] Nonetheless, the ordinary meaning (Article 31(1) VCLT) and thus a literal approach constitutes the logical starting point of any interpretation.[401] However, a literal approach to the interpretation of the refugee

399 On the VCLT's codifying pre-existing customary international law, see, e.g., ICJ, *Territorial Dispute (Libyan Arab Jamahiriya /Chad)*, Judgment, ICJ Reports 1994, para. 41. See also ICJ, *Maritime Delimitation and Territorial Questions between Qatar and Bahrain*, Jurisdiction and Admissibility, Judgment, ICJ Reports 1995, 21. Domestic courts have drawn on the VCLT in interpreting the refugee definition. See, e.g., *Revenko v. Secretary of State for the Home Department* [2001] QB 601 (Court of Appeal), 612 (UK) and *Applicant A v. Minister for Immigration and Ethnic Affairs* (1997) 190 CLR 225, 227 (Australia). Further: Jane McAdam, "Interpretation of the 1951 Convention", in *The 1951 Convention relating to the Status of Refugees and its 1967 Protocol: A Commentary*, edited by Andreas Zimmermann (editor), Jonas Dörschner, and Felix Machts (assistant editors) (Oxford: Oxford University Press, 2011), mn. 14, 82; Oliver Dörr, "Interpretation of Treaties", in *Vienna Convention on the Law of Treaties. A Commentary*, edited by Oliver Dörr and Kirsten Schmalenbach (Heidelberg et al.: Springer, 2012), mn. 6, 523.

400 See Richard K. Gardiner, *Treaty Interpretation* (Oxford: Oxford University Press, 2010), 10 and 36; and Matthias Herdegen, "Interpretation in International Law", in *Max Planck Encyclopedia of Public International Law*, edited by Rüdiger Wolfrum (Oxford: Oxford University Press, 2013, para. 14.

401 See Herdegen, "Interpretation", para. 11; Dörr, "Interpretation", mn. 38, 541; and Maarten Bos, "Theory and Practice of Treaty Interpretation", *Netherlands International Law Review* 27, no. 2 (1980): 135–170, 147. Gardiner notes that there is "a certain inherent logical sequence" in treaty interpretation. See Gardiner, *Treaty Interpretation*, 9. Authentic versions of the Refugee Convention exist in English and French, both of which are to be considered in treaty interpretation (see Article 33(1) VCLT).

definition risks going against the Refugee Convention's object and purpose.[402] The text of the refugee definition forms "the outer limits of its application" within which "plain meaning can only take us so far toward a workable interpretation of the refugee definition".[403] The ordinary meaning of the text must be established within the context of the treaty rather than in the abstract, as Article 31(1) VCLT makes clear.[404]

Pursuant to the teleological interpretative approach set out in Article 31(1) VCLT, a treaty is to be interpreted in light of its object and purpose. The object and purpose may *inter alia* be determined by recourse to its preamble.[405] A teleological approach can support a dynamic interpretation of a treaty.[406] The rule of effectiveness (*effet utile*) is part of the teleological approach. It provides that a treaty is to be interpreted so as to give fullest effect to its provisions.[407] Two objects could be discerned from the Refugee Convention's preamble: human rights protection and burden-sharing amongst States.[408] However, the text of the Refugee Convention in its entirety with its focus on refugees' entitlements reveals that its overall purpose is human rights protection.[409] The preamble also reveals that refugee protection is humanitarian in nature.[410] To achieve this object and purpose, the Refugee Convention must be understood as a "living treaty" and thus be interpreted dynamically.[411] It can also be deduced from this object and purpose that the refugee definition is to be interpreted in an inclusive rather than a restrictive way.[412]

402 See Foster, *International Refugee Law*, 45–46, basing this argument on an analysis of early Australian case law.

403 See Daniel J. Steinbock, "Interpreting the Refugee Definition", *UCLA Law Review* 45 (1998): 733–815, 763. Similarly: McAdam, "Interpretation", 83–84 and 86–87.

404 See Dörr, "Interpretation", mn. 39, 541.

405 See Gardiner, *Treaty Interpretation*, 197 and Hathaway, *The Rights of Refugees*, 52. Hathaway argues that a treaty's preparatory works constitute the starting point for determining its object and purpose. Hathaway, *The Rights of Refugees*, 56. However, this understanding is difficult to reconcile with a dynamic interpretation of the Refugee Convention.

406 See Dörr, "Interpretation", mn. 89, 560.

407 See Dörr, "Interpretation", mn. 35, 539; Hathaway, *The Rights of Refugees*, 62.

408 See first, second, fourth and fifth recital of the preamble of the Refugee Convention. See also Foster, *International Refugee Law*, 42–45 and McAdam, "Interpretation", mn. 43, 91. Hathaway argues that the first two operative paragraphs of the preamble establish a human rights purpose. See Hathaway, *The Rights of Refugees*, 53.

409 The Refugee Convention's structure of entitlements is described in Chapter 3. See also Foster, *International Refugee Law*, 46–47; and McAdam, "Interpretation", mn. 45–50, 92–93; UNHCR, "Interpreting Article 1 of the 1951 Convention relating to the Status of Refugees" (2001), available at www.refworld.org/docid/3b20a3914.html, accessed 10.03.2015, paras. 4–5.

410 The fifth preambular recital of the Refugee Convention refers to "the social and humanitarian nature of the refugee problem".

411 See Guy S. Goodwin-Gill, "The search for the one, true meaning...", in *The Limits of Transnational Law. Refugee Law, Policy Harmonization and Judicial Dialogue in the European Union*, edited by Guy S. Goodwin-Gill and Hélène Lambert (Cambridge: Cambridge University Press, 2010), 207 and UNHCR, *Note on International Protection (2011)*, para. 5.

412 See UNHCR, "Information Note".

The treaty context comprises the entire text of the treaty, its preamble and annexes, as well as other agreements or instruments as identified in Article 31(1) and (2) VCLT. The 1951 Final Act of the UN Conference of Plenipotentiaries on the Status of Refugees and Stateless Persons which adopted the Refugee Convention constitutes an "agreement relating to the treaty, which was made between all the parties in connection with the conclusion of the treaty" in the sense of Article 31(2)(a) VCLT.[413] State practice in the application of the refugee definition falls within Article 31(3)(b) VCLT if it establishes agreement of the parties regarding its interpretation. The Refugee Convention and its Protocol are multilateral treaties without treaty bodies. The refugee definition is typically interpreted by domestic refugee status decision-makers or adjudicators. While common law courts do refer to jurisprudence from other States in their interpretation and application of the refugee definition,[414] such transnational references are rarer elsewhere.[415] It is therefore difficult to identify State practice in the application of the refugee definition *that establishes agreement between the parties* as to the interpretation of the refugee definition. Hathaway argues that Article 31(3)(b) VCLT ought to be narrowly construed with regard to the Refugee Convention because this Convention was established to limit State conduct and to protect individuals:

> "This purpose could be fundamentally frustrated if the construction of the duties assumed by States were to be determined by the very State practice sought to be constrained."[416]

While there is merit in the result of this argument with respect to the Refugee Convention's definition of a refugee, it would be more in line with the premise that Article 31 VCLT sets out a single rule of interpretation to argue that State practice in the interpretation of the refugee definition must be taken into account alongside the Refugee Convention's object and purpose. This object and purpose may well act as a counterweight to restrictive State practice.

The Declaration of States Parties adopted at the 2001 Ministerial Meeting of the States Parties marking the fiftieth anniversary of the Refugee Convention

413 See Hathaway, *The Rights of Refugees*, 53. See also The Final Act of the Conference of the Plenipotentiaries on the Status of Refugees and Stateless Persons, 25 July 1951, UN Doc. A/CONF.2/108/Rev.1, available at www.refworld.org/docid/40a8a7394.html, accessed 10.03.2015.

414 See McAdam, "Interpretation", mn. 3, 78.

415 Regarding European States, see Hélène Lambert, "Transnational Judicial Dialogue, Harmonization and the Common European Asylum System", *International & Comparative Law Quarterly* 58, no. 3 (2009): 519–543. Concerning African States, see Marina Sharpe, "The 1969 OAU Convention and the Protection of People fleeing Armed Conflict and Other Situations of Violence in the Context of Individual Refugee Status Determination" (2011), available at www.refworld.org/docid/50fd3edb2.html, accessed 10.03.2015, 8–11.

416 Hathaway, *The Rights of Refugees*, 71.

(2001 Declaration) exhibits subsequent agreement between the parties on the meaning of the Refugee Convention and thus falls within Article 31(3)(b).[417] The ministerial communiqué adopted ten years later on the occasion of the Refugee Convention's sixtieth anniversary does not constitute such subsequent agreement because it was not adopted by the States parties to the Refugee Convention in this capacity.[418]

Furthermore, Article 31(3)(c) VCLT provides for a systemic approach to treaty interpretation in that any relevant rules of international law applicable in the relations between the parties are to be taken into account in the interpretation of a treaty.[419] It contains an implicit reference to the sources of international law as laid down in Article 38(1) of the Statute of the ICJ.[420] The term "applicable" suggests that legally non-binding documents cannot be resorted to in the interpretation of a treaty under Article 31(3)(c) VCLT.[421] Relevant rules include treaty or customary rules with a similar object, concerning the same subject matter or tackling the same or similar factual, legal or technical problems.[422] The term "parties" in Article 31(3)(c) VCLT could refer to parties to the dispute. But this understanding would not be pertinent with regard to the Refugee Convention because the refugee definition is typically not interpreted to resolve an inter-State dispute, but by national refugee status decision-makers or adjudicators.[423] Moreover, the definite article "the" could suggest that the relevant rules must be applicable between all parties to a treaty.[424] This would mean that recourse based on Article 31(3)(c) VCLT to relevant rules of international law is limited to those rules that are binding on all parties to the Refugee Convention. Very few treaties, if any, will have exactly the same parties as the Refugee Convention. This strict requirement would therefore have the effect of cutting off widely ratified multilateral treaties such as the Refugee Convention from developments of international treaty law.[425] Therefore, in some

---

417 See Hathaway, *The Rights of Refugees*, 54.

418 See Intergovernmental event at the ministerial level of Member States of the United Nations on the occasion of the 60th anniversary of the 1951 Convention relating to the Status of Refugees and the 50th anniversary of the 1961 Convention on the Reduction of Statelessness, 8 December 2011, UN Doc. HRC/MINCOMMS/2011/6, available at www.unhcr.org/4ee210d89.html, accessed 10.03.2015.

419 See Dörr, "Interpretation", mn. 89, 560. Hathaway notes that "it is important that treaties be interpreted in a way that reconciles them to their contemporary international legal context." Hathaway, *The Rights of Refugees*, 64.

420 See Dörr, "Interpretation", 561, mn. 92; Bos, "Theory and Practice of Treaty Interpretation", 145.

421 See Villiger, "The Rules on Interpretation", 112.

422 See Dörr, "Interpretation", mn. 93, 562 and mn. 98–99, 565.

423 As argued by Foster, *International Refugee Law*, 55–56.

424 See Foster, *International Refugee Law*, 55.

425 See Foster, *International Refugee Law*, 55 and Campbell McLachlan, "The Principle of Systemic Integration and Article 31(3)(c) of the Vienna Convention", *International and Comparative Law Quarterly* 54 (2005): 279–320, 314. French notes that "the requirement

circumstances reference to treaties that do not have co-extensive membership is justified, provided they are relevant in the sense of Article 31(3)(c) VCLT for the interpretation of the refugee definition. Where reference is made to customary international law, of course, this problem does not arise as it binds all States with the exception of persistent objectors.

Another issue is whether the phrase "relevant rules applicable between the parties" concerns rules applicable at the time the Refugee Convention was concluded or at the point in time when it is being interpreted. The text of the Refugee Convention and its object and purpose provide guidance on this matter.[426] An effective realisation of the Refugee Convention's object and purpose – protecting refugees – is only possible if the refugee definition is interpreted in a dynamic way, taking into account legal and factual developments.[427] Therefore, as regards the refugee definition, Article 31(3)(c) VCLT is to be understood as referring to rules applicable at the time of interpretation, not the time of the conclusion of the Refugee Convention.

Article 31(4) VCLT, which is the final element of the general rule of interpretation providing that a term is to be given a special meaning if this corresponds to the parties' intention, has no relevance for the interpretation of the refugee definition.[428] Article 32 VCLT allows resorting to supplementary means of interpretation as a way of confirming the meaning resulting from the interpretative methods listed in Article 31 VCLT or of determining the meaning if this interpretation "leaves the meaning ambiguous or obscure" (para. a) or if it "leads to a result which is manifestly absurd or unreasonable" (para. b). Preparatory work to the treaty and the circumstances surrounding its conclusion constitute such secondary means of interpretation. There may be a tension or even incompatibility between a dynamic interpretation of the refugee definition that places the Refugee Convention within present day law and circumstances on the one hand and recourse to the Refugee Convention's *travaux préparatoires*, even if only as secondary sources of interpretation, on the

---

of duality of treaty membership is often an almost impossible criterion to meet." Duncan French, "Treaty Interpretation and the Incorporation of Extraneous Legal Rules", *International and Comparative Law Quarterly* 55, no. 2 (2006): 281–314, 307.

426 The terms of a treaty and its object and purpose may provide evidence of the parties' intention to contemplate evolution. See, e.g., ICJ, *Legal Consequences for States of the Continued Presence of South Africa in Namibia (South West Africa) notwithstanding Security Council Resolution 276 (1970)*, Advisory Opinion, ICJ Reports 1971, para. 53. Further: McLachlan, "The Principle of Systemic Integration", 317.

427 On the dynamic interpretation of the refugee definition, see also Sternberg, *The Grounds of Refugee Protection*, 320.

428 McAdam provides an overview of how national courts have used the general rule of treaty interpretation with respect to the Refugee Convention and only points to a British case referring to Article 31(4) VCLT as regards the term "*refouler*". See McAdam, "Interpretation", mn. 72, 99.

other. Therefore, the latter are not a significant interpretative tool as regards the refugee definition.[429]

3.2. UNHCR AND ITS EXECUTIVE COMMITTEE

As previously noted, UNHCR has a supervisory role over the application of the Refugee Convention as a result of which it publishes a range of documents setting out its views on the interpretation of the refugee definition. Moreover, conclusions by its EXCOM are relevant for the interpretation of the refugee definition.[430] Hathaway argues that UNHCR's Handbook and the Conclusions on International Protection adopted by the State members of the EXCOM evidence subsequent agreement (in the sense of Article 31(3)(a) VCLT) between the parties of the Refugee Convention regarding the latter's interpretation or the application of its provisions. He contends that the overwhelming majority of States parties to the Refugee Convention and/or its Protocol are members of the EXCOM and that, practically speaking, this is the fairest way of generating agreement amongst parties to the Refugee Convention.[431] While Hathaway's argument may be praised for its pragmatism, it must be acknowledged that pursuant to Article 31(3)(a) VCLT such subsequent agreement would have to originate from or be agreed by all parties of the Refugee Convention. Moreover, the EXCOM is a subsidiary organ of the ECOSOC which guides UNHCR rather than States and which is not a treaty body of the Refugee Convention. Therefore, EXCOM conclusions do not fall within the purview of Article 31(3)(a) VCLT.[432]

---

429 See Tillmann Löhr, *Die kinderspezifische Auslegung des völkerrechtlichen Flüchtlingsbegriffs* (Baden-Baden: Nomos, 2009), 72–74. McAdam, however, notes that the *travaux préparatoires* may be drawn upon to confirm the meaning of a treaty provision established by the interpretative methods set out in Article 31 VCLT because they can reflect the parties' intentions. See McAdam, "Interpretation", mn. 75–77, 100.

430 The role of UNHCR and its EXCOM is set forth in the Introduction.

431 See Hathaway, *The Rights of Refugees*, 54–55 and footnote 146. Agreeing: Deschamp and Dowd, "Review of the Use of UNHCR Executive Committee Conclusions", 28. Goodwin-Gill considers that the Handbook and subsequent Guidelines are evidence of subsequent practice establishing agreement on interpretation mediated through the prism of UNHCR's supervisory role. See Goodwin-Gill, "The search for the one, true meaning", 212–213. Currently, 87 States are members of the EXCOM (see www.unhcr.org/pages/49c3646c89.html, accessed 10.03.2015), while 147 States are parties to the Refugee Convention and/or its Protocol (see www.unhcr.org/3b73b0d63.html, accessed 10.03.2015).

432 See Marjoleine Zieck, "Article 35 of the 1951 Convention/Article II of the 1967 Protocol", in *The 1951 Convention relating to the Status of Refugees. A Commentary*, edited by Andreas Zimmermann (editor), Jonas Dörschner, and Felix Machts (assistant editors) (Oxford: Oxford University Press, 2011), mn. 69, 1497. Alternatively, EXCOM conclusions might constitute subsequent practice in the application of the Refugee Convention which establishes the agreement of the parties regarding its interpretation pursuant to Article 31(3)(b) VCLT. This could be the case even though not all parties to the Refugee Convention are members of the EXCOM if the States that are not EXCOM members agree with the EXCOM practice. However, because of the variations in the practice of the Refugee Convention parties

The better view is that States must take the UNHCR Handbook, guidelines and other views of UNHCR on matters of law as well as the conclusions of the EXCOM into account when interpreting and applying the refugee definition because of their obligation to cooperate with UNHCR that stems from Article 35 of the Refugee Convention and Article II of the Protocol. Though not legally binding, UNHCR's views are to be considered as authoritative interpretations which national courts, as a result of the obligation to cooperate with UNHCR, must consider and deviation from which must be justified.[433] As regards the EXCOM, Member States are obliged to act in good faith and are bound by the prohibition of *venire contra factum proprium*. They must thus take into account the principles adopted through EXCOM conclusions within their domestic system and justify deviation from them.[434] In fact, the UNHCR Handbook, UNHCR guidelines and EXCOM conclusions have been amply used as reference tools in State practice.[435]

3.3. INTERPRETING THE REFUGEE DEFINITION IN LIGHT OF INTERNATIONAL LAW

This section examines whether pursuant to the general rule of treaty interpretation set forth in the VCLT, the refugee definition can be interpreted in light of international human rights law, customary IHL and international criminal law, respectively.

3.3.1. International Human Rights Law

The context of the refugee definition supports an interpretation in light of international human rights law. The Refugee Convention's preamble recalls that the UN Charter and the UDHR uphold the enjoyment of human rights without discrimination.[436] It also reiterates the UN's goal of ensuring that refugees enjoy

on refugee protection it is difficult to see how EXCOM conclusions could establish such agreement.

433 See Kälin, "Supervising the 1951 Convention", 627; Löhr, *Die kinderspezifische Auslegung*, 55. Also: Markard, *Kriegsflüchtlinge*, 25–26.

434 See Löhr, *Die kinderspezifische Auslegung*, 55; Markard, *Kriegsflüchtlinge*, 27.

435 See McAdam, "Interpretation", 110–114, mn. 109–122; Kälin, "Supervising the 1951 Convention", 625–627 and Erika Feller and Anja Klug, "Refugees, United Nations High Commissioner (UNHCR)", in *Max Planck Encyclopedia of Public International Law*, edited by Rüdiger Wolfrum (Oxford: Oxford University Press, 2007), available at www.mpepil.com, accessed 10.03.2015, para. 65. Specifically concerning EXCOM conclusions, see Deschamp and Dowd, "Review of the Use of UNHCR Executive Committee Conclusions", iv–v and 26–29.

436 See first recital of the preamble of the Refugee Convention.

"the widest possible exercise of these fundamental rights and freedoms".[437] The preamble demonstrates that the Refugee Convention's object and purpose also support reference to international human rights law in the interpretation of the refugee definition.[438] Subsequent State practice also affirms an interpretation in light of international human rights law. In the aforementioned 2001 Declaration, States parties of the Refugee Convention recognised that the Refugee Convention "sets out rights, including human rights".[439] Thus, the Refugee Convention's object and purpose, the context of the refugee definition and subsequent State practice support a human rights-based interpretation of the refugee definition. The interpretation of the Refugee Convention in light of international human rights law is generally accepted by UNHCR,[440] in State practice[441] and in the refugee law literature.[442] The question remains, though, exactly which international human rights law instruments can provide interpretative guidance.

The reference to the UDHR in the Refugee Convention's preamble establishes a connection between the UDHR and the Refugee Convention. Therefore, the

---

437 Second recital of the preamble of the Refugee Convention.

438 See Foster, *International Refugee Law*, 49.

439 Second preambular recital of the 2001 Declaration.

440 The UNHCR Handbook recommends resorting to international human rights law as regards the interpretation of persecution: UNHCR, *Handbook*, paras. 51 and 60. UNHCR's guidance on refugee claims relating to sexual orientation and gender-identity as well as those on gender-related persecution draw on progressive developments in international human rights law: UNHCR, *Guidelines on International Protection No. 1*, para. 2 and UNHCR, "Guidance Note on Refugee Claims Relating to Sexual Orientation and Gender Identity" (2008), available at www.refworld.org/docid/48abd5660.html, accessed 10.03.2015, paras. 5 and 9. The UNHCR guidelines on "particular social group" note that "the term membership of a particular social group should be read in an evolutionary manner, open to the diverse and changing nature of groups in various societies and evolving international human rights norms." UNHCR, *Guidelines on International Protection No. 2*, para. 3. See further UNHCR, *Guidelines on International Protection No. 4: 'Internal Flight or Relocation Alternative' within the Context of Article 1A(2) of the 1951 Convention and/or 1967 Protocol relating to the Status of Refugees*, UN Doc. HRC/GIP/03/04 (23 July 2003), para. 4; UNHCR, *Guidelines on International Protection No. 6. Religion-Based Refugee Claims under Article 1A(2) of the 1951 Convention and/or the 1967 Protocol relating to the Status of Refugees*, UN Doc. HRC/GIP/04/06 (28 April 2004), para. 2; UNHCR, *Guidelines on International Protection No. 7: The application of Article 1A(2) of the 1951 Convention and/or 1967 Protocol relating to the Status of Refugees to Victims of Trafficking and Persons at Risk of Being Trafficked*, UN Doc. HCR/GIP/06/07 (7 April 2006), 14 (regarding persecution).

441 Foster identifies such State practice, noting that although a human rights-based interpretative approach is the dominant one, it is not universally accepted in State practice: Foster, *International Refugee Law*, 28.

442 Ground-breaking in this respect was the study by James Hathaway: James C. Hathaway, *The Law of Refugee Status* (Toronto: Butterworths, 1991), 101–104. See also Grahl-Madsen, *Status of Refugees* 212–216; Pirkko Kourula, *Broadening the Edges. Refugee Definition and International Protection Revisited*, edited by Anne F. Bayefsky, Refugees and Human Rights (The Hague/Boston/London: Martinus Nijhoff, 1997), 92–93 and 132; Anker, "Refugee Law", 133–138; Binder, *Frauenspezifische Verfolgung*, 21–46; Löhr, *Die kinderspezifische Auslegung*, 61–65.

refugee definition may be interpreted in light of the rights set out in the UDHR, even though the UDHR as such is not legally binding. The previous section established that the Refugee Convention is to be interpreted in a dynamic way. It is therefore possible to draw on international human rights law as it stands today when interpreting the refugee definition, rather than merely as it was when the Convention or its Protocol were adopted. It has also been shown that under Article 31(3)(c) VCLT, recourse is not limited to treaties with co-extensive membership or to treaties whose norms are also part of customary international law. Widely ratified international human rights treaties set out how a large number of State parties to the Refugee Convention have defined unacceptable violations of human dignity and may therefore be drawn upon in the interpretation of the refugee definition.[443] Such treaties include the ICCPR, the CEDAW, the CAT, the CRC and its Optional Protocol, as well as the CERD and the ICESCR.[444] Resorting to regional human rights treaties in the interpretation of the refugee definition raises problems of fairness and consistency because different receiving States could interpret the refugee definition in light of varying regional human rights treaties.[445] They are therefore not considered here.

It is irrelevant whether the country of origin has ratified a specific human rights treaty which is used in the interpretation of the refugee definition. Such a requirement would undermine the Refugee Convention's object and purpose because it would mean that asylum-seekers from countries that have ratified few human rights treaties would be faced with a narrower scope of the refugee definition than those from countries who have widely ratified international human rights treaties.[446]

3.3.2. Customary International Humanitarian Law

While the human rights-based interpretation of the refugee definition in times of peace is widely accepted, situations of armed conflict in the country of origin pose the question of whether IHL can also provide interpretative guidance. Concerns have been raised that drawing on customary IHL in interpreting the refugee definition distorts refugee law by suggesting or even positing that violations of customary IHL create an independent basis for asylum.[447] However,

---

443 See Foster, *International Refugee Law*, 57, who bases her argument on Lauterpacht and Bethlehem, "The Principle of *Non-Refoulement*", 113.

444 See Foster, *International Refugee Law*, 64.

445 See Foster, *International Refugee Law*, 68.

446 See also Foster, *International Refugee Law*, 27–86.

447 Storey and Wallace note that in US case of *In re Medina*, a similar objection was made. See Storey and Wallace, "War and Peace", 355–356 and *In re Medina*, 19 I. & N. Dec. 734 (1988) (US). The case of *In re Medina* has since been qualified by *In re S-P-*, 21 I. & N. Dec. 486, Interim Decision 3287, 1996 WL 422990 (BIA) (US). In *Echeverria-Hernandez v. Immigration and Naturalization Service* 923 F.2d 688 (9th Cir. 1991) (US), the petitioner unsuccessfully

resorting to customary IHL as an interpretative aid to determine the meaning and scope of the refugee definition is conceptually different from claiming asylum on the basis of rules of customary IHL. Understanding elements of the refugee definition in light of customary IHL means that the rule of international law that is being applied is Article 1A(2) Refugee Convention, rather than any rules of customary IHL.

As set out above, the Refugee Convention's object and purpose is to provide protection to people who fulfil the refugee definition and to protect their human rights. The Refugee Convention's preamble stresses the need to protect fundamental rights and freedoms without discrimination. The Refugee Convention's preamble notes that refugee protection is a humanitarian "problem".[448] The previous analysis showed that customary IHL is similar to the Refugee Convention in that it confers certain obligations on States parties to armed conflict to protect their nationals and stateless persons on their territory in armed conflict. In armed conflict, the international public interest of protecting the individual person is shared by customary IHL and international human rights law.[449] The Refugee Convention, international human rights law and customary IHL share a concern for human dignity and worthiness. Therefore, violations of customary IHL rules can manifest a broken bond of protection between the country of origin and the refugee claimant in times of armed conflict.[450] Consequently, customary IHL can be drawn upon in a teleological interpretation of the refugee definition.

Yet it must be acknowledged that interpreting the refugee definition in light of customary IHL could restrict the scope of this definition and thus undermine the Refugee Convention by incorporating the "minimalistic" approach of customary IHL to protection in armed conflict that balances humanitarian considerations against military necessity as manifested, for example, in its rules

---

argued that an obligation to provide temporary protection flows from the Geneva Convention IV (paras. 22–27). Marx also contended that a prohibition of *refoulement* flows from common Article 3 of the Geneva Conventions. See Reinhard Marx, "Völkervertragsrechtliche Abschiebungshindernisse für Flüchtlinge", in *Aktuelle asylrechtliche Probleme der gerichtlichen Entscheidungspraxis in Deutschland, Österreich und der Schweiz*, edited by Klaus Barwig and Walter Brill (Baden-Baden: Nomos, 1996), 128–131. Agreeing with this argument: Cordula Droege, "Transfer of Detainees – Legal Framework, Non-refoulement and Contemporary Challenges", *International Review of the Red Cross* 90, no. 871 (2008): 669–701, 675. For the opposing view, see Karoline Kerber, "International Humanitarian Law as a Source of Protection for Refugees from Areas of Armed Conflict", *Refuge* 16, no. 6 (1997): 6–8.

448 Fifth preambular recital of the Refugee Convention.

449 See Pictet (editor), *Commentary on the Geneva Convention for the Amelioration of the Condition of the Wounded and Sick in Armed Forces in the Field*, 25. Von Sternberg argues that customary IHL guarantees human rights during armed conflict and therefore ought to be considered in the interpretation of the refugee definition. See Sternberg, *The Grounds of Refugee Protection*, 320.

450 On the broken bond of trust, loyalty and protection between and individual and the government in the context of refugee protection, see Grahl-Madsen, *Status of Refugees* 79.

on the use of lethal force during the conduct of hostilities, which are laxer than international human rights law.[451] In response to such concerns, it is important to recall the requirement examined above of an inclusive and dynamic interpretation which flows from the Refugee Convention's object and purpose. This rule for interpreting the refugee definition qualifies recourse to customary IHL in the sense that customary IHL can only provide interpretative guidance to the extent that it enhances, rather than restricts, refugee protection under the Refugee Convention. What is more, because of the difficulties that victims of armed conflict face in obtaining refugee status, it is important to explore whether IHL and international law can strengthen refugee protection in contexts of armed conflict.[452]

Though not sufficiently widespread to constitute "subsequent practice in the application of the treaty *which establishes the agreement of the parties* regarding its interpretation"[453] in the sense of Article 31(3)(b) VCLT, the State practice that draws on customary IHL in the interpretation of the refugee definition indicates that some States agree with such an interpretation. For example, the US Basic Law Manual acknowledges that violations of the 1949 Geneva Conventions may constitute the basis for an asylum claim.[454] The US Board of Immigration appeals noted that "the evidence must [*inter alia*] be evaluated in the context of the ongoing civil conflict [in Sri Lanka] to determine whether the motive for the abuse in the particular case … was part of the violence inherent in an armed conflict (i.e. lawful acts of war)."[455] The UK Asylum and Immigration Tribunal (AIT) held that "serious violations of peremptory norms of customary IHL and human rights" constitute persecution.[456] The Canadian Civil War Guidelines for refugee status decision-makers provide that in addition to international human rights law, customary IHL may assist in determining what constitutes permissible conduct.[457] These Guidelines, however, are rarely used presently.[458]

---

451 A similar concern has been voiced by Durieux, "Of War, Flows, Laws and Flaws", 166. For a sceptical view see also Chetail, "Armed Conflict and Forced Migration", 723. The use of lethal force is examined in detail in Chapter 5.

452 See introduction.

453 Emphasis added.

454 See US Immigration and Naturalization Service, *The Basic Law Manual: U.S. Law and INS Refugee/Asylum Adjudications* 22 (1995), cited by Sternberg, *The Grounds of Refugee Protection*, 37. See also *Montecino v. Immigration and Naturalization Service*, 915 F.2d 518, 520 (9th Cir. 1990) (US).

455 *In re S-P-*, 21 I. & N. Dec. 486, Interim Decision 3287, 1996 WL 422990 (BIA), 493–494 (US).

456 See *AM & AM v. Secretary of State for the Home Department* (armed conflict: risk categories) Somalia CG [2008] UKAIT 00091, para. 76 (UK).

457 See Immigration and Refugee Board of Canada, "Civilian Non-Combatants Fearing Persecution in Civil War Situations".

458 At least since September 2001, the few references that do exist in jurisprudence regarding the guidelines have omitted to specifically refer to their provisions on IHL. See, e.g., *Sheriff v. Canada (Minister of Citizenship and Immigration)* 2002 FCT 8; *Fi v. Canada (Minister of Citizenship and Immigration)* 2006 FC 1125; *Kanagaratnam v. Canada (Minister of*

As rules determining unacceptable infringements of human dignity in armed conflict, customary IHL rules are "relevant rules of international law applicable between the parties" in the sense of Article 31(3)(c) VCLT with respect to the interpretation of the Refugee Convention.[459] Parties to the Refugee Convention are obliged to interpret and apply the refugee definition in a way that is consistent with their other obligations under international law,[460] and thus with their obligation under customary IHL to ensure respect for customary IHL.[461] This obligation further strengthens the view that rules of customary IHL are "relevant rules applicable between the parties" for the purposes of Article 31(3)(c) VCLT. An interpretation of the refugee definition in light of customary IHL would not affect the receiving State's compliance with customary IHL *stricto sensu*. But it would contribute to the protective function of customary IHL because it would ensure that asylum-seekers are not exposed to customary IHL violations taking place in their country of origin. The interpretation of the refugee definition in light of customary IHL is tentatively supported by UNHCR[462] and its EXCOM[463] as well as more strongly in the literature.[464]

Citizenship and Immigration) 2006 FC 1205; *Navaratnam v. Canada (Minister of Citizenship and Immigration)* 2003 FCT 523; *Innocent v. Canada (Citizenship and Immigration)* 2009 FC 1019; *Kanagasabapathy v. Canada (Minister of Citizenship and Immigration)* 2003 FCT 78 (all Canada).

459 Some authors and the Canadian Civil War Guidelines suggest drawing on the Additional Protocol II in the interpretation of the refugee definition without discussing the implications of the Protocol's high threshold of applicability (for example, would the armed conflict in the country of origin have to meet the criteria set out in Article 1(1) Additional Protocol II?). Sternberg, *The Grounds of Refugee Protection*, 116; Storey and Wallace, "War and Peace", 359; Markard, *Kriegsflüchtlinge*, 159–161; Immigration and Refugee Board of Canada, "Civilian Non-Combatants Fearing Persecution in Civil War Situations".

460 This is based on the principle of good faith. See Villiger, "The Rules on Interpretation", 112; Dörr, "Interpretation", 561, mn. 90.

461 On this rule of customary IHL, see Henckaerts and Doswald-Beck, *Customary International Humanitarian Law*, 509.

462 See UNHCR, *Note on International Protection (2000)*, para. 32; UNHCR, *Note on International Protection (2003)*, para. 53; UNHCR, "Eligibility Guidelines for Asylum-Seekers from Afghanistan 2013", 30.

463 See UNHCR Executive Committee, *Conclusion on the Provision of International Protection Including Through Complementary Forms of Protection (Conclusion No. No. 103 [LVI])*, UN Doc. A/AC.96/1021 (7 October 2005), para. c.

464 See Durieux and Cantor, "Refuge from Inhumanity? Canvassing the Issues", 18; Storey and Wallace, "War and Peace", 359–366; Sternberg, *The Grounds of Refugee Protection*, 116–123, 31; Mark R. von Sternberg, "The Plight of the Non-Combatant in Civil War and the New Criteria for Refugee Status", *International Journal of Refugee Law* 9, no. 2 (1997): 169–195; Erik Møse, "The Criminality Perspective", *Georgetown Immigration Law Journal* 15, no. 3 (2000–2001): 463–478, 475; Jaquemet, "Cross-Fertilization"; Jerzy Sztucki, "Who Is a Refugee? The Convention Definition: Universal or Obsolete?", in *Refugee Rights and Realities. Evolving International Concepts and Regimes*, edited by Frances Nicholson and Patrick Twomey (Cambridge Cambridge University Press, 1999), 63; Brandl, "Die Anwendbarkeit des Flüchtlingsbegriffs", 192–196; Markard, *Kriegsflüchtlinge*, 158–167, 169 and Zimmermann and Mahler, "Article 1A, para. 2", mn. 319, 371.

In conclusion, an interpretation of the refugee definition in light of customary IHL is in accordance with the rules on treaty interpretation. The Refugee Convention's humanitarian object and purpose ensures that such an interpretation strengthens rather than weakens refugee protection.

3.3.3. *International Criminal Law*

The analysis of whether an interpretation in light of substantive norms of international criminal law is in line with the rules on treaty interpretation focusses on the objective elements of war crimes, namely acts or omissions contrary to rules of IHL (*actus reus*) rather than the subjective elements (*mens rea*).[465] The latter are irrelevant for the interpretation of the refugee definition because refugee status determination is not concerned with determining the individual criminal responsibility of the persecutor.

The strongest basis for drawing on international criminal law in interpreting the refugee definition is Article 31(3)(c) VCLT. As set out above,[466] international criminal law is concerned with the protection of the individual in armed conflict. International criminal law comprises relevant rules applicable in the relations between the parties because they address the same subject matter as the Refugee Convention, the protection of human dignity and physical integrity.[467] This indicates that drawing on international criminal law is also supported by a teleological interpretation. The intrinsic link between customary IHL and international criminal law, in particular the latter's role in clarifying and developing IHL, further strengthens this view.[468] The context of Article 1A(2) Refugee Convention also supports an interpretation in light of international criminal law. The exclusion clause in Article 1F(a) Refugee Convention refers to war crimes, thus showing that references to international criminal law are not alien to Article 1 Refugee Convention.[469] At the same time, the Refugee Convention's object and purpose, in particular the requirement to interpret the refugee definition inclusively and dynamically, qualifies recourse to international criminal law in the same way as it limits recourse to customary IHL. International criminal law can only provide interpretative guidance to the extent that it strengthens, rather than undermines, refugee protection.

---

465 On objective and subjective elements of international crimes, see Cassese, *International Criminal Law*, 53. Werle distinguishes between material and mental elements of international crimes: Werle, *Völkerstrafrecht*, mn. 405–408, 188–189.

466 See Chapter 3.

467 Similarly: Jaquemet, "Cross-Fertilization", 664–669.

468 On the development of IHL by international criminal tribunals, see generally Darcy, *Judges, War and Law*.

469 See Storey, "Armed Conflict in Asylum Law", 14.

UNHCR lends tentative and implicit support to an interpretation of the refugee definition in light of international criminal law, acknowledging:

> "If someone is forced to flee armed conflict in their country because of human rights violations and breaches of humanitarian law, these factors will be part of what determines that person's refugee status."[470]

UNHCR's EXCOM also indicated support of such an interpretation, noting that harm which causes cross-border forced displacement may constitute both a violation of international human rights law and IHL.[471] While a few refugee law scholars support an interpretation of the refugee definition in light of international criminal law in certain circumstances,[472] others are more cautious because of the differences between international criminal law and the Refugee Convention.[473]

Thus, pursuant to the rules on treaty interpretation, the refugee definition can be interpreted in light of international criminal law concerning the objective elements of war crimes. The Refugee Convention's humanitarian object and purpose serves to ensure that such an interpretation enriches rather than restricts refugee protection.

4. CONCLUSION

Since customary IHL and international criminal law can only provide interpretative guidance if a refugee protection claim is related to an armed conflict in the country of origin, refugee status decision-makers can and should

---

470 UNHCR, *Note on International Protection (2003)*, para. 53. UNHCR also considers that "the existence of serious violations of international humanitarian law which constitute threats to life or freedom or other serious harm" is a relevant for determining whether "the consequences of violence for civilians are sufficiently serious to meet the threshold of persecution." UNHCR, "Eligibility Guidelines for Asylum-Seekers from Afghanistan 2013", 30.

471 See UNHCR Executive Committee, *Conclusion No. 73 (XLIV) Refugee Protection and Sexual Violence* (1993), first preambular recital.

472 See Jaquemet, "Cross-Fertilization", 665–673; Møse, "The Criminality Perspective", 475; Sternberg, *The Grounds of Refugee Protection*, 116–123 and 313; and Markard, *Kriegsflüchtlinge*, 169–173.

473 The summary conclusions of the expert meeting convened by UNHCR and the ICTR on the complementarities between international refugee law, international criminal law and international human rights law note that although many of the same acts are considered persecution under international criminal law and international refugee law, "there are also important distinctions in the ways in which the concept has been applied and interpreted under each legal regime. In particular, the differing purposes of each branch of law need to be borne in mind." Expert Meeting on Complementarities between International Refugee Law, International Criminal Law and International Refugee Law, "Arusha Summary Conclusions", para. 13.

determine whether there was, is or is likely to be an armed conflict in the country of origin. Pursuant to Article 31(1) VCLT, the refugee definition is to be interpreted in good faith in accordance with the ordinary meaning to be given to its terms in their context and in light of its object and purpose. Due to the Refugee Convention's humanitarian object and purpose, the refugee definition must be interpreted inclusively and dynamically. It is intricate to identify State practice in the application of the refugee definition that establishes agreement between the parties as to the interpretation of the refugee definition. The 2001 Declaration adopted at a meeting of States parties to the Refugee Convention evidences subsequent agreement between the parties on the meaning of the Refugee Convention and thus falls within Article 31(3)(b). Pursuant to a systemic interpretation of the refugee definition, multilateral treaties and rules of customary international law in force at the time of interpretation can be drawn upon.

Interpreting the refugee definition in light of international human rights law, in particular the UDHR, the ICCPR, the CEDAW, the CAT, the CRC and its Optional Protocol, the CERD and the ICESCR, as well as in light of customary IHL and international criminal law, is in accordance with the rules on treaty interpretation set out in the VCLT. A human rights-based interpretation of the refugee definition is widely supported in State practice and also by UNHCR and its EXCOM. A few States have also drawn on IHL in interpreting the refugee definition. UNHCR has tentatively indicated acceptance of an interpretation of the refugee definition in light of IHL and international criminal law. The Refugee Convention's humanitarian purpose and the resultant requirement of an inclusive and dynamic interpretation counters concerns that recourse to IHL and international criminal law in interpreting the refugee definition undermines refugee protection by restricting the scope of the refugee definition.

CHAPTER 5

THE WELL-FOUNDED FEAR OF BEING PERSECUTED

1. INTRODUCTION

According to the refugee definition in Article 1A(2) Refugee Convention, a refugee must have a well-founded fear of being persecuted for reasons of a Refugee Convention ground. This chapter analyses the well-founded fear of being persecuted.

2. WELL-FOUNDED FEAR

To qualify for refugee status under the Refugee Convention, a person needs to demonstrate a well-founded fear of being persecuted, with "fear" entailing a "forward-looking expectation of risk".[474]

2.1. BURDEN OF PROOF AND STANDARD OF PROOF

In many States, the burden of proof in refugee status determination at first instance is on the refugee claimant,[475] while UNHCR argues that the

474 Zimmermann and Mahler, "Article 1A, para. 2", mn. 199, 341. Procedural aspects of refugee status determination (apart from the brief discussion of the burden of proof here) fall outside this book's scope. On well-founded fear, see also Holzer, "The 1951 Refugee Convention", 13–17.

475 See UNHCR, *Handbook*, para. 66. Wouters rightly notes that in the identification of the reason(s) for the possible persecution, the burden of proof is incumbent on the receiving State. Concerning the availability of an internal protection alternative, the burden of proof is also on the receiving State. See Wouters, *International Legal Standards for the Protection from Refoulement*, 95 and 97. Also: UNHCR, *Handbook*, para. 66. In the US, the burden of proof is in principle on the claimant. But in past persecution cases, there is a presumption of well-founded fear and the burden of proof shifts. See Deborah Anker, *Law of Asylum in the United States* (Thomson West, 2011), para. 2:22. In Germany, the refugee claimant incurs a burden to present the facts underlying his or her claim (*Darlegungslast*). See Kay Hailbronner, *Asyl- und Ausländerrecht*, 2nd ed. (Stuttgart: W. Kohlhammer, 2008), 323, mn. 659. Further: Rodger Haines, "Gender-related Persecution (Article 1A(2))", in *Refugee Protection in*

obligation to ascertain and analyse all relevant facts is shared by the applicant and the decision-maker.[476] A shared burden of proof is preferable because it acknowledges the numerous practical challenges which a refugee claimant faces in a foreign legal system and is therefore conducive to realising the Refugee Convention's humanitarian object and purpose of providing international protection. In Belgium, for example, the burden of proof is shared between the asylum applicant and the asylum authorities.[477] This shared obligation is particularly important if the country of origin is experiencing an armed conflict as this makes obtaining documentation more difficult for the refugee claimant.[478]

To prove a well-founded fear of persecution, the standard of "reasonable possibility or chance" is widely accepted in State practice.[479] It is also supported by UNHCR[480] and the literature.[481] However, in a few States, a higher standard of proof seems to be implicitly required regarding refugee claims arising out of armed conflict and other situations of violence. For example, with regard to claims to asylum by people fleeing conflict and violence in El Salvador in the 1980s, the US Board of Immigration Appeals was criticised for subjecting evidence to a higher standard of proof than the "reasonable possibility"

International Law. UNHCR's Global Consultations on International Protection, edited by Erika Feller, Volker Türk, and Frances Nicholson (Cambridge: Cambridge University Press, 2003), 338; Löhr, *Die kinderspezifische Auslegung*, 77; and more generally Gregror Noll, *Proof, Evidentiary Assessment and Credibility in Asylum Procedures* (Leiden/Boston: Martinus Nijhoff, 2005).

476 See UNHCR, *Handbook*, para. 197.

477 As noted by European Migration Network, "EU and Non-EU Harmonised Protection Statuses in Belgium" (2011), available at www.emnbelgium.be/sites/default/files/publications/eu_and_non-eu_harmonised_protection_statuses_in_belgium_0.pdf, accessed 10.03.2015, 29, citing *Raad van State* (Council of State), *No. 157.749*, 19 April 2006; *Raad voor Vreemdelingenbetwistingen* (Council for Alien Law Litigation), *No. 4460*, December 2007 and other decisions.

478 See Storey and Wallace, "War and Peace", 365.

479 See *INS v. Cardoza-Fonseca*, 480 US 421, 440 (1987) (US); *R v. Secretary of State for the Home Department, ex parte Sivakumaran* [1988] Imm AR 147, 150 per Lord Keith (UK); *Chan v. Minister for Immigration and Ethnic Affairs* (1989) 169 CLR 379, per Mason CJ ("real chance") (Australia); *Refugee Appeal No. 71404/99* [1999] NZRSAA (29 October 1999) (both New Zealand); *Adjei v. Canada (Minister of Employment and Immigration)* 1989 2 FC 680 (Canada). On the German standard of "beachtliche Wahrscheinlichkeit" (substantial likelihood), see Markard, *Kriegsflüchtlinge*, 217–218.

480 UNCHR considers that persecution "must prove to be reasonably possible": UNHCR, "Note on Burden and Standard of Proof in Refugee Claims" (1998), available at www.unhcr.org/refworld/docid/3ae6b3338.html, accessed 10.03.2015, para. 17. See also UNHCR, "Eligibility Guidelines for Asylum-Seekers from Afghanistan 2013", 5.

481 See Hathaway, *Law of Refugee Status*, 75–80; Jean-Yves Carlier, "The Geneva Refugee Definition and the 'Theory of the Three Scales'", in *Refugee Rights and Realities. Evolving International Concepts and Regimes*, edited by Frances Nicholson and Patrick Twomey (Cambridge: Cambridge University Press 1999), 41–43; Anker, *Law of Asylum in the United States*, para. 2:2; and Markard, *Kriegsflüchtlinge*, 215–220, who provides a very detailed analysis.

standard.[482] Such a higher standard of proof in contexts of armed conflict disregards the wording of the refugee definition which does not distinguish between times of peace and armed conflict and should therefore not be adopted.

2.2. RISK ASSESSMENT

The notion of well-founded fear entails an assessment of the refugee claimant's risk of being persecuted. Article 1A(2) Refugee Convention does not require the refugee applicant to already have experienced persecution. A well-founded fear of being persecuted may arise after his or her departure from the country of origin.[483] Past persecution should, however, be taken as probative of future risk of being persecuted.[484] Two central aspects of this risk assessment are examined here, namely whether a combination of subjective and objective factors or solely objective factors ought to be considered in the risk assessment and the necessary degree of individualisation of the risk.

2.2.1. Subjective-Objective Approach versus Objective Approach

There are two approaches to assessing whether a person has a well-founded fear of being persecuted: the subjective-objective approach and the objective approach. Two variations of the subjective-objective approach have been developed, with one version considering that the objective element, namely the actual risk of being persecuted, and the subjective element, i.e. the fear or emotional state of trepidation, must be cumulatively established. A different version of the subjective-objective approach departs from this cumulative requirement, understanding subjective fear as an element that can top up an otherwise insufficient objective risk of persecution.[485] In contrast, the objective approach understands the well-founded fear standard as solely entailing "an individuated, forward-looking appraisal of actual risk".[486] While the objective

---

482 See generally Peter Butcher, "Assessing Fear of Persecution in a War Zone", *Georgetown Immigration Law Journal* 5 (1991): 435–473. For a more recent US judgment concerning a Colombian refugee applicant whose evidence of death threats was not considered to prove a well-founded fear, see *Silva v. US Attorney General*, 448 F.3d 1299, 1233 (11th Cir. 2006) (US).

483 This refers to so-called refugees *sur place*. See Rainer Hofmann, "Nachfluchtgründe und Flüchtlingsvölkerrecht", *Neue Verwaltungszeitschrift* 6, no. 4 (1987): 299–301, 299; Goodwin-Gill and McAdam, *The Refugee in International Law*, 542; Zimmermann and Mahler, "Article 1A, para. 2", mn. 127–162, 324–332.

484 See Wouters, *International Legal Standards for the Protection from Refoulement*, 85–87; Hathaway, *Law of Refugee Status*, 87–89; Binder, *Frauenspezifische Verfolgung*, 232. Similarly: Zimmermann and Mahler, "Article 1A, para. 2", 342, mn. 207.

485 On both versions of the subjective-objective approach: James C. Hathaway and William S. Hicks, "Is There a Subjective Element in the Refugee Convention's Requirement of 'Well-Founded Fear'?", *Michigan Journal of International Law* 26 (2004–2005): 505–562, 510–511.

486 Hathaway and Hicks, "Is There a Subjective Element", 507.

approach does not consider the refugee claimant's state of mind, it does take into account the refugee claimant's individual circumstances.[487]

The application of the subjective-objective approach may result in denial of refugee status for persons whom the decision-makers do not deem to be fearful because their trepidation has not been identified. An assessment of a refugee claimant's state of mind involves various practical and often insurmountable challenges, ranging from communicating through an interpreter over cultural, gender and age differences to the effects of trauma experienced by the claimant. There are thus many practical reasons why a refugee claimant's state of mind may not be adequately assessed. Moreover, different individuals have different ways of experiencing and expressing fear.[488] In any case, the term "fear" is linguistically better understood as chance or possibility rather than trepidation.[489] The context of Article 1A(2) Refugee Convention supports this understanding: for cessation of refugee protection, Article 1C(5) Refugee Convention requires that "the circumstances in connexion with which he has been recognised as a refugee have ceased to exist." This focus on the circumstances implies an objective approach. Furthermore, the prohibition of *refoulement* in Article 33 Refugee Convention does not contain any indications of a subjective element either.[490] The objective approach is also more in line with the object and purpose of the Refugee Convention as it concentrates on protection from the actual risk of persecution, irrespective of the refugee applicant's emotional state of mind.[491] For these reasons, the objective approach is to be preferred.

As noted above, pursuant to the objective approach a claimant's risk of being persecuted must be assessed in the context of the situation in the country of

---

487 See Zimmermann and Mahler, "Article 1A, para. 2", mn. 196, 340.

488 See Zimmermann and Mahler, "Article 1A, para. 2", mn. 193, 339; Bridgette A. Carr, "We Don't Need to See Them Cry: Eliminating the Subjective Apprehension Element of the Well-Founded Fear Analysis for Child Refugee Applicants", *Pepperdine Law Review* 33 (2005–2006): 535–573, 544–555; Michael Bossin and Laila Demirdache, "A Canadian Perspective on the Subjective Component of the Bipartite Test for 'Persecution': Time for Re-evaluation", *Refuge* 22, no. 1 (2005): 108–118, 111–116; Hathaway and Hicks, "Is there a Subjective Element", 512 and 517. On the difficulties in assessing subjective fear: Hilary Evans Cameron, "Risk Theory and 'Subjective Fear': The Role of Risk Perception, Assessment, and Management in Refugee Status Determinations", *International Journal of Refugee Law* 20, no. 4 (2008): 567–585.
See Hathaway and Hicks, "Is there a Subjective Element", 534–535. Similarly: Carr, "We Don't Need", 544–555; Bossin and Demirdache, "A Canadian Perspective", 111–116.

489 See Hathaway and Hicks, "Is there a Subjective Element", 509 and Markard, *Kriegsflüchtlinge*, 210–211. Expressing a different view: Zimmermann and Mahler, "Article 1A, para. 2", mn. 176–178, 336–337.

490 See Markard, *Kriegsflüchtlinge*, 211.

491 See Wouters, *International Legal Standards for the Protection from Refoulement*, 83–84; Markard, Kriegsflüchtlinge, 211–212. Also supporting the objective approach: Hugo Storey, "Persecution: Towards a Working Definition", in *Research Handbook on International Law and Migration*, edited by Vincent Chetail and Céline Bauloz (Cheltenham/Northampton: Edward Elgar, 2014), 508–509.

origin, taking into consideration aspects of the individual's profile, experiences and activities.[492] A refugee claimant must therefore show a relationship between the general circumstances in the country of origin on the one hand and individualised facts on the other.[493] The relevant general circumstances in the country of origin include *inter alia* that country's human rights record and security situation,[494] including the existence of an armed conflict.[495] If the country of origin is experiencing an armed conflict, they also comprise the extent to which the parties to the conflict have complied with IHL. While in times of peace, the human rights situation in the country of origin offers important clues as to the refugee claimant's risk of being harmed, in times of armed conflict a consideration of IHL violations can provide additional guidance. This approach is, for instance, illustrated by the International Convention for the Protection of All Persons from Enforced Disappearance (Convention on Enforced Disappearances).[496] Article 16(1) of the Convention on Enforced Disappearances prohibits *refoulement* of an individual to a State where he or she would be at risk of being subjected to enforced disappearance. Article 16(2) of this Convention states:

> "For the purpose of determining whether there are such grounds, the competent authorities shall take into account all relevant considerations, including, where applicable, the existence in the State concerned of a consistent pattern of gross, flagrant or mass violations of human rights or of serious violations of international humanitarian law."

Premised on an understanding that enforced disappearance can result from violations of international human rights law and/or IHL, the approach to the risk assessment in Article 16(2) of the Convention on Enforced Disappearance takes into account patterns of violations of human rights and IHL in the country of origin. A similar approach should be adopted in assessing the risk of persecution. For example, UNHCR's 2005 Eligibility Guidelines on Colombia examine the human rights situation and the degree to which IHL is complied with for the purposes of assessing the risk of persecution and other forms of harm prompting the need for international protection of Colombian asylum-seekers.[497] Hence, in

492 See UNHCR, "Eligibility Guidelines for Asylum-Seekers from Sri Lanka 2009", 29; UNHCR, "Eligibility Guidelines for Iraqi Asylum-Seekers 2007", 134; UNHCR, "Eligibility Guidelines for Afghan Asylum-Seekers 2007", para. 63.

493 See Mark R. von Sternberg, "Outline of United States Asylum Law: Substantive Criteria and Procedural Concerns", *Defending Immigration Removal Proceedings* (2011): 31–76, 33.

494 See Wouters, *International Legal Standards for the Protection from Refoulement*, 91.

495 See Chetail, "Armed Conflict and Forced Migration", 722.

496 Adopted by UN General Assembly, *Resolution 61/177*, UN Doc. A/RES/61/177 (20 December 2006).

497 These guidelines contain a section titled "Indices of Violence, Violations of Human Rights and International Humanitarian Law". See UNHCR, "International Protection Considerations Regarding Colombian Asylum-Seekers 2005", 14.

cases where the country of origin has been experiencing an armed conflict, the objective approach to assessing whether an individual has a well-founded fear of being persecuted *inter alia* includes a consideration of the extent to which the parties to the conflict have complied with IHL.

2.2.2. Individualisation

During armed conflict, a large number of people may be at risk of serious harm. In refugee claims revolving around situations of armed conflict, the question of how individualised the risk of persecution must be is often particularly contentious.[498] Regarding the degree of individualisation and the level of risk recognised, State practice can be broadly divided into a restrictive approach (also known as "differential risk analysis")[499] and a liberal approach.

The judgment of the UK House of Lords in *Adan* epitomises the restrictive position. Lord Slynn of Hadley considered the situation in Somalia at a time when "law and order have broken down and where ... every group seems to be fighting some other group or groups in an endeavor to gain power." In such a context, he found that the claimant "must be able to show fear of persecution for [Refugee] Convention grounds *over and above* the risk to life and liberty inherent in the civil war."[500] The high level of violence in Somalia in the late 1990s and its group-based and widespread nature affected the risk assessment, leading their Lordships to require a higher level of risk than necessary in times of peace. In this view, an individualised risk of persecution results when a higher risk of persecution, compared with the rest of the population or other members of the group, is present.[501] The US Eighth Circuit Court of Appeals also adopted a restrictive approach to the risk assessment. The court held that "the harm suffered must be particularised to the individual. ... Harm arising from general conditions such as anarchy, civil war, or mob violence will not ordinarily support a claim of persecution."[502] This position requires a high level of individualisation of the threat irrespective of the characteristics of the underlying armed conflict and fails to acknowledge that the general situation in the country of origin forms

---

498 See Sternberg, *The Grounds of Refugee Protection*, 33.

499 See Storey, "Armed Conflict in Asylum Law", 11.

500 *Adan v. Secretary of State for the Home Department* [1998] 2 WLR 702, per Lord Slynn of Hadley. The UKIAT subsequently applied the requirement of a higher risk in *NM and Others (Lone Women – Ashraf) Somalia v. Secretary of State for the Home Department* CG [2005] UKIAT 00076, paras 118 and 135 (emphasis added) (UK).

501 See Markard, *Kriegsflüchtlinge*, 133, who also provides an analysis of the German jurisprudence on this matter. But see: Zimmermann and Mahler, "Article 1A, para. 2", mn. 314, 370.

502 *Mohamed v. Ashcroft*, 396 F.3d 999, 1006 (8th Cir. 2005) (US). Binder shows that Swiss jurisprudence adopts a similar restrictive approach focussing on the "singled out" requirement. See Binder, *Frauenspezifische Verfolgung*, 170–179.

part of the risk assessment. It appears to also conflate the risk element with the causal link to a Refugee Convention ground.[503]

The judgment in *Prophète v. Canada* rejects the differential risk requirement, stressing that there can be situations in which "an individual ... may have a personalised risk, but one that is shared by many other individuals."[504] Hence, the experiences of similarly situated persons can support a claim of being at risk of persecution. The jurisprudence in Australia and New Zealand,[505] as well as UNHCR,[506] also reject the "differential risk" or "singled out" requirement. For example, the Refugee Status Appeals Authority (RSAA) of New Zealand held that "the claimant must only establish the 'ordinary' real chance of being persecuted and not some increased level of risk or that he/she has been singled out for persecution".[507] Also UNHCR stressed:

> "Whole communities may risk or suffer persecution for [Refugee] Convention reasons. The fact that all members of the community are equally affected does not in any way undermine the legitimacy of any particular individual claim."[508]

There is nothing in the wording of the refugee definition to suggest that a refugee has to be singled out for persecution, either generally or over and above other persecuted persons.[509] A well-founded fear of persecution can result from numerous personal facts and general facts and circumstances that are unrelated to the individual refugee claimant. The experiences of similarly situated persons constitute significant evidence that the individual refugee claimant is at risk of persecution.[510] Membership of a group that is being

---

503 The problem of such conflation is addressed by *Refugee Appeal No. 71462* [1999] NZRSAA (27 September 1999), para. 52 (New Zealand). See also Markard, *Kriegsflüchtlinge*, 136. The nexus requirement is examined in Chapter 7.

504 *Prophète v. Canada (Minister of Citizenship and Immigration)* 2008 FC 331, para 18 (Canada). See also *Gonzales-Neyra v. INS*, 122 F.3d 1293, 1295 (9th Cir. 1997) (US), as amended on denial of rehearing, 133 F.3d 726 (9th Cir. 1998), acknowledging that the group of persons facing the same risk as the applicant is not limited in size.

505 See *Minister for Immigration and Multicultural Affairs v. Haji Ibrahim* [2000] HCA 55, para. 70 (also at para. 147), per Gummow J (Australia); *Refugee Appeal No. 71462* [1999] NZRSAA (27 September 1999), para. 77 (New Zealand); *Minister for Immigration and Multicultural Affairs v. Abdi* [1999] FCA 299, per O'Connor, Tamberlin and Mansfield JJ (Australia).

506 See UNHCR, "Eligibility Guidelines for Iraqi Asylum-Seekers 2007", 129.

507 *Refugee Appeal No. 76551* [2010] NZRSAA 103 (21 September 2010), para. 66 (New Zealand).

508 UNHCR, "Eligibility Guidelines for Iraqi Asylum-Seekers 2007", 129.

509 The requirement that a refugee claimant be singled out for persecution has been widely criticised by scholars. See, e.g., James Crawford and Patricia Hyndman, "Three Heresies in the Application of the Refugee Convention", *International Journal of Refugee Law* 1, no. 2 (1989): 155–179, 155 and 165–167; Kälin, "Refugees and Civil Wars", 441–443; Butcher, "Assessing Fear of Persecution", 453–458; Binder, *Frauenspezifische Verfolgung*, 182–186; Kagan and Johnson, "Persecution", 248; Jaquemet, "Cross-Fertilization", 667–668.

510 See Hathaway, *Law of Refugee Status*, 89–91. See also Markard, *Kriegsflüchtlinge*, 220–223, focussing on the persecution of third persons and group persecution. Similarly: Sternberg,

persecuted should be individual enough.[511] Moreover, the underlying rationale of requiring a higher level of risk may well be found in the political realm rather than in the legal sphere, namely in concerns that unless a higher level of risk is required, individuals on either side of a conflict could qualify for refugee protection, thus potentially leading to large numbers of refugee claimants.[512] For these reasons, the "differential risk" or "singled out" requirement is to be rejected.[513]

2.3. RESULT

In determining whether a refugee claimant has a well-founded fear of persecution, the burden of proof ought to be shared between the refugee claimant and the decision-maker. This shared burden of proof is particularly relevant in contexts of armed conflict which exacerbate the claimant's difficulties in obtaining sufficient documentation and evidence. The standard of proof is that of "reasonable possibility". In conducting the risk assessment, an objective approach is to be preferred over a subjective-objective approach. An individual's risk of being persecuted must be examined in light of the general situation in the country of origin, including the extent to which human rights and IHL are complied with if there is an armed conflict, and in view of the individual circumstances. The extent to which the risk of persecution must be individualised is contentious in State practice. A liberal approach to the degree of individualisation, which does not require that the claimant be singled out for persecution and which takes into account the experiences of similarly situated persons, is to be preferred.

The Grounds of Refugee Protection, 6–7, noting that the protected grounds refer to group traits rather than individualised characteristics.

511 See Wouters, *International Legal Standards for the Protection from Refoulement*, 87–88; Binder, *Frauenspezifische Verfolgung*, 160. On group persecution, see further: Binder, *Frauenspezifische Verfolgung*, 162–168.

512 In *Adan v. Secretary of State for the Home Department* [1998] 2 WLR 702, Lord Lloyd of Berwick guarded against an interpretation of the refugee definition that would result in "participants on both sides of the civil war … [being] entitled to protection under the [Refugee] Convention" (UK). See also *Isa v. Canada (Secretary of State)* [1995] FCJ No. 354, 72 (Canada). As noted by Storey and Wallace, "War and Peace", 351 and more recently Markard, *Kriegsflüchtlinge*, 131. Durieux identifies a "contamination of qualitative criteria by quantitative factors": Durieux, "Of War, Flows, Laws and Flaws", 164. Further: Jean-Francois Durieux and Agnès Hurwitz, "How Many is too Many? African and European Responses to Mass Influxes of Refugees", *German Yearbook of International Law* 47 (2004): 105–159.

513 Storey shows that the singled out-requirement has been rejected in the literature and case law. See Storey, "Persecution", 513.

3. THE HUMAN RIGHTS-BASED INTERPRETATION OF PERSECUTION

Persecution is not defined by the Refugee Convention or any other international refugee or human rights treaty.[514] Nevertheless, two main approaches to the human rights-based interpretation of persecution (the hierarchical and the two-tiered approach) have evolved.[515]

3.1. HIERARCHICAL APPROACH

Although Vernant had already suggested an interpretation of persecution in light of human rights in 1953,[516] the human rights-based interpretation of persecution gained its main impetus from Hathaway's analysis in 1991.[517] He defined persecution "as the sustained or systemic violation of basic human rights demonstrative of a failure of State protection".[518] Hathaway argued that the International Bill of Rights, comprising the UDHR, the ICCPR and the ICESCR, constitutes "a minimum condition of legitimacy"[519] of States which the

---

514 Article 7(2)(g) Rome Statute defines the crime against humanity of persecution as "the intentional and severe deprivation of fundamental rights contrary to international law by reason of the identity of the group or collectivity". There are various reasons why this definition is narrower than the definition of persecution in the refugee definition, including the contextual element of crimes against humanity (widespread or systematic attack against any civilian population) and the requirement of discriminatory intent. See Expert Meeting on Complementarities between International Refugee Law, International Criminal Law and International Refugee Law, "Arusha Summary Conclusions", para. 15; Löhr, *Die kinderspezifische Auslegung*, 86.

515 There are numerous studies that have examined the extent to which and the way in which domestic decision-makers in several States draw upon international human rights law to interpret persecution. See, e.g., Nicholas Sitaropoulos, *Judicial Interpretation of Refugee Status: In Search of a Principled Methodology Based on a Critical Comparative Analysis, with Special Reference to Contemporary British, French, and German Jurisprudence* (Baden-Baden: Nomos, 1999); Foster, *International Refugee Law* (concentrating on socio-economic rights); Binder, *Frauenspezifische Verfolgung* (focussing on gender-related persecution); Löhr, *Die kinderspezifische Auslegung* (on a child-specific interpretation of the refugee definition). For an older study comprising numerous States and with specific references to the use of international human rights law, see Jean-Yves Carlier et al. (editors), *Who Is a Refugee? A Comparative Case Law Study* (The Hague: Kluwer Law International, 1997).

516 Vernant stated that a refugee is defined as "anyone who can prove that his person or property is either threatened, or as good as threatened, with severe measures and sanctions of an arbitrary nature, incompatible with the principles set forth in the Universal Declaration of Human Rights" (footnotes in original omitted): Jacques Vernant, *The Refugee in the Post-War World* (London: George Allen & Unwin Ltd, 1953), 7–8. Atle Grahl-Madsen highlighted that the human rights-based interpretation of persecution was first advocated by Vernant as early as 1953. See Grahl-Madsen, *Status of Refugees* 193.

517 See Hathaway, *Law of Refugee Status*, 101–134.

518 Hathaway, *Law of Refugee Status*, 104–105.

519 Hathaway, *Law of Refugee Status*, 106.

international community has recognised. He subsequently broadened the range of international human rights treaties to which recourse can be made in the interpretation of persecution.[520]

Hathaway conceptualised the human rights-based understanding of persecution as a hierarchical model based on different types of obligations which exist under the International Bill of Rights.[521] In his view, the first two categories are based on human rights obligations which are immediately binding, while the remaining categories refer to human rights treaties that stipulate obligations which are not immediately binding.[522] The first category comprises the non-derogable rights in the ICCPR whose violation constitutes persecution under any circumstances. The second category consists of derogable rights enshrined in the ICCPR. A violation of these rights amounts to persecution unless the State lawfully derogated from them.[523] The third category contains rights stipulated in the ICESCR. Because of the particular nature of States' obligations under the ICESCR, persecution exists if "a government fails to ensure the non-discriminatory allocation of available resources to meet the most basic of socio-economic needs."[524] Violations of the rights in the fourth category, namely those rights that were included in the UDHR but not in the ICCPR or the ICESCR, do not amount to persecution.[525]

3.2. TWO-TIERED APPROACH

Various States,[526] UNHCR[527] and numerous scholars[528] adopt a two-tiered approach to the interpretation of persecution in light of international human

520 The additionally included international human rights treaties are: the CEDAW, the CERD and the CRC. See James C. Hathaway, "The Relationship Between Human Rights and Refugee Law: What Refugee Law Judges Can Contribute", in *Realities of Refugee Determination on the Eve of a New Millennium: The Role of the Judiciary. 3rd Conference of the International Association of Refugee Law Judges. October 1998 Ottawa*, edited by International Association of Refugee Law Judges (Haarlem: 1998), 87.

521 See Hathaway, *Law of Refugee Status*, 108.

522 See Foster, *International Refugee Law*, 169 and Hathaway, *Law of Refugee Status*, 110 and 116.

523 See Hathaway, *Law of Refugee Status*, 101–116.

524 Hathaway, *Law of Refugee Status*, 117.

525 See Hathaway, *Law of Refugee Status*, 109–111.

526 See James C. Hathaway and Michelle Foster, *The Law of Refugee Status*, 2nd ed. (Cambridge: Cambridge University Press, 2014), 196–197. Article 9(1) Qualification Directive and Article 9(1) Recast Qualification Directive. See further the analyses of State practice by, e.g., Löhr, *Die kinderspezifische Auslegung*, 93; Binder, *Frauenspezifische Verfolgung*, 89–90; and Markard, *Kriegsflüchtlinge*, 143.

527 See UNHCR, "Interpreting Article 1 of the 1951 Convention relating to the Status of Refugees", paras. 2–6 and UNHCR, *Guidelines on International Protection No. 1*, paras. 5 and 9.

528 See Zimmermann and Mahler, "Article 1A, para. 2", mn. 250, 354; Löhr, *Die kinderspezifische Auslegung*, 89; Jean-Yves Carlier, *Droit d'asile et des réfugiés. De la protection aux droits*, The Hague Academy of International Law, Recueil des Cours/Collected Courses, Vol. 332,

rights law, understanding persecution as a human rights violation of a certain intensity. The two-tiered approach examines on the one hand whether one or several human rights are violated and on the other hand the intensity of the human right violation or violations. There are various factors that indicate whether a human rights violation is of sufficient intensity. They comprise quantitative factors such as the duration, systematic nature, repetition, and repeatability of the infringement. They also include qualitative factors, such as the importance of the right violated, and the severity of the infringement. Further factors are the individual circumstances of the refugee claimant, such as family ties, gender, age, and state of health.[529] The cumulative effect of various human rights violations must also be taken into account. Even if single events do not surpass the intensity threshold, their cumulative effect may.[530] For example, UNHCR notes with reference to Afghanistan:

> "Regular exposure to measures such as security checks, raids, interrogation, personal and property searches, and restrictions on freedom of movement may, in some cases, result in undue hardship for the persons affected and cumulatively amount to persecution."[531]

3.3. DISCUSSION

3.3.1. General Observations

With its fixed categories, the hierarchical approach to the human rights-based interpretation of persecution fails to give adequate weight to the individual circumstances of the case at hand. It lacks the flexibility necessary for a dynamic interpretation of persecution, and it does not sufficiently acknowledge the indivisibility of all human rights.[532] Therefore, it is ill-suited

---

Collected Courses (The Hague et al.: Martinus Nijhoff, 2008), 190–237; Goodwin-Gill and McAdam, *The Refugee in International Law*, 92; Haines, "Gender-related Persecution", 327–329; Binder, *Frauenspezifische Verfolgung*, 79–80; Walter Kälin, "Flight in Times of War", *International Review of the Red Cross* 843 (2001): 629–650, 634. Foster's core obligations approach can be considered a variant of the two-tiered approach. According to this approach, "if the violation in question is not fundamental, key or grave, or, in other words, does not impinge on the core of the right, then it will not, at least alone, be considered sufficiently serious as to amount to persecution". Foster, *International Refugee Law*, 195.

529 Löhr identified these criteria for assessing the intensity of a human rights violation by analysing case law and doctrine: Löhr, *Die kinderspezifische Auslegung*, 90–91. Storey reiterates that the human rights-based understanding of persecution is person-specific and context-specific. See Storey, "Persecution", 476.

530 See, e.g., Carlier, "The Geneva Refugee Definition", 43. On cumulative harms and the human rights approach to persecution, see also Storey, "Persecution", 476.

531 UNHCR, "Eligibility Guidelines for Afghan Asylum-Seekers 2007", 17.

532 Similarly: Löhr, *Die kinderspezifische Auslegung*, 98–100; Foster, *International Refugee Law*, 190. More recently: Storey, "Persecution".

for the interpretation of persecution. Moreover, there are various reasons that speak for the two-tiered approach to the interpretation of persecution in light of international human rights law. The context of Article 1A(2) Refugee Convention supports the two-tiered approach: Article 33(1) Refugee Convention states that a refugee may not be expelled or returned to a State "where his life or freedom would be threatened on account of his race, religion, nationality membership of a particular social group or political opinion." This provision shows that persecution encompasses at least threats to life and freedom and the corresponding human rights, thus indicating that persecution is concerned with *serious* human rights violations. Moreover, the Refugee Convention's object and purpose, which is not to provide surrogate human rights protection in general, but merely in those situations in which continued presence in the country of origin would be intolerable, further supports the view that only human rights violations which surpass a certain intensity threshold qualify as persecution.[533] Furthermore, the two-tiered approach is flexible, allowing for reference to international human rights law as an objective normative standard whilst at the same time taking individual circumstances into account. It also incorporates the full range of human rights. For these reasons, the two-tiered approach is used in this book. It must be acknowledged, though, that since not all kinds of harm have been codified by international human rights law, it is conceivable that harm amounts to persecution even though there is no serious human rights violation.[534]

3.3.2. Material Scope in Peace and Armed Conflict

Having established that the two-tiered approach is most suitable for interpreting persecution in light of international human rights law, the question arises with respect to refugee protection claims that arise out of situations of armed conflict in the country of origin as to whether the human rights-informed scope of persecution is narrower in times of armed conflict than in times of peace.[535] This could be the case because, as shown in Chapter 3, the scope of protection under international human rights law could be considered as limited to non-derogable human rights in times of armed conflict. For example, the US Eleventh Circuit Court of Appeals considered death threats by a guerrilla group in Colombia, in a "place where the awful is ordinary",[536] of insufficient severity to constitute persecution,[537] possibly insinuating that in situations where abuse

533 See Löhr, *Die kinderspezifische Auslegung*, 99–100. See Storey, "Persecution", 475.

534 See Expert Meeting on Complementarities between International Refugee Law, International Criminal Law and International Refugee Law, "Arusha Summary Conclusions", para. 17.

535 This question was first explored in Holzer, "Persecution", 101–127.

536 *Silva v. US Attorney General*, 448 F.3d 1299 (11th Cir. 2006), 1242 (US).

537 See *Silva v. US Attorney General*, 448 F.3d 1299 (11th Cir. 2006), 1233 (US). Swedish authorities have been criticised for requiring a level of severity for persecutory acts that is too

is widespread, harm needs to surpass a higher threshold so as to constitute persecution.

It is correct that lawful derogations by the country of origin from its human rights obligations would not fall within the scope of persecution because they would not breach that country's human rights obligations. However, it cannot be generally assumed that the material scope of persecution in armed conflict is necessarily limited to non-derogable human rights. The Refugee Convention applies irrespective of whether the country of origin is in peace or armed conflict. There is nothing in the wording of the refugee definition that would indicate that a more restrictive interpretation is justified in a context of armed conflict. Giving persecution a narrower scope in armed conflict than in times of peace would be contrary to the Refugee Convention's humanitarian object and purpose because it would deny refugee protection for reasons unrelated to the refugee definition and in situations when typically large numbers of people require international protection. Furthermore, the Refugee Convention was developed against a backdrop of conflict-induced forced displacement. The drafters did not consider it necessary to limit its scope in situations of armed conflict as opposed to times of peace.[538] In addition, there are a number of instances in State practice acknowledging that an act can constitute persecution irrespective of whether it occurs in times of peace or armed conflict. For example, the US Board of Immigration Appeal held:

> "While inter-clan violence may arise during the course of civil strife, such circumstances do not preclude the possibility that harm inflicted during the course of such strife may constitute persecution."[539]

Moreover, UNHCR considers:

> "Human rights violations and other consequences of exposure to conflict-related violence may amount to persecution within Article 1A(2) of the 1951 [Refugee] Convention, either independently or cumulatively."[540]

UNHCR further states that when assessing whether the impact of conflict-related violence on civilians is sufficiently serious as to constitute persecution, it is necessary to take into account the impact of the armed conflict on the

---

high, though this practice is not limited to situations of conflict and violence. See UNHCR, "Quality in the Swedish Asylum Procedure: A Study of the Swedish Migration Board's Examination of and Decision on Applications for International Protection", 2011, 6–7 (on file with author).

538 See Chapter 2.

539 *In re H-*, 21 I. & N. Dec. 337, Interim Decision 3276, 1996 WL 291910 (BIA), 343 (US). See also *Minister for Immigration and Multicultural Affairs v. Haji Ibrahim* [2000] HCA 55, para. 18 per Gaudron J (Australia); *Matter of Villalta*, 20 I. & N. Dec. 142 (BIA 1990) (US).

540 UNHCR, "Eligibility Guidelines for Asylum-Seekers from Afghanistan 2013", 5.

human rights situation in the country of origin and on the State's ability to protect human rights.[541] Thus, UNHCR does not adopt a narrower human rights-based interpretation of persecution in times of armed conflict than in times of peace. In UNHCR's view, the fact that there is an armed conflict in the country of origin does not mean that the human rights standard of protection is lower for the purpose of interpreting persecution. To the contrary, the armed conflict can reduce or nullify the State's ability to provide protection from persecution.

For these reasons, the material scope of persecution ought not to be interpreted more restrictively in times of armed conflict than in times of peace.

3.3.3. Persecutors

The refugee definition in Article 1A(2) Refugee Convention does not expressly refer to the identity of the persecutors.[542] Where persecution emanates from the country of origin, it is generally understood to fall within the scope of the refugee definition.[543] This is because the refugee definition clearly recognises the link between a well-founded fear of persecution and protection, stipulating that owing to his or her fear of being persecuted, the refugee is unwilling to avail him- or herself of the protection of the country of origin.[544] Since refugee protection is not concerned with attributing State responsibility for persecution, the rules on State responsibility are not decisive in determining whether or not persecution originates from the country of origin.[545]

In non-international armed conflict, serious harm often originates from non-State actors. As regards the question of whether persecution by non-State actors falls within the scope of the refugee definition, State practice was in the

541 See UNHCR, "Eligibility Guidelines for Asylum-Seekers from Afghanistan 2013", 30.

542 This book does not employ the commonly used term "agent of persecution" because it is misleading: an "agent" usually acts for and on behalf of another person, the "principal". See Goodwin-Gill and McAdam, *The Refugee in International Law*, 98. It must be recalled that this book focusses on the country of origin, its agents or non-State actors as potential persecutors; the question of whether third States can be persecutors falls outside its scope. The book's scope is set forth in the Introduction.

543 The UNHCR Handbook notes: "Persecution is normally related to action by the authorities of a country." UNHCR, *Handbook*, 65. Further: UNHCR, "Opinion of UNHCR regarding the Question of Non-State Persecution, as Discussed with the Committee on Human Rights and Humanitarian Aid of the German Parliament (Lower House)" (1999), available at www.unhcr.org/refworld/docid/3df755477.html, accessed 10.03.2015, 12.

544 See Goodwin-Gill and McAdam, *The Refugee in International Law*, 98–99.

545 See Goodwin-Gill and McAdam, *The Refugee in International Law*, 99–100. Zimmermann and Mahler, however, draw on the general rules of State responsibility to identify, on the one hand, situations in which acts can be attributed to the State and therefore undoubtedly fall within the meaning of persecution and, on the other, the more contentious situations in which acts by non-State actors cannot be attributed to a State. See Zimmermann and Mahler, "Article 1A, para. 2", mn, 267, 358–359.

past divided into an "accountability approach" and a "protection approach". Under the accountability approach, persecution had to be attributable to a State or another subject of international law. Pursuant to the protection approach, the inability of the country of origin to provide protection was the decisive criterion.[546] The accountability approach was particularly prominent with respect to refugee claimants from countries experiencing civil wars whose claims to refugee protection did not involve persecution by the State and who were consequently denied refugee protection.[547]

It cannot be inferred from the wording of the refugee definition that only State agents are potential persecutors because, as previously noted, the identity of the persecutors is not mentioned at all. Rather, this choice of wording indicates an intention to refrain from limiting the range of potential persecutors. The Refugee Convention's object and purpose, the widest possible protection of refugees' fundamental rights, is best realised by acknowledging that persecution by non-State actors falls within the refugee definition if the country of origin is unable or unwilling to provide effective protection.[548] The protection approach is therefore to be preferred. It is now widely supported in State practice[549] and by UNHCR.[550] With respect to countries of origin experiencing armed conflict, armed groups which are parties to a conflict have been recognised as persecutors, as the example of the *Fuerzas Armadas Revolucionarias de Colombia* (Revolutionary Armed Forces of Colombia) illustrates.[551]

---

546 See UNHCR, "Opinion of UNHCR regarding the Question of Non-State Persecution", para. 19; Zimmermann and Mahler, "Article 1A, para. 2", mn. 292, 364; Daniel Wilsher, "Non-State Actors and the Definition of a Refugee in the United Kingdom: Protection, Accountability or Culpability?", *International Journal of Refugee Law* 15, no. 1 (2003): 68–112, 68, 71.

547 See UNHCR, "Opinion of UNHCR regarding the Question of Non-State Persecution", para. 46; Wilsher, "Non-State Actors", mn. 293, 364; Reinhard Marx, "The Notion of Persecution by Non-State Agents in German Jurisprudence", *Georgetown Immigration Law Journal* 15 (2000–2001): 447–461; Markard, *Kriegsflüchtlinge*, 188.

548 See UNHCR, "Agents of Persecution – UNHCR Position" (1995), available at www.refworld.org/docid/3ae6b31da3.html, accessed 10.03.2015, para. a; UNHCR, "Opinion of UNHCR regarding the Question of Non-State Persecution", paras. 6–13. Further: Zimmermann and Mahler, "Article 1A, para. 2", mn. 302–310, 367–368 and Storey, "Persecution", 484. Lack of protection is examined in Chapter 6.

549 See Hathaway and Foster, *The Law of Refugee Status*, 303–308; Löhr, *Die kinderspezifische Auslegung*, 100–102; Markard, *Kriegsflüchtlinge*, 193–194. As manifested in Article 6(c) Qualification Directive and Article 6(c) Recast Qualification Directive.

550 For UNHCR's views see, e.g., UNHCR, "Opinion of UNHCR regarding the Question of Non-State Persecution"; UNHCR, *Guidelines on International Protection No. 10: Claims to Refugee Status related to Military Service within the context of Article 1A(2) of the 1951 Convention and/or the 1967 Protocol relating to the Status of Refugees*, UN Doc. HCR/GIP/13/10 (3 December 2013), pars. 42–43.

551 See *Refugee Appeal No. 76289* [2009] NZRSAA 36 (8 May 2009), para. 43 (New Zealand); *Starred Gomez (Non-State Actors: Acero-Garces Disapproved) (Colombia)*, [2000] UKIAT 00007, para. 66 (UK); *Espinosa-Cortez and others v. Attorney General* 607 F3.d 101 (3rd Cir. 2010) (US).

Irrespective of whether the persecutor is a State or non-State agent, there is no requirement that there be evidence of

> "particularized enmity, malignity or animus on the part of the person or group responsible for infliction or threat of a relevant harm, or on the part of a State which withholds its protection."[552]

While evidence of such intent may establish a well-founded fear of persecution, the converse does not necessarily follow.[553]

3.3.4. Victims of Persecution

The wording of Article 1A(2) Refugee Convention does not limit the category of potential victims of persecution because it does not address this matter explicitly. In line with the Refugee Convention's humanitarian object and purpose, any person can become the victim of persecution. It is not only civilians who refrained from direct participation in hostilities who are entitled to claim refugee protection under the Refugee Convention. Members of the armed forces and individuals who directly participated in hostilities are also entitled to seek refugee protection provided they have genuinely and permanently laid down their arms – a requirement which flows from the civilian and humanitarian character of asylum.[554] For example, UNHCR considered former members of parties to the conflict in Colombia as persons facing a heightened risk of persecution and thus as potentially falling within the Refugee Convention's definition of a refugee.[555]

---

552 UNHCR, "Note on Issues related to Eligibility for International Protection in the Context of Fumigations" (2007), available at www.unhcr.org/refworld/pdfid/46b6d62f2.pdf, accessed 10.03.2015, para. 15. See also Goodwin-Gill and McAdam, *The Refugee in International Law*, 99–100.

553 See UNHCR, "Note on Issues related to Eligibility for International Protection in the Context of Fumigations", para. 15. See also Storey, "Persecution", 485.

554 On the requirement that refugee claimants must have genuinely and permanently laid down their arms, see Stéphane Jaquemet, "Under What Circumstances Can a Person Who Has Taken an Active Part in the Hostilities of an International or a Non-International Armed Conflict become an Asylum Seeker?", *UNHCR Legal and Protection Policy Research Series* (2004), available at www.unhcr.org/protect/PROTECTION/40ebf49a4.pdf, accessed 10.03.2015; Rosa da Costa, "Maintaining the Civilian and Humanitarian Character of Asylum" *Legal and Protection Policy Research Series* (2004), available at www.unhcr.org/protect/PROTECTION/40ebf51b4.pdf, accessed 10.03.2015; Chaloka Beyani, "International Legal Criteria for the Separation of Members of Armed Forces, Armed Bands and Militia from Refugees in the Territories of Host States", *International Journal of Refugee Law* 12 (2000): 251–271. But see Eric Fripp, "Inclusion of Refugees from Armed Conflict. Combatants and Ex-combatants", in *Refuge from Inhumanity? War Refugees and International Humanitarian Law*, edited by David James Cantor and Jean-François Durieux (Leiden: Koninklijke Brill, 2014), 140–153.

555 See UNHCR, "International Protection Considerations Regarding Colombian Asylum-Seekers 2005", 27.

3.4. RESULT

The two-tiered approach to a human rights-based interpretation of persecution is to be preferred over Hathaway's hierarchical approach. Accordingly, persecution entails a human rights violation or several human rights violations of a certain intensity. Relevant international human rights instruments are: the ICCPR, the ICESCR, the CEDAW, the CAT, the CRC and its Optional Protocol, the CERD and the UDHR. Criteria for determining whether a human rights violation surpasses the intensity threshold of persecution include quantitative considerations (duration, systematic nature, repetition and repeatability of the infringement), qualitative factors (the importance of the right breached and the severity of the infringement) as well as individual elements (the claimant's age, gender, state of health or family ties). Moreover, the cumulative effects of several human rights violations must be considered. Finally, the material scope of persecution is not narrower in times of armed conflict than in times of peace. Specifically, it is not limited to non-derogable human rights. The category of potential persecutors is not confined to agents of the country of origin but also includes non-State actors such as armed groups which are parties to an armed conflict. Not only can civilians who did not directly participate in hostilities claim refugee protection under the Refugee Convention, but so too can members of the armed forces or armed groups provided they have genuinely and permanently laid down their arms.

4. PERSECUTION IN LIGHT OF CUSTOMARY INTERNATIONAL HUMANITARIAN LAW AND INTERNATIONAL CRIMINAL LAW

While the interpretation of persecution in light of international human rights law in times of peace is widely accepted, the interpretation in contexts of armed conflict in the country of origin is more complex because the question arises of whether the human rights-based interpretation needs to be modified or complemented by recourse to customary IHL and international criminal law. This section examines whether violations of customary IHL can constitute persecution and whether war crimes can function as intensity yardsticks, signalling that violations of IHL have surpassed the intensity threshold necessary for harm to constitute persecution.

4.1. VIOLATIONS OF CUSTOMARY INTERNATIONAL HUMANITARIAN LAW IN GENERAL

At the outset, it ought to be examined why violations of IHL might *not* be considered persecution. One might argue that a State's military measures are not persecution because "they have a typical military character and serve to regain control over areas which, *de jure*, still belong to the State territory but are, *de facto*, controlled by insurgents."[556] This argument suggests that military measures designed to regain territorial control in an armed conflict fall outside the purview of persecution. Using the vague and ambiguous concept of military measures and selected legitimate military purposes to assess whether or not conduct is persecutory, this position does not provide a sufficiently clear and transparent analytical framework for assessing persecution in light of an objective standard. IHL offers a more suitable, objective normative yardstick which takes into account military necessity.[557]

There are a few instances in State practice in which persecution is solely considered in light of IHL. The US Basic Law Manual, for example, acknowledges that violations of the Geneva Conventions may constitute the basis for an asylum claim.[558] According to this approach, the Geneva Conventions assist in the interpretation of persecution by identifying conduct as persecutory when it breaches these Conventions. Moreover, the US Board of Immigration Appeals noted that "the evidence must [*inter alia*] be evaluated in the context of the ongoing civil conflict [in Sri Lanka] to determine whether the motive for the abuse in the particular case … was part of the violence inherent in an armed conflict (i.e. lawful acts of war)."[559] Though this statement seems to focus more on the causal link between a well-founded fear of persecution and a Refugee Convention ground, it nonetheless uses "lawful acts of war", i.e. acts which comply with IHL, as a normative yardstick for assessing persecution. Moreover, the Canadian Civil War Guidelines provide that in addition to international human rights law, the Geneva Convention IV, in particular Common Article 3, and the 1977 Additional Protocol II may assist in determining what constitutes permissible conduct.[560] Yet the topical relevance of these Guidelines may be curtailed because their provisions on IHL have rarely been referred to in post-2001 Canadian jurisprudence.[561]

---

556 Kälin, "Refugees and Civil Wars", 440. Markard shows a similar understanding in German jurisprudence. See Markard, *Kriegsflüchtlinge*, 167–168.

557 Similarly: Markard, *Kriegsflüchtlinge*, 168–169. On military necessity, see the analysis in Chapter 7.

558 See US Immigration and Naturalization Service, *The Basic Law Manual: U.S. Law and INS Refugee/Asylum Adjudications* 22 (1995), cited by Sternberg, *The Grounds of Refugee Protection*, 37. See also *Montecino v. Immigration and Naturalization Service*, 915 F.2d 518 (9th Cir. 1990) (US), 520.

559 *In re S-P-*, 21 I. & N. Dec. 486, Interim Decision 3287, 1996 WL 422990 (BIA) (US), 493–494.

560 See Immigration and Refugee Board of Canada, "Civilian Non-Combatants Fearing Persecution in Civil War Situations".

561 The following judgments refer to the Civil War Guidelines without specifically mentioning their provisions on IHL: *Sheriff v. Canada (Minister of Citizenship and Immigration)* 2002 FCT 8; *Fi v. Canada (Minister of Citizenship and Immigration)* 2006 FC 1125; *Kanagaratnam v. Canada (Minister of Citizenship and Immigration)* 2006 FC 1205; *Navaratnam v. Canada (Minister of Citizenship and Immigration)* 2003 FCT 523; *Innocent v. Canada (Citizenship*

However, there is also State practice which rejects the proposition to understand persecution in light of IHL. In the UK case of *Adan*, Lord Lloyd of Berwick held in 1998:

> "What ... is the critical factor which distinguishes persecution from the ordinary incidents of civil war? Mr Blake [counsel for the respondent] sought to draw a distinction between the armed forces of either side, who would, he said, be governed by the rules of war, and the targeting of individual civilians or groups of civilians. I doubt, however, whether, in the context of clan warfare in Somalia, it is realistic to think in terms of rules of war, or the conventional distinction between civilians and members of the armed forces."[562]

According to his Lordship, "ordinary incidents of civil war" would not constitute persecution, while extraordinary incidents would. Lord Lloyd of Berwick appeared to suggest that the lack of compliance with IHL, in particular with the principle of distinction, means that this IHL principle, and IHL more generally, cannot provide interpretative guidance regarding persecution. Ten years after the House of Lords' judgment in *Adan*, the UK AIT considered the notion of "ordinary risks of clan warfare" in light of subsequent legal developments. The AIT found that:

> "the most sensible content to be given to this distinction [between ordinary and extraordinary incidents of civil war] is between acts of armed conflict which accord with the laws of war and acts which do not."[563]

The AIT also held that while civilians caught in the crossfire would usually merely face ordinary incidents of civil war, deliberate violations of IHL constitute extraordinary incidents of civil war.[564] The AIT concluded that "serious violations of peremptory norms of international humanitarian law and human rights law" constitute persecution.[565] Thus, the AIT interpreted the House of Lords' earlier approach as drawing on IHL to demarcate the line between acts of violence in armed conflict that amount to persecution and those that do not.

As shown above,[566] an interpretation of the refugee definition, including the notion of persecution, in light of customary IHL is in line with the rules on

and Immigration) 2009 FC 1019; *Kanagasabapathy v. Canada (Minister of Citizenship and Immigration)* 2003 FCT 78 (all Canada).

562 *Adan v. Secretary of State for the Home Department* [1998] 2 WLR 702, per Lord Slynn of Hadley (UK).

563 *AM & AM v. Secretary of State for the Home Department* (armed conflict: risk categories) Somalia CG [2008] UKAIT 00091, para. 76 (UK).

564 See *AM & AM v. Secretary of State for the Home Department* (armed conflict: risk categories) Somalia CG [2008] UKAIT 00091, para. 76 (UK).

565 See *AM & AM v. Secretary of State for the Home Department* (armed conflict: risk categories) Somalia CG [2008] UKAIT 00091, para. 76 (UK).

566 See Chapter 4.

treaty interpretation. Similar to international human rights law, customary IHL is characterised by a concern for human dignity. As a party to an armed conflict, the country of origin incurs certain protection obligations under customary IHL with respect to its own nationals and stateless persons who habitually reside within its territory. Armed groups which are parties to a non-international armed conflict in the country of origin also incur such protection obligations.[567] Customary IHL strives to limit and mitigate human suffering and to restrict the use of violence to what is necessary to overcome the enemy.[568] In light of these considerations, it can be concluded that one or several violations of a rule of customary IHL can constitute persecution.[569]

As previously noted, there have been concerns that individuals on either side of a conflict could fall within the refugee definition,[570] possibly resulting in a copious number of refugee claimants. This concern might be used to argue against drawing on customary IHL in the interpretation of persecution because customary IHL binds and protects all sides of a conflict. However, this concern is of a political rather than a legal nature. In fact, violations of customary IHL rules can amount to persecution even if they affect a large number of individuals, as would be the case, for example, in a large-scale direct attack against civilians.[571] To say otherwise would go against the Refugee Convention's object and purpose of providing refugee protection, as it would result in a denial of refugee protection when large numbers of people need it. The historical evolution of international refugee law strengthens this view, as large numbers of people displaced by conflict and violence benefited from the refugee protection instruments drawn up in the early and mid-twentieth century.[572] Moreover, UNHCR underscores

---

567 As shown in Chapter 3.

568 See Sassòli, Bouvier and Quintin, *How does Law Protect in War?*, 1.

569 Several scholars argue that IHL can be drawn upon in the interpretation of persecution. See Markard, *Kriegsflüchtlinge*, 143, who notes that IHL and international war crimes law provide indications as to when the intensity threshold of persecution is met. See also Brandl, "Die Anwendbarkeit des Flüchtlingsbegriffs", 194–195. Butcher suggests "to incorporate the norms of humanitarian and human rights law, regarding minimum standards of treatment of civilians during war, into the assessment of persecution feared by those applicants who are fleeing a war zone." Butcher, "Assessing Fear of Persecution", 469. Further: Sternberg, *The Grounds of Refugee Protection*, 122; Roundtable on International Protection of Persons Fleeing Armed Conflict and Other Situations of Violence, "Cape Town Summary Conclusions", para. 12; and Rutinwa, "Refugee Claims Based on Violation of IHL". Storey and Wallace argue that IHL, in addition to international human rights law, IHL "helps elucidate which feared harms are sufficiently serious to constitute persecution." Storey and Wallace, "War and Peace", 355–356. See also Storey, "Persecution", 515–516.

570 Such concerns were voiced in *Isa v. Canada (Secretary of State)* [1995] FCJ No. 354, 72. As noted by Storey and Wallace, "War and Peace", 351.

571 See Henkel, "Who Is a Refugee? Refugees from Civil War and Other Internal Armed Conflicts", 19; Storey and Wallace, "War and Peace", 353.

572 On the historical evolution of international refugee law, see Chapter 2.

this point by considering persecution as comprising "more indiscriminate forms of violence such as suicide attacks and improvised explosive devices".[573]

Just as not all human rights violations amount to persecution, so not all breaches of customary IHL constitute persecution. In cases where the persecutor is the country of origin or one of its agents, only rules of customary IHL that address the relationship between the country of origin and its nationals or stateless persons on its territory are pertinent.[574] In cases where the persecutor is an armed group which is a party to the conflict taking place in the country of origin, violations of customary IHL rules whose beneficiaries are the nationals of the country of origin or stateless persons habitually residing in that country are relevant. Furthermore, violations of customary IHL must surpass an intensity threshold to amount to persecution. The rationale for the severity threshold is the same whether it concerns human rights infringements or violations of customary IHL, namely that the Refugee Convention solely provides for the surrogate protection of the receiving State if the claimant's stay in the country of origin has become intolerable. However, the intensity threshold is still vague with respect to violations of customary IHL. The subsequent section will therefore analyse if war crimes can provide a suitable yardstick for assessing whether a violation of customary IHL is of sufficient intensity to constitute persecution.

Zimmermann and Mahler, though acknowledging that rules of IHL must be taken into account in the interpretation of persecution, argue:

> "Even violations of norms of the laws of war cannot, however, per se be equated with persecution and it cannot be the interest of refugee law to have any illegal act of warfare revised in order to be able to decide on a refugee claim."[575]

It is correct that not every violation of IHL necessarily amounts to persecution. As previously noted, to constitute persecution, the rule of IHL in question must, in international or non-international armed conflict, govern the relationship between the country of origin and its nationals or stateless persons habitually residing within its territory or, in non-international armed conflict, between an armed group that is a party to the conflict and nationals of the country of origin within its territory or with stateless persons habitually residing within its territory. The IHL violation must also be of sufficient intensity to constitute persecution. The question of whether international refugee law ought to be concerned with reviewing the lawfulness of warfare points to concerns about the nature of asylum. It is important to recall that an interpretation of persecution in light of international human rights law is not tantamount to attributing

573 UNHCR, "Eligibility Guidelines for Afghan Asylum-Seekers 2007", para. 63. See also UNHCR, "Information Note", in which UNHCR notes that indiscriminate shelling and bombardment can give rise to refugee status.

574 These rules were identified in Chapter 3.

575 Zimmermann and Mahler, "Article 1A, para. 2", mn. 319, 371.

responsibility for human rights violations in the country of origin.[576] Asylum is a neutral and humanitarian act in inter-State relations.[577] It is hence not the purpose of international refugee law to review the lawfulness of acts or omissions by or within the country of origin, whether in times of peace or armed conflict. Indeed, the UNHCR Handbook notes that the "competent authorities that are called upon to determine refugee status are not required to pass judgement on conditions in the applicant's country of origin."[578] Therefore, concerns about reviewing acts of warfare in the course of refugee status determination do not preclude an interpretation of persecution in light of customary IHL.

Understanding persecution as encompassing certain violations of customary IHL raises the question of whether it can be concluded from conduct in armed conflict that complies with IHL that a refugee claimant is not at risk of being persecuted. Zimmermann and Mahler state that "acts in accordance with applicable norms of international humanitarian law, even if they cause damage to civilians or civilian objects, cannot amount to persecution."[579] It is true that IHL legitimises conduct during armed conflict and could therefore remove it from the scope of persecution if persecution were solely understood in light of IHL. There are instances in State practice where conduct is not considered persecution because it complies with IHL. For example, the 1996 Joint Position of the Council of the European Union suggested that conduct is not persecution by a State's armed forces if it complies with IHL: "the use of the armed forces does not constitute persecution where it is in accordance with international rules of war".[580]

However, this understanding is not entirely correct. It must be recalled that the interpretation and application of the refugee definition requires a comprehensive assessment of all pertinent individual and general circumstances in the country of origin. For instance, civilians may have been compelled by parties to an armed conflict to participate in hostilities. A case in point is Colombia, where villagers are often threatened by guerrillas to provide food, shelter or information.[581] If and when these villagers are directly participating in hostilities, their death as a result of a direct attack would not violate customary

---

576 Similarly: Zimmermann and Mahler, "Article 1A, para. 2", mn. 226, 347–348.

577 See UN General Assembly, *Declaration on Territorial Asylum. Resolution 2312 (XXII)*, UN Doc. A/6716 (14 December 1967), second preambular recital. The Refugee Convention's preamble emphasises the humanitarian nature of refugee protection and that refugee protection ought not to become a source of tension in inter-State relations (fifth recital).

578 UNHCR, *Handbook*, para. 42.

579 Zimmermann and Mahler, "Article 1A, para. 2", mn. 319, 371.

580 Council of the European Union, "Joint Position", para. 6.

581 In Colombia, security forces, paramilitaries and guerrilla groups are reported to have caused harm to civilians who refuse to participate in hostilities. See UNHCR, "Eligibility Guidelines for Asylum-Seekers from Colombia 2010", 7. See also *Escobar v. Holder* 2011 U.S. App. LEXIS 18538 (7th Cir. 2011) (US), which concerned a Colombian truck driver compelled by FARC to transport goods for them.

IHL (if the attack is carried out by lawful means). However, the fact that they were compelled to participate in hostilities could in and of itself constitute persecution. Furthermore, use of force can be lawful under IHL, but may for other reasons constitute persecution, for example because the overall purpose of the conflict is to expel or destroy a certain group. Hence, it cannot automatically be deduced from the absence of IHL violations that a refugee claimant is not at risk of persecution in an armed conflict.[582]

4.2. WAR CRIMES AS INTENSITY YARDSTICK

As set out above, not all IHL violations constitute persecution; they must be of sufficient intensity. In this respect, war crimes are of particular interest because, broadly speaking, they are IHL violations of a certain intensity. Since refugee status determination is not concerned with determining the persecutor's individual criminal responsibility, only the objective elements of war crimes are relevant for the interpretation of persecution. Conversely, the subjective elements (or *mens rea* elements) are not pertinent.[583]

The jurisprudence of the ICTY offers a number of criteria for the assessment of the seriousness of a violation of IHL. The ICTY Appeals Chamber in the *Tadić case* identified four conditions which must be fulfilled for a violation of IHL to constitute a violation of the laws and customs of war under Article 3 ICTY statute, i.e. a war crime.[584] Albeit identified with a view to delimiting the ICTY's jurisdiction under Article 3 of its Statute, these conditions are relevant more generally because the finding of the ICTY's jurisdiction presupposes the existence of the corresponding war crimes in international law.[585] According to the ICTY, in international or non-international armed conflict, the criteria are as follows:

"(i) the violation must constitute an infringement of a rule of international humanitarian law;

(ii) the rule must be customary in nature or, if it belongs to treaty law, the required conditions must be met …;

582 This counters Durieux's concern that drawing on IHL in the interpretation of persecution limits the protective scope of the refugee definition. See Durieux, "Of War, Flows, Laws and Flaws", 166.

583 In this respect, refugee law decision-makers have "a selective interest" in international criminal law: Storey, "Armed Conflict in Asylum Law", 32. On the objective and subjective elements of war crimes, see Werle, *Völkerstrafrecht*, mn. 405–408, 188–189. See also the analysis of international war crimes law in Chapter 3.

584 See ICTY, *The Prosecutor v. Duško Tadić aka "Dule"*, Decision on the Defence Motion for Interlocutory Appeal on Jurisdiction, Appeals Chamber, 2 October 1995, Case No. IT-94-1-AR72, para. 94. The ICTY Statute was adopted by Security Council, *Resolution 827*, UN Doc. S/RES/827 (25 May 1993) and subsequently amended by a number of UN Security Council Resolutions.

585 See Werle, *Völkerstrafrecht*, mn. 1054, 466.

(iii) the violation must be 'serious', that is to say, it must constitute a breach of a rule protecting important values, and the breach must involve grave consequences for the victim. Thus, for instance, the fact of a combatant simply appropriating a loaf of bread in an occupied village would not amount to a 'serious violation of international humanitarian law' although it may be regarded as falling foul of the basic principle laid down in Article 46, paragraph 1, of the Hague Regulations (and the corresponding rule of customary international law) whereby 'private property must be respected' by any army occupying an enemy territory;

(iv) the violation of the rule must entail, under customary or conventional law, the individual criminal responsibility of the person breaching the rule."[586]

Paragraph (iii) addresses the question of how to examine the seriousness of a violation of an IHL rule. It states that the values which the norm protects and the consequences for the victim are the decisive criteria. These criteria are similar to the ones employed by the two-tiered human rights-based interpretation of persecution which *inter alia* encompass qualitative factors such as the importance of the right violated or the severity of the infringement and which take into account the individual circumstances including age, gender and state of health. Moreover, UNHCR considers that "the existence of serious violations of international humanitarian law which constitute threats to life or freedom or other serious harm" is relevant for determining whether "the consequences of violence for civilians are sufficiently serious to meet the threshold of persecution."[587] UNHCR is thus using serious IHL violations as intensity yardsticks in assessing whether harm amounts to persecution. For these reasons, violations of customary IHL which constitute war crimes surpass the intensity threshold of persecution and can assist in determining whether conduct amounts to persecution.[588]

4.3. RESULT

Violations of customary IHL which are of sufficient intensity can constitute persecution. The absence of a violation of customary IHL in an individual case related to an armed conflict, however, is not necessarily tantamount to the lack of persecution. War crimes can serve as a yardstick for assessing whether IHL violations are serious enough to amount to persecution. More specifically,

---

586 ICTY, *The Prosecutor v. Duško Tadić aka "Dule"*, Decision on the Defence Motion for Interlocutory Appeal on Jurisdiction, Appeals Chamber, 2 October 1995, Case No. IT-94-1-AR72, para. 94.

587 UNHCR, "Eligibility Guidelines for Asylum-Seekers from Afghanistan 2013", 30.

588 See Brandl, "Die Anwendbarkeit des Flüchtlingsbegriffs", 194; Markard, *Kriegsflüchtlinge*, 175. Jaquemet states: "War crimes are offensive to human dignity and, as such, always constitute persecution." Jaquemet, "Cross-Fertilization", 667.

the criterion developed by the ICTY to determine whether an IHL violation is of sufficient intensity to constitute a war crime, namely that the breached rule must protect important values and that its infringement must have grave consequences for the victim, can assist in assessing whether an IHL violation amounts to persecution.

5. A COMPLEMENTARY APPROACH TO UNDERSTANDING PERSECUTION IN ARMED CONFLICT

Having conducted a separate analysis of persecution in light of international human rights law on the one hand and customary IHL and international criminal law on the other, this section develops a complementary approach by examining persecution in armed conflict in light of all of these branches of international law.[589]

5.1. OVERVIEW

When developing a complementary approach to persecution that draws on all branches of international law pertinent for the protection of the individual in armed conflict, the necessary starting point is the identification and discussion of any existing similar approaches in State practice or in the publications of UNHCR.

There are few instances where States draw on both international human rights law and IHL in interpreting persecution. The Canadian Civil War Guidelines state that in addition to international human rights law, "international instruments exist that relate to the protection of civilians in time of war",[590] namely the Geneva Convention IV and the Additional Protocol II, provide interpretative guidance as regards persecution. The Canadian Civil War Guidelines hence understand these IHL treaties as complementing an interpretation of persecution in light of international human rights law. Moreover, the UK AIT held that "serious violations of peremptory norms of international humanitarian law and human rights" constitute persecution.[591] The AIT drew on both customary IHL and human rights law in conceptualising persecution without, however, offering more detailed guidance.

---

589 This complementary approach was first elaborated in Holzer, "Persecution", 101–127.

590 Immigration and Refugee Board of Canada, "Civilian Non-Combatants Fearing Persecution in Civil War Situations".

591 See *AM & AM v. Secretary of State for the Home Department* (armed conflict: risk categories) Somalia CG [2008] UKAIT 00091, para. 76 (UK).

UNHCR infrequently refers to both international human rights law and IHL in interpreting persecution. Though cautious as regards references to IHL in interpreting the refugee definition, UNHCR acknowledged:

> "If someone is forced to flee armed conflict in their country because of human rights violations and breaches of humanitarian law, these factors will be part of what determines that person's refugee status."[592]

In a few Eligibility Guidelines concerning Colombia, UNHCR refers to violations of human rights and IHL in the context of identifying individuals who are eligible for international protection. For example, UNHCR concluded that because of the massive and widespread violations of human rights and IHL during the armed conflict in Colombia, many Colombian asylum-seekers fall within the Refugee Convention's refugee definition.[593] Neither UNHCR nor the Canadian Civil War Guidelines provide any detail on how to interpret persecution in light of both IHL and international human rights law, nor do they refer to international criminal law. Further analysis is therefore required.

At the outset, the need to distinguish between three different kinds of situations during armed conflict, whether international or non-international in character, must be acknowledged. There are situations in which only international human rights law applies. There are also situations that fall exclusively within the remit of IHL. And there are situations that fall within the purview of both IHL and international human rights law.[594] Concerning persecution, this means that even if a country of origin is experiencing an armed conflict, there can be claims to refugee protection by individuals who have fled from this country which need not be framed in light of IHL and international criminal law.[595] For example, concerning claims to protection under the Refugee Convention relating to

592 UNHCR, *Note on International Protection (2003)*, para. 53.

593 See UNHCR, "International Protection Considerations regarding Colombian Asylum-seekers and Refugees 2002", para. 83. Similarly: UNHCR, "UNHCR Eligibility Guidelines for Assessing the International Protection Needs of Asylum-Seekers from Somalia (2010)", 39–40 (attacks on civilians). However, in several Eligibility Guidelines, UNHCR considers the situation in the country of origin as an armed conflict, but frames the forms of harm prevalent in the country of origin as human rights violations rather than violations of IHL when considering inclusion within the refugee definition. For example, UNHCR stated: "In view of the serious and widespread human rights violations and ongoing armed conflict in many parts of the country … a significant number of Afghan asylum-seekers are in need of international protection." UNHCR, "Eligibility Guidelines for Asylum-Seekers from Afghanistan 2009", 11. See also UNHCR, "Position on Asylum-Seekers from Sri Lanka 2006", para. 5; UNHCR, "Eligibility Guidelines for Asylum-Seekers from Sri Lanka 2009", 5–7 and 15; UNHCR, "Eligibility Guidelines for Asylum-Seekers from Afghanistan 2010", 2.

594 See ICJ, *Legal Consequences of the Construction of a Wall in the Occupied Palestinian Territory*, Advisory Opinion (2004) ICJ Reports 136 at 177 para. 106.

595 Storey and Wallace poignantly state: "Recognition of the relevance of IHL norms to civil war and armed conflict cases does not mean that they must be applied to the case of every claimant from a country facing civil war." Storey and Wallace, "War and Peace", 359.

infringements of freedom of expression, freedom of assembly or discrimination based on sexual orientation, international human rights law provides the relevant international legal framework; IHL and international criminal law are hardly pertinent here. Determining which situations are exclusively governed by IHL and also pertinent for the assessment of persecution is more challenging, but such situations may include the use of certain weapons or the combatant privilege according to which combatants in international armed conflict cannot be punished for participating in hostilities.[596]

5.2. *LEX SPECIALIS DEROGAT LEGI GENERALI?*

As noted in Chapter 3, the relationship between IHL and international human rights law is generally considered as being governed by the principle *lex specialis derogat legi generali*. In situations in which both customary IHL and international human rights law provide the pertinent legal framework for assessing persecution, the question arises of what role, if any, this principle plays in the interpretation of persecution in armed conflict. Indeed, Fripp argues that IHL informs the scope of persecution indirectly because the human rights-based interpretation of persecution is open to IHL through the principle of *lex specialis*.[597]

Traditionally, the *lex specialis* maxim was understood as a tool to resolve a conflict of norms by stipulating that the more specific norm prevails over the more general norm.[598] During refugee status determination when the refugee definition is being interpreted and applied, there is no conflict of norms because only one norm is being applied, namely Article 1A(2) Refugee Convention. Customary IHL and international human rights law are not applied concurrently; they are merely interpretative aids to determine the meaning and

---

596 On the combatant privilege, see Knut Ipsen, "Combatants and Non-Combatants", in *Handbook of International Humanitarian Law*, edited by Dieter Fleck (Oxford: Oxford University Press, 2008), mn. 304, 86; Knut Dörmann, "The Legal Situation of 'Unlawful/Unprivileged Combatants'", *International Review of the Red Cross* 85, no. 849 (2003): 45–74, 45; Henckaerts and Doswald-Beck, *Customary International Humanitarian Law*, 384.

597 See Eric Fripp, "International Humanitarian law and the Interpretation of 'Persecution' in Article 1A(2) CSR51", *International Journal of Refugee* Law 26, no. 3 (2014): 382–403, 396–401.

598 As shown by Prud'homme, "*Lex Specialis*", 369, who traces this meaning of *lex specialis* back to Emerich de Vattel. More recently, Schabas considered *lex specialis* as a rule of interpretation that assists in resolving conflicts in laws. Schabas, "*Lex Specialis*? Belt and Suspenders?", 597. On this meaning of *lex specialis*, see also Study Group of the International Law Commission, *Fragmentation of International Law*, para. 57. Müller provides an overview of the development of the relationship between IHL and international human rights law and the role *of lex specialis*: Müller, *The Relationship between Economic, Social and Cultural Rights and International Humanitarian Law*, 13–38.

scope of persecution. Therefore, this notion of *lex specialis* has no bearing on the interpretation of persecution.

Yet the understanding of *lex specialis* has expanded. The maxim is now also considered as operating without the existence of a norm conflict, governing the relationship between a general rule and a specific rule so that the general rule is interpreted in light of the specific rule.[599] In its Advisory Opinion on the Legality of the Threat or Use of Nuclear Weapons, the ICJ found that what constitutes an arbitrary deprivation of life under Article 6(1) ICCPR in armed conflict must be determined in light of the *lex specialis* of IHL.[600] The ICJ further stated in its Advisory Opinion on the Legal Consequences of the Construction of a Wall in the Palestinian Occupied Territories that IHL does not only constitute the *lex specialis* as regards the right not to be arbitrarily deprived of one's life, but more generally with respect to the entire body of international human rights law.[601] In these Advisory Opinions, the ICJ was concerned with the concurrent application of IHL and international human rights law.[602] Nonetheless, the ICJ's stance has been understood as employing the *lex specialis* principle as an interpretative device, as Pauwelyn notes:

> "This is an instance where *lex specialis* is used to interpret the terms of another, more general norm (*in casu,* the words 'arbitrarily deprived'). It does not conflict with nor, *a fortiori,* overrule the other norm."[603]

Resorting to the *lex specialis* principle as a tool for the interpretation of persecution in light of international human rights law and IHL is problematic for various reasons. The *lex specialis* maxim lacks clarity as to its normative status and precise meaning.[604] It does not provide guidance on which norm or branch of international law is general and which is special.[605] Originally developed in a context of domestic law, the maxim of *lex specialis* is ill-suited as

---

599 See Study Group of the International Law Commission, *Fragmentation of International Law,* 56; Anja Lindroos, "Addressing Norm Conflicts in a Fragmented Legal System: The Doctrine of *Lex Specialis*", *Nordic Journal of International Law* 74 (2005): 27–66, 46; Droege, "Elective affinities?", 524; Prud'homme, "*Lex Specialis*", 369.

600 See ICJ, *Legality of the Threat or Use of Nuclear Weapons,* Advisory Opinion of 8 July 1996, ICJ Reports 1996, para. 25. Hathaway and Foster seem to use this understanding in noting that civilians' loss of life due to IHL violations would constitute arbitrary deprivations of liberty and thus persecution. See Hathaway and Foster, *The Law of Refugee Status,* 209–210.

601 See ICJ, *Legal Consequences of the Construction of a Wall in the Occupied Palestinian Territory,* Advisory Opinion, ICJ Reports 2004, 178, para. 106.

602 See Prud'homme, "*Lex Specialis*", 372.

603 Joost Pauwelyn, *Conflict of Norms in Public International Law: How WTO Law Relates to other Rules of International Law* (2003), 410. Agreeing: Prud'homme, "*Lex Specialis*", 374.

604 See, e.g., Erich Vranes, "*Lex Superior, Lex Specialis, Lex Posterior* – Zur Rechtsnatur der 'Konfliktlösungsregeln'", *Zeitschrift für ausländisches öffentliches Recht und Völkerrecht* 65 (2005): 391–405.

605 See Study Group of the International Law Commission, *Fragmentation of International Law,* para. 111; Prud'homme, "*Lex Specialis*", 381.

an interpretative tool for the fragmented international legal system that lacks a central legislator.[606]

The general rule on treaty interpretation, set forth in Chapter 4, provides more suitable guidance on how to draw on both international human rights law and customary IHL in the interpretation of persecution. Of particular relevance are the systemic and teleological interpretation methods. To recall, the Refugee Convention's humanitarian object and purpose requires an inclusive and dynamic interpretation of persecution. Article 31(3)(c) VCLT allows for the interpretation of persecution in light of international human rights law and customary IHL. Article 31(3)(c) VCLT thus comes very close to the principle of *lex specialis* in the sense of interpreting a more general rule in light of the more specific one, thereby operationalising the complementarity between customary IHL and international human rights law.[607] Recourse to customary IHL and international criminal law in interpreting persecution pursuant to Article 31(3)(c) VCLT is controlled by the Refugee Convention's humanitarian object and purpose, as well as the refugee definition's wording. Therefore, if in interpreting persecution in light of international human rights law and customary IHL, the protection standards under international human rights law and customary IHL differ, interpretative guidance is to be obtained from whichever branch of international law provides the higher standard of protection for the individual in armed conflict.[608] This approach ensures that the scope of persecution is not narrower in times of armed conflict than in times of peace. It counters concerns that drawing on customary IHL in the interpretation of the refugee definition would narrow that definition's scope and undermine refugee protection.[609]

This approach of giving greater weight to the more protective branch of international law when interpreting persecution in contexts of armed conflict gains support from the Human Rights Committee's understanding of the relationship of IHL and international human rights law. The Human Rights Committee stated:

606 On *lex specialis*, see Lindroos, "Addressing Norm Conflicts", 28 and Prud'homme, "*Lex Specialis*", 308–381. Chetail also notes that *lex specialis* does not offer a satisfactory conceptualisation of the relationship between human rights and IHL: Chetail, "Armed Conflict and Forced Migration", 702.

607 See Droege, "Elective affinities?", 521 and 524. It appears to be in this sense that Storey understands the *lex specialis* maxim, arguing that "the only meaning [of the *lex specialis* principle] that can apply [in the interpretation of the refugee definition] is as a supplement, so as to provide scope and content to its protective provisions." Storey, "Armed Conflict in Asylum Law", 15.

608 Storey argues: "Given the subject-matter of refugee law and the imperative of protection, the correct approach should be to apply IHL or IHRL [international human rights law] norms, whichever ensures more protection." Storey, "The 'War Flaw' and Why it Matters", 53.

609 Agreeing: Storey, "The 'War Flaw' and Why it Matters", 45.

> "During armed conflict, whether international or non-international, rules of international humanitarian law become applicable and help, in addition to the provisions in article 4 and article 5, paragraph 1, of the Covenant, [i.e. the ICCPR] to prevent abuse of a State's emergency powers."[610]

According to this view, IHL and international human rights law complement one another in restraining a State's emergency powers, filling gaps in the respective other regime.[611] As Schabas stated: "The paradigm is not one of *lex specialis* and *lex generalis* but rather that of belt and suspenders."[612] The norm that provides the higher standard of protection is the appropriate normative benchmark for assessing whether harm constitutes persecution in armed conflict. This understanding is similar to the aforementioned *pro homine* principle advocated as an interpretative tool by Cançado Trindade's conceptualisation of the international law for humankind.[613] Yet, although the result is the same, the underpinning argumentation is different because the result is not derived from a separate maxim originating from Roman law or from an understanding of the international legal framework of the Refugee Convention as the international law for humankind. Rather, it is grounded in the rules of treaty interpretation in general and a teleological and systematic interpretation in particular.

5.3. SELECTED FORMS OF PERSECUTION

Applying the previously developed complementary approach to persecution in armed conflict that draws on international human rights law, customary IHL and international criminal law, this section examines selected types of harm that are frequent in armed conflict and widely considered to constitute persecution. Emphasis is placed on an analysis in light of international human rights law and customary IHL, with international war crimes jurisprudence being drawn upon to illustrate particular arguments.

5.3.1. Use of Lethal Force

The use of lethal force is an essential characteristic of armed conflict. Violence to life constitutes the most fundamental form of persecution.[614] Threats resulting

---

610 Human Rights Committee, *General Comment 29: States of Emergency (Article 4)*, 29.

611 The Human Rights Committee considers IHL and international human rights law as complementary spheres of law. See Human Rights Committee, *General Comment 31: Nature of the General Legal Obligation on States Parties to the Covenant*, para. 11.

612 Schabas, "*Lex Specialis*? Belt and Suspenders?", 598.

613 On the international law for humankind, see Chapter 3.

614 In the US, the Board of Immigration Appeals included threats to life in the definition of persecution. See *In re Acosta* (1985) 191 I. & N. Dec. 211, paras. 222–223 (US). Further: Binder, *Frauenspezifische Verfolgung*, 93. The Canadian Civil War Guidelines state that persecution

from the use of lethal force in armed conflict can take many forms. For example, UNHCR reported deliberate attacks on civilians in Colombia,[615] indiscriminate attacks and attacks against schools in Afghanistan,[616] and the use of improvised explosive devices in Iraq.[617] The use of lethal force is regulated by international human rights law on the hand and customary IHL and international criminal law on the other, prompting the question of how to assess the use of lethal force for the purposes of interpreting persecution.

There is very little State practice that examines the use of lethal force in armed conflict in light of IHL. A noteworthy example can be found in the Canadian Civil War Guidelines. These Guidelines, which only apply to situations of non-international armed conflict in the country of origin, recommend that IHL be considered in addition to international human rights law in interpreting the refugee definition. They further state that any violations of Article 3 common to the Geneva Conventions "would likely lead to a finding of persecution".[618] This includes Common Article 3(1)(a) of the Geneva Conventions which protects persons not directly participating in hostilities from violence to life, in particular murder of all kinds. The Canadian Civil War Guidelines also note that interpretative guidance can be obtained from the Additional Protocol II,[619] without going into further detail. The Additional Protocol II contains some provisions on the use of lethal force, for example Article 13(2) which prohibits making the civilian population and individual civilians the object of attack. The Civil War Guidelines do not, however, provide guidance on how to relate the provisions on the use of lethal force in the Additional Protocol II to the notion of persecution. Nor do they address the high threshold of application of the

---

is to be interpreted in light of international human rights law and IHL, expressly quoting the prohibition of violence to life in Common Article 3 of the Geneva Conventions. See Immigration and Refugee Board of Canada, "Civilian Non-Combatants Fearing Persecution in Civil War Situations". See also UNHCR, *Handbook*, para. 51, reiterated in UNHCR, "Eligibility Guidelines for Afghan Asylum-Seekers 2007", 6; UNHCR, "Eligibility Guidelines for Iraqi Asylum-Seekers 2007", 134; UNHCR, "Eligibility Guidelines for Asylum-Seekers from Afghanistan 2009", 13. Deprivation of life is also understood as persecution in the literature. See, e.g., Goodwin-Gill and McAdam, *The Refugee in International Law*, 93; Foster, *International Refugee Law*, 197 (noting that violations of the right to life always constitute persecution); Zimmermann and Mahler, "Article 1A, para. 2", mn. 252, 354.

615 See UNHCR, "International Protection Considerations regarding Colombian Asylum-seekers and Refugees 2002", para. 22.

616 See UNHCR, "Eligibility Guidelines for Afghan Asylum-Seekers 2007", 34–35 (indiscriminate attacks by anti-government groups); UNHCR, "Eligibility Guidelines for Afghan Asylum-Seekers 2007", 35 (attacks on schools).

617 UNHCR, "Eligibility Guidelines for Assessing the International Protection Needs of Asylum-Seekers from Iraq" (2012), available at www.unhcr.org/refworld/docid/4fc77d522.html, accessed 10.03.2015, 14.

618 Immigration and Refugee Board of Canada, "Civilian Non-Combatants Fearing Persecution in Civil War Situations".

619 See Immigration and Refugee Board of Canada, "Civilian Non-Combatants Fearing Persecution in Civil War Situations".

Additional Protocol II.[620] Lastly, they also fail to reconcile the different standards on the use of lethal force under international human rights law and IHL.

Several UNHCR's Eligibility Guidelines address the use of lethal force in armed conflict by drawing on international human rights law and IHL. For example, regarding Colombia UNHCR noted a decrease in the number of massacres defined as "the (nearly) simultaneous killing of three or more persons not actively participating in hostilities at a single location or several nearby locations",[621] thereby resorting to the IHL concept of participation in hostilities. In examining eligibility for refugee protection, UNHCR further noted the threats to civilians' lives in Afghanistan that result from attacks which violate IHL.[622] While some of UNHCR's Eligibility Guidelines tentatively indicate that the use of lethal force which breaches IHL constitutes persecution, the IHL framework employed in relation to using lethal force is not directly tied to persecution.

The Canadian Civil War Guidelines and some of UNHCR's Eligibility Guidelines support an understanding of persecution in light of international human rights law and IHL as regards the use of lethal force in armed conflict. However, it remains to be determined how exactly the different standards on the use of lethal force under these branches of international law are to be reconciled. At the outset, it is helpful to briefly consider what these standards are.

Under international human rights law, lethal force by a State is lawful if it fulfils a set of cumulative criteria. First, the use of lethal force must be based on a sufficient legal basis, which means that deprivation of life is arbitrary if it lacks a basis in a law or if it rests on a law that does not strictly circumvent the conditions of the use of legal force by a State. Second, the force used must fulfil the criterion of necessity in qualitative, quantitative and temporal terms. Third, the force used must be proportionate to the actual danger present. Fourth and finally, deprivation of life is arbitrary if it could have been avoided by reasonable precautionary measures.[623]

---

620 Article 1(1) Additional Protocol II states: "This Protocol ... shall apply to all armed conflicts ... which take place in the territory of a High Contracting Party between its armed forces and dissident armed forces or other organized armed groups which, under responsible command, exercise such control over a part of its territory as to enable them to carry out sustained and concerted military operations and to implement this Protocol." Article 1(1) Additional Protocol II *inter alia* requires a high degree of organisation from the armed group which is a party to an armed conflict as well as territorial control, thereby setting the threshold of applicability fairly high.

621 UNHCR, "International Protection Considerations Regarding Colombian Asylum-Seekers 2005", para. 49, footnote 74.

622 See UNHCR, "Eligibility Guidelines for Afghan Asylum-Seekers 2007", 34–35 (indiscriminate attacks by anti-government groups); UNHCR, "Eligibility Guidelines for Afghan Asylum-Seekers 2007", 35 (attacks on schools); UNHCR, "Eligibility Guidelines for Asylum-Seekers from Afghanistan 2009", 7 (excessive use of force).

623 All these criteria are developed by Melzer, *Targeted Killing*, 100–120. See also Marco Sassòli and Laura M. Olson, "The Relationship between Humanitarian Law and Human Rights

Customary IHL also regulates the use of lethal force in international and non-international armed conflict. In any armed conflict, in line with the principle of distinction, attacking civilians is unlawful,[624] while combatants may be attacked.[625] In any armed conflict, customary IHL also prohibits:

> "Launching an attack which may be expected to cause incidental loss of civilian life, injury to civilians, damage to civilian objects, or a combination thereof, which would be excessive in relation to the concrete and direct military advantage anticipated."[626]

Further, customary IHL prohibits perfidious killing,[627] ordering that no quarter shall be given or conducting hostilities on this basis,[628] and attacking persons *hors de combat* who refrain from hostile acts.[629] However, the practical application of the principle of distinction faces two main and interrelated challenges. First, combatant status exists only in international armed conflict. The ICRC commentary to the customary IHL rule on distinction in non-international armed conflict states that for the purposes of the principle of distinction members of State armed forces may be considered combatants.[630] Yet State practice is ambiguous as to whether members of armed opposition groups are civilians who lose their protection from attack if and for as long as they directly participate in hostilities, or whether they are liable to attack as such.[631] Second, in any armed conflict, pursuant to customary IHL civilians lose their protection from attack if and when they directly participate in hostilities. A clear definition of the notion "direct participation in hostilities" under customary IHL has not (yet) developed in State practice.[632]

Law where It Matters: Admissible Killing and Internment of Fighters in Non-International Armed Conflict", *International Review of the Red Cross* 90, no. 871 (2008): 599–627, 610–612; Jelena Pejic, "Conflict Classification and the Law Applicable to Detention and the Use of Force", in *International Law and the Classification of Conflicts*, edited by Elizabeth Wilmshurst (Oxford: Oxford University Press, 2012), 110–112. The Basic Principles on the Use of Force and Firearms by Law Enforcement Officials, Eighth United Nations Congress on the Prevention of Crime and the Treatment of Offenders ((1990), UN Doc. A/CONF.144/28/Rev.1 at 112) constitute a soft law instrument delimiting the criteria for the use of lethal force by law enforcement officials. However, they only apply to officers, including military officers, exercising police powers.

624 See Henckaerts and Doswald-Beck, *Customary International Humanitarian Law*, 3.

625 See Henckaerts and Doswald-Beck, *Customary International Humanitarian Law*, 3.

626 Henckaerts and Doswald-Beck, *Customary International Humanitarian Law*, 46.

627 See Henckaerts and Doswald-Beck, *Customary International Humanitarian Law*, 221. On perfidy in non-international armed conflict, see Richard B. Jackson, "Perfidy in Non-International Armed Conflicts", in *International Law Studies*, edited by Kenneth Watkin and Andrew J. Norris (Newport, RI: US Naval War College, 2012).

628 See Henckaerts and Doswald-Beck, *Customary International Humanitarian Law*, 161.

629 See Henckaerts and Doswald-Beck, *Customary International Humanitarian Law*, 164.

630 See Henckaerts and Doswald-Beck, *Customary International Humanitarian Law*, 12.

631 See Henckaerts and Doswald-Beck, *Customary International Humanitarian Law*, 12 and 19.

632 See Henckaerts and Doswald-Beck, *Customary International Humanitarian Law*, 12 and 23. The ICRC sought to clarify the notion of direct participation in hostilities (though not with

The Canadian Civil War Guidelines and the views of UNHCR set out above concern the use of lethal force against civilians who are not directly participating in hostilities or who are not being suspected of such participation. Such use of lethal force is unlawful under both international human rights law and customary IHL.[633] In this respect, international human rights law and customary IHL are mutually reinforcing, obviating the need for refugee status decision-makers to decide which branch of international law is pertinent. Therefore, direct attacks against civilians not directly participating in hostilities constitute persecution.[634]

The ICTY Trial Chamber underscores this point by emphasising the various adverse effects of direct attacks on civilians:

> "[A]ttacks on civilians jeopardise the lives or health of persons who do not take active part in combat. ... [T]he imminent risk of falling victim of an unlawful attack is in itself an acute experience for civilians, who, unarmed and defenceless, find themselves facing an army that has chosen them as its target. The Chamber emphasises that the categorical nature of the prohibition of such attacks and its prominent place among the rules of international humanitarian law make it evident that the purpose of this prohibition is not only to save lives of civilians, but also to spare them from the risk of being subjected to war atrocities. The Chamber is of the opinion that the experiencing of such a risk by a civilian is in itself a grave consequence of an unlawful attack, even if he or she, luckily, survives the attack with no physical injury."[635]

However, in situations where lethal force is used against persons who do not fall into the category of civilians not directly participating in hostilities, the question remains of how to assess the use of lethal force for the purposes of interpreting persecution in armed conflict. Specifically, it must be examined whether it is necessary for the interpretation of persecution to identify the pertinent international legal framework, namely whether it comprises international human rights law, IHL or both, and if both branches of international law are pertinent, how to reconcile them.

---

a specific focus on customary international law): ICRC, "Interpretative Guidance on the Notion of Direct Participation in Hostilities under International Humanitarian Law" (2009), available at https://www.icrc.org/eng/resources/documents/article/review/review-872-p991.htm, accessed 10.03.2015. This interpretative guidance has generated debate. See, e.g., Michael Bothe, "Direct Participation in Hostilities in Non-International Armed Conflict", *Expert Paper for the Second Expert Meeting on the Notion of Direct Participation in Hostilities, The Hague, 25–26 October 2004* (2004), available at www.icrc.org/eng/assets/files/other/2004-05-expert-paper-dph-icrc.pdf, accessed 10.03.2015; Michael N. Schmitt, "The Interpretative Guidance on the Notion of Direct Participation in Hostilities: A Critical Analysis", *Harvard National Security Journal* 1, no. 1 (2010): 5–44.

633 See Sassòli, "The Role of Human Rights", 78 (referring to "harmless civilians").

634 See also Sternberg, *The Grounds of Refugee Protection*, 121–123.

635 ICTY, *The Prosecutor v. Pavle Strugar*, Judgment, Trial Chamber II, 31 January 2005, Case No. IT-01-42-T, para. 221.

To recall, the Refugee Convention's humanitarian object and purpose warrants an inclusive interpretation of the refugee definition, including the notion of persecution. A possible understanding of persecution as regards the use of lethal force in armed conflict which combines international human rights law and customary IHL in a complementary way might be to apply the more protective standard on the use of lethal force, namely the stricter criteria under international human rights law. This might strengthen the Refugee Convention's humanitarian object and purpose by ensuring a broad understanding of persecution as any use of lethal force that does not fulfil these strict criteria would be persecution. However, even though the human rights-based interpretation of persecution acknowledges persecution by non-State actors without requiring that their acts incur the responsibility of the country of origin under international human rights law, it is difficult to see how human rights standards can regulate the use of lethal force by non-State actors in armed conflict.[636] Moreover, this approach would ignore the fact that IHL forms an inseparable part of the Refugee Convention's international legal framework in contexts of armed conflict. Therefore, it is not a suitable solution.

A better solution is to adopt a flexible approach to persecution and the use of lethal force in armed conflict. This approach proceeds in three steps from the strictest and highest standard for using lethal force in armed conflict to more liberal standards on a sliding scale. According to this approach, the first step considers the human rights standard on lethal force. Any use of lethal force which can be assessed in the context of law enforcement and which is in breach of international human rights law amounts to persecution. If the use of lethal force cannot be assessed within the human rights framework or if it is not unlawful pursuant to this framework, the second step is to assess the lawfulness of the use of lethal force under customary IHL. If the use of lethal force violates customary IHL, for example because it is targeted at civilians who are not directly participating in hostilities, it *a fortiori* constitutes persecution. If the use of lethal force in the case at hand is found to be in accordance with customary IHL, the analysis must consider in a third step whether there are other reasons why it could amount to persecution. As the UNHCR EXCOM emphasised, war is often the chosen instrument of persecutors to destroy or displace entire groups.[637] Thus, lethal force may be lawful under customary IHL, but may nonetheless constitute persecution.

For example, civilians may have been compelled by parties to an armed conflict to participate in hostilities. In Colombia, for instance, villagers are often threatened by guerrillas to provide food, shelter or information.[638] If and when these villagers are directly participating in attacks, their death as a result of an

---

636 This assumes that non-State actors are not directly bound by international human rights law. The duty bearers under international human rights law are examined in Chapter 3.

637 See UNHCR Executive Committee, *Conclusion No. 85 (XLIX)* (1998), para. 4.

638 See UNHCR, "Eligibility Guidelines for Asylum-Seekers from Colombia 2010", 7. See also *Escobar v. Holder* 2011 U.S. App. LEXIS 18538 (7th Cir. 2011) (US).

attack would not amount to persecution understood in light of customary IHL. However, the fact that they were compelled to directly participate in hostilities could in and of itself constitute persecution. This example shows that while customary IHL can be instructive in the assessment of deprivation of life during hostilities, in particular as regards protection from attack, customary IHL cannot be prescriptive in terms of the scope of persecution because it does not and cannot provide a comprehensive framework for assessing an individual's predicament during armed conflict.

Thus, using lethal force in violation of customary IHL amounts to persecution, in particular if directed against civilians not directly participating in hostilities. The converse proposition, however, is not necessarily correct. Lethal force that complies with customary IHL must not be equated to a lack of persecution because this would fall short of the comprehensive assessment of the objective and individual circumstances. Furthermore, a State's use of lethal force for the purposes of law enforcement must abide by the stricter criteria under international human rights law.

5.3.2. Torture

Torture has reportedly been used in many armed conflicts, including in Afghanistan,[639] the DRC[640] and Sri Lanka.[641] For example, Colombian paramilitary groups have in the past been reported to use torture as a means of warfare with the objective of terrorising the civilian population.[642] Torture is absolutely prohibited under international human rights law[643] and customary IHL in any armed conflict;[644] it is a war crime in international and non-international armed conflict.[645] Torture undoubtedly constitutes persecution.[646]

---

639 For example, UNHCR voiced concerns about the use of torture in Afghan detention facilities: UNHCR, "Eligibility Guidelines for Afghan Asylum-Seekers 2007", 48; UNHCR, "Eligibility Guidelines for Asylum-Seekers from Afghanistan 2009", 26 and 60; UNHCR, "Eligibility Guidelines for Asylum-Seekers from Afghanistan 2010", 16.

640 See UNHCR, "Background Paper on Refugees and Asylum Seekers from the Democratic Republic of Congo" (2000), available at www.unhcr.org/refworld/docid/3ae6a6574.html, accessed 10.03.2015, 15, 17, 19, 20 and 22.

641 UNHCR noted in 2004: "During the civil war government security forces, state-backed Sinhalese and Muslim civilian militias, and armed Tamil groups ... committed massacres, disappearances, extra-judicial executions, rape, and torture against civilians, mainly Tamils." UNHCR, "Background Paper", para. 141. See also UNHCR, "Position on Asylum-Seekers from Sri Lanka 2006", para. 14.

642 See UNHCR, "International Protection Considerations regarding Colombian Asylum-seekers and Refugees 2002", paras. 15–16.

643 See Articles 7 and 4(2) ICCPR, Article 2(2) CAT and Article 37(a) CRC.

644 See Henckaerts and Doswald-Beck, *Customary International Humanitarian Law*, 315.

645 See Article 8(2)(a)(ii) and (iii) Rome Statute (international armed conflict) and Article 8(2)(c)(i) Rome Statute (non-international armed conflict).

646 This understanding results form an interpretation of persecution in light of the CAT, in particular its Article 3(1) which prohibits *refoulement* to a State where there are substantial

Although international human rights law, customary IHL and international criminal law intersect in the prohibition of torture, the definition of torture is not identical under these branches of international law. Article 1(1) CAT defines torture as follows:

> "For the purposes of this Convention, the term 'torture' means any act by which severe pain or suffering, whether physical or mental, is intentionally inflicted on a person for such purposes as obtaining from him or a third person information or a confession, punishing him for an act he or a third person has committed or is suspected of having committed, or intimidating or coercing him or a third person, or for any reason based on discrimination of any kind, when such pain or suffering is inflicted by or at the instigation of or with the consent or acquiescence of a public official or other person acting in an official capacity. It does not include pain or suffering arising only from, inherent in or incidental to lawful sanctions."

The Elements of Crimes for the International Criminal Court define the war crime of torture as the infliction of:

> "severe physical or mental pain or suffering ... for such purposes as: obtaining information or a confession, punishment, intimidation or coercion or for any reason based on discrimination of any kind."[647]

This definition of torture is broader than the one under the CAT because it omits the requirement that "such pain or suffering is inflicted by or at the instigation of or with the consent or acquiescence of a public official or other person acting in an official capacity."[648] Given that IHL not only binds States but also non-State parties to an armed conflict, the omission of this requirement in the definition of torture in international criminal law and IHL is sound. Thus, if persecution is interpreted in reference to the definition of torture under IHL and international criminal law rather than to the narrower definition in Article 1(1) CAT, a broader material scope of persecution in armed conflict could result. IHL and international criminal law would provide a higher standard of protection. However, the difference in the definition of torture under CAT as opposed to

---

grounds for believing that the person in question would be in danger of being subjected to torture. See also UNHCR, "UNHCR Position on Claims for Refugee Status Under the 1951 Convention relating to the Status of Refugees Based on a Fear of Persecution Due to an Individual's Membership of a Family or Clan Engaged in a Blood Feud" (2006), available at www.unhcr.org/refworld/docid/44201a574.html, accessed 10.03.2015, para. 4; Goodwin-Gill and McAdam, *The Refugee in International Law*, 93; Zimmermann and Mahler, "Article 1A, para. 2", mn. 252, 354–355.

647 ICC, Elements of Crime, UN Doc. PCNICC/2000/1/Add.2 (2000), Article 8(2)(a)(ii)-1, paras. 1 and 2.

648 See ICTY, *The Prosecutor v. Dragoljub Kunarac, Radomir Kovač and Zoran Vuković*, Judgment, Trial Chamber II, 22 February 2001, Case Nos. IT-96-23-T and IT-96-23/1-T, para. 496.

IHL and international criminal law may be insignificant for the purposes of interpreting the refugee definition. This is because it is now widely recognised that non-State actors can be persecutors, and therefore the strict torture definition in Article 1(1) CAT would not be directly imported into the refugee definition even under a human rights-based interpretation.

To conclude, international human rights law, customary IHL, international war crimes law, and international criminal law are mutually reinforcing in assessing torture as persecution. The definition of torture under IHL and international criminal law is broader than under international human rights law.[649] However, this does not result in a broader scope of persecution if interpreted in light of IHL and international criminal law because in contrast to the definition of torture in Article 1(1) CAT, the refugee definition accepts that non-State actors can be perpetrators of torture.

5.3.3. *Rape and Other Forms of Sexual Violence*

Rape and other forms of sexual violence are a recurrent phenomenon in armed conflicts around the world, as the Special Representative of the UN Secretary-General on Sexual Violence in Conflict poignantly noted:

> "In contemporary wars, it has become more dangerous to be a woman fetching water or collecting firewood than a fighter on the frontline."[650]

Sexual violence amounts to persecution.[651] While rape was historically considered legitimate spoils of war, international law has seen a development over the last decades that decidedly outlaws and criminalises rape and other forms of sexual violence in any armed conflict.[652] Rape and other forms of

---

649 Similarly: Manfred Nowak, "Torture and Other Cruel, Inhuman, or Degrading Treatment or Punishment", in *The Oxford Handbook of International Law in Armed Conflict*, edited by Andrew Clapham, Paola Gaeta (editors), Tom Haeck and Alice Priddy (assistant editors) (Oxford: Oxford University Press: 2014), 407–409.

650 Special Representative of the Secretary-General on Sexual Violence in Conflict, *Statement before the Security Council*, UN Doc. S/PV.6722 (23 February 2012), 3. Men also experience rape and other forms of sexual violence in armed conflict. See Sandesh Sivakumaran, "Sexual Violence against Men in Armed Conflict", *European Journal of International Law* 18, no. 2 (2007): 253–277; Christine Chinkin, "Gender and Armed Conflict", in *The Oxford Handbook of International Law in Armed Conflict*, edited by Andrew Clapham, Paola Gaeta (editors), Tom Haeck and Alice Pritty (assistant editors) (Oxford: Oxford University Press, 2014), 689.

651 See Markard, *Kriegsflüchtlinge*, 177; Oosterveld, "Women and Girls", 19–31; Haines, "Gender-related Persecution", 330–331; and Binder, *Frauenspezifische Verfolgung*, 290–315. Further: UNHCR, *Guidelines on International Protection No. 1*, para. 9.

652 See Kelly D. Askin, "Prosecuting Wartime Rape and Other Gender-Related Crimes under International Law: Extraordinary Advances, Enduring Obstacles", *Berkeley Journal of International Law* 21 (2003): 288–349; Anne-Marie L.M. Brouwer, *Supranational Criminal Prosecution of Sexual Violence. The ICC and the Practice of the ICTY and the ICTR* (Antwerp/Oxford: Intersentia, 2005); Theodor Meron, "Rape as a Crime under International

violence are now prohibited under customary IHL[653] and constitute war crimes.[654] Yet recent research has shown that refugee law jurisprudence has not fully caught up with these developments.[655] Claims to refugee protection based on rape and other forms of sexual violence during armed conflict face several obstacles: for example, rape is characterised by some adjudicators as mere lust or solely a private act outside the realm of persecution, rather than as a method of warfare.[656] Other refugee status decision-makers fail to acknowledge the consequences of rape and other forms of sexual violence, such as societal stigma, which may persist after the end of the armed conflict.[657]

Customary IHL and international war crimes jurisprudence can serve to mitigate these erroneous findings in refugee status determination by reaffirming and clarifying the prohibition of rape and other forms of sexual violence in armed conflict.[658] They can strengthen the human rights-based interpretation of persecution by emphasising that rape and sexual violence are not only prohibited in times of peace, but also in armed conflict.

5.3.4. Enforced Disappearance

Recent armed conflicts such as those in Afghanistan,[659] Colombia,[660] and Iraq[661] have seen parties to the conflict resort to enforced disappearances. For example,

---

Humanitarian Law", *American Journal of International Law* 87 (1993); and Chinkin, "Gender and Armed Conflict", 681–683.

653 See Henckaerts and Doswald-Beck, *Customary International Humanitarian Law*, 323.

654 See Article 8(2)(b)(xxii) and (e)(vi) Rome Statute. On the application of the legal provisions relating to violence against women in conflict situations by international criminal tribunals, see Chinkin, "Gender and Armed Conflict", 686–693.

655 See the studies by Oosterveld, "Women and Girls" and Markard, *Kriegsflüchtlinge*.

656 See Oosterveld, "Women and Girls", 23–24, citing the *NS* Afghanistan CG [2004] UKIAT 00328 (30 December 2004) (UK), *Najjemba v. Secretary of State for the Home Department* [2002] EWCA Civ 1082, (15 July 2002) (UK), *PS (Sri Lanka) v. Secretary of State for the Home Department* [2008] EWCA (UK), and *VA9-00148* [2010] RPDD No. 512 (30 June 2010) (Canada).

657 See Oosterveld, "Women and Girls", 24, citing *NS* Afghanistan CG [2004] UKIAT 00328 (30 December 2004) (UK), *JXV (Re)* [2008] RPDD No. 3 (23 January 2008) (Canada), *LM* Republic of Congo (Congo-Brazzaville) CG [2008] UKAIT 00064 (14 August 2008) (UK) and *In re B (FC) (Appellant) (2002) Regina v. Special Adjudicator (Respondent) ex parte Hoxha (FC) (Appellant)* [2005] UKHL 19 (10 March 2005) (UK).

658 Similarly: Oosterveld, "Women and Girls", 26. On the definition of rape as a war crime (which is identical to the definition of rape as an underlying act of crimes against humanity), see Mettraux, *International Crimes*, 107–110.

659 In 2010, UNHCR noted: "Members of military, police and security services, as well as high-ranking Government officials during the Taraki, Hafizullah Amin, Babrak Karmal, and Najibullah regimes, were involved in operations subjecting civilians to arrest, disappearances, torture, inhuman and degrading treatment and punishment." UNHCR, "Eligibility Guidelines for Asylum-Seekers from Afghanistan 2010", 42 (footnote in original omitted).

660 See UNHCR, "International Protection Considerations Regarding Colombian Asylum-Seekers 2005", paras. 68, 108, 119, and 124.

661 See UNHCR, "Eligibility Guidelines for Iraqi Asylum-Seekers 2009", 31.

UNHCR reported in 2012 that parties to the armed conflict in Iraq used enforced disappearances.[662] Article 2 of the Convention on Enforced Disappearances defines enforced disappearances as:

> "[T]he arrest, detention, abduction or any other form of deprivation of liberty by agents of the State or by persons or groups of persons acting with the authorization, support or acquiescence of the State, followed by a refusal to acknowledge the deprivation of liberty or by concealment of the fate or whereabouts of the disappeared person, which place such a person outside the protection of the law."

Enforced disappearances have devastating effects for the victims, who are often tortured and fear for their lives, as well as for their families, who do not know what has become of the victim. The Office of the High Commissioner for Human Rights summarised the impact of enforced disappearance on the victims by stating:

> "Having been removed from the protective precinct of the law and 'disappeared' from society, they are in fact deprived of all their rights and are at the mercy of their captors. Even if death is not the final outcome and the victim is eventually released from the nightmare, the physical and psychological scars of this form of dehumanization and the brutality and torture which often accompany it remain."[663]

Both international human rights law[664] and customary IHL[665] directly prohibit enforced disappearance in any armed conflict. An "offence to human dignity",[666] enforced disappearance also violates a range of other international human rights[667] and other rules of customary IHL.[668] The severity of enforced

---

662 See UNHCR, "UNHCR Eligibility Guidelines for Asylum-Seekers from Iraq 2012", 57.

663 Office of the United Nations High Commissioner for Human Rights, "Enforced or Involuntary Disappearance. Fact Sheet No. 6/Rev. 3" (2009), available at www.ohchr.org/Documents/Publications/FactSheet6Rev3.pdf, accessed 10.03.2015, 1.

664 See Article 1(1) Convention on Enforced Disappearances. Article 1(2) of this Convention states: "No exceptional circumstances whatsoever, whether a state of war or a threat of war, internal political instability or any other public emergency, may be invoked as a justification for enforced disappearance."

665 See Henckaerts and Doswald-Beck, *Customary International Humanitarian Law*, 340.

666 Article 1(1) Declaration on the Protection of All Persons from Enforced Disappearances (Declaration on Enforced Disappearance), adopted by UN General Assembly, *Resolution 133*, UN Doc. A/47/133 (18 December 1992).

667 Namely the right to recognition as a person before the law, the right to liberty and security of the person and the right not to be subjected to torture and other cruel, inhuman or degrading treatment or punishment. It also violates or constitutes a grave threat to the right to life. See Article 1 Declaration on Enforced Disappearance. The Human Rights Committee has confirmed this in, e.g., Human Rights Committee, *Communication No. 950/2000, S. Jagatheeswara Sarma v. Sri Lanka*, Views under Article 5(4) of the Optional Protocol, 31 July 2003, UN Doc. CCPR/C/78/D/950/2000, para. 9.3; Human Rights Committee, *Communication No. 992/2001, Louisa Bousroual v. Algeria*, Views under Article 5(4) of the Optional Protocol, 24 April 2006, UN Doc. CCPR/C/86/D/992/2001, para. 9.2.

668 Namely the prohibition of arbitrary deprivation of liberty, the prohibition of torture and other cruel or inhuman treatment and the prohibition of murder. See Henckaerts and Doswald-Beck, *Customary International Humanitarian Law*, 340.

disappearance, even if it does not lead to the victim's death, is such that it constitutes persecution.[669]

Enforced disappearance thus constitutes a type of harm regarding which international human rights law and customary IHL overlap. In contrast to customary IHL, international human rights law provides a clear definition of enforced disappearance that can guide refugee status decision-makers. On the other hand, there are various rules of customary IHL designed to prevent the occurrence of forced displacement in armed conflict, such as the prohibition of arbitrary deprivation of liberty,[670] the obligation to register persons deprived of their liberty,[671] and the obligation of each party to the conflict to "take all feasible measures to account for persons reported missing as a result of armed conflict".[672] Violations of these rules of customary IHL can indicate the existence of a risk of persecution in the form of enforced disappearance.

Thus, international human rights law and customary IHL are mutually reinforcing in the prohibition of enforced disappearance and in the interpretation of persecution. International human rights law provides more detailed interpretative guidance than customary IHL regarding the definition of enforced disappearance, while customary IHL contains rules designed to prevent enforced disappearance in armed conflict.

5.3.5. Forced Recruitment or Participation of Children in Hostilities

Highlighting the crippling impact of armed conflict on children, the 1996 report by Graça Machel stated:

> "One of the most alarming trends in armed conflict is the participation of children as soldiers. Children serve armies in supporting roles, as cooks, porters, messengers and spies. Increasingly, however, adults are deliberately conscripting children as soldiers. Some commanders have even noted the desirability of child soldiers because they are 'more obedient, do not question orders and are easier to manipulate than adult soldiers'."[673]

---

669 Several UNHCR Eligibility Guidelines support this view. See, e.g., UNHCR, "Background Paper", para. 152, suggesting that enforced disappearance violate the right to life, personal security and physical integrity. Similarly: UNHCR, "Refugees and Asylum Seekers from the DRC", 19; UNHCR, "International Protection Considerations regarding Colombian Asylum-seekers and Refugees 2002", para. 54.

670 See Henckaerts and Doswald-Beck, *Customary International Humanitarian Law*, 344.

671 See Henckaerts and Doswald-Beck, *Customary International Humanitarian Law*, 439.

672 See Henckaerts and Doswald-Beck, *Customary International Humanitarian Law*, 421.

673 Graça Machel, *Impact of Armed Conflict on Children. Report of the Expert of the Secretary-General submitted pursuant to Resolution 48/157*, UN Doc. A/51/306 (1996), para. 34 (footnote in original omitted).

There have been reports on the recruitment and participation of children in many recent armed conflicts.[674] For example, UNHCR reported that during the armed conflict in Sri Lanka, the Liberation Tigers of Tamil Eelam (LTTE) resorted to the forced recruitment of children.[675]

International human rights law[676] and customary IHL[677] prohibit the recruitment of children into the armed forces or armed groups. According to the Rome Statute, "conscripting or enlisting children under the age of fifteen years" into armed forces or groups constitutes a war crime in international and non-international armed conflicts.[678] Using children to actively participate in hostilities is also prohibited under international human rights law[679] and customary IHL;[680] it constitutes a war crime.[681] The forced recruitment of children into the armed forces of a State or by a non-State armed group and the use of children for direct participation in hostilities constitutes persecution.[682]

Hence, international human rights law, customary IHL and international criminal law overlap in the prohibition of recruiting children into the armed forces or armed groups and in the prohibition of using them to actively participate in hostilities. However, the age limit for recruitment and participation in hostilities differs. International human rights law, in particular the Optional Protocol on the Involvement of Children in Armed Conflict, provides a higher standard of protection than IHL because it sets the age limit at 18 years,[683] while the Rome Statute and the Additional Protocols stipulate

---

674 See, UN Secretary-General, *Report of the Secretary General on Children and Armed Conflict*, UN Doc. A/68/878-S/2014/339 (15 May 2014), paras. 23 (on Afghanistan), 59 (on the DRC), 71 (on Iraq), 116 (on Somalia), 165 (on Colombia). See also regarding the DRC: UNHCR, "Refugees and Asylum Seekers from the DRC", 15 and 26. Concerning Afghanistan: UNHCR, "Eligibility Guidelines for Asylum-Seekers from Afghanistan 2009", 35 and UNHCR, "Eligibility Guidelines for Asylum-Seekers from Afghanistan 2010", 25–26. On Sri Lanka: UNHCR, "Eligibility Guidelines for Asylum-Seekers from Sri Lanka 2009", 6; UNHCR, "Background Paper", paras. 264–270; UNHCR, "Eligibility Guidelines for Asylum-Seekers from Sri Lanka 2009", 6. More generally, see: Coalition to Stop the Use of Child Soldiers, *Child Soldiers Global Report*, 2008, available at www.hrw.org/sites/default/files/reports/Child_Soldiers_Global_Report_Summary.pdf, accessed 10.03.2015. See also Löhr, *Die kinderspezifische Auslegung*, 193–198.

675 See UNHCR, "Background Paper", para. 264.

676 See Article 38(3) CRC; Articles 2–4 Optional Protocol to the CRC.

677 See Henckaerts and Doswald-Beck, *Customary International Humanitarian Law*, 452.

678 See Articles 8(2)(b)(xxvi) and 8(2)(e)(vii) Rome Statute.

679 See Article 38(2) CRC, Articles 1 and 4 Optional Protocol to the CRC.

680 See Henckaerts and Doswald-Beck, *Customary International Humanitarian Law*, 485.

681 See Article 8(2)(b)(xxvi) and (e)(vii) Rome Statute.

682 See UNHCR, *Guidelines on International Protection No. 8: Child Asylum Claims under Articles 1(A)2 and 1(F) of the 1951 Convention and/or 1967 Protocol relating to the Status of Refugees*, UN Doc. HCR/GIP/09/08 (22 December 2009), para. 21; Matthew Happold, "Excluding Children from Refugee Status: Child Soldiers and Article 1F of the Refugee Convention", *American University International Law Review* 17 (2002): 1131–1176, 1139; Markard, *Kriegsflüchtlinge*, 185–186; Löhr, *Die kinderspezifische Auslegung*, 198–209.

683 See Articles 1 and 4 Optional Protocol to the CRC. In contrast, Article 38(2) CRC sets the age limit at 18 years.

an age limit of 15 years.[684] There is no uniform State practice as regards the age limit under customary IHL.[685] This age limit exemplifies an instance where international human rights law provides more suitable interpretative guidance regarding persecution than IHL and international criminal law because of its higher standard of protection.[686]

International criminal law provides instructive insights for the interpretation of persecution by considering the meaning of children's "active participation in hostilities". The ICC Pre-Trial Chamber, in its decision on the confirmation of charges in the *Lubanga* case, stated:

> "261. 'Active participation' in hostilities means not only direct participation in hostilities, combat in other words, but also covers active participation in combat-related activities such as scouting, spying, sabotage and the use of children as decoys, couriers or at military check-points.
>
> 262. In this respect, the Chamber considers that this article does not apply if the activity in question is clearly unrelated to hostilities. Accordingly, this article does not apply to food deliveries to an airbase or the use of domestic staff in married officers' quarters.
>
> 263. Nevertheless, the Chamber finds that articles 8(2)(b)(xxvi) and 8(d)(e)(vii) [of the Rome Statute] apply if children are used to guard military objectives, such as the military quarters of the various units of the parties to the conflict, or to safeguard the physical safety of military commanders (in particular, where children are used as bodyguards). These activities are indeed related to hostilities in so far as i) the military commanders are in a position to take all the necessary decisions regarding the conduct of hostilities, ii) they have a direct impact on the level of logistical resources and on the organisation of operations required by the other party to the conflict whose aim is to attack such military objectives."[687]

This definition can clarify the range of activities that constitute participation in hostilities for the purposes of identifying persecution. However, it must be borne in mind that this definition of children's active participation in hostilities was developed as part of a war crime definition in a criminal trial. This normative context, governed *inter alia* by the principles of legality and specificity,[688] differs

---

684 See Article 77(2) Additional Protocol I, Article 4(3)(c) Additional Protocol II, Articles Article 8(2)(b)(xxvi) and (e)(vii) Rome Statute.

685 See Henckaerts and Doswald-Beck, *Customary International Humanitarian Law*, 485. Breau argues that although the military handbooks of several States stipulate 15 as the minimum age, the ratification of the widespread CRC and other State practice mean that special protection is to be granted to children under 18. Breau, "Protected Persons and Objects", 201.

686 UNHCR also argues that the more favourable age limit should be used: UNHCR, *Guidelines on International Protection No. 10: Claims to Refugee Status related to Military Service within the context of Article 1A(2) of the 1951 Convention and/or the 1967 Protocol relating to the Status of Refugees*, UN Doc. HCR/GIP/13/10 (3 December 2013), para. 12.

687 ICC, *The Prosecutor v. Thomas Lubanga Dyilo, Decision on the confirmation of charges*, Pre-Trial Chamber I, 29 January 2007, Case No. ICC-01/04–01/06, paras. 261–263.

688 As also noted in Chapter 3.

from the normative context of the refugee definition. Since the refugee definition in general and persecution in particular must be interpreted in a dynamic and inclusive way, it cannot be concluded that activities which fall outside the scope of active participation in hostilities for the purposes of defining a war crime are necessarily also outside the purview of persecution. Thus, while acts that fall within the objective elements of the war crime of forcefully recruiting children into the armed forces or armed groups or of using them to participate in hostilities *a fortiori* constitute persecution, the converse proposition that acts which fall outside the scope of the war crimes do not amount to persecution is incorrect. Indeed, UNHCR emphasises that:

> "in addition to taking an active part in hostilities, children are also used as spies, messengers, porters, servants, slaves ... and/or to lay or clear landmines. Regardless of the function held by the child, they may be exposed to serious or multiple forms of harm."[689]

In conclusion, international human rights law, customary IHL and international criminal law intersect in the prohibition of recruiting children into the armed forces or armed groups and of using them to participate in hostilities. Thereby, they reinforce the understanding that such acts amount to persecution. International human rights law provides a higher standard of protection and thus a broader scope of persecution by setting a higher age limit than IHL and international criminal law. The latter, on the other hand, provides some interpretative guidance regarding persecution by exploring what amounts to active participation in hostilities.

5.3.6. *Starvation as a Method of Warfare*

Hunger is a frequent phenomenon during armed conflicts. The UN Special Representative on the Right to Food succinctly observed: "During situations of armed conflict, many more people die directly from starvation and malnutrition than from bullets and bombs."[690] Hunger has been deliberately used as a method of warfare, for instance by destroying or poisoning crops or by blocking relief

689 UNHCR, *Guidelines on International Protection No. 10: Claims to Refugee Status related to Military Service within the context of Article 1A(2) of the 1951 Convention and/or the 1967 Protocol relating to the Status of Refugees,* UN Doc. HCR/GIP/13/10 (3 December 2013), para. 40.

690 Special Rapporteur on the Right to Food, *The Right to Food. Preliminary Report of the Special Rapporteur of the Commission on Human Rights on the Right to Food,* UN Doc. A/56/210 (23 July 2001), para. 39. Agreeing: Farrell and Schmitt, "The Causes, Character and Conduct of Armed Conflict, and the Effects of on Civilian Populations, 1990–2010", 10. Armed conflicts interfere with all aspects of food production and consumption, from farming over the procurement, allocation and preparation of food to its consumption. See Jelena Pejic, "The Right to Food in Situations of Armed Conflict: The Legal Framework", *International Review of the Red Cross* 83, no. 844 (2001): 1097–1109, 1097.

supplies.[691] For example, deliberate starvation was used as a strategy during the armed conflicts in Somalia[692] and the former Yugoslavia.[693]

As previously shown in this chapter, persecution can and must be interpreted in light of economic, social and cultural rights. While not all violations of economic, social or cultural rights are tantamount to persecution, breaches of the core obligations under the ICESCR are.[694] To clarify, under the ICESCR, States parties are obliged to progressively realise the stipulated rights, whilst being directly bound by a "minimum core obligation to ensure the satisfaction of, at the very least, minimum essential levels of each of the rights".[695] The ICESCR includes the right to adequate food.[696] The ICESCR applies in armed conflict and does not provide for derogations.[697] If a State uses starvation as a method of warfare this would, at the very least, breach its obligation to respect the right to adequate food as it denies access to adequate food. Indeed, the Special Rapporteur of the Commission on Human Rights on the right to food noted that in armed conflict the obligation to respect means that "the Government and other armed groups must not destroy productive resources and must not block, delay or divert relief food supplies to civilian populations."[698] Depriving any significant number of individuals of essential foodstuffs constitutes a violation of a State's core obligations under the ICESCR,[699] and thus amounts to persecution.[700]

Using the starvation of the civilian population as a method of warfare is also prohibited under customary IHL in any armed conflict.[701] It is also a war

---

691 See Special Rapporteur on the Right to Food, *The Right to Food*, para. 39.

692 See UN Secretary-General, *Report of the Secretary-General on the Protection of Civilians in Armed Conflict*, UN Doc. S/2001/331 (30 March 2001), para. 14.

693 See UN Commission on Human Rights, *Periodic Report by the Special Rapporteur on the Situation of Human Rights in the Former Yugoslavia*, UN Doc. S/1995/933-A/50/727 (4 October 1995), para. 54.

694 See Foster, *International Refugee Law*, 197–198.

695 Committee on Economic, Social and Cultural Rights, *General Comment 3*, para. 10.

696 Article 11(1) ICESCR states: "The States Parties to the present Covenant recognise the right of everyone to an adequate standard of living for himself and his family, including adequate food, clothing and housing, and to the continuous improvement of living conditions. The States Parties will take appropriate steps to ensure the realization of this right, recognizing to this effect the essential importance of international co-operation based on free consent."

697 See Chapter 3.

698 Special Rapporteur on the Right to Food, *The Right to Food*, para. 27.

699 See Committee on Economic, Social and Cultural Rights, *General Comment 3*, para. 10.

700 On starvation as persecution, see Markard, *Kriegsflüchtlinge*, 181; Storey and Wallace, "War and Peace", 359 (regarding starvation); Sternberg, *The Grounds of Refugee Protection*, 303; and Foster, *International Refugee Law*, 198 (concerning the prevention of access to humanitarian relief in armed conflict).

701 See Henckaerts and Doswald-Beck, *Customary International Humanitarian Law*, 186. This rule was introduced by the Additional Protocols in 1977 (see Article 54(1) of the 1977 Additional Protocol I and Article 14 of the 1977 Additional Protocol II).

crime.[702] The ICRC commentary to the corresponding provision in Additional Protocol I sheds light on the meaning of starvation, noting that using starvation as a method of warfare means to provoke starvation deliberately, "causing the population to suffer hunger, particularly by depriving it of its sources of food and supplies."[703] Starvation is prohibited not only when it results in death, but also when it causes hunger.[704] The deliberate infliction of hunger on the civilian population is thus prohibited.

Hence, starvation as a method of warfare is an area where a human rights-based understanding of persecution and an interpretation of persecution in light of customary IHL reinforce one another. Other customary IHL rules further clarify the prohibition of starvation of the civilian population as a method of warfare. For example, customary IHL prohibits attacking civilian objects,[705] including "foodstuffs, agricultural areas for the production of foodstuffs, crops, livestock, drinking water installations and supplies and irrigation works."[706] This rule of customary IHL can provide guidance for refugee status decision makers by pinpointing unlawful ways of conducting hostilities that can indicate that starvation is being used as a method of warfare. The same could be said for the prohibition under customary IHL of "[a]ttacking, destroying, removing or rendering useless objects indispensable to the survival of the civilian population are prohibited."[707] However, such objects can be attacked if they are military objectives. Another exception to this rule applies in international armed conflict only and allows for "scorched earth policies" in defence of the national territory against invasion.[708] At the same time, such measures on a State's own territory in international armed conflict cannot be reconciled with a State's core obligation under the right to adequate food set out in Article 11(1) ICESCR. In this respect, international human rights law provides the higher standard of protection and ought to be preferred in the interpretation of persecution over an understanding in light of customary IHL. Thus, rules of customary IHL complement, strengthen and clarify the right to adequate food in international human rights

---

702 Pursuant to Article 8(2)(b)(xxv) of the Rome Statute, "[i]ntentionally using starvation of civilians as a method of warfare by depriving them of objects indispensable to their survival" constitutes a war crime in international armed conflicts.

703 Sandoz, Swinarski, and Zimmermann (editors), *Commentary on the Additional Protocols of 8 June 1977 to the Geneva Conventions of 12 August 1949*, para. 2089.

704 See Sandoz, Swinarski and Zimmermann (editors), *Commentary on the Additional Protocols of 8 June 1977 to the Geneva Conventions of 12 August 1949*, para. 2089.

705 See Henckaerts and Doswald-Beck, *Customary International Humanitarian Law*, 25.

706 Pejic, "The Right to Food", 1098.

707 Henckaerts and Doswald-Beck, *Customary International Humanitarian Law*, 189.

708 See Henckaerts and Doswald-Beck, *Customary International Humanitarian Law*, 192. Article 54(5) Additional Protocol I states: "In recognition of the vital requirements of any Party to the conflict in the defence of its national territory against invasion, derogation from the prohibitions contained in paragraph 2 may be made by a Party to the conflict within such territory under its own control where required by imperative military necessity." Article 14 Additional Protocol II does not include such a caveat. See also Chapter 3.

law in armed conflict,[709] with one exception, namely "scorched earth policies" on a State's own territory in international armed conflict which are unlawful under the ICESCR and therefore would amount to persecution.

5.3.7. Use of Chemical Weapons

Chemical weapons have indiscriminate and devastating effects, as the example of Iraq illustrates.[710] In the late 1980s, during and after the Iran–Iraq war, the Iraqi regime conducted various attacks with chemical weapons, including mustard gas, within its territory against locations where Kurds lived whom the Iraqi regime suspected of collaborating with Iran. As a result of these attacks, thousands of civilians died. The attacks, which breached international law,[711] also caused permanent and severe health problems for survivors.[712] Such health problems were highlighted by the Special Rapporteur of the UN Commission on Human Rights on Violence against Women, Its Causes and Consequences, who stated with respect to victims of chemical weapons in Vietnam:

> "The victims have suffered disabilities related to their reproductive organs and have given birth to children with severe disabilities. The consequences resulting from the use of chemical weapons can be devastating, not only for the victim concerned but also for the next generation, unborn at the time of the armed conflict."[713]

While it must be acknowledged that the use of chemical weapons appears to breach a number of international human rights obligations, customary IHL regulates the matter in a more direct, detailed and explicit way. Customary IHL prohibits the use of chemical weapons in international and non-international

---

709 See Pejic, "The Right to Food", 1098.

710 The use of chemical weapons has also been reported in the Syrian armed conflict. See, e.g., UN Mission to Investigate Allegations of the Use of Chemical Weapons in the Syrian Arab Republic, "Report on the Alleged Use of Chemical Weapons in the Ghouta Area of Damascus on 21 August 2013" (2013), available at www.un.org/disarmament/content/slideshow/Secretary_General_Report_of_CW_Investigation.pdf, accessed 10.03.2015.

711 See ICRC, "Press Release No. 1567, Iran-Iraq conflict: The ICRC condemns the use of chemical weapons" (1988), available at www.icrc.org/customary-ihl/eng/docs/v2_rul_rule74, accessed 10.03.2015; Security Council, *Resolution 582,* UN Doc. S/RES/582 (24 February 1986), para. 2. By using chemical weapons, Iraq violated the 1925 Protocol for the Prohibition of the Use of Asphyxiating, Poisonous or Other Gases, and of Bacteriological Methods of Warfare (adopted 17 June 1925, entered into force 8 February 1928, printed in Dietrich Schindler and Jiri Toman, *The Laws of Armed Conflicts* (The Hague: Martinus Nijhoff, 1988), 116.

712 Iraq also used chemical weapons in attacks against installations in Iran. See Hague District Court, *Landelijk Jurispr Nr: AX6406*, Judgment of 23 December 2005. The court found that the defendant had supplied Iraq on numerous occasions with large quantities of a precursor for mustard gas, thus enabling Iraq to use chemical weapons.

713 UN Special Rapporteur on Violence against Women, *Report on violence against women perpetrated and/or condoned by the State during times of armed conflict (1997–2000),* UN Doc. E/CN.4/2001/73 (23 January 2001), para. 46.

armed conflict.[714] Such use is also a war crime,[715] which shows that using chemical weapons surpasses the intensity threshold of persecution. Drawing on customary IHL and international criminal law to interpret persecution as regards the use of chemical weapons in armed conflict thus means to obtain straightforward and specific guidance that such use constitutes persecution in international and non-international armed conflict.

5.3.8. Forced Displacement as a Method of Warfare

In armed conflict, civilians are often deliberately uprooted by parties to the conflict. In Colombia, for example, parties to the conflict have used forced displacement of the civilian population as a deliberate strategy. The *Fuerzas Armadas Revolucionarias de Colombia* (Revolutionary Armed Forces of Colombia, FARC) have reportedly forcibly displaced civilians in order to delay the opposing paramilitaries.[716] Forced displacement typically has a devastating impact on the affected civilians in various respects, including access to food, health care and education as well as family life.[717] Employing forced displacement as a method of warfare amounts to persecution.[718]

International human rights law does not expressly prohibit arbitrary displacement. Nonetheless, protection against arbitrary displacement can be inferred from various norms of international human rights law, including the right to freedom of movement and choice of residence.[719] The UN

---

714 On the customary IHL prohibition of chemical weapons, see Henckaerts and Doswald-Beck, *Customary International Humanitarian Law*, 259.

715 Reacting to the use of chemical weapons by Iraq in Kurdish villages, the ICTY held: "It is … clear that, whether or not Iraq really used chemical weapons against its own Kurdish nationals … there undisputedly emerged a general consensus in the international community on the principle that the use of those weapons is also prohibited in internal armed conflicts": ICTY, *The Prosecutor v. Duško Tadić aka "Dule"*, Decision on the Defence Motion for Interlocutory Appeal on Jurisdiction, Appeals Chamber, 2 October 1995, Case No. IT-94-1-AR72, para. 124. See also Darcy, *Judges, War and Law*, 199–202. Using chemical weapons is not expressly listed as a war crime in the Rome Statute, but may be subsumed under Article 8(2)(b)(xviii) of the 1998 ICC Statute, "[e]mploying asphyxiating, poisonous or other gases, and all analogous liquids, materials or devices" is a war crime in international armed conflict. At the 12th plenary meeting of the States parties to the Rome Statute in 2010, an amendment to the Rome Statute was adopted (Resolution RC/Res.5) which incorporates into the Rome Statute a further war crime in non-international armed conflict, namely "employing asphyxiating, poisonous or other gases, and all analogous liquids, materials or devices" (Article 8(2)(b)(xiv) Rome Statute).

716 See Jaques, *Armed Conflict and Displacement*, 56. Another example relates to the policy of forced displacement pursued in El Salvador in the 1980s. See Sternberg, *The Grounds of Refugee Protection*, 119.

717 See the detailed description by Jaques, *Armed Conflict and Displacement*, 185–208.

718 See UNHCR, *Note on International Protection*, UN Doc. A/AC.96/882 (2 July 1997), 169; Sternberg, *The Grounds of Refugee Protection*, 119–120.

719 As noted by Jaques, *Armed Conflict and Displacement*, 21. Article 12(1) ICCPR reads: "Everyone lawfully within the territory of a State shall, within that territory, have the right

Sub-Commission on Prevention of Discrimination and Protection of Minorities emphasised this by stating:

> "[P]ractices of forcible exile, mass expulsion and deportation, population transfer, forcible population exchange, unlawful forcible evacuation, eviction and forcible relocation, 'ethnic cleansing' and other forms of forcible displacement of populations within a country or across borders deprive the affected populations of their right to freedom of movement."[720]

Other human rights provisions also protect against arbitrary displacement or transfer,[721] namely provisions on privacy, including the prohibition of arbitrary interference with one's home,[722] and the right to adequate housing.[723] Yet the right to freedom of movement and the right to privacy are derogable.[724] In armed conflict, protection of these rights may thus be limited. Since the ICESCR does not allow for derogations,[725] the right to adequate housing applies in armed conflict. But limitations may be imposed on the right to adequate housing in accordance with Article 4 ICESCR according to which any limitations must be "determined by law only insofar as this may be compatible with the nature of these [economic, social and cultural] rights and solely for the purpose of promoting the general welfare in a democratic society".[726] The right to adequate housing continues to protect from arbitrary displacement in armed conflict, albeit with certain limitations. Hence, international human rights law provides

to liberty of movement and freedom to choose his residence." Article 13 ICCPR governs expulsions, but only with respect to aliens lawfully within the territory of State party to the ICCPR. This provision falls outside the scope of the present analysis which focusses on the protection of a State's own nationals or stateless persons.

720 Sub-Commission on Prevention of Discrimination and Protection of Minorities, *The Right to Freedom of Movement. Sub-Commission Resolution 1996/9*, UN Doc. E/CN.4/SUB.2/RES/1996/9 (28 August 1997), as noted by Jaques, *Armed Conflict and Displacement*, 21.

721 As noted by Jaques, *Armed Conflict and Displacement*, 21.

722 Article 17 ICCPR states: "1. No one shall be subjected to arbitrary or unlawful interference with his privacy, family, home or correspondence, nor to unlawful attacks on his honour and reputation. 2. Everyone has the right to the protection of the law against such interference or attacks."

723 Article 11(1) ICESCR *inter alia* states: "The States Parties to the present Covenant recognize the right of everyone to an adequate standard of living for himself and his family, including adequate food, clothing and housing". The Committee on Economic, Social and Cultural Rights noted: "Although the practice of forced evictions might appear to occur primarily in heavily populated urban areas, it also takes place in connection with forced population transfers, internal displacement, forced relocations in the context of armed conflict, mass exoduses and refugee movements. In all of these contexts, the right to adequate housing and not to be subjected to forced eviction may be violated through a wide range of acts or omissions attributable to States parties." Committee on Economic, Social and Cultural Rights, "General Comment No. 7", para. 6.

724 Article 4(2) ICCPR only exempts the following provisions from derogation: Articles 6, 7, 8 (paragraphs 1 and 2), 11, 15, 16 and 18 ICCPR.

725 As shown in Chapter 3.

726 See Committee on Economic, Social and Cultural Rights, "General Comment No. 7", para. 6.

interpretative guidance as regards persecution in the form of forced displacement in armed conflict because a number of human rights serve to prohibit arbitrary displacement or transfer, although some are subject to derogations or other limitations in armed conflict.

Customary IHL also prohibits the use of forced displacement as a method of warfare in armed conflict. In international armed conflict, customary IHL focusses on forced displacement in occupied territories.[727] Since this book does not examine situations of belligerent occupations,[728] this customary IHL rule is not further examined here. Rather, the analysis concentrates on non-international armed conflict, with respect to which customary IHL provides that parties to the conflict

> "may not order the displacement of the civilian population, in whole or in part, for reasons related to the conflict, unless the security of the civilians involved in or imperative military reasons so demand."[729]

Even though pursuant to its wording, this rule only prohibits *ordering* the forced displacement of the civilian population, the carrying out of such displacement is also prohibited. True, ordering forced displacement and carrying out forced displacement are different concepts.[730] However, the protection from forced displacement would be significantly curtailed, if not to say rendered futile, if customary IHL merely prohibited the ordering of forced displacement but not the actual forced displacement.[731] Moreover, some of the State practice supporting this rule of customary IHL refers to forced displacement in general.[732]

---

727 See Henckaerts and Doswald-Beck, *Customary International Humanitarian Law*, 457.

728 On the book's scope, see the Introduction.

729 Henckaerts and Doswald-Beck, *Customary International Humanitarian Law*, 457. In support: Piotrowicz, "Displacement", 347; Jaques, *Armed Conflict and Displacement*, 71.

730 See Piotrowicz, "Displacement", 347. The wording of this rule of customary IHL is very similar to Article 17(1) Additional Protocol II (first sentence), which states: "The displacement of the civilian population shall not be ordered for reasons related to the conflict unless the security of the civilians involved or imperative military reasons so demand."

731 See Jan Willms, "Without Order, Anything Goes? The Prohibition of Forced Displacement in Non-international Armed Conflict", *International Review of the Red Cross* 91, no. 875 (2009): 547–565, 551–553 and Jaques, *Armed Conflict and Displacement*, 58–62, both discussing Article 17 Additional Protocol II.

732 See, e.g., *Manuel de droit des conflits armés, Ministère de la Défense, Direction des Affaires Juridiques, Sous-Direction du droit international humanitaire et du droit européen, Bureau du droit des conflits armés* (Manual on the Law of Armed Conflict, Ministry of Defence, Legal Affairs Directorate, Sub-Directorate on International Humanitarian Law and European Law, Bureau on the Law of Armed Conflict), 2001, 65 (France); *Humanitair Oorlogsrecht: Handleiding, Voorschift No. 27–412, Koninklijke Landmacht, Militair Juridische Dienst* (Humanitarian Law Manual, Regulations No. 27–412, Royal Netherlands Army, Military Legal Services), 2005, para. 1040 (Netherlands). Further practice can be accessed on the ICRC Database on Customary IHL: www.icrc.org/customary-ihl/eng/docs/v2_rul_rule129, accessed 08.09.2013. See also Jaques, *Armed Conflict and Displacement*, 60–61.

Under customary IHL, there are two exceptions to the prohibition of forced displacement in non-international armed conflict. First, the civilian population may be forcefully displaced in the sense of being evacuated if its security so requires.[733] Indeed, parties to the conflict are obliged to remove civilians and civilian objects under their control from the vicinity of military objects to the extent possible.[734] The second exception to the prohibition of forced displacement, imperative military reasons, must be assessed in light of the information available to the commander at the time rather than with the benefit of hindsight.[735] Imperative military reasons do not justify the removal of civilians in order to persecute them.[736] Zayas concludes:

> "The defense of military necessity is therefore restricted to situations where army commanders judge that the safety of the civilian population requires that they be removed from the battle zone, and not when the same army commanders decide that military advantage would be gained by removing the population and scorching earth behind them."[737]

Military necessity does not involve considerations of political motives. Consequently, displacing a population to gain control over a rebellious ethnic group is unlawful.[738] It must be noted that customary IHL solely addresses forced displacement related to armed conflict, acknowledging that displacement may be necessary for other reasons such as epidemics or natural disasters.[739]

With respect to persecution in the form of forced displacement during armed conflict, it can be concluded that customary IHL reinforces the prohibition of arbitrary displacement in international human rights law in armed conflict, thereby strengthening the view that such displacement amounts to persecution. In order to constitute persecution, displacement must not be voluntary but forced. The jurisprudence of the ICTY identified a range of factors that assist in determining whether there was a lack of genuine choice on the part of the

733 See Henckaerts and Doswald-Beck, *Customary International Humanitarian Law*, 460.

734 See Henckaerts and Doswald-Beck, *Customary International Humanitarian Law*, 74. This rule of customary IHL applies in international armed conflict and arguably also in non-international armed conflict.

735 See Jaques, *Armed Conflict and Displacement*, 31.

736 See Henckaerts and Doswald-Beck, *Customary International Humanitarian Law*, 461.

737 Alfred M. Zayas, "International Law and Mass Population Transfers", *Harvard International Law Journal* 16 (1975): 207–258, 219. Very similar: Jean-Marie Henckaerts, "Deportation and Transfer of Civilians in Time of War", *Vanderbilt Journal of Transnational Law* 26 (1993–1994), 475. Affirmative: Jaques, *Armed Conflict and Displacement*, 32.

738 See Sandoz, Swinarski, and Zimmermann (editors), *Commentary on the Additional Protocols of 8 June 1977 to the Geneva Conventions of 12 August 1949*, para. 4854. This commentary on Article 17(1) Additional Protocol II sheds light on the meaning of the prohibition of forced displacement in non-international armed conflict under customary IHL because the customary rule is very similar in wording to Article 17(1) Additional Protocol II.

739 See Sandoz, Swinarski, and Zimmermann (editors), *Commentary on the Additional Protocols of 8 June 1977 to the Geneva Conventions of 12 August 1949*, para. 4855.

displaced civilian population. For example, the ICTY Trial Chamber stated in the *Slobodan Miloševic case*:

> "A lack of genuine choice may be inferred from, *inter alia*, threatening and intimidating acts that are calculated to deprive the civilian population of exercising its free will, such as the shelling of civilian objects, the burning of civilian property, and the commission of – or the threat to commit – other crimes 'calculated to terrify the population and make them flee the area with no hope of return.'"[740]

These factors can also assist refugee status decision-makers in determining whether there was a genuine lack of choice as regards the refugee claimant's displacement and thus whether the use of such forced displacement amounts to persecution. The prohibition of forced displacement under customary IHL is thus not only pertinent for the notion of persecution, but also the requirement that persecution be causally linked to a Refugee Convention ground, which is why it is further examined in Chapter 7.

In sum, international human rights law and customary IHL on the one hand and international criminal law on the other complement one another with respect to the prohibition of forced displacement in non-international armed conflict. They reinforce the Refugee Convention by outlawing forced displacement as a method of warfare. As regards persecution in the form of forced displacement, customary IHL provides more specific guidance in the context of non-international armed conflict than international human rights law.

5.3.9. Arbitrary Deprivation of Liberty

Arbitrary deprivation of liberty is a frequent form of harm in armed conflict. It is often used to suppress supporters of the adverse party or to spread fear amongst the civilian population.[741] For example, during the civil war in Sri Lanka, the LTTE carried out numerous arbitrary arrests and detentions.[742] In some areas of

740 *The Prosecutor v. Slobodan Milošević, Decision on Motion for Judgment of Acquittal*, Trial Chamber, 16 June 2004, Case No. IT-02-54-T, para. 74. Milošević was charged with three counts of deportation as a crime against humanity (Article 5(d) of the ICTY Statute), three counts of unlawful deportation or transfer as grave breaches of the Geneva Conventions (Article 2(g) ICTY Statute) and two counts of inhumane acts (forcible transfers) as crimes against humanity (Article 5(i) ICTY Statute). On the factors indicating a lack of choice, see also Expert Meeting on Complementarities between International Refugee Law, International Criminal Law and International Refugee Law, "Arusha Summary Conclusions", para. 11.

741 The notions "arbitrary deprivation of liberty" and "detention" are used interchangeably in this book. This section is not concerned with the material conditions of detention.

742 See UNHCR, "Background Paper", paras. 24, 44 and 47–48. See also Hathaway and Foster, *The Law of Refugee Status*, 242.

Afghanistan[743] and Iraq,[744] members of ethnic minorities have faced detention and intimidation by local power-holders. In Colombia, there have been mass detentions of persons suspected of being linked with the guerrillas.[745] Arbitrary deprivation of liberty constitutes persecution.[746] This section focusses on deprivation of liberty for reasons related to an armed conflict.

Both international human rights law and customary IHL address arbitrary deprivation of liberty in armed conflict. The ICCPR prohibits arbitrary deprivation of liberty in Article 9(1). Though applying to all forms of deprivation of liberty,[747] Article 9(1) ICCPR can be subject to derogation "in times of public emergency which threatens the life of the nation".[748] However, States parties may not invoke states of emergencies to justify violations of IHL such as arbitrary deprivation of liberty.[749] Children are especially protected from deprivation of liberty under international human rights law: Article 37 CRC states:

> "[N]o child shall be deprived of his or her liberty unlawfully or arbitrarily. The arrest, detention or imprisonment of a child shall be in conformity with the law and shall be used as a measure of last resort and for the shortest appropriate period of time."[750]

---

743 See UNHCR, "Eligibility Guidelines for Afghan Asylum-Seekers 2007", 66.

744 See UNHCR, "Eligibility Guidelines for Iraqi Asylum-Seekers 2007", 11.

745 See UNHCR, "International Protection Considerations Regarding Colombian Asylum-Seekers 2005", para. 40.

746 Article 33(1) Refugee Convention *inter alia* prohibits expulsion or return to countries where the refugee's freedom would be threatened. By definition, arbitrary deprivation of liberty impinges on the affected individual's freedom. The context of Article 1A(2) Refugee Convention therefore shows that arbitrary deprivation of liberty amounts to persecution. See also Zimmermann and Mahler, "Article 1A, para. 2", mn. 252, 355; Goodwin-Gill and McAdam, *The Refugee in International Law*, 93. See further: UNHCR, "Refugees and Asylum Seekers from the DRC", 19; UNHCR, "Background Paper", paras. 24, 44 and 47–48; UNHCR, "Eligibility Guidelines for Iraqi Asylum-Seekers 2007", 11; UNHCR, "International Protection Considerations Regarding Colombian Asylum-Seekers 2005", para. 40.

747 See Human Rights Committee, *General Comment No. 8: Right to Liberty and Security of the Persons (Art. 9)*, UN Doc. HRI/GEN/1/Rev.9 (1982), para. 1.

748 Article 4(1) ICCPR. Article 4(2) ICCPR, which lists the provisions of the ICCPR which are not subject to derogation, does not refer to Article 9 ICCPR.

749 See Human Rights Committee, *General Comment 29: States of Emergency (Article 4)*, para. 11.

750 Legally non-binding UN guidelines emphasise that the detention of children should be the last resort and limited to exceptional cases. See United Nations Rules for the Protection of Juveniles Deprived of their Liberty, adopted by UN General Assembly, *Resolution 45/113*, UN Doc. A/RES/45/113 (14 December 1990); United Nations Standard Minimum Rules for the Administration of Juvenile Justice ("The Beijing Rules") and UN General Assembly, *Resolution 40/33*, UN Doc. A/RES/40/33 (29 November 1985). When depriving children of their liberty, States parties to the CRC must make the best interests of the child a primary consideration. Article 3(1) CRC states: "In all actions concerning children, whether undertaken by public or private social welfare institutions, courts of law, administrative authorities or legislative bodies, the best interests of the child shall be a primary consideration."

In any armed conflict, customary IHL also prohibits arbitrary deprivation of liberty.[751] Unlawful confinement in international armed conflict is a war crime pursuant to Article 8(2)(a)(vii) of the Rome Statute. Contrastingly, in non-international armed conflict, unlawful deprivation of liberty is not a war crime under the Rome Statute nor under customary international law.[752]

Deprivation of liberty can be arbitrary because it is not based on a sufficient legal basis or because it violates procedural safeguards. Both situations are examined in the following in light of international human rights law on the one hand and customary IHL and international criminal law on the other with a view to clarifying the notion of persecution. First, the legal bases for deprivation of liberty in international armed conflict are examined. Neither the ICCPR nor the CRC spell out lawful bases for deprivation of liberty. In a case that was not related to a situation of armed conflict, the Human Rights Committee clarified the notion of "arbitrariness":

> "The drafting history of article 9, paragraph 1 [of the ICCPR], confirms that 'arbitrariness' is not to be equated with 'against the law', but must be interpreted more broadly to include elements of inappropriateness, injustice, lack of predictability and due process of law. … [T]his means that remand in custody pursuant to lawful arrest must not only be lawful but reasonable in all the circumstances … Remand in custody must further be necessary in all the circumstances, for example to prevent flight, interference with evidence or the recurrence of crime."[753]

Arrest or detention must hence be reasonable and necessary and in accordance with the due process of law, though the Human Rights Committee did not elaborate what this means in armed conflict. IHL is concerned with deprivation of liberty for reasons related to an armed conflict, in particular security reasons. The ICRC study on customary IHL did not identify customary grounds of detention in international armed conflict. However, the ICRC commentary on the rule of customary IHL which prohibits arbitrary deprivation of liberty points to the four Geneva Conventions which include provisions on the reasons for which certain individuals may be deprived of their liberty.[754] In order to delimit the scope of persecution, it is necessary to examine whether the Geneva Conventions provide grounds for the deprivation of liberty of a State's own nationals in international armed conflict. The Geneva Conventions I and II address the retention of the enemy's medical or religious personnel which

---

751 See Henckaerts and Doswald-Beck, *Customary International Humanitarian Law*, 344.

752 See Werle, *Völkerstrafrecht*, 525, mn. 1203.

753 *Communication No. 458/1991, Alber Womah Mukong v. Cameroon*, Views under Article 5(4) of the Optional Protocol, adopted on 8 July 1992, UN Doc. A/49/40, para. 9.8. See also *Communication No. 305/1988, Hugo van Alphen v. The Netherlands*, Views adopted on 23 July 1990, paragraph 5.8. On arbitrary deprivation of liberty as persecution, see further Hathaway and Foster, *The Law of Refugee Status*, 238–243.

754 See Henckaerts and Doswald-Beck, *Customary International Humanitarian Law*, 344.

typically will have enemy nationality. The Geneva Convention III allows for the internment of prisoners of war. Prisoners of war are in most cases not nationals of the detaining power.[755] Thus, Geneva Conventions I, II and III are not relevant for understanding arbitrary deprivation of liberty (and persecution) of a State's own nationals or stateless persons during armed conflict. Article 42(1) Geneva Convention IV, which concerns internment or placing in assigned residence of civilians "if the security of the Detaining Power makes it absolutely necessary", could be of interest for delimiting the scope of persecution. However, this provision is located in a Section of Geneva Convention IV which addresses aliens in the territory of a party to the conflict. Thus, Article 42(1) Geneva Convention IV is not relevant for the interpretation of the refugee definition which is concerned with intolerable harm within the country of nationality or, for stateless persons, the country of habitual residence.[756]

Another IHL treaty provision that addresses internment in international armed conflict can be found in Article 75 Additional Protocol I, which reflects customary international law.[757] This provision covers "persons who are in the power of a Party to the conflict and who do not benefit from more favourable treatment under the Conventions or under this Protocol".[758] Though addressing persons arrested, detained or interned for actions related to the armed conflict, Article 75(3) Additional Protocol I does not provide specific lawful grounds for depriving an individual of his or her liberty.[759] Thus, customary IHL, the Geneva Conventions and the Additional Protocol I do not identify the lawful reasons for which a State party to an international armed conflict may detain its nationals or stateless persons within its territory of their liberty in relation to an armed conflict.[760] Consequently, they offer no interpretative guidance as

755 This is notwithstanding the finding in Chapter 3 that prisoners of war may very occasionally be nationals of the detaining power.

756 Article 78(1) Geneva Convention IV addresses internment or assigned residence in occupied territory, but is not further examined here because this book does not analyse situations of belligerent occupation.

757 On the customary status of Article 75 Additional Protocol I, see Jelena Pejic, "Procedural Principles and Safeguards for Internment/Administrative Detention in Armed Conflict and Other Situations of Violence", *International Review of the Red Cross* 87, no. 858 (2005): 375–391, 37; ICRC, "International Humanitarian Law", 16. Tentatively also Henckaerts and Doswald-Beck, *Customary International Humanitarian Law*, 346 (concerning the obligation to inform a detained or interned person promptly and in a language that he or she understands of the reasons for this measure). Chapter 3 also examined Article 75 Additional Protocol I and showed that it provides protection for the nationals of a party to an international armed conflict and for stateless persons.

758 Article 75(1) Additional Protocol I.

759 See Marco Sassòli, "Internment", in *Max Planck Encyclopedia of Public International Law*, edited by Rüdiger Wolfrum (Oxford: Oxford University Press, 2013), available at www.mpepil.com, accessed 10.03.2015, para. 14.

760 See Hans-Peter Gasser, "Protection of the Civilian Population", in *The Handbook of International Humanitarian Law*, edited by Dieter Fleck (Cambridge: Cambridge University Press, 2008), mn. 582, 319. The ICRC purports to close this normative gap in IHL with legally

regards persecution in the form of arbitrary deprivation of liberty by the country of origin during international armed conflict. Only international human rights law is therefore relevant for the interpretation of persecution in this respect.

Having examined the lawful bases for depriving individuals of their liberty in international armed conflict, the analysis now turns to non-international armed conflicts. Common Article 3 of the Geneva Conventions and Additional Protocol II do not address the legal bases for deprivation of liberty.[761] Customary IHL is also silent on this matter.[762] The ICRC proposes that "imperative reasons of security" ought to constitute the minimum legal standard informing any internment decision,[763] striking a practicable balance "between the need to protect personal liberty and the detaining authority's need to protect against activity that is seriously prejudicial to its security."[764] This standard could also inform the meaning of persecution in non-international armed conflict when assessing arbitrary deprivation of liberty. However, the notion of "imperative reasons of security" is rather vague and would be difficult to assess in the context of refugee status determination, particularly given the forward-looking nature of such determinations. Moreover, "imperative reasons of security" would seem to not constitute an acceptable ground for deprivation of liberty under the ICCPR because it lacks specificity.[765] Consequently, also in non-international armed conflict, international human rights law provides more instructive interpretative guidance as regards the legal bases for deprivation of liberty and for persecution. This illustrates the limits of drawing on IHL to interpret persecution.

Having considered the legal bases for deprivation of liberty in armed conflict, it is next pertinent to examine procedural safeguards whose violation

---

non-binding procedural principles and safeguards for internment or administrative detention in armed conflict and other situations of violence. See Pejic, "Procedural Principles".

761 See Knut Dörmann, "Detention in Non-International Armed Conflict", in *Non-International Armed Conflict in the Twenty-first Century*, edited by Kenneth Watkin and Andrew J. Norris (Newport: US Naval War College, 2012), 356.

762 The ICRC noted with regard to non-international armed conflict: "The relevant rules of customary law are by necessity formulated in general terms, and thus do not provide sufficient guidance to detaining authorities on how an adequate detention regime may be created and operated." ICRC, "Strengthening Legal Protection for Victims of Armed Conflict. Draft Resolution and Report prepared for the 31st International Conference of the Red Cross and Red Crescent", 31IC/11/5.1.1 (2011), available at www.icrc.org/eng/assets/files/red-cross-crescent-movement/31st-international-conference/31-int-conference-strengthening-legal-protection-11-5-1-1-en.pdf, accessed 10.03.2015, 11.

763 See Dörmann, "Detention", 356. Pejic elaborates that internment "is a measure of control aimed at dealing with persons who pose a real threat to State security, currently or in the future, in situations of armed conflict ...; it is not a measure to replace criminal proceedings." Pejic, "Procedural Principles", 381.

764 Dörmann, "Detention", 356.

765 See Els Debuf, "Expert Meeting on Procedural Safeguards for Security Detention in Non-International Armed Conflict. Chatham House and International Committee of the Red Cross, 22–23 September 2008", *International Review of the Red Cross* 91, no. 876 (2009): 859–881, 864.

would render deprivation of liberty arbitrary. International human rights law provides for such procedural guarantees to ensure that detention of a State's own nationals or stateless persons in international armed conflict and detention in non-international armed conflict is not arbitrary. Customary IHL does not set out such procedural safeguards, and international humanitarian treaty law is largely silent on this matter too.[766] In its commentary on the customary rule prohibiting arbitrary deprivation of liberty, the ICRC noted that international human rights law establishes the following four procedural safeguards which inform the prohibition of arbitrary deprivation of liberty under customary IHL:

> "(i) an obligation to inform a person who is arrested of the reasons for arrest, (ii) an obligation to bring a person arrested on a criminal charge promptly before a judge, and (iii) an obligation to provide a person deprived of liberty with an opportunity to challenge the lawfulness of detention (so-called writ of *habeas corpus*)."[767]

Although the obligations in paragraphs (i) and (ii) are derogable, human rights bodies have established that they may not be completely foregone.[768] The ICRC emphasised the complementary nature of international human rights law *vis-à-vis* IHL in this respect, stating:

> "The rights of persons interned for security reasons in armed conflict - whether international or non-international - may be said to fall into the category of rights that, in the ICJ's wording, are 'matters' of both branches of law [i.e. IHL and international human rights law]."[769]

For the meaning of persecution, this means that international human rights law provides the more instructive interpretative guidance as to whether deprivation of liberty in armed conflict is arbitrary because it fails to comply with basic procedural safeguards and therefore constitutes persecution. Customary IHL is ill-suited to providing interpretative guidance on this matter for the notion of persecution.

---

766 With the exception of the aforementioned Article 75(3) Additional Protocol I. The ICRC identified the lack of procedural safeguards concerning deprivation of liberty as an area where IHL "falls short of the needs observed in the field." See ICRC, "Strengthening Legal Protection", 7.

767 Henckaerts and Doswald-Beck, *Customary International Humanitarian Law*, 349. See also Article 9(2)–(4) ICCPR and, with respect to the obligation to inform the person concerned of the reasons for the deprivation of liberty, see also Article 75(3) Additional Protocol I. Krieger discusses the approach to human rights law of the ICRC Study on Customary IHL: Heike Krieger, "A Conflict of Norms: The Relationship between Humanitarian Law and Human Rights Law in the ICRC Customary Law Study", *Journal of Conflict & Security Law* 11 (2006): 265–291.

768 See Henckaerts and Doswald-Beck, *Customary International Humanitarian Law*, 349. Whether and, if so, to what extent these procedural guarantees may be suspended in armed conflict remains controversial. See Sassòli, "Internment", paras. 22 and 38.

769 Pejic, "Procedural Principles", 377–378.

To conclude, although international human rights law and customary IHL overlap in prohibiting arbitrary deprivation of liberty in armed conflict, thereby reinforcing the prohibition of arbitrary deprivation of liberty, the paucity of customary IHL concerning the permissible legal bases for deprivation of liberty and the required procedural safeguards limits the usefulness of this branch of international law for the interpretation of persecution. International human rights law provides more instructive guidance, in particular as regards children.

5.4. RESULT

International human rights law, customary IHL and international criminal law can complement one another in the interpretation of persecution, with the overall guiding principle lying in the Refugee Convention's humanitarian object and purpose which requires a dynamic and inclusive interpretation. The complementary relationship between these branches of international law as regards the meaning and scope of persecution plays out in different ways regarding different forms of persecution.

Concerning various forms of persecution in armed conflict, international human rights law, customary IHL, and international criminal law mutually reinforce one another, thereby strengthening the position that these types of harm amount to persecution. These forms of persecution include, but are not limited to, torture, enforced disappearance, and rape and other forms of sexual violence. Customary IHL and international criminal law can rectify erroneous understandings by some refugee law decision-makers about the lawfulness of rape and other forms of sexual violence in armed conflict. Regarding some forms of persecution, customary IHL and international criminal law provide interpretative clarity. For example, what constitutes children's active participation in hostilities has been clarified by the ICC. Customary IHL and international criminal law also state unambiguously that the use of chemical weapons in any armed conflict and the use of forced displacement of the civilian population as a method of warfare in non-international armed conflict constitutes persecution.

As regards some types of harm, international human rights law grants a higher standard of protection than customary IHL and ought therefore to prevail in the interpretation of persecution. For instance, the definition of a child under the Optional Protocol to the CRC is broader than under IHL, and in contrast to customary IHL international human rights law does not allow for "scorched earth policies" in international armed conflict on a State's own territory. With respect to certain forms of harm that may amount to persecution, such as arbitrary deprivation of liberty, gaps in the normative framework of IHL limit the extent to which this branch of international law can give meaning to persecution. In such contexts, international human rights law is the main point of reference. In some cases, such as the use of lethal force, violations of customary IHL *a fortiori* constitute persecution, while the absence of such breaches must not be equated with a lack of persecution.

6. CONCLUSION

This chapter explored the notion of "well-founded fear of being persecuted" in armed conflict, focussing on the question of what insights can be gained from customary IHL and international criminal law. In determining whether a refugee claimant has a well-founded fear of being persecuted, the burden of proof ought to be shared between the claimant and the decision-maker, with the standard of proof being that of "reasonable possibility". An objective approach to assessing a refugee claimant's risk of persecution which takes into account the general circumstances in the country of origin, including patterns of IHL violations during armed conflict, is to be preferred over a subjective-objective approach. There is no requirement that the refugee claimant be singled out for persecution or be more at risk of persecution than others.

A two-tiered interpretation of persecution in light of international human rights law according to which persecution entails one or several human rights violation(s) that surpass an intensity threshold is widely accepted. There are various criteria for assessing such intensity, including qualitative and quantitative factors taking into consideration the individual specificities as well as cumulative effects of several events. If the country of origin is experiencing an armed conflict, the refugee definition's wording and object and purpose do not justify narrowing the material scope of persecution to non-derogable human rights. This understanding is also supported by some State practice and UNHCR. The category of potential victims of persecution is broad, encompassing members of armed forces and armed groups as well as civilians, irrespective of whether they have been directly participating in hostilities. Potential persecutors comprise agents of the country of origin and non-State actors such as armed groups which are parties to a non-international armed conflict.

In order to amount to persecution, violations of customary IHL must be of sufficient intensity and, if the persecutor is the country of origin in an international armed conflict, they must confer protection obligations on this country as a party to the conflict *vis-à-vis* its nationals or stateless persons on its territory. War crimes, in particular the criterion established by the ICTY that the breached rule of IHL must protect important values with the breach entailing grave consequences for the victim, constitute instructive yardsticks for assessing whether the intensity threshold is surpassed. Although the principle of *lex specialis derogat legi generali* is generally considered to govern the relationship of international human rights law and IHL, it is ill-suited for the interpretation of persecution in light of international human rights law and IHL. Rather, a complementary approach to the interpretation of persecution in contexts of armed conflict that draws on international human rights law, customary IHL and international criminal law can be developed based on the general rule of treaty interpretation. In the event of varying protection standards under international human rights law on the one hand and customary IHL on the other, the higher standard is to be used in interpreting persecution pursuant to the Refugee Convention's humanitarian object and purpose. Customary IHL and international criminal law cannot and ought not replace international human rights law as the branch of international law providing guidance on the meaning and scope of persecution; rather, they complement international human rights law in this respect. The absence of violations of customary IHL cannot be equated with a lack of persecution because the circumstances of the case must be considered.

International human rights law, customary IHL and international criminal law can supplement one another in the interpretation of persecution. Regarding some forms of persecution in armed conflict, customary IHL and international criminal law provide detailed and comprehensive guidance that reinforces the human rights-based interpretation (e.g. concerning rape and other forms of sexual violence). Customary IHL and international criminal law also offer armed conflict-specific interpretative guidance on unlawful means and methods of warfare that amount to persecution (such as forced displacement, starvation or the use of chemical weapons). However, concerning other types of persecution, customary IHL and international criminal law fall short of the necessary interpretative clarity (e.g. arbitrary deprivation of liberty). In such cases, international human rights law provides more instructive guidance. While violations of customary IHL *a fortiori* amount to persecution regarding the use of lethal force, the converse is not necessarily true. If lethal force complies with customary IHL, further case-by-case analysis is necessary to determine whether it amounts to persecution. The interpretative guidance that can be obtained from customary IHL and international criminal law is not comprehensive because for some forms of persecution in armed conflict international human rights law provides for a higher or more specific standard of protection, as the example of forced recruitment of children into the armed forces or armed groups illustrates.

CHAPTER 6
LACK OF PROTECTION IN THE COUNTRY OF ORIGIN

1. INTRODUCTION

International refugee protection is surrogate protection in cases in which the country of origin fails to provide protection from persecution for one of the Refugee Convention grounds.[770] Thus, international refugee protection is premised on the absence of national protection. This chapter examines such lack of protection in countries of origin which are experiencing an armed conflict.

2. LACK OF PROTECTION

2.1. TEXTUAL AND CONCEPTUAL BASES

The refugee definition in Article 1A(2) Refugee Convention states that a refugee claimant must be outside the country of his or her nationality or, in the case of stateless persons, the country of habitual residence and must be unable or, owing to such well-founded fear, unwilling to avail him- or herself of the protection of that country. Thus, a refugee claimant must lack the protection of the country of origin, either because such protection is unavailable or because of an unwillingness to avail him- or herself of such protection. The requirement of lack of protection in the country of origin is linked to the well-founded fear of persecution clause because the existence of a well-founded fear of persecution

---

770 See Reinhard Marx, "The Criteria of Applying the 'Internal Flight Alternative' Test in National Refugee Status Determination Procedures", *International Journal of Refugee Law* 14 (2002): 179–218, 184; James C. Hathaway, "International Refugee Law: The Michigan Guidelines on the Internal Protection Alternative", *Michigan Journal of International Law* 21 (1999–2000): 131–133, 131; First Colloquium on Challenges in International Refugee Law. Convened by the Program in Refugee and Asylum Law of the University of Michigan Law School, "The Michigan Guidelines on the Internal Protection Alternative", *Michigan Journal of International Law* 21 (1999–2000): 133–140, para. 1; Zimmermann and Mahler, "Article 1A, para. 2", mn. 607, 446.

presupposes the lack of national protection from persecution.[771] The context of Article 1A(2) Refugee Convention further emphasises the requirement of lack of protection by the country of origin: Article 1C addresses cessation of refugee status in cases where protection by the country of origin becomes available again,[772] thereby showing that refugee protection presupposes the lack of national protection. Moreover, the Refugee Convention's object and purpose of providing for international protection imply that States parties to the Refugee Convention are only obliged to provide refugee protection if adequate national protection is lacking.[773] Hence, the textual and conceptual bases of the requirement that a refugee must lack the protection of the country of origin can be found in the refugee definition's wording, context and object and purpose.

It is important to distinguish between refugee protection claims which concern persecution at the hands of the country of origin and claims that relate to persecution by non-State actors. In cases in which persecution emanates from the State, the State's unwillingness to provide protection is presumed.[774] If persecution is feared or experienced at the hands of non-State actors, the individual is required to at least attempt to obtain protection from the country of origin, except if it is evident that protection will not be granted or will not be effective.[775] However, there is no basis in the Refugee Convention in general or the refugee definition in particular to deny refugee protection on the grounds that the country of origin is a failed State.[776] Rather,

---

771 See UNHCR, *Handbook*, 98; Zimmermann and Mahler, "Article 1A, para. 2", mn. 595, 444; Wouters, *International Legal Standards for the Protection from Refoulement*, 99.

772 Article 1C(1), (3) and (5) Refugee Convention reads: "This Convention shall cease to apply to any person falling under the terms of section A if: (1) He has voluntarily re-availed himself of the protection of the country of his nationality; or … (3) He has acquired a new nationality, and enjoys the protection of the country of his new nationality; or … (5) He can no longer, because the circumstances in connexion with which he has been recognized as a refugee have ceased to exist, continue to refuse to avail himself of the protection of the country of his nationality."

773 See *Attorney-General of Canada v. Ward* [1993] 2 SCR 689 (Canada); *Conseil d'Etat* (Council of State), *Esshak Danka, Decision No. 42.074* (27 May1983) (France). See also Hathaway, *Law of Refugee Status*, 124; Zimmermann and Mahler, "Article 1A, para. 2", mn. 598, 445; Wouters, *International Legal Standards for the Protection from Refoulement*, 99; UNHCR, *Handbook*, para. 97. For Grahl-Madsen, refugee protection is premised on the normal bond of loyalty, trust and protection between a country and its citizen being ruptured. See Grahl-Madsen, *Status of Refugees*, 79.

774 See UNHCR, *Guidelines on International Protection No. 4*, para. 13; Löhr, *Die kinderspezifische Auslegung*, 120. This assumption of State protection can be rebutted. For example, in areas of Somalia not affected by armed conflict, effective protection by governing authorities may be available. See UNHCR, "UNHCR Eligibility Guidelines for Assessing the International Protection Needs of Asylum-Seekers from Somalia (2010)", 31; Wouters, *International Legal Standards for the Protection from Refoulement*, 100.

775 See Wouters, *International Legal Standards for the Protection from Refoulement*, 101.

776 See Zimmermann and Mahler, "Article 1A, para. 2", mn. 307–310, 368–369; Goodwin-Gill and McAdam, *The Refugee in International Law*, 100; Tara Magner, "Does a Failed State Country of Origin Result in a Failure of International Protection? A Review of Policies

in such cases the inability of the country of origin to provide protection is self-evident.

As previously noted, the refugee definition entails the requirement that a refugee claim must be unable or unwilling to avail themselves to the protection of the country of origin. The refugee claimant's inability to avail him- or herself of the country of origin's protection means that circumstances in the country of origin are such that it is impossible for the individual to obtain protection.[777] In this respect, the existence of an armed conflict in the country of origin is pertinent because it may mean that seeking protection from the country of origin is unfeasible.[778] Due to an armed conflict, a refugee claimant may be *unable* to avail him- or herself of the protection of the country of origin. The only permissible reason why a refugee claimant may be *unwilling* to avail him- or herself of the country of origin's protection is his or her well-founded fear of persecution.[779]

Though historically understood as external or diplomatic protection by the country of origin,[780] protection has come to be conceived as human rights protection within the country of origin.[781] This understanding corresponds to a human rights-based interpretation of persecution.[782] As a party to an armed conflict, the country of origin not only incurs protection obligations under international human rights law, but also under customary IHL.[783] As previously shown, persecution also encompasses serious violations of customary IHL rules.[784] Consequently, due to a well-founded fear of human rights violations and/or violations of customary IHL rules, a refugee claimant can be unwilling to seek the protection of the country of origin.

Toward Asylum-Seekers in Leading Asylum Nations", *Georgetown Immigration Law Journal* 15 (2001): 703–726.

777 See Wouters, *International Legal Standards for the Protection from Refoulement*, 99.

778 See Wouters, *International Legal Standards for the Protection from Refoulement*, 99–100.

779 See Zimmermann and Mahler, "Article 1A, para. 2", mn. 599, 445; UNHCR, *Handbook*, para. 100; Wouters, *International Legal Standards for the Protection from Refoulement*, 100.

780 See Weis, "Legal Aspects", 480. Fortin still favours this understanding of protection: Antonio Fortin, "The Meaning of 'Protection' in the Refugee Definition", *International Journal of Refugee Law* 12, no. 4 (2001): 548–576. However, understanding protection as diplomatic protection in today's world is not only contrary to the refugee definition's wording, but also to its object and purpose of human rights protection. See Zimmermann and Mahler, "Article 1A, para. 2", mn. 596, 444.

781 See James C. Hathaway and Michelle Foster, "Internal Protection/Relocation/Flight Alternative as an Aspect of Refugee Status Determination", in *Refugee Protection in International Law. UNHCR's Global Consultations on International Protection*, edited by Erika Feller, Volker Türk and Frances Nicholson (Cambridge: Cambridge University Press, 2003), 373–380. On refugee protection as human rights protection, see also Chapter 3.

782 The human rights-based interpretation of persecution is examined in detail in Chapter 5.

783 See Chapter 3.

784 The interpretation of persecution in light of customary IHL is analysed in Chapter 5.

2.2. PROVIDERS OF PROTECTION

The country of origin is the archetypical provider of protection, as the wording of the refugee definition in Article 1A(2) Refugee Convention confirms by referring to "the protection of *that* country".[785] The country of origin is bound under international human rights law to protect the human rights of its nationals and stateless persons on its territory.[786] As noted above, as party to an international or non-international armed conflict, it also incurs certain obligations *vis-à-vis* its nationals and stateless persons under customary IHL.[787] It is pertinent to examine whether other entities, namely non-State actors such as clans, tribes or armed groups,[788] international organisations including, for example UN peacekeeping forces,[789] and third States such as multi-national forces[790] or occupying powers can also be providers of protection within the country of origin.

Article 1A(2) Refugee Convention refers to the "protection of that country", namely the country of origin, thereby strongly suggesting that the refugee definition is premised on a State-centred understanding of protection.[791] This understanding would mean that only the country of origin can be a provider

785 Emphasis added. See, e.g., *Adan v. SSHD* [1999] 1 AC 293, 304 per Lord Lloyd of Berwick (UK); *Horvath v. SSHD* [2000] 3 WLR 379, 496–500 per Lord Hope of Craighead (UK); *Gardi v. SSHD* [2002] EWCA Civ 759 (UK); *Canada (Attorney General) v. Ward* [1993] 2 SCR 689 (Canada); *Svecs v. MIMA* [1999] FCA 1507, per Hely J. at 26 (Australia). See also UNHCR, "Interpreting Article 1 of the 1951 Convention relating to the Status of Refugees", paras. 14–15; UNHCR, *Handbook*, para. 166.

786 See Chapter 3.

787 See Chapter 3.

788 Article 7(1) Qualification Directive states: "Protection can be provided by: (a) the State; or (b) parties or organizations, including international organizations, controlling the State or a substantial part of the territory of the State." Some States accept non-State actors as providers of protection. See, e.g., *Bundesverwaltungsgericht* (Federal Administrative Court, Germany), *10 C 33.07*, 7 February 2008, para. 27. For further jurisprudence, see Maria O'Sullivan, "Acting the Part: Can Non-State Entities Provide Protection Under International Refugee Law?", *International Journal of Refugee Law* 24, no. 1 (2012): 85–110, 101.

789 See the aforementioned Article 7(1) Qualification Directive. UNHCR documented French, German, Greek and Swedish practice revealing the preparedness of decision-makers to consider international organizations as protectors. See UNHCR, "Asylum in the European Union. A Study of the Implementation of the Qualification Directive" (2007), available at www.refworld.org/docid/473050632.html, accessed 10.03.2015, 48. See also *Canaj and Vallaj v. SSHD* [2001] EWCA Civ. 782 (UK). Further: Penelope Mathew, James C. Hathaway and Michelle Foster, "The Role of State Protection in Refugee Analysis. Discussion Paper No. 2, Advanced Refugee Law Workshop, International Association of Refugee Law Judges, Auckland, New Zealand, October 2002", *International Journal of Refugee Law* 15 (2003): 444–460, 457.

790 See *Bundesverwaltungsgericht* (Federal Administrative Court), 10 C 34.06, 20 March 2007, para. 27 (Germany); European Court of Justice, Joined Cases C-175/08, C-176/08, C-178/08 and C-179/08, *Salahadin Abdulla, Hasan, Adem and Rashi, Jama v. Bundesrepublik Deutschland*, 2 March 2010, European Court Reports 2010, I-01493 (in the context of cessation of refugee protection). As noted by O'Sullivan, "Acting the Part", 95–97.

791 See Löhr, *Die kinderspezifische Auslegung*, 115.

of protection. The context of Article 1A(2) Refugee Convention supports this view. The Refugee Convention's cessation clause in Article 1C Refugee Convention expressly refers to the protection of the country of nationality or, regarding stateless persons, the country of habitual residence. Moreover, it must be recalled that the Refugee Convention's object and purpose is to ensure human rights protection. Consequently, entities which are not directly bound by international human rights law or which otherwise lack accountability under international human rights law cannot be providers of protection for the purposes of the refugee definition.[792] Even though the UN is bound by international human rights law,[793] it lacks accountability for human rights violations due to the unavailability of judicial remedies.[794] Multi-national

[792] See Mathew, Hathaway and Foster, "The Role of State Protection in Refugee Analysis", 456; O'Sullivan, "Acting the Part", 102. Accountability can be defined as "an overarching term, which covers both the substantive obligations of the relevant actors and their responsibility for breaches of these obligations. The applicable substantive rules and the rules on responsibility operate as a coherent body of law." Zegveld, *Accountability of Armed Opposition Groups*, 5. UNHCR opines that "refugee status should not be denied on the basis of an assumption that the threatened individual could be protected by parties or organizations, including international organizations, if that assumption cannot be challenged or assailed. It would, in UNHCR's view, be inappropriate to equate national protection provided by States with the exercise of a certain administrative authority and control over territory by international organizations on a transitional or temporary basis. Under international law, international organizations do not have the attributes of a State. In practice, this generally has meant that their ability to enforce the rule of law is limited." UNHCR, "Annotated Comments on the EC Council Directive", 18. Also: Löhr, *Die kinderspezifische Auslegung*, 115.

[793] International organisations are not signatories to international human rights treaties. See Mathew, Hathaway and Foster, "The Role of State Protection in Refugee Analysis". Nonetheless, the UN is bound to comply with human rights law due to the references to human rights in Articles 1(3), 55 and 56 UN Charter and because it is a subject of international law with respect to customary international human rights law. See Annette Simon, *UN-Schutzzonen – Ein Schutzinstrument für verfolgte Personen? Eine Analyse anhand der internationalen Schutzzonen im Irak, in Ruanda und Bosnien-Herzegowina mit besonderem Blick auf die schweren Menschenrechtsverletzungen in der safe area Srebrenica* (Berlin et al.: Springer, 2005), 110. More generally: Jochen Frowein, "United Nations (UN)", in *Max Planck Encyclopedia of Public International Law*, edited by Rüdiger Wolfrum (Oxford: Oxford University Press, 2009), available at www.mpepil.com, accessed 10.03.2015, para. 43. Exploring the issue in detail: Frédéric Mégret and Florian Hoffmann, "The UN as a Human Rights Violator? Some Reflections on the United Nations Changing Human Rights Responsibilities", *Human Rights Quarterly* 25, no. 2 (2003): 314–342 who at 317–318 point out ways in which the UN can possibly be bound by human rights standards. See also Clapham, *Human Rights Obligations*, 109–137.

[794] Although international organisations provide the best possible support and protection, their efforts are curtailed by restricted resources and legal authority. As a result, UNHCR argues, they cannot control territory or provide protection in a way similar to a State. See Madeleine Garlick, "UNHCR and the Implementation of Council Directive 2004/83/EC on Minimum Standards for the Qualification and Status of Third Country Nations or Stateless Persons as Refugees or as Persons who Otherwise Need International Protection and the Content of the Protection Granted (The EC "Qualification Directive")", in *The Qualification Directive: Central Themes, Problem Issues, and implementation in Selected Member States*, edited by Karin Zwaan (Nijmegen: Wolf Legal Publishers, 2007), 65. On the accountability of the UN, see also Frowein, "United Nations (UN)", para. 43. More comprehensively: Rainer Hofmann,

forces and occupying powers may incur certain human rights obligations in their extra-territorial actions.[795] They also have obligations under customary IHL. Non-State actors are not directly bound by international human rights law.[796] As parties to a non-international armed conflict, however, they do incur obligations under customary IHL. This might mean that these actors can be providers of protection for the purposes of the refugee definition. Nevertheless, the objections to accepting them as providers of protection which flow from the refugee definition's wording and context remain. Furthermore, from a conceptual viewpoint, protection by entities other than the country of origin cannot repair or replace the severed bond between a refugee and his or her country of origin.[797] In addition, protection obligations under customary IHL are limited in the sense that they do not provide for the protection from armed conflict as such, or even from violence during armed conflict as such, and in the sense that they are temporarily limited to the duration of the armed conflict.[798] For these reasons, entities other than the country of origin cannot be providers of protection for the purpose of the refugee definition, be it in times of peace or in armed conflict.[799]

2.3. EFFECTIVENESS OF PROTECTION

Protection in the country of origin must be effective in order to be meaningful. This does not mean that each and every risk of harm must be eliminated, a requirement that would be unrealistic. Rather, an overall system of protection must exist that reduces the risk of harm.[800] Whether protection is effective depends on the State's *de jure* and *de facto* ability and willingness

---

"Die Rechtskontrolle von Organen der Staatengemeinschaft", in *Die Rechtskontrolle von Organen der Staatengemeinschaft. Vielfalt der Gerichte – Einheit des Prozessrechts?*, edited by Rainer Hofmann, et al. (Heidelberg: C.F. Müller Verlag, 2007).

795 On the extra-territorial applicability of human rights law, see generally Karen da Costa, *The Extraterritorial Application of Selected Human Rights Treaties* (Leiden: Martinus Nijhoff, 2012); Marco Milanović, *Extraterritorial Application of Human Rights Treaties: Law, Principles, and Policy* (Oxford: Oxford University Press, 2011); Michal Gondek, *The Reach of Human Rights in a Globalizing World: Extraterritorial Application of Human Rights Treaties* (Antwerp: Intersentia, 2009).

796 See McCorquodale, "Non-State Actors", 97; Thomas Buergenthal, *International Human Rights in a Nutshell* (St. Paul: West, 1988), 1; Henry J. Steiner, Philip Alston and Ryan Goodman, *International Human Rights in Context. Law, Politics, Morals* (Oxford: Oxford University Press, 2008), 1385–1386. See also Chapter 3.

797 O'Sullivan makes this argument with respect to protection by non-State actors, but it can be considered as applying to other entities as well. See O'Sullivan, "Acting the Part", 102.

798 This is explained further in Chapter 3.

799 Zimmermann and Mahler, however, accept that other entities can be providers of protection. See Zimmermann and Mahler, "Article 1A, para. 2", mn. 663–670, 459–460.

800 See Zimmermann and Mahler, "Article 1A, para. 2", mn. 303, 367; Mathew, Hathaway, and Foster, "The Role of State Protection in Refugee Analysis", 448.

to provide protection.[801] In the literature and State practice,[802] two tests have been devised for establishing whether there is a lack of protection in the country of origin, namely the "due diligence test" and the "no well-founded fear test".

The due diligence test requires refugee status to be denied where the applicant's country of origin has done everything it can be reasonably expected to do to protect the applicant from persecution.[803] This test focusses on the reasonableness of the home country's efforts in an objective way, rather than on a fact-specific basis. It does not investigate whether the fear of persecution has actually ceased to be well founded.[804] In contrast, the no well-founded fear test focusses on the reality of the risk of being persecuted for a Refugee Convention ground and assesses whether or not the protection afforded by the country of origin actually brings the risk of being persecuted below the standard of well-founded fear.[805] The due diligence test has its origins in the law of State responsibility.[806] Yet the interpretation of the refugee definition is structurally different from an assessment of the country of origin's responsibility under general international law. Moreover, the due diligence test cannot be reconciled with a teleological interpretation of the refugee definition, in particular the *effet utile* principle, as it could result in the return of refugee claimants to countries where they effectively do not enjoy the protection from persecution.[807] This tests risks undermining the prohibition of *refoulement* in Article 33 Refugee Convention whose wording solely refers to the objective dangers, not the measures taken to mitigate them.[808] UNHCR supports the no well-founded fear

[801] See Wouters, *International Legal Standards for the Protection from Refoulement*, 100.

[802] For an overview and analysis of State practice in this respect, see Mathew, Hathaway, and Foster, "The Role of State Protection in Refugee Analysis", 451–453; Anker, "Refugee Law", 147. On the implementation of the test under Article 7(2) and (3) Qualification Directive, see UNHCR, "Asylum in the European Union", 50–52.

[803] See generally *Horvath v. Secretary of State for the Home Department* [2000] UKHL 37 (UK). Article 7 Qualification Directive and Article 7 Recast Qualification Directive closely resemble the due diligence test, as noted by Jonah Eaton, "The Internal Protection Alternative Under European Union Law: Examining the Recast Qualification Directive", *International Journal of Refugee Law* 24, no. 4 (2012): 765–792, 780. Article 7(2) Recast Qualification Directive, however, adds that protection against persecution must be effective and non-temporary. The due diligence test is also used in Australian and in part in Canadian jurisprudence: See Löhr, *Die kinderspezifische Auslegung*, 117.

[804] See Mathew, Hathaway, and Foster, "The Role of State Protection in Refugee Analysis", 449–453.

[805] See RSAA, *Refugee Appeal No. 71427/99*, 16 August 2000 (New Zealand); *Bobrik v. MCI* (F.C.T.D., no. IMM-5519-93) [1994] FTR 13 (Canada); Mathew, Hathaway, and Foster, "The Role of State Protection in Refugee Analysis", 449–450.

[806] See generally Timo Koivurova, "Due Diligence", in *Max Planck Encyclopedia of Public International Law*, edited by Rüdiger Wolfrum (Oxford: Oxford University Press, 2007), available at www.mpepil.com, accessed 10.03.2015.

[807] See Mathew, Hathaway, and Foster, "The Role of State Protection in Refugee Analysis", 448; Löhr, *Die kinderspezifische Auslegung*, 118.

[808] See Löhr, *Die kinderspezifische Auslegung*, 119.

of persecution test, noting that the effectiveness, accessibility and adequacy of available protection must be assessed with a view to determining whether the fear of persecution continues to be well-founded irrespective of the measures taken to prevent persecution or serious harm.[809]

These considerations suggest that the no well-founded fear test is to be preferred. If the country of origin is experiencing an armed conflict, however, an additional issue arises: noting that an armed conflict in the country of origin "may entitle the State, subject to certain safeguards, to give less by way of protection",[810] Storey contends:

> "[I]international law does not require States to succeed in protecting its citizens from the violence arising from such armed conflicts, only to take all reasonable steps to minimise the violence and seek to bring it to an end: the principle of proportionality. International law prevents the targeting of civilians but does not proscribe the collateral killings of civilians as such."[811]

Storey's argument is a variation of the due diligence approach specifically designed for situations of armed conflict. He argues that as a party to an armed conflict, the country of origin is merely required to take all reasonable steps to minimise violence, to limit its attacks to military objectives and to refrain from attacking when civilian casualties would be disproportionate to the concrete and direct military advantage anticipated. It is correct that under IHL, attacks may only be directed against military objectives and are prohibited if they violate the principle of proportionality. However, this approach reduces the scope of the country of origin's obligations to provide protection in situations of armed conflict to respect for IHL, specifically the principles of distinction and proportionality, in the conduct of hostilities. It fails to consider that the focus of the analysis of lack of protection for the purposes of the refugee definition is on protection from persecution and that persecution may take many forms in armed conflict. Storey's approach does not take into account that for the purposes of the refugee definition, the country of origin must provide protection from persecution by non-State actors. As previously noted, there is nothing in the wording, context or object and purpose of Article 1A(2) Refugee Convention that would justify a narrower scope of the refugee definition in armed conflict as opposed to peacetime situations.[812]

For these reasons, the no well-founded fear test for assessing the effectiveness of protection by the country of origin is to be preferred not only in times of peace, but also in cases in which there is an armed conflict in the country of origin. An armed conflict in the country of origin may well adversely affect the

---

809 See UNHCR, "Annotated Comments on the EC Council Directive", 18.
810 Storey, "Armed Conflict in Asylum Law", 12.
811 Storey, "Armed Conflict in Asylum Law", 12. See also Storey, "Persecution", 487–488.
812 On the interpretation of the refugee definition, see Chapter 4.

effectiveness of the protection provided by the country of origin,[813] for instance because the country of origin lacks control over part of its territory or because it fails to provide protection from IHL violations by armed opposition groups. For example, UNHCR noted in 2007 concerning Iraq that "[p]ervasive violence, institutional weaknesses, and a general lack of rule of law seriously impede the ability of Iraqi authorities to provide protection to its citizens."[814] UNHCR Eligibility Guidelines show that a considerable number of civilian casualties,[815] internal displacement,[816] and lack of compliance with IHL[817] are factors indicating that protection by the country of origin during armed conflict is not effective.

2.4. RESULT

The refugee definition requires a lack of protection from persecution by the country of origin, that is from violations of human rights or customary IHL rules that amount to persecution. Only the country of origin can provide such protection. Third parties such as non-State actors, multi-national forces or international organisations are not potential providers of protection for the purposes of the refugee definition. It is not sufficient that the country of origin carries out due diligence in attempting to remove the risk of persecution. Rather, protection from persecution must be provided effectively. An armed conflict can adversely affect the effectiveness of such protection.

---

813 See UNHCR, *Handbook*, para. 98; UNHCR, *Guidelines on International Protection No. 3: Cessation of Refugee Status under Article 1C(5) and (6) of the 1951 Convention relating to the Status of Refugees (the "Ceased Circumstances" Clauses)*, UN Doc. HRC/GIP/03/03 (23 February 2003), para. 15; UNHCR, *Guidelines on International Protection No. 2*, para. 20; UNHCR, "Eligibility Guidelines for Asylum-Seekers from Afghanistan 2013", 30.

814 UNHCR, "Eligibility Guidelines for Iraqi Asylum-Seekers 2007", 35. Similarly: UNHCR, "UNHCR Eligibility Guidelines for Assessing the International Protection Needs of Asylum-Seekers from Somalia (2010)", 31.

815 See UNHCR, "Eligibility Guidelines for Asylum-Seekers from Afghanistan 2009", 8; UNHCR, "Eligibility Guidelines for Asylum-Seekers from Afghanistan 2010", 3; UNHCR, "International Protection Considerations regarding Colombian Asylum-seekers and Refugees 2002", para. 23; UNHCR, "Eligibility Guidelines for Asylum-Seekers from Colombia 2010", 1 and 3; UNHCR, "Eligibility Guidelines for Iraqi Asylum-Seekers 2007", 23.

816 See UNHCR, "Eligibility Guidelines for Asylum-Seekers from Afghanistan 2010", 4; UNHCR, "Eligibility Guidelines for Iraqi Asylum-Seekers 2007", 25.

817 See UNHCR, "Eligibility Guidelines for Asylum-Seekers from Afghanistan 2009", 7; UNHCR, "International Protection Considerations regarding Colombian Asylum-seekers and Refugees 2002", para. 17 (also referring to human rights violations); UNHCR, "Eligibility Guidelines for Asylum-Seekers from Colombia 2010", 3; UNHCR, "Eligibility Guidelines for Iraqi Asylum-Seekers 2007", 35 (noting that non-State actors and increasingly also the Iraqi armed forces violate IHL).

3. INTERNAL PROTECTION ALTERNATIVE

A refugee claimant need not show that he or she has a well-founded fear of being persecuted in the entire country of origin.[818] However, cases where the well-founded fear of being persecuted is confined to a specific part of the country, for instance because an armed conflict is geographically limited,[819] may give rise to the question of whether the refugee claimant has an internal protection alternative (IPA) within the country of origin.[820] This is normally only required where the persecutor is a non-State agent, as it is presumed that in State persecution cases the State has control throughout the territory.[821]

3.1. TEXTUAL AND CONCEPTUAL BASES

There is no explicit basis for the IPA analysis in the refugee definition.[822] While it is generally accepted that the IPA is based on the principle that international refugee protection is surrogate protection where the country of origin fails to provide protection from persecution for one of the Refugee Convention grounds,[823] no clear consensus has emerged regarding the textual basis of the IPA in Article 1A(2) Refugee Convention.

---

818 See Goodwin-Gill and McAdam, *The Refugee in International Law*, 123; UNHCR, *Handbook*, para. 91; UNHCR, *Guidelines on International Protection No. 4*, paras. 4 and 6. On the IPA, see also Holzer, "The 1951 Refugee Convention", 39–41.

819 See UNHCR, *Handbook*, para. 91.

820 The term IPA is used here rather than the alternative notions "internal flight alternative" or "internal relocation alternative" because it more adequately reflects the Refugee Convention's object and purpose of providing protection. See Hathaway and Foster, "Internal Protection Alternative", 381–389.

821 This presumption can be rebutted if it is clearly established that the power of the State authority which is the persecutor is geographically confined. See Zimmermann and Mahler, "Article 1A, para. 2", mn. 633, 451. Further: UNHCR, *Guidelines on International Protection No. 4*, para. 13; Expert Roundtable Organized by the United Nations High Commissioner for Refugees and the International Institute of Humanitarian Law, "Summary Conclusions: Internal Protection / Relocation / Flight Alternative", in *Refugee Protection in International Law. UNHCR's Global Consultations on International Protection*, edited by Erika Feller, Volker Türk, and Frances Nicholson (Cambridge: Cambridge University Press, 2001), 419, para. 2; Ninette Kelley, "Internal Flight / Relocation / Protection Alternative: Is It Reasonable?", *International Journal of Refugee Law* 14 (2002): 4–43, 16–17; Marx, "The Criteria of Applying the 'Internal Flight Alternative' Test", 189–191; Löhr, *Die kinderspezifische Auslegung*, 120.

822 Article 8 of the Qualification Directive and Article 8 of the Recast Qualification Directive, however, codify the IPA requirement.

823 See Marx, "The Criteria of Applying the 'Internal Flight Alternative' Test", 184; Hathaway, "International Refugee Law: The Michigan Guidelines", 131; First Colloquium on Challenges in International Refugee Law. Convened by the Program in Refugee and Asylum Law of the University of Michigan Law School, "The Michigan Guidelines on the Internal Protection Alternative", para. 1; Zimmermann and Mahler, "Article 1A, para. 2", mn. 607, 446.

There are two potential bases for the IPA analysis in the refugee definition: the well-founded fear clause, i.e. the requirement that a refugee must have a well-founded fear of being persecuted, or the protection clause, that is the requirement that the refugee must be unable or, owing to his or her well-founded fear of persecution, unwilling to avail him- or herself of the protection of the country of origin. Basing the IPA on the refugee definition's well-founded fear clause would mean requiring the refugee claimant to show that he or she has a country-wide well-founded fear of persecution for a Refugee Convention ground. This would introduce an additional requirement into the text of the refugee definition according to which the well-founded fear of being persecuted must be experienced throughout the country of origin.[824] Not only is such an interpretation not justified by the wording of Article 1A(2),[825] it also entails the risk of pre-empting an in-depth assessment of whether the refugee claimant has a well-founded fear of persecution by prompting decision-makers to instead examine the existence of an IPA.[826] The wording of the refugee definition's protection clause provides a more suitable basis for an IPA analysis. A refugee claimant must be unable to avail him- or herself of the protection of the country of origin. The existence of an IPA may mean that he or she is in fact able to obtain such protection within the country of origin.[827]

3.2. CRITERIA FOR THE EXISTENCE OF AN INTERNAL PROTECTION ALTERNATIVE

A proposed area of relocation within the country of origin must cumulatively fulfil three criteria. First, the area of relocation must be accessible. Second, protection in the narrow sense, i.e. protection from persecution, must be available in the area of relocation. Third, there must be protection in the broader sense, i.e. protection beyond persecution, in the suggested area of relocation. The refugee claimant's personal situation, such as their age or gender, and the general situation in the country of origin must be taken into account.[828] Regarding the

---

824 See Hathaway and Foster, "Internal Protection Alternative", 365–371. Eaton notes that reading an IPA requirement into the well-founded fear clause risks that the IPA becomes a threshold requirement, resulting in a higher burden of proof for the refugee claimant. See Eaton, "The Internal Protection Alternative", 769–770. Similarly: Marx, "The Criteria of Applying the 'Internal Flight Alternative' Test", 183.

825 The refugee definition does not require a "well-founded fear of being persecuted in the entire country of origin". See Hathaway and Foster, "Internal Protection Alternative", 369.

826 See Hathaway and Foster, "Internal Protection Alternative", 370–371.

827 See First Colloquium on Challenges in International Refugee Law. Convened by the Program in Refugee and Asylum Law of the University of Michigan Law School, "The Michigan Guidelines on the Internal Protection Alternative", paras. 11–13; Hathaway and Foster, "Internal Protection Alternative", 370–372.

828 See Marx, "The Criteria of Applying the 'Internal Flight Alternative' Test", 187. Article 8(2) Qualification Directive states: "In examining whether a part of the country of origin is in

possible providers of protection, for the same reasons as identified above, only the country of origin can provide protection. Since the IPA analysis is premised on the existence of a well-founded fear of persecution, the burden of proof to establish that an IPA exists lies on the receiving country.[829]

3.2.1. Accessibility

The proposed area of relocation must be practically, safely and legally accessible in order to be relevant.[830] Accessibility must be determined from the State undertaking the refugee status determination.[831] Practical accessibility means that the refugee applicant must in fact have access to the location. The area must be genuinely accessible,[832] not merely theoretically or abstractly.[833] Safe accessibility involves an assessment of the physical risks *en route* to the IPA. Security threats arising from an armed conflict "such as mine fields, factional fighting, shifting war fronts, banditry and other forms of harassment or exploitation"[834] render an IPA inaccessible. For example, concerning Afghanistan, the UK Border Agency noted: "In many areas insurgent violence, banditry, land mines, and improvised explosive devices make travel extremely dangerous, especially at night."[835] Regarding Sri Lanka, the Canadian Federal Court of Appeal held:

accordance with paragraph 1, Member States shall at the time of taking the decision on the application have regard to the general circumstances prevailing in that part of the country and to the personal circumstances of the applicant." See also Article 8(2) Recast Qualification Directive.

829 See First Colloquium on Challenges in International Refugee Law. Convened by the Program in Refugee and Asylum Law of the University of Michigan Law School, "The Michigan Guidelines on the Internal Protection Alternative", para. 14.

830 See Expert Roundtable Organized by the United Nations High Commissioner for Refugees and the International Institute of Humanitarian Law, "Summary Conclusions: Internal Protection", 419, para. 3; Hathaway and Foster, "Internal Protection Alternative", 390–392; Marx, "The Criteria of Applying the 'Internal Flight Alternative' Test", 185–187; Kelley, "Internal Flight / Relocation / Protection Alternative: Is It Reasonable?", 14; UNHCR, *Guidelines on International Protection No. 4*, paras. 10–12.

831 See Kelley, "Internal Flight / Relocation / Protection Alternative: Is It Reasonable?", 14–15.

832 See Marx, "The Criteria of Applying the 'Internal Flight Alternative' Test", 185–186 who refers to German and Austrian jurisprudence on this matter.

833 See Hathaway and Foster, "Internal Protection Alternative", 390; Hugo Storey, "The Internal Flight Alternative Test: The Jurisprudence Re-examined", *International Journal of Refugee Law* 10, no. 3 (1998): 499–532, 523; Kelley, "Internal Flight / Relocation / Protection Alternative: Is It Reasonable?", 14.

834 UNHCR, *Guidelines on International Protection No. 4*, paras. 10–12. Similarly: Zimmermann and Mahler, "Article 1A, para. 2", mn. 630, 450; Storey, "The Internal Flight Alternative Test", 523; Marx, "The Criteria of Applying the 'Internal Flight Alternative' Test ", 185–186.

835 UK Border Agency, *Considering the Protection (Asylum) Claim and Assessing Credibility*, para. 2.12. See also UNHCR, "Eligibility Guidelines for Asylum-Seekers from Afghanistan 2013", 73.

> "The claimant cannot be required to encounter great physical danger or to undergo undue hardship in travelling there or in staying there. For example, claimants should not be required to cross battle lines where fighting is going on at great risk to their lives in order to reach a place of safety."[836]

An armed conflict in the country of origin may thus render a relocation area inaccessible. Importantly, this may be the case even if the armed conflict has ended, for example because of destroyed infrastructure or explosive remnants of war. Moreover, an IPA must be legally accessible. This is the case if the refugee claimant has the legal right to travel there, to enter, and to remain.[837] Legal accessibility must be determined pursuant to *inter alia* visa and transit requirements, and the availability of travel documents.[838]

3.2.2. Protection in the Narrow Sense

For the proposed location to be considered relevant, the refugee claimant must be able to find protection in the narrow sense, namely protection from persecution.[839] This includes an assessment of whether the fear of being persecuted that existed in the original place of residence or abode continues in the proposed area of relocation, whether there is a risk of being forced to leave the IPA and to return to this original place of residence and whether any new well-founded fear of persecution for a Refugee Convention ground may arise in the IPA.[840] In this respect, the prevalence of human rights and IHL violations in the proposed area of relocation may indicate a risk of persecution, rendering the area irrelevant as an IPA. Protection in the narrow sense includes, but is not limited to, protection from experiencing or being subjected to war crimes.[841]

An armed conflict may prevent a country of origin from providing protection or may render such protection ineffective.[842] The intensity of a conflict and the

---

836 *Thirunavukkarasu v. Canada (Minister of Employment and Immigration)* [1994] 1 FC 589 (C.A.) (Canada).

837 See UNHCR, *Guidelines on International Protection No. 4*, para. 12.

838 See Marx, "The Criteria of Applying the 'Internal Flight Alternative' Test", 186–187.

839 See Zimmermann and Mahler, "Article 1A, para. 2", mn. 637–644, 452–453; First Colloquium on Challenges in International Refugee Law. Convened by the Program in Refugee and Asylum Law of the University of Michigan Law School, "The Michigan Guidelines on the Internal Protection Alternative", paras. 15–19, requiring that the IPA be an "antidote" to the primary risk of persecution and that no additional risk of persecution or of harm equivalent to persecution exist.

840 See Zimmermann and Mahler, "Article 1A, para. 2", mn. 637–644, 452–453; Hathaway and Foster, "Internal Protection Alternative", 392. UNHCR Executive Committee, *Conclusion No. 87 (L)* (1999), para. j, cautioning that an application of the IPA requirement must not violate the principle *of non-refoulement*.

841 See Jaquemet, "Cross-Fertilization", 669.

842 See UNHCR, *Handbook*, para. 98; UNHCR, "Eligibility Guidelines for Iraqi Asylum-Seekers 2007", 9; UNHCR, "UNHCR Eligibility Guidelines for Assessing the International Protection Needs of Asylum-Seekers from Somalia (2010)", 31.

volume of threats to citizens may indicate a State's inability to provide protection to the claimant.[843] In several States,[844] territorial control is considered a crucial factor in assessing the ability of the country of origin to provide protection. While territorial control is a prerequisite for effective State protection,[845] during armed conflict State protection may be ineffective despite the State's territorial control over an area.[846] Territorial control is thus a necessary but not sufficient factor in determining the availability of State protection in a proposed area of relocation. Canadian jurisprudence, for example, presumes State protection except in situations of complete breakdown of the State apparatus.[847] Armed conflict may lead to such a breakdown. Nevertheless, this understanding may be too narrow. Even if the State can no longer provide meaningful protection, its armed forces may still function. The State apparatus could hence be understood as not having broken down completely. It would be more appropriate to assume a lack of State protection if the armed conflict exhibits very intense, frequent and geographically widespread violence.[848]

In ascertaining whether a proposed area of relocation offers protection in the narrow sense, the reach of non-State agents of persecution is a relevant consideration.[849] A finding by the Immigration and Refugee Board of Canada (IRB) illustrates this point. The IRB held that even though an armed group was not physically present throughout all of Colombia, it could locate targeted individuals anywhere in the country.[850] Thus, that a non-State persecutor does not

843 See *X (Re) 2004 CanLII 56786* (Canada).

844 See *Bundesverwaltungsgericht* (Federal Administrative Court), BVerwG 10 C 43.07 - VGH 13 a B 05.30833 (24 June 2008), 25 (Germany); *Lara Deheza v. Canada (Citizenship and Immigration)* 2010 FC 521, para. 36 (Canada); X (Re) 2004 CanLII 56786 (IRB) (Canada); X (Re) 2009 CanLII 90052 (IRB) (Canada); X (Re) 2003 CanLII 55250 (IRB) (Canada). The US Asylum Office notes: "A government in the midst of a civil war, or one that is unable to exercise its authority over portions of the country (e.g. Colombia, Indonesia, Somalia) will be unable to control the persecutor in areas of the country where its influence does not extend." US Citizenship and Immigration Services, "Refugee, Asylum and International Operations Directorate, Officer Training: Definition of Persecution and Eligibility based on Past Persecution" (2012), available at www.uscis.gov/portal/site/uscis/menuitem.5af9bb95919f35e66f614176543f6d1a/?vgnextoid=17412765b826f310VgnVCM100000082ca60aRCRD&vgnextchannel=e88514c0cee47210VgnVCM100000082ca60aRCRD, accessed 10.03.2015. Highlighted by Anker, *Law of Asylum in the United States*, para. 2:14, footnote 23.

845 See UNHCR, "Eligibility Guidelines for Asylum-Seekers from Sri Lanka 2009", 9.

846 See UNHCR, "Eligibility Guidelines for Asylum-Seekers from Sri Lanka 2009", 9.

847 See *Canada (Attorney General) v. Ward* [1993] 2 SCR 689, 724–725 (Canada); see also *Balasingam v. Canada (Minister for Employment and Immigration)* 2004 FC 1465, paras. 30 and 33 (Canada).

848 See also Holzer, "The 1951 Refugee Convention", 40.

849 See *AM & AM v. Secretary of State for the Home Department* (armed conflict: risk categories) Somalia CG [2008] UKAIT 00091, para. 190 (UK).

850 See *X (Re)* 2004 CanLII 56786 (IRB) (Canada). See also *Rodriguez Gutierrez v. Canada* (Minister of Citizenship and Immigration) 2010 FC 1010, paras. 22 and 26 (Canada). Similarly: UK Border Agency, *Considering the Protection (Asylum) Claim and Assessing Credibility*, para. 2.13.

have territorial control over a portion of the country does not necessarily mean that the refugee claimant would be safe there from harm by this persecutor.[851]

3.2.3. Protection in the Broader Sense

Lastly, a refugee claimant must be able to find protection in the broader sense, i.e. protection beyond persecution,[852] in the proposed area of relocation.[853] One approach to assessing such protection examines whether a minimum standard of protection, i.e. the rights set out in Articles 2 to 33 of the Refugee Convention, would be secured in the proposed area of relocation.[854] However, this approach is structurally problematic because the rights entailed in the Refugee Convention differ according to the level of allegiance between the beneficiary and the host State, with most of them additionally being contingent on the host State's treatment of other groups such as other aliens.[855] It is difficult to use the rights set out in the Refugee Convention to assess protection within the country or origin which is concerned with the rights granted and protected by a State *vis-à-vis* its nationals.

An alternative approach is therefore more suitable, examining whether relocation to a different place within the country of origin is a reasonable alternative to international refugee protection.[856] This approach requires that the refugee claimant's basic civil, political and socio-economic rights must be protected at the proposed site,[857] including his or her safety and security as

---

851 See also Vanessa Holzer, "The 1951 Refugee Convention", 40.

852 See Zimmermann and Mahler, "Article 1A, para. 2", mn. 645, 453. See also First Colloquium on Challenges in International Refugee Law. Convened by the Program in Refugee and Asylum Law of the University of Michigan Law School, "The Michigan Guidelines on the Internal Protection Alternative", paras. 20–23 requiring "the existence of a minimalist commitment to affirmative protection".

853 See Expert Roundtable Organized by the United Nations High Commissioner for Refugees and the International Institute of Humanitarian Law, "Summary Conclusions: Internal Protection", 419, para. 5; Marx, "The Criteria of Applying the 'Internal Flight Alternative' Test", 200; Kelley, "Internal Flight / Relocation / Protection Alternative: Is It Reasonable?", 23; UNHCR, *Guidelines on International Protection No.* 4, paras. 18–21 and 27–30; UNHCR, "Asylum in the European Union", 58 and 60; UNHCR, "Interpreting Article 1 of the 1951 Convention relating to the Status of Refugees", para. 13.

854 See First Colloquium on Challenges in International Refugee Law. Convened by the Program in Refugee and Asylum Law of the University of Michigan Law School, "The Michigan Guidelines on the Internal Protection Alternative", para. 22; Hathaway and Foster, "Internal Protection Alternative", 405–411; Zimmermann and Mahler, "Article 1A, para. 2", mn. 651, 455.

855 For a detailed analysis of the Refugee Convention's structure, see Hathaway, *The Rights of Refugees*, 154–277.

856 As used in, e.g., *Thirunavukkarasu v. Canada* (Minister of Employment and Immigration) [1994] 1 FC 589 (Canada). See also Zimmermann and Mahler, "Article 1A, para. 2", mn. 647–648, 454–455; Kelley, "Internal Flight / Relocation / Protection Alternative: Is It Reasonable?", 24; UNHCR, *Guidelines on International Protection No. 4*, paras. 22–30.

857 See Marx, "The Criteria of Applying the 'Internal Flight Alternative' Test", 200; Kelley, "Internal Flight / Relocation / Protection Alternative: Is It Reasonable?"; Expert Roundtable

well as basic livelihood.[858] If a refugee claimant can be reasonably expected to relocate to an alternative location within the country of origin, he or she is able to avail him- or herself of the protection of the country of origin. Protection in the alternative location must be durable and stable.[859]

An armed conflict in the country of origin typically affects all of these factors, possibly rendering protection in the proposed area of relocation ineffective.[860] Indeed, UNHCR considers that an IPA "is not available in areas affected by active conflict".[861] A proposed area of relocation would need to be reasonable in all the circumstances, taking into account the volatility and fluidity of the armed conflict.[862] The lack of adequate security is a primary reason why, for example, France's National Court of Asylum (*Cour Nationale du Droit d'Asile*) has often rejected the existence of an IPA.[863] The existence of an armed conflict in the country of origin should not mean that the viability of a proposed IPA is solely assessed as regards safety risks. Other factors must also be considered such as "the destruction of socio-economic infrastructure",[864] the "inadequacy of essential services"[865] and "continued economic and security restrictions ... which prevent civilians from accessing locations used for agriculture, fishing and cattle grazing and other livelihood activities."[866]

3.3. RESULT

Based on the refugee definition's protection clause, the IPA analysis examines whether an area within the country of origin offers protection that obviates the need for international refugee protection. An IPA must fulfil three cumulative

Organized by the United Nations High Commissioner for Refugees and the International Institute of Humanitarian Law, "Summary Conclusions: Internal Protection", 419, para. 5; Storey, "The Internal Flight Alternative Test", 529–530; Löhr, *Die kinderspezifische Auslegung*, 129–131.

858 See UNHCR, *Guidelines on International Protection No. 4*, paras. 29–39; Marx, "The Criteria of Applying the 'Internal Flight Alternative' Test", 207; Storey, "The Internal Flight Alternative Test", 530.

859 See Kelley, "Internal Flight / Relocation / Protection Alternative: Is It Reasonable?", 22.

860 See UNHCR, *Handbook*, para. 98; UNHCR, "Eligibility Guidelines for Iraqi Asylum-Seekers 2007", 9.

861 UNHCR, "Eligibility Guidelines for Asylum-Seekers from Afghanistan 2013", 74.

862 See UNHCR, "Eligibility Guidelines for Asylum-Seekers from Afghanistan 2013", 8.

863 See, e.g., *Cour nationale du droit d'asile* (National Asylum Court, CNDA), decision no 574495, *Mlle N.*, 2 April 2008; *Commission des recours des réfugiés*, No. 585846, *Mlle S.*, 15 March 2007; *Commission des recours des réfugiés*, SR, No. 573815, *T.*, 16 February 2007 (all France). See also Title 8 Code of Federal Regulations §208 31(3)(b) (US).

864 *X (Re)* 2004 CanLII 56786 (IRB) (Canada).

865 UNHCR, "Eligibility Guidelines for Assessing the International Protection Needs of Asylum-Seekers from Sri Lanka" (2010), available at www.unhcr.org/refworld/docid/4c31a5b82.html, accessed 10.03.2015, 10.

866 UNHCR; "Eligibility Guidelines for Asylum-Seekers from Sri Lanka 2010", 10.

criteria: First, it must be practically, safely and legally accessible. Second, it must provide protection in the narrow sense, that is protection from persecution. Protection in the narrow sense includes protection from being subjected to or experiencing IHL violations and war crimes. Third, the proposed area of relocation must provide protection in the broader sense, namely protection of basic civil and political rights and a basic livelihood. An armed conflict in the country of origin is relevant for all three criteria.

4. CONCLUSION

International refugee protection provides surrogate protection if protection by the country of origin is lacking. This is normally the case if persecution emanates from the State. In the case of non-State persecution, the State must be unable or unwilling to provide protection from persecution. The only legitimate provider of protection in the context of the refugee definition is the country of origin. An armed conflict may adversely affect the ability of the country of origin to provide effective protection from persecution. Such protection is not to be understood more narrowly in times of armed conflict (e.g. by limiting protection to compliance with IHL) than in times of peace. Rather than assessing the effectiveness of protection by using a due diligence test, the no well-founded fear test is to be used which examines whether *de facto* protection from persecution exists. If the well-founded fear of persecution is geographically confined, for example because an armed conflict is limited to a certain region of the country of origin, the existence of an IPA may be examined. The proposed area of relocation must not only be practically, safely and legally accessible, but must also provide protection in the narrow sense – protection from persecution – and protection in the broader sense – protection of basic civil and political rights and basic livelihood. An armed conflict can undermine or nullify all three criteria which the IPA must cumulatively fulfil.

Customary IHL plays a limited role in assessing whether protection in the country of origin during armed conflict is absent. An armed conflict in the country of origin does not result in a lower standard of protection being required than in times of peace. It does not follow from the international legal framework for the protection of the individual in armed conflict that in the context of the refugee definition, protection in armed conflict in the country of origin can be equated to protection from IHL violations and war crimes. Conversely, however, a lack of compliance with IHL or the commission of war crimes by any party to the conflict strongly indicate that protection by the country of origin is ineffective. IHL violations in a proposed area of relocation negate the availability of an IPA.

CHAPTER 7
THE NEXUS TO A REFUGEE CONVENTION GROUND IN ARMED CONFLICT

1. INTRODUCTION

The refugee definition in Article 1A(2) Refugee Convention states that a refugee must have a well-founded fear of being persecuted *for reasons of* race, religion, nationality, membership of a particular social group or political opinion and that he or she must be unable or, owing to such fear, unwilling to avail him- or herself of the country of origin's protection. Armed conflicts are often rooted in political, ethnic or religious differences with different groups facing heightened risks of harm,[867] thus suggesting the applicability of the Refugee Convention grounds. In contexts of armed conflict in which a number of people are typically at risk of harm for various reasons, the nexus requirement (or causal link) is one of the main issues that courts grapple with.[868] This chapter explores the interpretation and application of the refugee definition's nexus requirement with respect to refugee protection claims of individuals forced to flee from their country of origin due to an armed conflict or who fear return to a country that is experiencing armed conflict.

---

867 See UNHCR, "Eligibility Guidelines for Asylum-Seekers from Sri Lanka 2009", 31–32 (noting that individuals may be at risk on various grounds because the armed conflict is rooted in ethnic and political differences). Farrell and Schmitt emphasise that in most cases, conflicts are driven by a mix of factors, and not only ethnic differences. See Farrell and Schmitt, "The Causes, Character and Conduct of Armed Conflict, and the Effects of on Civilian Populations, 1990–2010", 2. Markard provides a detailed analysis of the characteristics of armed conflict: Markard, *Kriegsflüchtlinge*, 57–111. See also the present book's Introduction.

868 Sternberg notes that "establishing persecutory motive … during armed conflict constitutes one of the most formidable challenges of refugee protection." Sternberg, *The Grounds of Refugee Protection*, 83. Similarly: Markard, *Kriegsflüchtlinge*, 272. On the nexus requirement, see also Holzer, "The 1951 Refugee Convention", 22–38.

2. THE NEXUS REQUIREMENT IN INTERNATIONAL REFUGEE LAW

The wording of the refugee definition's nexus requirement poses the question of precisely what kind of causal relationship and which causal standard should be used. It is also pertinent to examine whether or not the refugee claimant's predicament ought to be compared to that of others in the country of origin and what inferences can be drawn from the characteristics of an armed conflict.

2.1. THE CAUSAL RELATIONSHIP

The refugee definition states that the well-founded fear of being persecuted must be for reasons of a Refugee Convention ground. While the notion "for reasons of" denotes a causal relationship, the wording of Article 1A(2) Refugee Convention offers few clues as to the precise nature of this causal relationship.[869] The use of passive voice ("being persecuted") indicates that the focus is on the causal link between the refugee claimant's predicament and one or more Refugee Convention grounds, inquiring why the individual is in the predicament of fearing persecution.[870] The Refugee Convention's object and purpose is to provide refugee protection, rather than to attribute responsibility for persecution. Therefore, the determination of the causal link must be premised on an objective assessment of the reasons underpinning the well-founded fear of persecution, not on the persecutor's subjective motivation.[871] Evidence of the persecutor's motivation being connected to a Refugee Convention ground may suffice to fulfil the nexus requirement, but lack of such intent does not mean that the nexus requirement is necessarily not fulfilled.[872] A persecutor's intent may be to harm the refugee claimant because of his or her beliefs or activities – and hence for reasons of a Refugee Convention ground – irrespective or regardless of whether the refugee claimant in fact holds such beliefs or carries out such activities.[873] Where persecution emanates from non-State actors, such persecution, the failure of the country of origin to provide protection from

869 Article 9(3) Recast Qualification Directive specifies that there must be a connection between the grounds and the acts of persecution or the absence of protection from such acts.

870 See Second Colloquium on Challenges to International Refugee Law, "The Michigan Guidelines on Nexus to a Convention Ground", *Michigan Journal of International Law* 23 (2001–2002): 211–221, para. 6; UNHCR, "Guidance Note on Refugee Claims Relating to Sexual Orientation", para. 28.

871 See Zimmermann and Mahler, "Article 1A, para. 2", mn. 331, 373–374.

872 See Goodwin-Gill and McAdam, *The Refugee in International Law*, 101; Markard, *Kriegsflüchtlinge*, 283.

873 See Goodwin-Gill and McAdam, *The Refugee in International Law*, 102; James C. Hathaway and Michelle Foster, "The Causal Connection ("Nexus") to a Convention Ground", *International Journal of Refugee Law* 15, no. 3 (2003): 461–476, para. 8.

persecution, or both, can be causally linked to a Refugee Convention ground.[874] Thus, the nexus requirement encapsulates a causal relationship between one or more Refuge Convention grounds and the refugee claimant's predicament, with such predicament encompassing the persecutor's intention, the country of origin's failure to provide protection and the persecutory acts.[875]

2.2. THE STANDARD OF CAUSATION

In contexts of armed conflict, there are typically multiple causes for a refugee claimant's predicament.[876] Some causes, such as parties to the conflict seeking economic gains, are unrelated to a Refugee Convention ground.[877] Refugee status decision-makers across and within jurisdictions have used different causal standards,[878] ranging from the Refugee Convention ground as the sole reason,[879] over the requirement that but for a Refugee Convention ground there would be no well-founded fear of persecution[880] and considering that a Refugee Convention ground must be the central reason of the refugee claimant's predicament,[881] to inferences from anti-discrimination law.[882] The wording of the refugee definition, which does not include "sole reason", and the Refugee Convention's humanitarian object and purpose mean that a Refugee Convention ground must not be required

874 See Second Colloquium on Challenges to International Refugee Law, "The Michigan Guidelines on Nexus", para. 9; Zimmermann and Mahler, "Article 1A, para. 2", mn. 332, 374; Hathaway and Foster, "The Causal Connection", paras. 16–17; UNHCR, *Guidelines on International Protection No. 2*, paras. 21–23; Markard, *Kriegsflüchtlinge*, 284–285.

875 In support of the predicament-based understanding of the nexus requirement: UNHCR, "Guidance Note on Refugee Claims Relating to Sexual Orientation", para. 28; Wouters, *International Legal Standards for the Protection from Refoulement*, 80; Roundtable on International Protection of Persons Fleeing Armed Conflict and Other Situations of Violence, "Cape Town Summary Conclusions", para. 14; Markard, *Kriegsflüchtlinge*, 292.

876 See *Refugee Appeal No. 71462/99*, 27 September 1999, para 30 (New Zealand); Michelle Foster, "Causation in Context: Interpreting the Nexus Clause in the Refugee Convention", *Michigan Journal of International Law* 23 (2001–2002): 296.

877 As noted by Markard, *Kriegsflüchtlinge*, 271.

878 Markard analyses the different causal standards in detail in a context of armed conflict and other situations of violence: Markard, *Kriegsflüchtlinge*, 272–303. Foster provides a comprehensive overview of the different causal standards used by refugee status decision-makers: Foster, "Causation in Context", 269–297. More generally, see Zimmermann and Mahler, "Article 1A, para. 2", mn. 326–329, 372–373; Hathaway and Foster, *The Law of Refugee Status*, 362–394.

879 See, e.g., CNDA, Decision no. 08008523, *M.S*, 2 November 2010, in which the CNDA denied refugee status to a Tamil asylum-seeker *inter alia* because Tamils are not targeted for persecution by the governmental authorities solely for the reason of their ethnic origin (France).

880 See, e.g., *Velsco v. Secretary of State for the Home Department*, 2000 LEXIS (C.A. April 2000), para. 7, quoted after Foster, "Causation in Context", 276.

881 Section 91R(1)(c) of Australia's Migration Act (1958) states that the Refugee Convention reason must be "the essential and significant reason … for the persecution".

882 Markard advocates an understanding of the causal relationship in light of anti-discrimination law. See Markard, *Kriegsflüchtlinge*, 294–303.

to be the sole or even essential, substantial or central reason for the refugee claimant's predicament.[883] The refugee claimant's predicament often has a variety of underlying causes and information about the individual's circumstances and the general situation in the country of origin may be incomplete, in particular in contexts of armed conflict.[884] The causal standard used for interpreting "for reasons of" must reflect these realities. Indeed, it is important to understand "for reasons of" in its unique context of refugee status determination. To recall, the notion of "well-founded fear" entails the relatively lenient risk element of "reasonable chance".[885] Demanding that the refugee claimant identify the precise role played by the Refugee Convention ground in his predicament would be tantamount to demanding a degree of certainty beyond that of "reasonable chance", thus creating inconsistencies in the interpretation of different elements of the refugee definition.[886] At the same time, the fact that the phrase "for reasons of" is included in the refugee definition means that the causal standard cannot be interpreted in such a broad way that the Refugee Convention ground is only so remotely linked to the refugee claimant's predicament as to be virtually irrelevant.[887]

In light of the above, a Refugee Convention ground need not be the sole or even the dominant cause of the refugee's predicament, but a contributing factor.[888] This understanding is supported by UNHCR.[889] Since the wording of the refugee definition does not distinguish between contexts of peace and armed conflict, this standard of causation is pertinent regardless of whether the country of origin is experiencing armed conflict.[890]

2.3. COMPARATIVE VERSUS NON-COMPARATIVE APPROACH

In the context of armed conflict, the nexus requirement has been conflated in some jurisprudence with the risk assessment which forms part of the notion of

883 See Foster, "Causation in Context", 335–337; Hathaway and Foster, "The Causal Connection", para. 10.

884 See Hathaway and Foster, "The Causal Connection", para. 24; Second Colloquium on Challenges to International Refugee Law, "The Michigan Guidelines on Nexus", para. 12.

885 On the well-founded fear of being persecuted, see Chapter 5.

886 See Foster, "Causation in Context", 337.

887 See Second Colloquium on Challenges to International Refugee Law, "The Michigan Guidelines on Nexus", para. 13; Foster, "Causation in Context", 339; Hathaway and Foster, "The Causal Connection", para. 18.

888 See Second Colloquium on Challenges to International Refugee Law, "The Michigan Guidelines on Nexus", para. 13; Hathaway and Foster, *The Law of Refugee Status*, 391.

889 See UNHCR, "Guidance Note on Refugee Claims relating to Victims of Organized Gangs" (2010), available at www.refworld.org/docid/4bb21fa02.html, accessed 10.03.2015, para. 29; UNHCR, "Guidance Note on Refugee Claims Relating to Sexual Orientation", para. 28.

890 Similarly: Second Colloquium on Challenges to International Refugee Law, "The Michigan Guidelines on Nexus", para. 17.

a "well-founded fear".[891] This conflation may result in comparing the refugee claimant's predicament to that of other individuals or groups in the country of origin. Such a comparative approach may give rise to additional requirements which must be fulfilled in cases relating to flight from armed conflict. The RSAA of New Zealand summarised this problem:

> "One must not confuse equality of *risk* of harm with the equality of *reason* for that harm. The well-foundedness element (ie, the risk issue) is a separate inquiry to that of the 'for reason of' element (ie, the nexus issue). So while it is convenient to speak in the short-hand of a differential risk in order to emphasize the specific focus of the 'for reason of' element, the very phrasing of the short-hand expression can, unfortunately, lead to a conflation of the risk element with the 'for reason of' or nexus requirement. If this happens, a person at real risk of serious harm for reason of his or her religion will be required to establish that he or she is *more* at risk of serious harm for reason of his or her religion than others who are equally at real risk of serious harm for reason of their religion. This is a requirement to establish a double-differential risk. Such approach, we believe, amounts to a misdirection in law."[892]

A similar conflation of the nexus requirement and the risk assessment can be observed, for example, in some US jurisprudence in which the nexus requirement in its entirety is equated with the necessity that the refugee claimant be "singled out" for a Refugee Convention ground. For example, in *Trujillo Jabba and others*, the Court of Appeal for the Eleventh Circuit found that the applicants "failed to show that, upon return to Colombia, they will be 'singled out' for persecution on account of a protected ground."[893] The phrase "singled out" continues to be used as a shorthand for the nexus requirement even though *Matter of H* already established in 1996 that the refugee claimant need not show individualised persecution, but merely a causal link to a refugee ground.[894] This standard has since been further developed in US regulations. A refugee claimant need not show that he or she would be singled out for persecution if a nexus to a Refugee Convention ground can be established through a pattern or practice in the country of origin that shows that a group to which the applicant belongs is being persecuted for a Refugee Convention ground.[895] Nevertheless, the US Court of Appeals for the Sixth Circuit compared the petitioner's predicament to that of other groups in Iraq, requiring that the petitioner "must establish that

891 "Well-founded fear of being persecuted" is discussed in Chapter 5.

892 *Refugee Appeal No. 71462* [1999] NZRSAA (27 September 1999), para. 52 (emphasis in original) (New Zealand).

893 *Jabba and others v. US Attorney General,* 195 F. Appx. 883, 7 (11th Cir. 2006) (US). See also *Sepulveda v. US Attorney General,* 401 F.3d 1226, 1231 (11th Cir. 2004) (US).

894 See *In re H-*, 21 I. & N. Dec. 337, Interim Decision 3276, 1996 WL 291910 (BIA) (US), 345–346. The "singled out" doctrine is also prevalent in Dutch jurisprudence. See Kazimierz Bem, "Defining the Refugee. American and Dutch Asylum Case-Law 1975–2005" (Vrije Universiteit Amsterdam, 2007), 170.

895 See 8 Code of Federal Regulations para. 208.13(b)(2)(iii) (US).

he is at particular risk as a Christian and that his predicament is appreciably different from the dangers faced by other non-Christian Iraqis".[896]

However, pursuant to the plain wording of the refugee definition, the fact that the refugee claimant's predicament is linked to his or her religion suffices to fulfil the nexus requirement. The predicament of other groups in the country of origin is irrelevant for the interpretation of the nexus requirement. Otherwise, refugee claimants from countries in which various groups are being persecuted would be disadvantaged. An understanding that there is no nexus to a Refugee Convention ground where a large number of people face persecution would go against the object and purpose of the Refugee Convention.[897] Moreover, the Refugee Convention grounds refer to characteristics or beliefs typically shared by groups of people.[898] As previously noted, the requirement of individually experienced persecution does not mean that a person has been or will be persecuted because of his or her individual activities.[899] Being part of a persecuted group should be individual enough.[900] For instance, membership of a persecuted group may suffice to fulfil the nexus requirement; this is often the case when there is a general pattern of persecution putting all members of the targeted group in danger.[901] As a result, the individual applicant does not have to show that he or she is individually targeted but only that he or she is a member of the targeted group. Being personally at risk of persecution should merely mean that the person is purposefully, rather than accidentally, at risk of being harmed.[902] There is no requirement that a refugee claimant must fear "a form or degree of harm above that suffered by other individuals with the same profile."[903] For a finding

896 *Elias v. Gonzales,* 212 F. Appx 441, 448 (6th Cir. 2007). See also *Hanona v. Gonzales,* 243 F. Appx 158, 163 (6th Cir. 2007); *Shasha v. Gonzales,* 227 F. Appx 436, 440 (6th Cir. 2007); *Aoraha v. Gonzales,* 209 F. Appx 473, 476 (6th Cir. 2006); *Toma v. Gonzales,* 179 F. Appx 320, 324 (6th Cir. 2006) (all US).

897 See Storey and Wallace, "War and Peace", 353.

898 See Kälin, "Refugees and Civil Wars", 438, footnote 6; Second Colloquium on Challenges to International Refugee Law, "The Michigan Guidelines on Nexus", para. 15.

899 The analysis of "well-founded fear" in Chapter 5 showed that the experiences of similarly situated persons can support a claim of being at risk of persecution.

900 See Wouters, *International Legal Standards for the Protection from Refoulement*, 87. See also Kälin, "Refugees and Civil Wars", 437–438, and Jaquemet, "Cross-Fertilization", 668.

901 See, e.g., Federal Constitutional Court (*Bundesverwaltungsgericht*), judgment of 21 April 2009 – 10 C 11.08. See also Higher Administrative Court (*Verwaltungsgerichtshof*) (VGH) Baden-Württemberg, RSpDienst 1991, Annex (*Beilage*) 8, B4. The German concept of "group persecution" (*Gruppenverfolgung*) is only exceptionally applied. See Hailbronner, *Asyl- und Ausländerrecht*, 331, 676. UNHCR emphasises that "entire communities may have a well-founded fear of persecution for one or more of the 1951 [Refugee] Convention grounds". UNHCR, "Eligibility Guidelines for Asylum-Seekers from Afghanistan 2013", 5.

902 See Kälin, "Refugees and Civil Wars", 437–438. There is no requirement to show that the refugee claimant is more at risk than other persons or groups in the country of origin. See Second Colloquium on Challenges to International Refugee Law, "The Michigan Guidelines on Nexus", para. 16.

903 UNHCR, "Eligibility Guidelines for Asylum-Seekers from Afghanistan 2013", 30.

of a nexus to a Refugee Convention ground, it is not necessary that the asylum-seeker be known to, and sought or targeted personally, by the persecutor(s).[904]

For these reasons, the refugee claimant's predicament must not be compared to the predicament of other groups in the country of origin for the purpose of establishing whether it is causally linked to a Refugee Convention ground.[905] Rather, the non-comparative approach to the nexus requirement, enunciated by the Canadian Federal Court of Appeal, is to be preferred:

> "[A] situation of civil war in a given country is not an obstacle to a claim provided the fear felt is not that felt indiscriminately by all citizens as a consequence of the civil war, but that felt by the applicant himself, by a group with which he is associated, or, even, by all citizens on account of a risk of persecution based on one of the reasons stated in the definition."[906]

2.4. CONTEXT OF ARMED CONFLICT

Since the armed conflict which is taking place in the country of origin can be part and parcel of a refugee claimant's predicament, it is important to consider the characteristics of the armed conflict when interpreting and applying the nexus requirement. Indeed, UNHCR emphasises that methods of warfare such as bombing, shelling, suicide attacks and using improvised explosive devices can be employed "against targets or in areas where civilians of specific ethnic or political profiles predominantly reside or gather, and for this reason, may be linked to a Refugee Convention ground."[907]

However, not all refugee status decision-makers take into account the implications of the causes and characteristics of the armed conflict in the country of origin for the refugee claimant's predicament. For instance, the Australian High Court rejected the proposition that a decision-maker would be required, in a case involving a situation of armed conflict, to determine whether the objective of a war is directed against persons because of a Refugee Convention ground.[908]

---

904 See UNHCR, "Eligibility Guidelines for Asylum-Seekers from Sri Lanka 2009", 31–32; UNHCR, "Eligibility Guidelines for Asylum-Seekers from Afghanistan 2013", 29.

905 Various scholars also support the non-comparative approach. See, e.g., Kagan and Johnson, "Persecution", 24; Sternberg, "The Plight of the Non-Combatant", 171; Roundtable on International Protection of Persons Fleeing Armed Conflict and Other Situations of Violence, "Cape Town Summary Conclusions", para. 19; Markard, *Kriegsflüchtlinge*, 137–139.

906 *Salibian v. Canada (Minister of Employment and Immigration)* 1990 3 FC 250, 259 (Canada).

907 UNHCR, "Eligibility Guidelines for Asylum-Seekers from Sri Lanka 2009", 32. See also UNHCR, "Eligibility Guidelines for Asylum-Seekers from Afghanistan 2013", 29; UNHCR Executive Committee, *Conclusion No. 85 (XLIX)* (1998), para. c; Second Colloquium on Challenges to International Refugee Law, "The Michigan Guidelines on Nexus", para. 17. Markard also emphasises this point: Markard, *Kriegsflüchtlinge*, 286.

908 See *Minister for Immigration and Multicultural Affairs v. Haji Ibrahim* [2000] HCA 55, para. 102 per McHugh J and para. 146 per Gummow J, Gleeson CJ and Hayne J agreeing (Australia).

Nevertheless, the Australian Refugee Review Tribunal did subsequently examine the nature of the conflict in a certain Afghan province, concluding that "the violence continues to manifest itself … on ethnic, political and or religious lines; and thus comes well within the grounds provided for by the Refugee Convention."[909] Indeed, there is jurisprudence which exhibits awareness of the different ways in which an armed conflict may reveal a nexus between the refugee claimant's predicament and a Refugee Convention ground. For example, the UK AIT held that "when … [the] attack [experienced by the appellant] is looked at in the context of violence in Ituri [DRC], the appellant was not simply a victim of civil war but the attack was motivated by the ethnic conflicts in that region."[910] In this case the character and causes of the conflict, identified by considering the broader context of a single attack, revealed a nexus between the claimant's predicament and a Refugee Convention ground.[911] In New Zealand, the RSAA stressed the various ways in which a nexus between the refugee claimant's predicament and a Refugee Convention ground may be manifest:

> "Cases from civil war countries raise complex factual issues and are highly context dependent, turning on the particular characteristics, attributes, and background of the claimant viewed against the underlying drivers of the civil war and the resulting human rights landscape."[912]

These "conflict-sensitive" approaches to the nexus requirement in contexts of armed conflict acknowledge that a refugee's predicament may be affected by the causes, character and impact of the armed conflict in the country of origin, making these elements relevant for the interpretation of the nexus requirement.

2.5. RESULT

The refugee definition's nexus requirement denotes a causal relationship between, on the one hand, the refugee claimant's predicament and, on the other hand, one or more Refugee Convention grounds. Though a Refugee Convention ground need not be the sole or even the dominant cause of the refugee's predicament, it must be a contributing factor. There is no basis in the refugee definition for requiring that the refugee claimant be singled out for persecution.

---

909 Refugee Review Tribunal, *Case no. 071329032* [2007] RRTA 82 (23 April 2007) (Australia).

910 *NA (Risk Categories – Hema) Democratic Republic of Congo v. Secretary of State for the Home Department* CG [2008] UKAIT 00071, para. 37 (UK). However, the House of Lords found that a nexus to a Refugee Convention ground in the context of clan-based warfare cannot be established by looking at the overall context of the conflict alone. See *Adan v. Secretary of State for the Home Department* [1998] 2 WLR 702, per Lord Lloyd of Berwick (UK).

911 A similar view is expressed by Immigration and Refugee Board of Canada, "Civilian Non-Combatants Fearing Persecution in Civil War Situations".

912 *Refugee Appeal No. 76551* [2010] NZRSAA 103 (21 September 2010), para. 62 (New Zealand).

The non-comparative approach to the nexus requirement which focusses on the causal link between a Refugee Convention ground and the refugee claimant's predicament without comparing it to the situation of others in the country of origin is preferable over a comparative approach. The causes, characteristics and impact of the armed conflict in the country of origin must be considered because they can reveal that the refugee claimant's predicament is causally linked to a Refugee Convention ground.

3. THE NEXUS REQUIREMENT IN LIGHT OF CUSTOMARY INTERNATIONAL HUMANITARIAN LAW AND INTERNATIONAL CRIMINAL LAW

This section explores whether and, if so, how customary IHL and international criminal law can assist in determining the existence of a causal link to a Refugee Convention ground in contexts of armed conflict.[913] The nexus requirement is not ordinarily interpreted in light of international human rights law, which is why this branch of international law is not considered here.

3.1. GENERAL OBSERVATIONS

There are no rules of customary IHL which directly correspond to the refugee definition's nexus requirement. One could even argue that IHL cannot inform the interpretation of the nexus requirement because IHL regulates *how* hostilities are fought, not *why*.[914] The strict separation of IHL from the *ius ad bellum* supports this proposition. However, pursuant to the principle of military necessity, IHL limits the use of violence *inter alia* by "restricting it to the amount necessary to achieve the aim of the conflict, which – independently of the causes fought for – can only be to weaken the military potential of the enemy."[915] Therefore, IHL violations could indicate that the refugee claimant's predicament is not causally linked to what is necessary to weaken the enemy's military potential but to other reasons, which in turn may encompass a Refugee Convention ground. Indeed, the US Board of Immigration Appeals considered the refugee definition's nexus requirement in light of IHL and held:

> "Although the Board has ruled that violations of the Geneva Conventions do not create an independent basis for asylum … there may be situations in which the

913 For a first enunciation of this approach, Holzer, "Persecution", 101–127.
914 On this role of IHL in regulating armed conflict see Lawand, "Internal Conflicts".
915 Sassòli, Bouvier, and Quintin, *How does Law Protect in War?*, 1 (footnotes in original omitted).

> severity of the violations of the Geneva Convention[s] may support an inference that the abuse is grounded in one of the protected grounds under asylum law."[916]

This finding suggests that inferences can be drawn from IHL as regards the refugee definition's nexus requirement. The Board of Immigration Appeals' focus on the severity of violations of the Geneva Conventions is in line with the finding in Chapter 5 that for a violation of IHL to amount to persecution, it must surpass the required severity threshold. It is plausible that drawing any inferences from minor or isolated violations of IHL as regards the victims' predicament would be difficult. However, limiting the analysis, as the US Board of Immigration Appeals does, to the Geneva Conventions is problematic because the Geneva Conventions only concern international armed conflicts with the exception of Common Article 3 and because they entail very few provisions on the conduct of hostilities. A broader approach that draws on customary IHL is therefore advisable.[917]

UNHCR indicates that patterns of IHL violations may reveal a nexus to a Refugee Convention ground:

> "[M]any conflicts take place against a political background which may involve serious violations of human rights, including the targeting of particular ethnic or religious groups. In a situation of internal armed conflict, the aims of the warring parties, including a government's need to protect itself, do not justify the use of indiscriminate shelling or bombardment, torture or arbitrary punishment against certain sectors of the population. Such acts may be considered, therefore, as giving rise to refugee status under the Refugee Convention."[918]

Hence, it is pertinent to examine what inferences can be drawn from customary IHL as regards the refugee definition's nexus requirement, focussing on key IHL principles, namely military necessity, distinction and proportionality.

3.2. THE PRINCIPLE OF MILITARY NECESSITY

This section clarifies the notion of military necessity and explores both rules of IHL which implicitly refer to military necessity and rules of IHL which include explicit references to military necessity.

---

916 *Matter of S-P-*, 21 I. & N. 486, 494 (BIA 1996) (US), footnote 3. Von Sternberg highlights this case and pioneered an interpretation of the nexus requirement in light of IHL, arguing: "Violations of international humanitarian law carried out against those who are perceived to be identified with another party to the conflict may … give rise to a finding that the victims of the violation have been persecuted within the meaning of the Refugee Convention and that the persecution relates to a Convention ground." Sternberg, *The Grounds of Refugee Protection*, 119.

917 On persecution in light of customary IHL, see Chapter 5.

918 UNHCR, "Information Note".

3.2.1. *The Notion of Military Necessity*

IHL balances military necessity with considerations of humanity.[919] The principle of military necessity reflects the long-standing rule that the right of the parties to a conflict to choose means and methods of warfare is not unlimited.[920] The 1863 Lieber Code, which represents the first written reference to military necessity in IHL, states:

> "Art. 14. Military necessity, as understood by modern civilized nations, consists in the necessity of those measures which are indispensable for securing the ends of the war, and which are lawful according to the modern law and usages of war.
>
> Art. 15. Military necessity admits of all direct destruction of life or limb of armed enemies, and of other persons whose destruction is incidentally unavoidable in the armed contests of the war ...
>
> Art. 16. Military necessity does not admit of cruelty – that is, the infliction of suffering for the sake of suffering or for revenge, nor of maiming or wounding except in fight, nor of torture to extort confessions."[921]

Pursuant to the Lieber Code, considerations of military necessity are confined by "the modern law and usages of war"; they do not permit violating IHL. Military necessity solely justifies measures necessary to achieve the object of the war. Another influential definition of military necessity can be found in the 1948 judgment of an American Military Tribunal in the *Hostages case*, in which the tribunal stated:

> "Military necessity permits a belligerent, subject to the laws of war, to apply any amount and kind of force to compel the complete submission of the enemy with the least possible expenditure of time, life, and money."[922]

---

919 See Bothe, Partsch, and Solf, *New Rules for Victims of Armed Conflicts*, 194–195. On protection under IHL, see Chapter 3. Since this book does not address the *ius ad bellum*, this section does not examine the principle of necessity under the *ius ad bellum*. The book's scope is set forth in the Introduction.

920 This principle is laid down in Article 22 Hague Regulations and Article 35(1) Additional Protocol I. See also Michael N. Schmitt, "Military Necessity and Humanity in International Humanitarian Law: Preserving the Delicate Balance", *Virginia Journal of International Law* 50 (2010): 795–838, 798; Melzer, *Targeted Killing*, 280.

921 Instructions for the Government of Armies of the United States in the Field, promulgated by General Orders No. 100 by President Lincoln, 24 April 1863, prepared by Francis Lieber, available at www.icrc.org/applic/ihl/ihl.nsf/Treaty.xsp?action=openDocument&documentId =A25AA5871A04919BC12563CD002D65C5, accessed 10.03.2015.

922 *Hostage Case* (*United States v. List*), Judgment, 19 February 1948, printed in: *Trials of War Criminals before the Nuernberg Military Tribunals*, Vol. 11 (Washington DC 1950: US Government Printing Office), 1230, at 1253. Dinstein considers this definition of military necessity to be authoritative. See Dinstein, "Military Necessity", para. 1. Apparently also Schmitt, "Military Necessity", 797.

This definition also emphasises that military necessity does not allow breaching IHL. Apparently drawing on these definitions of military necessity, recent State practice[923] and legal doctrine[924] consider the principle of military necessity as requiring that military action be necessary for achieving the legitimate military object and that it be carried out in a way that does not violate IHL.

In armed conflict, military necessity plays a permissive role because it allows the use of force within the confines of IHL. It also exerts a restrictive function because it states that only those military operations that are necessary for achieving the legitimate object of the armed conflict are permissible.[925] IHL does not provide belligerents with absolute or unfettered permission to achieve their political aims with military might.[926] Already in the period when the Lieber

[923] See, e.g., The Manual of the Law of Armed Conflict, Australian Defence Doctrine Publication 06.4, Australian Defence Headquarters, 11 May 2006, paras. 2.6 and 5.5–5.7 (Australia); *Règlement n° 98 sur le droit international humanitaire, Ministère de la Défense Nationale et des Anciens Combattants, Projet "Moralisation"* (Regulation No. 98 on International Humanitarian law, Ministry of National Defence and Veterans, Project "Increase Ethical Standards") (BDI/B-05), August 2007, Part I bis, 54 (Burundi); *Droit des conflits armés et droit international humanitaire, Manuel de l'instructeur en vigeur dans les forces de défense, Ministère de la Défense, Présidence de la République, Etat-major des Armées* (Law of Armed Conflict and International Humanitarian Law, Manual for Instructors in the Defence Forces, Ministry of Defence, Presidency of the Republic, Chief of Staff), 2006, 223, para. 223 and 224, para. 231 (Cameroon); *Manuel de droit des conflits armés, Ministère de la Défense, Direction des Affaires Juridiques, Sous-Direction du droit international humanitaire et du droit européen, Bureau du droit des conflits armés* (Manual on the Law of Armed Conflict, Ministry of Defence, Directorate for Legal Affairs, Sub-Directorate for International Humanitarian Law and European Law, Bureau on the Law of Armed Conflict), 2001, 86–87 (France); *Humanitair Oorlogsrecht: Handleiding, Voorschift No. 27-412, Koninklijke Landmacht, Militair Juridische Dienst* (Humanitarian Law Manual, Regulations No. 27-412, Royal Netherlands Army, Military Legal Services), 2005, paras. 0223*bis*, 0225–0226, 0233 and 33 (Netherlands); *Manual de Derecho Internacional Humanitario y Derechos Humanos para las Fuerzas Armadas, Resolución Ministerial No. 049-2010/DE/VPD* (Manual on International Humanitarian Law and Human Rights for the Armed Forces, Ministerial Resolution No. 049-2010/DE/VPD), Lima, 21 May 2010, 409–410 and 224 (Peru); The Manual of the Law of Armed Conflict, Ministry of Defence, 1 July 2004, as amended by Amendment 3, Ministry of Defence, September 2010, para. 2.2. (UK).

[924] See, e.g., Hans-Peter Gasser and Nils Melzer, *Humanitäres Völkerrecht* (Zürich: Schluthess Juristische Medien, 2012), 27–28; Thürer, *International Humanitarian Law*, 68; Schmitt, "Military Necessity", 797–799; Michael Bothe, "Friedenssicherungsrecht und Kriegsrecht", in *Völkerrecht*, edited by Wolfgang Graf Vitzthum (Berlin: De Gruyter, 2010), mn. 64, 697; Dinstein, "Military Necessity", para. 1; Melzer, *Targeted Killing*, 285; Burrus M. Carnahan, "Lincoln, Lieber and the Laws of War: The Origins and Limits of the Principle of Military Necessity", *The American Journal of International Law* 92, no. 2 (1998): 213–231, 213 (emphasising the restrictive role of the principle of military necessity); William Gerald Downey, Jr., "The Law of War and Military Necessity", *The American Journal of International Law* 47, no. 2 (1953): 251–262, 254.

[925] See Melzer, *Targeted Killing*, 286–289 (noting that the principle of military necessity plays both a restrictive and a permissive role); Carnahan, "Lincoln, Lieber and the Laws of War", 213; Downey, "The Law of War", 254. Thürer stresses that the principle of military necessity is not a blank cheque: Thürer, *International Humanitarian Law*, 69.

[926] See Ian Henderson, *The Contemporary Law of Targeting. Military Objectives, Proportionality and Precautions in Attack under Additional Protocol I* (Leiden/Boston: Martinus Nijhoff, 2009), 65.

Code was adopted, the only legitimate objective of an armed conflict under IHL was to weaken the enemy military forces.[927] Pursuant to the principle of military necessity, objectives which are military in nature are legitimate, while political or personal goals do not justify military actions.[928] Therefore, customary IHL permits attacks against military objectives defined as objects "whose partial or total destruction, capture or neutralization, in the circumstances ruling at the time, offers a definite military advantage".[929] An object is only a military objective if an attack against it directly or indirectly weakens the enemy's military capability; objects do not constitute military objectives solely because attacking them would contribute to the political or strategic goals of an armed conflict.[930] Although some State practice exhibits a tendency to understand the notion of military objectives broadly as not only gaining ground on or defeating the enemy but also ensuring the security of one's own forces,[931] the term "overall" in the definition of military objectives does not refer to the entire armed conflict but rather to the advantage of a military attack as a whole as opposed to isolated or individual parts of the attack.[932]

3.2.2. Rules Implicitly Referring to Military Necessity

Most IHL rules balance military necessity and humanity implicitly. For example, the customary IHL principle of distinction, which is discussed in

927 The 1868 Declaration of St. Petersburg states in its second preambular recital "[t]hat the only legitimate object which States should endeavour to accomplish during war is to weaken the military forces of the enemy." Declaration Renouncing the Use, in Time of War, of Explosive Projectiles Under 400 Grammes Weight. Saint Petersburg, 29 November/11 December 1868, available at www.icrc.org/applic/ihl/ihl.nsf/Article.xsp?action=openDocument&documentId=568842C2B90F4A29C12563CD0051547C, accessed 10.03.2015. As noted by Melzer, *Targeted Killing*, 283. See also Thürer, *International Humanitarian Law*, 69.

928 See Dinstein, "Military Necessity", paras. 20 and 25–26. The prohibition of pillage illustrates that personal motives are not relevant considerations within IHL. See also Carnahan, "Lincoln, Lieber and the Laws of War", 219.

929 Henckaerts and Doswald-Beck, *Customary International Humanitarian Law*, 29.

930 See Henderson, *The Contemporary Law of Targeting*, 43.

931 See Manual on Law of Armed Conflict, Australian Defence Force Publication, Operations Series, ADFP 37 – Interim Edition, 1994, paras. 525 and 916c (noting that "[m]ilitary advantage includes the security of friendly forces") (Australia); *Aspectos Importantes del Derecho Internacional Marítimo que Deben Tener Presente los Comandantes de los Buques, Academia de Guerra Naval* (Important Aspects of International Maritime Law which Ship Commanders Must Know, Academy of Naval Warfare), 1989, para. 8.1.1 (stating that "[m]ilitary advantage may involve a variety of considerations, including the security of the attacking forces") (Ecuador); The Commander's Handbook on the Law of Naval Operations, NWP 1-14M/MCWP 5-2.1/COMDTPUB P5800.7, issued by the Department of the Navy, Office of the Chief of Naval Operations and Headquarters, US Marine Corps, and Department of Transportation, US Coast Guard, October 1995 (formerly NWP 9 (Rev. A)/FMFM 1-10, October 1989), para. 8.1.1 (containing a statement identical to the one in Ecuador's manual) (US).

932 See Jean-Marie Henckaerts, "Proportionality", in *The Oxford Companion to International Criminal Justice*, edited by Antonio Cassese (Oxford: Oxford University Press, 2009), 470.

more detail below, pays heed to military necessity by allowing attacks against combatants and to humanity by prohibiting attacks against civilians not directly participating in hostilities.[933] Another example is the principle of proportionality, which pursuant to customary IHL states:

> "Launching an attack which may be expected to cause incidental loss of civilian life, injury to civilians, damage to civilian objects, or a combination thereof, which would be excessive in relation to the concrete and direct military advantage anticipated, is prohibited."[934]

This principle acknowledges military necessity by allowing for the injury or death of civilians and/or damage to civilian objects as a side-effect of an attack against military objective. It takes humanity into account by prohibiting any such injury, death or damage that would be disproportionate. The principle of proportionality is also examined separately below.

The rules of customary IHL prescribing humane treatment, such as the prohibition of torture, inhuman and degrading treatment,[935] and the prohibition of rape and other forms of sexual violence,[936] also reflect a balance between humanity and military necessity. The above quoted Article 16 of the Lieber Code states that military necessity does not allow for cruelty in the sense of inflicting suffering for the sake of it, for reasons of revenge or to coerce confession. Such reasons do not constitute military necessity. Consequently, if an armed conflict in the country of origin is characterised by parties to the conflict resorting to inhuman treatment, torture, sexual violence, and/or maiming, these violations of customary IHL rules indicate causes, intentions or objectives that go beyond military necessity as confined by customary IHL. Therefore, the predicament of victims of such customary IHL violations cannot be justified by military necessity.

The prohibition under customary IHL in any armed conflict of "[a]cts or threats of violence the primary purpose of which is to spread terror among the civilian population"[937] further illustrates this point. Intended to keep the inhabitants of an area in a constant state of terror,[938] such acts cannot be justified by military necessity. Their purpose is to terrorise the civilian population, a purpose which is unlawful under customary IHL. Examples of such acts

---

933 Schmitt states that military necessity restricts the principle of distinction: Schmitt, "Military Necessity", 803.

934 Henckaerts and Doswald-Beck, *Customary International Humanitarian Law*, 46. Schmitt notes that the most conspicuous balancing of military necessity and humanity appears in the principle of proportionality: Schmitt, "Military Necessity", 804.

935 See Henckaerts and Doswald-Beck, *Customary International Humanitarian Law*, 315.

936 See Henckaerts and Doswald-Beck, *Customary International Humanitarian Law*, 323.

937 Henckaerts and Doswald-Beck, *Customary International Humanitarian Law*, 8.

938 See ICTY, *The Prosecutor v. Stanislav Galić, Judgment on Appeal*, 30 November 2006, Case No. 98-29-A, para. 102.

are:[939] mass killings;[940] bombardments of towns and cities;[941] assault, rape, abuse and torture of women and children;[942] direct attacks against civilians;[943] indiscriminate attacks;[944] and prolonged shelling and sniping of civilian areas.[945] Such acts may be indicative of the persecutor's intent to terrorise the civilian population, which in turn can be connected to a Refugee Convention ground, for instance because the civilians concerned are of a particular ethnicity.

The law of weaponry also strikes a balance between military necessity and humanity.[946] For example, the use of chemical weapons cannot be vindicated by reference to military necessity;[947] it amounts to persecution.[948] The use of prohibited weapons exceeds the boundaries of military necessity to the detriment of humanitarian considerations. Such use does not strive to achieve legitimate military objects but is motivated by other aims or purposes that are not legitimate under customary IHL. Whether or not as a result the victims' predicament is causally linked to a Refugee Convention ground depends on the precise nature of these aims or purposes and is to be assessed in each individual case.

In the US case of *Hernandez-Ortiz v. Immigration and Naturalization Service*, the US Ninth Circuit Court of Appeals held that where a government exercises its might against a family without such force being accompanied by criminal prosecution, a presumption arises that the government's actions are motivated by political considerations.[949] Von Sternberg argues that violations of IHL by the government give rise to a similar presumption that the government's

---

939 Some of these examples are also listed by Henckaerts and Doswald-Beck, *Customary International Humanitarian Law*, 11.

940 See Organization for Security and Co-operation in Europe, "Kosovo/Kosova. As Seen, As Told. An Analysis of the Human Rights Findings of the OSCE Kosovo Verification Mission October 1998 to 1999" (1999), available at www.osce.org/odihr/17772, accessed 10.03.2015, executive summary.

941 See *Humanitair Oorlogsrecht: Handleiding*, Voorschift No. 27–412, Koninklijke Landmacht, Militair Juridische Dienst (Humanitarian Law Manual, Regulations No. 27–412, Royal Netherlands Army, Military Legal Services), 2005, para. 0514 (Netherlands).

942 See Commission on Human Rights, *Contemporary Forms of Slavery. Systematic rape, sexual slavery and slavery-like practices during armed conflict*, UN Doc. E/CN.4/Sub.2/2000/21 (6 June 2000), para. 20.

943 See ICTY, *The Prosecutor v. Stanislav Galić, Judgment on Appeal*, 30 November 2006, Case No. 98–29-A, para. 102; ICTY, *Prosecutor v. Dragomir Milošević*, Judgment, Appeals Chamber, 12 November 2009, Case No. IT-98–29/1-A.

944 See ICTY, *The Prosecutor v. Stanislav Galić, Judgment on Appeal*, 30 November 2006, Case No. 98–29-A, para. 102.

945 ICTY, *Dragomir Milošević case*, Prosecution's Submission of Amended Indictment Pursuant to Rule 50 and Trial Chamber's Decision dated 12 December 2006, 18 December 2006, para. 22, Count 1.

946 On the balance between humanitarian considerations and military necessity in IHL, see Chapter 3.

947 Customary IHL prohibits the use of chemical weapons in any armed conflict. See Henckaerts and Doswald-Beck, *Customary International Humanitarian Law*, 259.

948 Persecution and the use of chemical weapons is examined in Chapter 5.

949 See *Hernandez-Ortiz v. INS*, 777 F.2d 517 (9th Cir. 1985) (US), 516.

actions are motivated by a Refugee Convention ground.[950] It is correct that the failure to comply with IHL shows that the perpetrators' motives or, more generally, the victims' predicament are not based on legitimate reasons of military necessity, thereby pointing to the presence of other causes. However, there is a multitude of such other causes which may or may not include a Refugee Convention ground. It is therefore not justified to argue that a presumption of a causal link to a Refugee Convention ground arises in such cases. The better view is that violations of customary IHL constitute strong indicia of the presence of other causes which are possibly related to a Refugee Convention ground. They can assist refugee status decision-makers in determining whether the nexus requirement is fulfilled in a context of armed conflict.

To conclude, serious violations of customary IHL rules which implicitly balance military necessity and humanity indicate the presence of motives or causes unrelated to legitimate military objects.[951] Where actions by parties to a conflict are not legitimately justified by military necessity, the resulting IHL violations constitute strong indications that the victims' predicament has other causes which, in turn, may or may not relate to race, religion, nationality, membership of a particular social group or political opinion. Violations of customary IHL in the country of origin should be taken into account in the assessment of the refugee definition's nexus requirement because they show that the refugee claimant's predicament cannot be justified by military necessity. Violations of customary IHL can point to a causal link between the refugee claimant's predicament and a Refugee Convention ground. They cannot, however, in and of themselves identify the pertinent Refugee Convention ground. Such an assessment depends on the specific circumstances of the case.

3.2.3. Rules Explicitly Referring to Military Necessity

Some rules of IHL entail express caveats for military necessity. For instance, in any armed conflict customary, IHL prohibits the destruction or seizure of the adversary's property unless required by imperative military necessity.[952] The tribunal in the aforementioned *Hostage case* emphasised:

---

950 See Sternberg, *The Grounds of Refugee Protection*, 122–123.

951 This approach was indicated in the US case *In re S-P-*, 21 I. & N. Dec. 486, Interim Decision 3287, 1996 WL 422990 (BIA), 493. See Storey and Wallace, "War and Peace", 361–364; Sternberg, *The Grounds of Refugee Protection*, 191.

952 See Henckaerts and Doswald-Beck, *Customary International Humanitarian Law*, 175. The ICRC chose to include the adjective "imperative" in formulating this prohibition. However, this characterisation can be considered obvious as military necessity only qualifies if it is imperative. See Dinstein, "Military Necessity", para 13. There is another rule of customary IHL specifically addressing the destruction and seizure of public or private property in occupied territory (see Henckaerts and Doswald-Beck, *Customary International Humanitarian Law*, 178). However, this book is merely concerned with acts

> "Destruction as an end in itself is a violation of international law. There must be some reasonable connection between the destruction of property and the overcoming of the enemy forces."[953]

The jurisprudence of the ICC shows that destruction not justified by military necessity can indicate that the victims' predicament is causally linked to a Refugee Convention ground. With respect to the destruction of property as a war crime in non-international armed conflict under Article 8(2)(e)(xii) Rome Statute, the ICC Pre-Trial Chamber found that there were reasonable grounds to consider that the accused had contributed to the destruction of property belonging primarily to the Fur population in a number of villages and towns in the Darfur region of Sudan, including the burning of food storages, mosques and dwellings as well as the destruction of crops and farms.[954] This example illustrates that if military necessity does not vindicate the destruction of property, a pattern of such destruction in violation of customary IHL can reveal a causal link between the victims' predicament and a Refugee Convention ground because it can show that the destruction of property was targeted at a particular ethnic group.[955]

Another example relates to the prohibition of forced displacement under customary IHL in non-international armed conflict, which includes an express caveat of military necessity.[956] Customary IHL provides:

> "Parties to a non-international armed conflict may not order the displacement of the civilian population, in whole or in part, for reasons related to the conflict, unless the security of the civilians involved or imperative military reasons so demand."[957]

This prohibition under customary IHL is modelled on Article 17(1) Additional Protocol II. Therefore, the ICRC commentary on this provision can shed

---

or omissions within the territory of the country of origin by State authorities or non-State actors. Acts or omissions on occupied territory by the occupying power fall outside this book's scope.

953 *Hostage Case* (*United States v. List*), Judgment, 19 February 1948, printed in: *Trials of War Criminals before the Nuernberg Military Tribunals*, Vol. 11 (Washington DC 1950: US Government Printing Office), 1230, at 1253–1254 (which relates to an international armed conflict). As noted by Dinstein, *The Conduct of Hostilities*, 6.

954 See ICC, *The Prosecutor v. Ahmad Muhammad Harun ("Ahmad Harun")*, Warrant of Arrest, Pre-Trial Chamber I, 27 April 2007, Case No. ICC-02/05–01/07–2-Corr, Counts 8, 19, 38 and 50; ICC, *The Prosecutor v. Ali Muhammad Ali Abd-al-Rahman ("Ali Kushayb")*, Warrant of Arrest, Pre-Trial Chamber I, 27 April 2007, Case No. ICC-02/05–01/07–3-Corr, Counts 8, 19, 38 and 50.

955 Similarly: Sternberg, *The Grounds of Refugee Protection*, 121–122.

956 Chapter 5 examines the use of forced displacement as a method of warfare and as persecution.

957 Henckaerts and Doswald-Beck, *Customary International Humanitarian Law*, 457. Sternberg noted that inferences can be drawn from this rule of IHL as regards the nexus requirement: See Sternberg, *The Grounds of Refugee Protection*, 119–120.

further light on the notion of "imperative military reasons" in this context. This commentary states:

> "Clearly, imperative military reasons cannot be justified by political motives. For example, it would be prohibited to move a population in order to exercise more effective control over a dissident group."[958]

Hence, political considerations cannot be invoked to vindicate forced displacement of the civilian population in non-international armed conflict. Therefore, the occurrence of forced displacement of the civilian population for reasons related to the conflict which cannot be justified by military necessity (or the security of the civilian population) suggests the presence of other causes that can relate to a Refugee Convention ground.[959] Ethnic cleansing, which can be defined as "rendering an area ethnically homogeneous by using force or intimidation to remove persons of given groups from the area",[960] is a manifestation of forced displacement for reasons of race, religion or nationality. Indeed, the UNHCR EXCOM strongly deplored

> "that systematic violations of human rights, blatant disregard of international humanitarian law, and policies of wholesale expulsions of populations and 'ethnic cleansing' have caused significant displacement both internally and across borders in many regions of the world."[961]

To summarise, violations of rules expressly containing caveats of military necessity such as the prohibition of destruction of the adversary's property or the prohibition of forced displacement in non-international armed conflict mean that the victims' predicament cannot be justified by military necessity. They indicate the presence of other causes which may, depending on the facts of the case, include Refugee Convention grounds.

3.3. THE PRINCIPLE OF DISTINCTION

A cardinal principle of customary IHL,[962] the principle of distinction, provides that parties to any armed conflict must distinguish at all times between civilians

---

958 Sandoz, Swinarski, and Zimmermann (editors), *Commentary on the Additional Protocols of 8 June 1977 to the Geneva Conventions of 12 August 1949*, 1473.

959 Similarly: Sternberg, *The Grounds of Refugee Protection*, 119–120.

960 UN Commission of Experts, *Final Report of the United Nations Commission of Experts Established pursuant to Security Council Resolution 780 (1992)*, UN Doc. S/1994/674 (27 May 1994), para. 55.

961 UNHCR Executive Committee, *Conclusion No. 87 (L)* (1999), para. a.

962 As noted by the ICJ in *Legality of the Threat or Use of Nuclear Weapons*, Advisory Opinion of 8 July 1996, ICJ Reports 1996, paras. 78–79.

and combatants, as well as between civilian objects and military objectives. Its principal purpose is to protect civilians and civilian objects.[963] While attacks may be directed against combatants and military objectives, civilians not directly participating in hostilities and civilian objects may not be attacked.[964] To recall, military objectives are objects "whose partial or total destruction, capture or neutralization, in the circumstances ruling at the time, offers a definite military advantage."[965] Civilian objects are objects which are not military objectives.[966]

In order to explore what inferences can be drawn from the customary IHL principle of distinction for the refugee definition's nexus requirement, it is necessary to determine the meaning of "combatants" and "civilians" in international and non-international armed conflict. In international armed conflict, all members of armed forces with the exception of medical and religious personnel are combatants under customary IHL.[967] Conversely, civilians are defined as persons who are not members of the armed forces, with the civilian population comprising all persons who are civilians.[968] The previous analysis has shown that the term "civilians" in international armed conflict includes a State's own nationals.[969] While the respective statuses of civilians and combatants in international armed conflict are thus clearly defined, the same cannot be said in non-international armed conflict. The term "combatant" in the aforementioned formulation of the principle of distinction as applicable in non-international armed conflict under customary IHL is used in a generic sense referring to persons who do not enjoy the protection against attack that is granted to civilians, without implying a right to combatant (and thus prisoner of war) status.[970] For the purpose of interpreting and applying the principle of distinction, members of a State's armed forces can be considered combatants in non-international armed conflict, except for medical and religious personnel.[971] However, State practice is ambiguous as regards the status of members of armed opposition groups in non-international armed conflict, specifically as regards

963 See Thürer, *International Humanitarian Law*, 81.

964 See Henckaerts and Doswald-Beck, *Customary International Humanitarian Law*, 3, 19 and 25. It is also prohibited to attack persons *hors de combat*. See Henckaerts and Doswald-Beck, *Customary International Humanitarian Law*, 164.

965 Henckaerts and Doswald-Beck, *Customary International Humanitarian Law*, 29.

966 See Henckaerts and Doswald-Beck, *Customary International Humanitarian Law*, 32.

967 See Henckaerts and Doswald-Beck, *Customary International Humanitarian Law*, 11. Combatant status (and entitlement to prisoner of war status upon capture) only exists in international armed conflict.

968 See Henckaerts and Doswald-Beck, *Customary International Humanitarian Law*, 17.

969 See Chapter 3.

970 See Henckaerts and Doswald-Beck, *Customary International Humanitarian Law*, 3. Also: Jean-François Quéguiner, "The Principle of Distinction: Beyond an Obligation of Customary International Humanitarian Law", in *The Legitimate Use of Military Force. The Just War Tradition and the Customary Law of Armed Conflict*, edited by Howard M. Hensel (Aldershot: Ashgate, 2008), 168.

971 See Henckaerts and Doswald-Beck, *Customary International Humanitarian Law*, 11.

the question of whether they are civilians losing protection from attack if and when they directly participate in hostilities, or whether they are liable to attack as such.[972]

The ICRC commentary to the customary rule of IHL on civilians' loss of protection from attack favours an understanding of members of armed opposition groups as either civilians continuously participating in hostilities or as lacking civilian status. If members of armed opposition groups were civilians directly participating in hostilities, they would only lose protection from attack if and when they are directly participating in hostilities, as opposed to members of a State's armed forces who are liable to attack at any time (unless they are *hors de combat*). The result would be an imbalance between the State party to the conflict and the armed group which is a party to the conflict.[973] For the purposes of interpreting the refugee definition's nexus requirement, the question of whether members of armed opposition groups lack civilian status or are civilians continuously participating in hostilities need not be resolved because only the consequence – loss of protection from attack at any time rather than only when they are directly participating in hostilities – is relevant for the interpretation of the nexus requirement.[974] Thus, attacks against members of armed opposition groups in non-international armed conflict are justified by military necessity not only if and when they are participating in hostilities but at any time under the principle of distinction, subject to the other rules of customary IHL.

It follows from the definition of military objectives which requires a military advantage that attacks against civilian objects do not yield a legitimate military advantage. Similarly, attacks against individual civilians or the civilian population cannot be justified by military necessity.[975] Therefore, civilians' predicament resulting from attacks against individual civilians, the civilian population or civilian objects is not based on lawful military causes, which indicates the presence of other causes that might be related to a Refugee Convention ground. The jurisprudence of the ICTY shows that various factors can indicate that an attack is directed against civilians, including:

> "the means and methods used in the course of the attack, the status of the victims, their number, the discriminatory nature of the attack, the nature of the crimes committed in its course, the resistance to the assailants at the time and the extent to

---

972 See Henckaerts and Doswald-Beck, *Customary International Humanitarian Law*, 12 and 19.

973 See Henckaerts and Doswald-Beck, *Customary International Humanitarian Law*, 21.

974 There is no definition of the notion "direct participation in hostilities" in customary IHL. See Henckaerts and Doswald-Beck, *Customary International Humanitarian Law*, 22. As previously noted, the ICRC purported to clarify the notion of "direct participation in hostilities" (though not under customary international law): ICRC, "Interpretative Guidance on Direct Participation".

975 As confirmed by ICTY, *The Prosecutor v. Dario Kordić and Mario Čerkez*, Judgment, Appeals Chamber, 17 December 2004, Case No. IT-95-14/2-A, para. 54; ICTY, *The Prosecutor v. Stanislav Galić*, Judgment on Appeal, 30 November 2006, Case No. 98-29-A, para. 30.

> which the attacking force may be said to have complied or attempted to comply with the precautionary requirements of the laws of war."[976]

When examining the refugee definition's nexus requirement, these factors together with the context of the armed conflict and of the attack can also indicate that the civilian's predicament is causally linked to a Refugee Convention ground. For example, UNHCR stated with regard to Sri Lanka that:

> "many ordinary civilians may be at risk of harm from bombs, shelling, suicide attacks, and improvised explosive devices. ... [T]hese methods of violence may be used against targets or in areas where civilians of specific ethnic or political profiles predominantly reside or gather, and for this reason, may be linked to a 1951 [Refugee] Convention ground."[977]

Moreover, the jurisprudence of the ICC shows that if the pattern or characteristics of the attack is taken into consideration, a causal link to a Refugee Convention ground can be inferred from attacks which violate the principle of distinction. In the *Harun case* and in the *Kushyab case*, the ICC Pre-Trial Chamber I considered that there were reasonable grounds to believe that the accused contributed to the commission of attacks against civilians from the ethnic Fur group of certain towns and villages.[978]

Having considered attacks directed at civilians or civilian objects, the analysis now turns to indiscriminate attacks. Prohibited under customary IHL,[979] indiscriminate attacks are attacks:

> "(a) which are not directed at a specific military objective;
> (b) which employ a method or means of combat which cannot be directed at a specific military objective; or

---

976 ICTY, *The Prosecutor v. Dragoljub Kunarac, Radomir Kovač and Zoran Vuković*, Judgment on Appeal, Appeal Chamber, 22 February 2001, Case Nos. IT-96-23 and IT-96-23/1-A, para. 91. Affirmed in ICTY, *The Prosecutor v. Tihomir Blaškić*, Judgment, Appeals Chamber, 29 July 2004, Case No. IT-95-14-A, para. 106. These cases discuss attacks directed against a civilian population in the context of the *chapeau* requirement of crimes against humanity. The ICTY noted that the same observations are pertinent for an analysis of whether attacks are directed against a civilian population under IHL. See ICTY, *The Prosecutor v. Stanislav Galić*, Judgment on Appeal, 30 November 2006, Case No. 98-29-A, para. 132.

977 UNHCR, "Eligibility Guidelines for Asylum-Seekers from Sri Lanka 2009", 32. Sternberg notes "that the most critical evidence of linking persecution to a protected ground is to be found in systematic violations of the laws of war being practiced against a discernible group." Sternberg, *The Grounds of Refugee Protection*, 116.

978 See ICC, *The Prosecutor v. Ahmad Muhammad Harun ("Ahmad Harun")*, Warrant of Arrest, Pre-Trial Chamber I, 27 April 2007, Case No. ICC-02/05-01/07-2-Corr, Counts 6, 15, 32 and 44; ICC, *The Prosecutor v. Ali Muhammad Ali Abd-al-Rahman ("Ali Kushayb")*, Warrant of Arrest, Pre-Trial Chamber I, 27 April 2007, Case No. ICC-02/05-01/07-3-Corr, Counts 6, 7, 51, 16, 32, 33, 44 and 45.

979 See Henckaerts and Doswald-Beck, *Customary International Humanitarian Law*, 37.

(c) which employ a method or means of combat the effects of which cannot be limited as required by international humanitarian law; and consequently, in each such case, are of a nature to strike military objectives and civilians or civilian objects without distinction."[980]

The ICTY jurisprudence shows that indiscriminate attacks can also be qualified as direct attacks against civilians.[981] For example, the use of a cluster bomb warhead was considered as evidencing an intent to deliberately attack the civilian population.[982] The characteristics of the armed conflict or the attack may reveal that the targeted civilian population belonged to an ethnic or religious group. In this case there may well have been a nexus between the perpetrator's motive and a Refugee Convention ground.[983] Hence, the use of indiscriminate weapons and, more generally, evidence that indiscriminate attacks can be qualified as direct attacks against civilians can be relevant for the evaluation of whether the victims' predicament is causally connected to a Refugee Convention ground.

To conclude, for the purpose of interpreting and applying the nexus requirement of the refugee definition, direct attacks against civilians who are not directly participating in hostilities and indiscriminate attacks are indicia that the victims' predicament is linked to causes which are not justified by military necessity and which may include a Refugee Convention ground.

3.4. THE PRINCIPLE OF PROPORTIONALITY

As previously noted, the customary IHL principle of proportionality states:

> "Launching an attack which may be expected to cause incidental loss of civilian life, injury to civilians, damage to civilian objects, or a combination thereof, which would be excessive in relation to the concrete and direct military advantage anticipated, is prohibited."[984]

The principle of proportionality concerns incidental loss of civilian casualties, incidental damage to civilian objects or both, which result from attacks against military objectives. To recall, customary IHL defines military objectives as:

---

980 Henckaerts and Doswald-Beck, *Customary International Humanitarian Law*, 40.

981 See ICTY, *The Prosecutor v. Stanislav Galić*, Judgment on Appeal, 30 November 2006, Case No. 98-29-A, para. 132.

982 See ICTY, *The Prosecutor v. Stanislav Galić*, Judgment on Appeal, 30 November 2006, Case No. 98-29-A, para. 132.

983 Similarly: Sternberg, *The Grounds of Refugee Protection*, 101; Immigration and Refugee Board of Canada, "Civilian Non-Combatants Fearing Persecution in Civil War Situations".

984 Henckaerts and Doswald-Beck, *Customary International Humanitarian Law*, 46. Since the book does not address the *ius ad bellum*, this section does not examine the principle of proportionality under the *ius ad bellum*.

> "objects which by their nature, location, purpose or use make an effective contribution to military action and whose partial or total destruction, capture or neutralization, in the circumstances ruling at the time, offers a definite military advantage."[985]

That the military advantage must be direct and concrete excludes potential or indeterminate military advantages.[986] "Concrete" stands for specific, in contrast to general. "Direct" refers to causation in the sense that the advantage must not be too remote from the attack itself.[987] A direct and concrete military advantage need not solely be determined in terms of immediate tactical gain from an isolated attack, but may take into account related actions and may arise in the future.[988] Consequently, attacks which violate the principle of proportionality indicate the presence of motives on the part of the attackers which are not related to or exceed the legitimate military advantage. Disproportionate attacks can therefore indicate the presence of persecutory motives.[989] For instance, UNHCR noted that the parties to the Colombian armed conflict often resorted to disproportionate attacks on military objectives which resulted in a number of civilian casualties. UNHCR considered this relevant for refugee status decision-makers.[990] By considering the context of the Colombian armed conflict, it may be possible to conclude from such disproportionate attacks that they were in fact also, or possibly even exclusively, directed at the civilians for reasons related to a Refugee Convention ground such as political opinion.

However, when making inferences from the principle of proportionality for the refugee definition's nexus requirement, the time element of proportionality should not be forgotten: the principle of proportionality must be assessed in light of real-time information rather than with the benefit of hindsight,[991] and from the perspective of "a reasonably well-informed person … making reasonable use of the information available at the time".[992] Civilian casualties or damage to civilian objects do not necessarily mean that the attack violated the principle of proportionality.[993] For the purposes of proportionality, the military advantage

985 Henckaerts and Doswald-Beck, *Customary International Humanitarian Law*, 29.

986 See Sandoz, Swinarski, and Zimmermann (editors), *Commentary on the Additional Protocols of 8 June 1977 to the Geneva Conventions of 12 August 1949*, para. 2024, 636.

987 See Bothe, Partsch and Solf, *New Rules for Victims of Armed Conflicts*, 365.

988 See Henderson, *The Contemporary Law of Targeting*, 65–66.

989 Similarly: Storey and Wallace, "War and Peace", 362; Sternberg, *The Grounds of Refugee Protection*, 190–194.

990 See UNHCR, "International Protection Considerations regarding Colombian Asylum-seekers and Refugees 2002", para. 24.

991 See Henderson, *The Contemporary Law of Targeting*, 202.

992 ICTY, *The Prosecutor v. Stanislav Galić*, Judgment, Trial Chamber I, 5 December 2003, Case No. IT-98-29-T, para. 58.

993 See A.P.V. Rogers, "The Principle of Proportionality", in *The Legitimate Use of Military Force. The Just War Tradition and the Customary Law of Armed Conflict*, edited by Howard M. Hensel (Aldershot: Ashgate, 2007), 209.

is the sole relevant reason for which an attack is carried out. An attack can be disproportionate if the attacker considered aspects that go beyond the *direct and concrete* military advantage but nonetheless concern the military advantage. Moreover, proportionality seeks to measure and balance the dissimilar quantities of civilian lives and physical integrity and damage to civilian objects on the one hand and military advantage on the other. Such balancing is hardly possible in a reasonably exact or objective way.[994] Evaluating the relative values of human lives and a particular military advantage such as capturing a bridge is difficult.[995] Proportionality entails a degree of ambiguity, as the Committee set up by the ICTY prosecutor to assess the NATO bombing campaign against the Federal Republic of Yugoslavia noted: "The main problem with the principle of proportionality is not whether or not it exists but what it means and how it is to be applied."[996] This inherent ambiguity restricts the usefulness of proportionality for interpreting the refugee definition's nexus requirement.

Nonetheless, it is possible to infer from disproportionate attacks as regards their underpinning motives. For instance, the ICTY Trial Chamber found "that certain apparently disproportionate attacks may give rise to the inference that civilians were actually the object of attack. This is to be determined on a case-by-case basis in light of the available evidence."[997] The Trial Chamber further held that:

> "in case of repeated attacks, all or most of them falling within the grey area between indisputable legality and unlawfulness, it might be warranted to conclude that the cumulative effect of such acts entails that they may not be in keeping with international law."[998]

---

994 See William J. Fenrick, "The Rule of Proportionality and Protocol I in Conventional Warfare", *Military Law Review* 98 (1982): 91–127, 102; Kenneth Watkin, "Assessing Proportionality: Moral Complexity and Legal Rules", *Yearbook of International Humanitarian Law* 8 (2005): 3–53, 23; ICTY, "Final Report to the Prosecutor by the Committee Established to Review the NATO Bombing Campaign Against the Federal Republic of Yugoslavia", *International Legal Materials* 39 (2000): 1257–1283, para. 48. Similarly: Enzo Cannizzaro, "Proportionality in the Law of Armed Conflict", in *The Oxford Handbook of International Law in Armed Conflict*, edited by Andrew Clapham, Paola Gaeta (editors), Tom Haeck and Alice Priddy (assistant editors) (Oxford: Oxford University Press: 2014), 337.

995 See Fenrick, "The Rule of Proportionality", 94–95, 102.

996 ICTY, "Final Report to the Prosecutor", para. 48. Kretzmer noted that the principle of proportionality is "notoriously difficult to apply": David Kretzmer, "Targeted Killing of Suspected Terrorists: Extra-Judicial Executions or Legitimate Means of Defence?", *European Journal of International Law* 16, no. 2 (2005): 171–212, 200. Wright seeks to operationalise the principle of proportionality by proposing a seven-step targeting methodology: Jason D. Wright, "'Excessive' Ambiguity: Analysing and Refining the Proportionality Standard", *International Review of the Red Cross* 94, no. 775 (2012): 819–854.

997 ICTY, *The Prosecutor v. Stanislav Galić*, Judgment, Trial Chamber I, 5 December 2003, Case No. IT-98-29-T, para. 60.

998 ICTY, *The Prosecutor v. Zoran Kupreškić, Mirjan Kupreškić, Vlatko Kupreškić, Drago Josipović, Dragan Papić, Vladimir Šantić aka "Vlado"*, Judgment, Trial Chamber II, 14 January 2000, Case No. IT-95-16-T, para. 526.

This judgment illustrates that an overall analysis of the civilian victims *vis-à-vis* the goals of the military campaign is required. A similar evaluation should be carried out when assessing the situation in the country of origin in order to determine whether disproportionate attacks are linked to a Refugee Convention ground.

To summarise, in the interpretation and application of the refugee definition's nexus requirement, disproportionate attacks constitute indicia that the attackers' motives or the victims' predicament are causally linked to causes that go beyond military necessity and that may include a Refugee Convention ground.

3.5. RESULT

Some inferences can be drawn from the principles of military necessity, distinction and proportionality as regards the causes of the victims' predicament. Violations of customary IHL not permitted by military necessity can by definition neither be vindicated by political or other objectives of the parties to the conflict. Consequently, violations of customary IHL indicate that the victims' predicament has other causes which may include a Refugee Convention ground. Violations of customary IHL do not in and of themselves identify a causal link to a Refugee Convention ground, but they constitute relevant indicia highlighting that an assessment of the causes, character and impact of the armed conflict ought to be included in the interpretation and application of the nexus requirement.

In particular, violations of rules of customary IHL implicitly balancing humanity and military necessity, such as the rule prohibiting the use of chemical weapons or the rules proscribing human treatment, including the prohibitions on torture, rape and other sexual violence, mean that the victims' predicament is militarily unjustified and may be causally linked to a Refugee Convention ground. Moreover, patterns of destruction not justified by military necessity may indicate that certain groups are targeted for a Refugee Convention ground. In non-international armed conflict, forced displacement of the civilian population for reasons related to the armed conflict which cannot be vindicated by military necessity or the security of the civilian population suggests the presence of other causes that can relate to a Refugee Convention ground. Direct attacks against civilians not participating in hostilities, indiscriminate attacks and disproportionate attacks mean that the civilians' predicament is not justified by military necessity, indicating the presence of other causes related to armed conflict and possibly to a Refugee Convention ground. An armed conflict in the country of origin that is characterised by patterns of violations of rules of customary IHL can be considered as indicating that the predicament of the victims of such customary IHL violations is causally linked to causes other than military necessity. These causes, in turn, may relate to the Refugee Convention grounds. Whether this is the case and which Refugee Convention ground is pertinent must be assessed on a case-by-case basis in light of the respective armed conflict in the country of origin.

4. THE REFUGEE CONVENTION GROUNDS

The Refugee Convention grounds are race, religion, nationality, membership of a particular group and political opinion. The obligation to identify the correct Refugee Convention ground does not rest on the refugee claimant alone, but is shared with the decision-maker.[999] A Refugee Convention ground may be identified through the claimant's behaviour, but this is not necessary. It may also be that the Refugee Convention ground is imputed to the refugee claimant,[1000] which is particularly relevant in contexts of armed conflict as will be shown below. Though independent from one another,[1001] the Refugee Convention grounds may overlap and are not mutually exclusive. More than one Refugee Convention ground is frequently relevant in a refugee protection claim.[1002]

4.1. RACE, RELIGION, NATIONALITY

In contexts of armed conflict, race, religion and nationality are pertinent Refugee Convention grounds, for example because the parties involved are grouped along ethnic or religious lines. Civilians of a certain ethnicity or religion may be perceived as affiliated with "their" party to the conflict. As a result, they may be

999 See Second Colloquium on Challenges to International Refugee Law, "The Michigan Guidelines on Nexus", para. 3; Hathaway and Foster, "The Causal Connection", para. 6; UNHCR, *Handbook*, paras. 66–67. See also the analysis of the burden of proof in refugee status determination in Chapter 5.

1000 Hathaway and Foster, *The Law of Refugee Status*, 291.

1001 See Hathaway and Foster, *The Law of Refugee Status*, 391.

1002 See, e.g., *Refugee Appeal No. 76006* NZRSAA (16 July 2007) (country of origin: Sri Lanka; grounds: ethnicity and imputed political opinion) (New Zealand); *Refugee Appeal No. 74686* NZRSAA (29 November 2004) (country of origin: Iraq; grounds: religion and imputed political opinion) (New Zealand); *Refugee Appeal No. 76457* NZRSAA (15 March 2010) (country of origin: Iraq; grounds: religion and membership of a particular social group (women)) (New Zealand). In France, the CNDA seems to consider in cases concerning refugee claimants from Afghanistan that an ethnic background of such claims alone is insufficient for establishing a Refugee Convention ground; often, refugee status is granted for reasons of ethnicity and political opinion. See, e.g., CNDA, *decision no. 08000815, M. Husseini*, 25 June 2010; CNDA *decision no. 0915005. M. Yusefi*, 1 September 2010; CNDA, *decision no. 09012012, M. Hussaini*, 2 November 2010; CNDA, *decision no. 08010018, M. Yaguby*, 2 November 2010 (all France). See also UNHCR, "Eligibility Guidelines for Iraqi Asylum-Seekers 2007", 20.

forced to provide support or participate in hostilities, or they may be subject to attacks by the adverse party.[1003]

Race should be broadly interpreted and encompasses persons of common descent who typically form a minority within a certain population.[1004] Race often overlaps with other Convention grounds.[1005] Indeed, there are few refugee protection claims that only relate to the Refugee Convention ground of race. Usually, racial or ethnic claims are framed and decided on other grounds, for example membership of a particular social group. The ground of political opinion may also be relevant in such cases. Tamil refugee protection claimants fleeing from the armed conflict in Sri Lanka, for example, have been considered to have a well-founded fear of persecution for reasons of their ethnicity and their imputed political opinion.[1006] This illustrates that ethnic groups can be affiliated with movements that strive for power, equality or independence.[1007] Group members may be perceived as affiliated with such movements even though they are not directly involved in the conflict.[1008]

1003 See Blanche Tax, "Refugee by Association", in *Forced Migration Review* 47 (2014): 26 (in relation to the Syrian conflict); Markard, *Kriegsflüchtlinge*, 233–234; Farrell and Schmitt, "The Causes, Character and Conduct of Armed Conflict, and the Effects of on Civilian Populations, 1990–2010", 3–5. On ethnically and religiously motivated conflicts, see also UNHCR, *Note on International Protection (1998)*, para. 4.

1004 See UNHCR, *Handbook*, para. 68. See also Article 10(1)(a) Qualification Directive and Article 10(1)(a) Recast Qualification Directive. Markard provides a detailed discussion of "race": Markard, *Kriegsflüchtlinge*, 234–235. On the broad understanding of race, see also Hathaway and Foster, *The Law of Refugee Status*, 394–397.

1005 See James C. Hathaway and Michelle Foster, *The Law of Refugee Status*, 2nd ed. (Cambridge: Cambridge University Press, 2014), 397.

1006 See *Refugee Appeal No. 76006 NZRSAA* (16 July 2007); *Refugee Appeal No. 76199 NZRSAA* (11 November 2008) (both New Zealand). See also UNHCR, "Eligibility Guidelines for Asylum-Seekers from Sri Lanka 2009", 31–32.

1007 See Anker, *Law of Asylum in the United States*, paras. 5:83–5:86. In France, recognition of refugee status for Afghans is usually not based on ethnicity alone, but also on the ground of political opinion. See, e.g., CNDA, *decision no. 08000815, M. Husseini*, 25 June 2010; CNDA *decision no. 09015005, M. Yusefi*, 1 September 2010; CNDA, *decision no. 09012012*, M. Hussaini, 2 November 2010; CNDA, *decision no. 08010018*, M. Yagbuby, 2 November 2010 (all France). Further: UK Border Agency, *Considering the Protection (Asylum) Claim and Assessing Credibility*, 27; US Citizenship and Immigration Services, "Asylum Officer Basic Training Course, Asylum Eligibility Part III: Nexus and the Five Protected Characteristics" (2009), available at www.uscis.gov/portal/site/uscis/menuitem.5af9bb95919f35e66f614176543f6d1a/?vgnextoid=2a1d1a877b4bc110VgnVCM1000004718190aRCRD&vgnextchannel=3a82ef4c766fd010VgnVCM1000000ecd190aRCRD, accessed 10.03.2015, 17; UNHCR, *Handbook*, para. 75.

1008 See US Citizenship and Immigration Services, "Asylum Officer Basic Training", 17. The US Court of Appeal for the Third Circuit indicated that a female member of the Bemba tribe who was found to be at risk of being arbitrarily detained and raped during detention feared persecution on account of her tribal identity. The Court noted the government of the DRC considers members of the Bemba tribe as its enemies and that members of this tribe have been targeted by armed groups supporting the government. See *Zubeda v. Ashcroft*, 333F.3d 462 (3rd Cir. 2003) (US), para. 102.

Nationality should also be widely construed and relates to a refugee claimant's "identification as a member of a culturally, ethnically, linguistically, or otherwise distinct 'social' group."[1009] Thus the grounds of race and nationality both include ethnicity. Somali minority clans,[1010] Tamils in Sri Lanka,[1011] and the Hazara in Afghanistan[1012] are examples of ethnic groups whose members were found to be persecuted for reasons of ethnicity in situations of conflict. Moreover, the Refugee Convention ground of nationality is pertinent when a refugee claimant is affiliated or perceived to be affiliated with a country that supports an armed group. For example, the UK AIT held that being a national of a country hostile to the DRC such as Rwanda, or being perceived as such a national, constitutes a risk category.[1013]

Religion has a wide meaning, encompassing a belief or non-belief, an identity and/or a way of life.[1014] There are various ways in which religion may be relevant in refugee protection claims related to armed conflicts. A refugee claimant may fear persecution for reasons of religion when a religious belief is imputed to him or her, even though he or she does not actually hold this belief.[1015] Affiliation to a party to the conflict may be imputed on religious grounds. For example, violence against Christians in Iraq has in the past in part been fuelled by their perceived affiliation with the occupying forces. This gave rise a well-founded fear of persecution due to religion and imputed political opinion.[1016]

1009 Hathaway and Foster, *The Law of Refugee Status*, 399. See also UNHCR, *Handbook*, para. 74; James C. Hathaway and Michelle Foster, *The Law of Refugee Status*, 2nd ed. (Cambridge: Cambridge University Press, 2014), 398, as well as Article 10(1)(c) Qualification Directive and Article 10(1)(c) Recast Qualification Directive. Further: Markard, *Kriegsflüchtlinge*, 237–238.

1010 See UNHCR, "UNHCR Eligibility Guidelines for Assessing the International Protection Needs of Asylum-Seekers from Somalia (2010)", 16. UNHCR also notes that in Afghanistan, members of ethnic groups such as the Pashtuns are at risk of persecution because of their ethnicity in areas where they constitute a minority. See UNHCR, "Eligibility Guidelines for Asylum-Seekers from Afghanistan 2010", 30.

1011 In *Refugee Appeal Nos. 76294 and 76295* NZRSAA (30 June 2009), a Tamil was found to be at risk of persecution because of his ethnicity (New Zealand).

1012 See *Refugee Appeal Nos. 76294 and 76295* NZRSAA (30 June 2009) (New Zealand). The UKAIT considered that members of their Hema tribe may be at risk because of their ethnicity, though membership in this tribe alone is insufficient. See *NA (risk categories – Hema) Democratic Republic of Congo CG* [2008] UKAIT 00071 (UK).

1013 See *AB and DM (Risk categories reviewed, Tutsis added) Democratic Republic of Congo CG* [2005] UKIAT 00118, para. 51, though whether the nexus requirement is fulfilled depends on the circumstances of the case (UK).

1014 See UNHCR, *Guidelines on International Protection No. 6*, paras. 4–5. See also Article 10(1)(b) Qualification Directive and Article 10(1)(b) Recast Qualification Directive, discussed by Markard, *Kriegsflüchtlinge*, 236. For a detailed analysis of the meaning of "religion", see Zimmermann and Mahler, "Article 1A, para. 2", mn. 335–379, 380–387. On the broad interpretation of "religion", see also Hathaway and Foster, *The Law of Refugee Status*, 400–405.

1015 See Hathaway and Foster, *The Law of Refugee Status*, 401.

1016 See *Refugee Appeal No. 74686* [2004] NZRSAA (29 November 2004), paras. 38 and 41 (New Zealand). There are few cases in Dutch jurisprudence that acknowledge refugee status based

4.2. MEMBERSHIP OF A PARTICULAR SOCIAL GROUP

Although membership of a particular social group is considered to be "the ground with least clarity",[1017] there is wide agreement on a number of definitional aspects: A particular social group need not be homogeneous or internally coherent.[1018] The group size does not matter.[1019] Not all group members need to be at risk.[1020] However, the group cannot be solely defined by a shared risk of persecution.[1021]

There are two approaches in State practice for determining a particular social group.[1022] Under the "protected characteristics approach", membership of a particular social group means that "an individual who is a member of a group of persons all of whom share a common, immutable characteristic."[1023] This immutable characteristic may be innate or unalterable for other reasons, for instance because the alteration would require a renunciation of basic human rights.[1024] The "social perception approach" defines a particular social group as "a collection of persons who share a certain characteristic or element which unites them and enables them to be set apart from society at large."[1025] In line

---

on religious persecution. See Bem, "Defining the Refugee. American and Dutch Asylum Case-Law 1975–2005", 172.

1017 Expert Roundtable Organized by the United Nations High Commissioner for Refugees and the International Institute of Humanitarian Law, "Summary Conclusions: membership of a particular social group", in *Refugee Protection in International Law. UNHCR's Global Consultations on International Protection*, edited by Erika Feller, Volker Türk, and Frances Nicholson (Cambridge: Cambridge University Press, 2001), 312, para. 1. Emphasised by Michelle Foster, "The 'Ground with the Least Clarity': A Comparative Study of Jurisprudential Developments relating to 'Membership of a Particular Social Group'", *UNHCR Legal and Protection Policy Research Series* 25 (2012), available at www.unhcr.org/4f7d8d189.html, accessed 10.03.2015.

1018 See *Minister for Immigration and Cultural Affairs v. Khawar* [2002] HCA 14 per Gleeson CJ (Australia). See also Zimmermann and Mahler, "Article 1A, para. 2", mn. 409–410, 394–395; Hathaway and Foster, *The Law of Refugee Status*, 425.

1019 See *Applicant A and Anor v. Minister for Immigration and Cultural Affairs* (1997) 190 CLR 225 per Dawson J (Australia). See also Zimmermann and Mahler, "Article 1A, para. 2", mn. 408, 394; Hathaway and Foster, *The Law of Refugee Status*, 425.

1020 See *Khawar* [2002] HCA 14 (Australia). See also UNHCR, *Guidelines on International Protection No. 2*, 18; Hathaway and Foster, *The Law of Refugee Status*, 425.

1021 See *Applicant A v. Minister for Immigration and Ethnic* Affairs [1997] HCA 4, 242 per Dawson J (Australia).

1022 See generally Andreas Zimmermann and Claudia Mahler, "Article 1A, para. 2", in *The 1951 Convention relating to the Status of Refugees and its 1967 Protocol*, edited by Andreas Zimmermann (editor), Jonas Dörschner and Felix Machts (assistant editors) (Oxford: Oxford University Press, 2011), 399–407. See also Markard, *Kriegsflüchtlinge*, 238–265. Hathaway and Foster distinguish between the *ejusdem generis* and the social perception approach: Hathaway and Foster, *The Law of Refugee Status*, 426.

1023 *In re Acosta* (1985) 191 I. & N. Dec. 211 (US), para. 10.

1024 See *Canada (Attorney General) v. Ward* [1993] 2 SCR 689, 737 (Canada).

1025 *Applicant A v. Minister for Immigration and Ethnic Affairs* [1997] HCA 4, per Dawson J (Australia). See also UNHCR, *Guidelines on International Protection No. 2*, para. 14.

with an inclusive and purposeful interpretation of the refugee definition, the two approaches can be reconciled in an alternative, non-cumulative way.[1026]

Civilians are frequently directly attacked in armed conflict. This poses the question of whether civilians can constitute a particular social group, although it must be acknowledged that no State practice has been identified which addresses this question. While referring to "civilian non-combatants fearing persecution in civil war situations",[1027] the Canadian Civil War Guidelines do not discuss this issue. Civilians can be defined in international armed conflict as persons who are not members of the armed forces. Members of the armed forces are also not viewed as civilians in non-international armed conflicts.[1028] Whether members of armed opposition groups are considered as members of armed forces or as civilians remains unclear in customary IHL.[1029] For the sake of this argument, they are understood as being members of the armed forces of the non-State party in a functional sense and thus not civilians.

Civilians would form a potentially large and heterogeneous group not all of whose members would necessarily be at risk of harm. As noted above, these findings do not rule out a definition of civilians as a particular social group. For civilians to form a particular social group according to the protected characteristics approach, they would have to share a characteristic that is innate, unchangeable, or so fundamental to their identity, conscience or exercise of human rights that they cannot be required to alter it. Membership in armed forces may change over time.[1030] Persons who refuse to be recruited into the armed forces or who desert would probably fall into a group that is not defined by reference to civilian status.[1031] Thus, civilians would not constitute a particular social group pursuant to the protected characteristics approach.

1026 As done by UNHCR: UNHCR, *Guidelines on International Protection No. 2*, para. 14. Supporting: Markard, *Kriegsflüchtlinge*, 258–264. But Hathaway and Foster, *The Law of Refugee Status*, 432–436, who argue that the *ejusdem generis* approach is to be preferred over the social perceptions approach.

1027 Immigration and Refugee Board of Canada, "Civilian Non-Combatants Fearing Persecution in Civil War Situations".

1028 See Henckaerts and Doswald-Beck, *Customary International Humanitarian Law*, 12.

1029 See Henckaerts and Doswald-Beck, *Customary International Humanitarian Law*, 17.

1030 This definition of a civilian under customary IHL relates to the application of the principle of distinction. See Henckaerts and Doswald-Beck, *Customary International Humanitarian Law*, 17. The principle of distinction concerns the identification of individuals (civilians) or a group (the civilian population), and therefore can also form the basis for discussing the identification of civilians as a particular social group.

1031 UNHCR argues that conscientious objectors are a particular social group and that draft evaders or deserters may also form such a group: UNHCR, *Guidelines on International Protection No. 10: Claims to Refugee Status related to Military Service within the context of Article 1A(2) of the 1951 Convention and/or the 1967 Protocol relating to the Status of Refugees*, UN Doc. HCR/GIP/13/10 (3 December 2013), para. 58. For a discussion of conscientious objectors, which falls outside this book's scope, see, e.g., Martin Jones, "The Refusal to Bear Arms as Grounds for Refugee Protection in the Canadian Jurisprudence", *International Journal of Refugee Law* 20, no. 1 (2008): 123–165; Cecilia M. Baillet, "Assessing *Jus Ad Bellum*

For civilians to form a particular social group under the social perceptions approach, they would have to be perceived as such by society. Civilians are negatively defined as people who are not members of the armed forces. While a Belgian judgment found the armed forces to constitute a particular social group clearly distinguished from the rest of society,[1032] the proposition that non-members of the armed forces also are a particular social group does not automatically hold true. Since a social group must be distinguished from the relevant society at large, it is difficult to establish that civilians would be perceived as a social group. This might be the case in exceptional circumstances in which the society in question is strongly militarised and in which membership in the armed forces is so prevalent that non-membership is objectively cognisable.[1033] It is likely that the group would have to be defined by more criteria than simply "civilian" for it to constitute a particular social group in the sense of the refugee definition.

4.3. POLITICAL OPINION

Political opinion can be defined as "any opinion on any matter in which the machinery of the State, government, society, or policy may be engaged."[1034] Its content depends on the historical, political and socio-cultural context in the home country.[1035] A variety of acts can express political opinion in situations of armed conflict. This point is particularly relevant for female refugee claimants whose acts risk being perceived as entirely private. Because of their traditional role in society, they may express political opinions by providing shelter or food, acting as messengers, or caring for wounded fighters.[1036]

The Refugee Convention ground of political opinion is salient in contexts of armed conflict, in particular because it not only encompasses political opinions

---

and *Jus in Bello* within the Refugee Status Determination Process: Contemplations on Conscientious Objectors Seeking Asylum", *Georgetown Immigration Law Journal* 20 (2006): 337–384; and Mark R. von Sternberg, "Political Asylum and the Law of Internal Armed Conflict: Refugee Status, Human Rights and Humanitarian Concerns", *International Journal of Refugee Law* 5, no. 2 (1993): 153–185.

1032 See, e.g., *Commission Permanente de Recours des Réfugiés* (Permanent Refugee Appeals Commission), *Decision No. 01-1019/F1369/cd (Russe)*, 15 March 2002 (Belgium), recognising Russian conscripts as a particular social group.

1033 On the requirement that a group be objectively cognisable, see *Applicant S* (2004) 217 CLR 387, 410–411 (69) per McHugh J (Australia) and Foster, "The 'Ground with the Least Clarity'", 9.

1034 Goodwin-Gill and McAdam, *The Refugee in International Law*, 87. See also UNHCR, *Guidelines on International Protection No. 1*, para. 32. On the endorsement of this definition see also Goodwin-Gill and McAdam, *The Refugee in International Law*, 87.

1035 See UNHCR, "Guidance Note on Refugee Claims relating to Victims of Organized Gangs", para. 46. See also *Starred Gomez (Non-State Actors: Acero-Garces Disapproved) (Colombia)* [2000] UKIAT 00007, paras. 40–41 (UK); *Jerez-Spring v. Canada* [1981] 2 FC 527 [FCA] (Canada).

1036 See Hathaway and Foster, *The Law of Refugee Status*, 411 and Markard, *Kriegsflüchtlinge*, 267.

held or expressed by refugee protection claimants but also those imputed on them.[1037] Whether or not such opinions are in fact the victim's is immaterial in such cases.[1038] It is not the persecutor's own political opinions that are relevant, but the persecutor's perception of the victim's political opinion.[1039] There are a number of bases on which a political opinion may be attributed to a refugee claimant in conflicts such as profession,[1040] affiliation with a hostile State[1041] or the international community,[1042] ethnicity,[1043] or place of residence.[1044] Indeed, depending on the nature of the armed conflict, entire neighbourhoods, villages

---

[1037] On the attribution of political opinion, see e.g. Hathaway and Foster, *The Law of Refugee Status*, 406–407 (footnote 276).

[1038] See, e.g., *Noune v. Secretary of State for the Home Department* before the Court of Appeal (Civil Division), 2000 WL 1791543, 6 December 2000, para. 8 (UK).

[1039] See also *Starred Gomez (Non-State Actors: Acero-Garces Disapproved) (Colombia)* [2000] UKIAT 00007, para. 37 (UK); *Sangha v. INS*, 103 F.3d 1482, 1488 (9th Cir. 1997) (US). Non-State actors may also impute political opinions to their victims. See Mark Symes and Peter Jorro, *Asylum Law and Practice*, 2nd ed. (Haywards Heath: Bloomsbury Professional, 2010), 222.

[1040] See *Verwaltungsgerichtshof* (Higher Administrative Court) Baden-Württemberg, VGH BWA 2 S 229/07, NVwZ 2008, 447 (8 August 2007) (regarding journalists and members of the intellectual elite such as academics, physician or artists), *Bundesverwaltungserisht* (Federal Administrative Court) BVerwG, Judgment of 24 June 2008 – 10 C 43/07, NVwZ 2008, 1241 (1245) (all Germany), quoted by Markard, *Kriegsflüchtlinge*, 268. Also: *X (Re)* 2004 CanLII 56786 (IRB) (regarding a Colombian who previously worked government and was considered to be attributed a pro-government/anti-ELN opinion) (Canada); *Verwaltungsgericht* (Administrative Court), VG Frankfurt, 7 K 3373/09.F.A. (16 September 2010) (Germany) (regarding *inter alia* a female teacher in a girls school); UK Border Agency, *Considering the Protection (Asylum) Claim and Assessing Credibility*, 30. But see *Tamara-Gomez v. Gonzalez*, 447 F.3d 343, 15 (5th Cir. 2006) in which being targeted as a member of the police was held to be part of a policeman's role and not related to political opinion even though the claimant was not a policeman but a civilian helicopter mechanic) (US). The UK AIT expressed caution in noting that "it cannot be said as a universal proposition that those on the side of law and order and justice who face persecution from non-State actors … [such as] guerrilla organisations … will have a political opinion imputed on them." *Starred Gomez (Non-State Actors: Acero-Garces Disapproved) (Colombia)* [2000] UKIAT 00007, para. 47 (UK).

[1041] See *Al-Harbi v. INS* 242 F.3d 882 (9th Cir. 2001) (regarding Iraqis airlifted by the US) (US).

[1042] See *Bayrisches Verwaltungsgericht* (Bavarian Administrative Court), *M 23 K 09.50296* (19 January 2011) in which a claimant from Afghanistan who had worked for international organisations was held to have a well-founded fear of being persecuted for reasons of his imputed political opinion (Germany). See also UNHCR, "Eligibility Guidelines for Afghan Asylum-Seekers 2007", 64.

[1043] See UNHCR, "Eligibility Guidelines for Asylum-Seekers from Sri Lanka 2009", 31.

[1044] See *Garcia-Martinez v. Ashcroft*, 371 F.3d 1066, 1069–1070 (9th Cir. 2004) (US). See also Anker, *Law of Asylum in the United States*, para. 5:31, and UNHCR, "International Protection Considerations Regarding Colombian Asylum-Seekers 2005", para. 89. But see *Cediel and others v. US Attorney General*, 170 Fed. Appx. 89 (11th Cir. 2006) (US), in which the Court rejected the petitioners' argument that the paramilitaries imputed a pro-guerrilla opinion on one of the petitioners because of his home town which was known as a guerrilla stronghold, finding that the petitioner had not been singled out and that the paramilitaries generally harassed people.

or towns can be targeted by association.[1045] Moreover, religious groups often have political agendas or are affiliated with political movements, as the case of an Assyrian Christian from Iraq illustrates who claimed persecution by the then ruling Ba'ath Party on account of political opinions imputed to his ethno-religious group.[1046] In addition, armed groups may impose religious rules in an area under their control, with deviation being perceived as manifesting religious (non-)belief and/or a political opinion.[1047]

Civilians may also have a well-founded fear of being persecuted because of other Refugee Convention grounds, in particular political opinion. For example, Afghan civilians perceived as providing support to anti-government groups may be arbitrarily detained and ill-treated. Hence they are at risk of persecution because of their imputed political opinion.[1048]

Any actor of persecution can impute political opinions, including non-State armed groups.[1049] Political opinion should be construed widely.[1050] However, the notion is not so broad that it would include any opinion which a non-State persecutor may impute on its victim,[1051] as the UK AIT demonstrates:

> "To qualify as political the opinion in question must relate to the major power transactions taking place in that particular society. It is difficult to see how a political opinion can be imputed by a non-State actor who (or which) is not itself a political entity."[1052]

The persecutor's broad aims in the conflict are not as such sufficient for establishing imputed political opinion.[1053] The challenge is to take into

---

1045 See Blanche Tax, "Refugee by Association", *Forced Migration Review* 47 (2014): 26–27 in relation to the conflict in Syria.

1046 See *Youkhana v. Gonzalez*, 460 F.3d 927 (7th Cir. 2006) (US). See also Anker, *Law of Asylum in the United States*, para. 7:79.

1047 See, e.g., UNHCR, "UNHCR Eligibility Guidelines for Assessing the International Protection Needs of Asylum-Seekers from Somalia (2010)", 13 on Somalia. Regarding Afghanistan, see UNHCR, "Eligibility Guidelines for Asylum-Seekers from Afghanistan 2009", 35. Non-conformity with religious norms may also give rise to a well-founded fear of being persecuted for reasons of political opinion, for example if it is perceived as opposition to traditional power structures in a given society. See Markard, *Kriegsflüchtlinge*, 237.

1048 See UNHCR, "Eligibility Guidelines for Asylum-Seekers from Afghanistan 2010", 16–17. Similarly in relation to Syria: Blanche Tax, "Refugee by Association", *Forced Migration Review* 47 (2014): 26–27.

1049 See UNHCR, *Guidelines on International Protection No. 10: Claims to Refugee Status related to Military Service within the context of Article 1A(2) of the 1951 Convention and/or the 1967 Protocol relating to the Status of Refugees*, UN Doc. HCR/GIP/13/10 (3 December 2013), para. 51.

1050 See UNHCR, *Guidelines on International Protection No. 1*, para. 32. See also Goodwin-Gill and McAdam, *The Refugee in International Law*, 87.

1051 See *Starred Gomez (Non-State Actors: Acero-Garces Disapproved) (Colombia)* [2000] UKIAT 00007, para. 73(VI) (UK).

1052 *Starred Gomez (Non-State Actors: Acero-Garces Disapproved) (Colombia)* [2000] UKIAT 00007, para. 73(VII) (UK).

1053 See *Starred Gomez (Non-State Actors: Acero-Garces Disapproved) (Colombia)* [2000] UKIAT 00007, para. 73(XI); see also para. 67 regarding the FARC in Colombia (UK).

consideration the armed conflict's political dimension and its effects on the individual refugee claimant. The characteristics of the conflict, for example the polarised situation in Colombia,[1054] may assist in determining whether an opinion attributed to a victim by a non-State actor is political. Another relevant factor is the nature of the armed group in question, such as the FARC which has been found to have had so much power that it carried out State-like functions.[1055]

Parties to armed conflict often also have economic or criminal motives. For example, the RSAA in New Zealand found:

> "[T]he FARC is an extreme left-wing political movement which categorizes its victims as enemies of the working class. Its actions are confused, often contradictory and usually criminal, but the underlying political current is sufficient to satisfy the Authority that any harm to the appellant would be for reasons, at least in part, of political opinion."[1056]

This case illustrates that it may be difficult to determine whether a non-State party to a conflict seeks to achieve its political objectives without consideration of the victims' political views or whether it imputes political opinions on them.[1057] The case further shows that criminal motives may also be involved. Cases involving resistance to extortion or recruitment into an armed group are frequently examined by inquiring whether they either relate to motives of criminality, revenge, or retribution, or whether they reveal expressions or attributions of political opinion.[1058] Another case in point is the UK Border Agency, which found:

> "Even if a rebel group has a broad political aim (e.g. overthrowing the Government), individual attacks on particular individuals might simply be retaliatory or criminal and not necessarily linked to an overriding political aim."[1059]

1054 See UNHCR, "International Protection Considerations regarding Colombian Asylum-seekers and Refugees 2002", para. 22.

1055 See *Starred Gomez (Non-State Actors: Acero-Garces Disapproved) (Colombia)* [2000] UKIAT 00007, para. 21 (UK).

1056 *Refugee Appeal No. 76289* [2009] NZRSAA 36 (8 May 2009), para. 43 (New Zealand). On the FARC, the *Ejército de Liberación Nacional* (National Liberation Army, ELN) and imputed political opinion, see also *Starred Gomez (Non-State Actors: Acero-Garces Disapproved) (Colombia)* [2000] UKIAT 00007, para. 66 (UK). In *Guerrero-Gomez and others v. Attorney General*, 218 Fed. Appx. 921 (11th Cir. 2007) (US), in which the Court held that the FARC's harassment of the petitioner was merely extortion rather than based on a political opinion attributed to him. In *Espinosa-Cortez and others v. Attorney General* 607 F3.d 101 (3rd Cir. 2010) (US), the Court found that the petitioners' fear of persecution was at least in part based political opinion imputed on them by the FARC because a petitioner had made his anti-FARC views known.

1057 See Anker, *Law of Asylum in the United States*, para. 5:55.

1058 See Hathaway and Foster, *The Law of Refugee Status*, 419.

1059 UK Border Agency, *Considering the Protection (Asylum) Claim and Assessing Credibility*, 31.

However, as previously noted, multiple motives do not rule out the existence of a nexus to a Refugee Convention ground.[1060] Even though not every act by an armed group is necessarily political, retaliation may be political, requiring an examination of the individual circumstances and societal contexts.[1061] Cases involving opinions imputed by non-State actors require an analysis of the actor's characteristics, its objectives and how they impact on the victim, the context of the conflict, and the individual circumstances.

Perceived opposition or support for the adversary is often the reason why civilians are at risk.[1062] For example, the Canadian IRB held that a Colombian feared persecution for reasons of his pro-government/anti-guerrilla political opinion,[1063] and, in a different case, that the guerrilla was political in nature.[1064] Moreover, refusing to join or support a party to a conflict or to take sides may express political neutrality, which in certain circumstances can constitute a political opinion.[1065]

1060 Schiemann LJ found: "The motives of the persecutor may be mixed and they can include non-Convention reasons: it is not necessary to show that they are purely political". *Noune v. Secretary of State for the Home Department* before the Court of Appeal (Civil Division), 2000 WL 1791543, 6 December 2000, para. 8 (UK). See also Hathaway and Foster, *The Law of Refugee Status*, 419.

1061 In *Dalit Sing v. Minister for Immigration and Multicultural Affairs* [1999] FCA 1599, Mansfield J noted at para. 35: "Revenge may be personal or it may be political" (Canada). The US Court of Appeal for the Second Circuit found that "the conclusion that a cause of persecution is economic does not necessarily imply that there cannot exist other causes of the persecution." *Osorio v. INS*, 18 F.3d 1017, 1028 (2nd Cir. 1994) (US). See also *Starred Gomez (Non-State Actors: Acero-Garces Disapproved) (Colombia)* [2000] UKIAT 00007, para. 42 (UK). See also Hathaway and Foster, *The Law of Refugee Status*, 420.

1062 See in relation to Syria: Blanche Tax, "Refugee by Association", *Forced Migration Review* 47 (2014): 26–27.

1063 See *X (Re)* 2004 CanLII 56786 (IRB) (Canada).

1064 See *X (Re)* 2004 CanLII 56786 (IRB) (Canada).

1065 In *Sangha v. INS*, 103 F.3d 1482, 1488 (9th Cir. 1997) (US), the US Court of Appeals for the Ninth Circuit held that "an applicant can establish a 'political opinion' ... [by] show[ing] political neutrality in an environment in which political neutrality is fraught with hazard, from governmental or uncontrolled anti-governmental forces." See also *Elias-Zacarias v. INS*, 112 S.Ct 812 (1992); *Rivera-Moreno v. INS* (No, 98–71463) (9th Cir. 2000), *Maldonado-Cruz v. INS*, 883 F.2d 788, 791 (9th Cir. 1989) (all US). Further: Sternberg, *The Grounds of Refugee Protection*, 82–122. UK jurisprudence seems to adopt a broader approach. In the case of *Noune v. Secretary of State for the Home Department* before the Court of Appeal (Civil Division), 2000 WL 1791543, 6 December 2000, Schiemann LJ stated at para. 8 that "in order to show persecution on account of political opinion it is not necessary to show political action or activity by the victim: in some circumstances, mere inactivity and unwillingness to co-operate can be taken as an expression of political opinion" (UK). See also *Secretary of State for the Home Department (Appellant) v. RT (Zimbabwe), SM (Zimbabwe) and AM (Zimbabwe) (Respondents) and the United Nations High Commissioner for Refugees (Intervener)* – Case for the Intervener, 25 May 2012, 2011/0011, para. 10 (UK). UNHCR, however, argues that political opinion encompasses political neutrality in all cases. See UNHCR, *Guidelines on International Protection No. 10: Claims to Refugee Status related to Military Service within the context of Article 1A(2) of the 1951 Convention and/or the 1967 Protocol relating to the Status of Refugees*, UN Doc. HCR/GIP/13/10 (3 December 2013), para. 51.

5. CONCLUSION

The refugee definition's nexus requirement refers to a causal link between, on the one hand, the refugee claimant's predicament and, on the other hand, one or more Refugee Convention grounds. A Refugee Convention ground must be a contributing cause to the refugee claimant's predicament, but it need not be the sole or dominant cause. The causes, character and impact of the armed conflict in the country of origin must be taken into consideration in the interpretation and application of the nexus requirement. This context includes patterns of serious IHL violations. Since IHL only permits violence if it is pursuing a legitimate military objective, violations of customary IHL reveal that the causes of the victims' predicament exceed legitimate military necessity. The political objectives of the parties to a conflict do not vindicate violations of IHL. While customary IHL does not itself identify a pertinent Refugee Convention ground, serious violations of customary IHL provide indicia that may assist in the determination of whether the nexus requirement is fulfilled. These indicia include patterns of rape, inhuman treatment, mutilations, destruction and forced displacement in non-international armed conflict not justified by military necessity, the use of unlawful weapons such as chemical weapons, direct attacks against civilians, indiscriminate attacks, and disproportionate attacks. The grounds listed in the Refugee Convention are to be interpreted broadly and with reference to the causes, characteristics or impact of the armed conflict in the country of origin. Customary IHL provides little interpretative guidance as to their meaning.

Customary IHL and international criminal law play an indicative role in the interpretation of the refugee definition's nexus requirement and the stipulated grounds by identifying patterns of violence that can point to a causal link between the victims' predicament and a Refugee Convention ground. Inferences can be drawn from violations of customary IHL as to the fulfilment of the nexus requirement. Customary IHL does not, however, provide comprehensive guidance concerning the nexus requirement and the Refugee Convention grounds because it does not itself give meaning to these grounds or assist in identifying the pertinent ground in individual cases.

CHAPTER 8
CONCLUSION

This book examined the refugee definition in Article 1A(2) Refugee Convention in light of international human rights law, customary IHL and international criminal law with respect to refugee protection claims of individuals who had to leave their country of origin due to armed conflict or who fear return to their country of origin because of armed conflict. The book sought to calibrate the extent to which and the way in which customary IHL and international criminal law should be drawn upon in the interpretation of the refugee definition as regards such claims to refugee protection.

International refugee law, international human rights law, IHL and international criminal law are distinct yet interrelated branches of international law that interact in a variety of ways to further the protection of the individual in armed conflict. Customary IHL and international criminal law cannot and should not replace international human rights law as a source of insight with respect to conflict-related claims to refugee protection. Rather, these bodies of international law complement the human rights-based interpretation of the refugee definition. They can assist national refugee status decision-makers by providing armed conflict-specific interpretative guidance on certain matters.

Refugee status decision-makers ought to determine whether a situation of violence in the country of origin was, is or is likely to be an armed conflict since customary IHL and international criminal law can only provide interpretative guidance if the refugee protection claim relates to an armed conflict in the country of origin. A suitable definition of armed conflict was provided by the ICTY in the *Tadić case*, with subsequent ICTY jurisprudence offering a set of indicators to determine whether a situation of violence constitutes an armed conflict. Refugee status decision-makers can draw on this definition of armed conflicts and these indicators in assessing whether there is, was or is likely to be an armed conflict in the country of origin.

The general rule on treaty interpretation set forth in the VCLT allows for an interpretation of the refugee definition in light of international human rights law, customary IHL and international criminal law. Of particular relevance in this respect is the requirement to interpret the refugee definition in an inclusive and dynamic way which flows from the Refugee Convention's humanitarian object and purpose. Consequently, customary IHL and international criminal law can only provide interpretative guidance if they serve to strengthen rather than undermine refugee protection based on the Refugee Convention. Customary IHL and international criminal law do not shed light on all elements of the refugee definition. Rather, most insights can be gained from these branches of international law with respect to persecution and the causal link between a refugee claimant's predicament and a Refugee Convention ground. To a lesser extent, customary IHL and international criminal law also inform other elements of the refugee definition such as the lack of protection in the country of origin and the notion of membership of a particular social group as regards civilians.

Not only may civilians who did not directly participate in hostilities claim refugee protection, but also civilians who did take up arms, members of armed opposition groups and members of the armed forces. The passive personal scope of the refugee definition is not limited in times of armed conflict, although pursuant to Article 1F Refugee Convention the term "refugee" does not apply to persons with regard to whom there are serious reasons for considering that they committed a war crime or other stipulated crimes.

In determining whether the refugee protection claimant has a well-founded fear of persecution, the burden of proof must be shared between the receiving country and the claimant, with the standard of proof being that of "reasonable possibility". In assessing the claimant's "well-founded fear", an objective approach is to be adopted that considers the individual's risk of being persecuted in the context of the situation in the country of origin, including violations of international human rights law and IHL. The refugee claimant need not show that they would be singled out for persecution or that they are in any way more at risk than other persons or groups in the country of origin. Both agents of the country of origin and non-State actors can be persecutors.

Persecution encompasses one or more human rights violations of sufficient intensity. The human rights-based scope of persecution is not narrower in times of armed conflict than in times of peace even though human rights protection in the country of origin might be curtailed due to the armed conflict. Moreover, in armed conflict, violations of customary IHL can constitute persecution in and of themselves, provided they are serious enough. International criminal law, in particular the requirement that the breached rule of IHL must protect important values and that its breach must result in grave consequences for the victims, provides helpful benchmarks for assessing whether the intensity threshold required for persecution is surpassed. Although the relationship between international human rights law and IHL is usually perceived in terms of the *lex specialis* principle, this principle is not suitable for informing the way in which persecution ought to be interpreted in light of international human rights law and IHL. More instructive is the requirement to interpret the refugee definition in an inclusive and dynamic way. Consequently, in cases in which the standards of protection under international human rights law and customary IHL differ and the scope of persecution would be narrower if interpreted in light of one branch of international law as opposed to the other, the branch of international law that results in the broader scope of persecution is to be preferred.

Customary IHL and international criminal law can reinforce a human rights-based understanding of persecution in contexts of armed conflict. For instance, although rape and other forms of sexual violence are clearly prohibited under international human rights law in times of peace and armed conflict, refugee jurisprudence has at times failed to recognise rape as persecution in armed conflict. The prohibition of rape and other forms of sexual violence under customary IHL and their constituting a war crime can serve to rectify this misapprehension. Customary IHL and international criminal law can also pinpoint unlawful means and methods of warfare that constitute persecution, such as the use of chemical weapons, starvation or forced displacement in non-international armed conflict. With respect to certain forms of harm, such as the minimum age for the recruitment of children into the armed forces or armed groups or concerning "scorched earth policies" in international armed conflict, the standard of protection provided by international human rights law in armed conflict is higher than that under customary IHL and must therefore be preferred in the interpretation of persecution. As regards other forms of harm such as arbitrary deprivation of liberty in armed conflict, IHL's paucity means that international human rights law provides more instructive interpretative guidance, in particular as regards children. The use of lethal force which violates rules of customary IHL, such as direct attacks against civilians, amounts to persecution. However, the use of lethal force that complies with customary IHL does not necessarily fall outside the scope of persecution but ought to be further examined in light of international human rights law and the individual circumstances of the case at hand in order to determine whether it constitutes persecution.

Customary IHL and international criminal law cannot provide comprehensive interpretative guidance for the refugee definition with regard to refugee protection claims arising out of situations of armed conflict. The absence of a risk of being subjected to a violation of customary IHL is not necessarily tantamount to the lack of a well-founded fear of being persecuted. For example, an attack against child civilians who are directly participating in hostilities might not be unlawful and thus not persecutory, but these children may nonetheless have been persecuted because they may have been forced to participate in the hostilities in the first place.

International refugee protection is surrogate protection for individuals who lack the protection of their country of origin. In times of armed conflict, such protection is not only to be understood in light of international human rights law, but also by taking into consideration customary IHL and international criminal law. Violations of customary IHL indicate the absence of national protection. Yet compliance with customary IHL is not tantamount to effective protection by the country of origin as a range of other factors must also be considered. If persecution is feared or was experienced at the hands of agents of the country of origin, lack of protection from such persecution is assumed. If persecution emanates from non-State actors, protection by the country of origin from such persecution must be such that it removes the well-founded fear of persecution. A refugee claimant need not show a country-wide well-founded fear of persecution. But in cases in which the fear of persecution at the hands of a non-State actor is geographically confined, for instance because of a regionally limited armed conflict, an internal protection alternative may be available if the proposed area of relocation is accessible and if protection from persecution – namely protection from serious violations of human rights, customary IHL and war crimes – and protection in the broader sense is available there.

Moreover, it must be determined whether the refugee claimant's predicament is causally linked to a Refugee Convention ground. Pursuant to customary IHL, parties to an armed conflict do not possess an absolute or unfettered right to achieve their political or other aims with military might. Customary IHL only recognises the weakening of the enemy's military force as legitimate objective. With respect to the refugee definition's nexus requirement, patterns of violations of customary IHL rules in the country of origin mean that the victims' predicament is not justified by military necessity but has other causes, which in turn may relate to a Refugee Convention ground. Thus, customary IHL does not provide comprehensive interpretative guidance as regards the causal link between a refugee claimant's predicament and a Refugee Convention ground. It does, however, offer an instructive set of indicia, in particular if persecution is also considered in light of customary IHL. For example, using the forced displacement of the civilian population as a method of warfare in contravention of customary IHL cannot be justified by military necessity, which indicates the presence of other causes such as political oppression or even ethnic cleansing that can in turn relate to a Refugee Convention ground.

It is important to take into account the causes, character and impact of an armed conflict when interpreting and applying the nexus requirement. For instance, international war crimes jurisprudence shows that attacks against civilians, which breach customary IHL, may mostly affect civilians belonging to a certain ethnic or religious group. Indiscriminate attacks may in fact be directed at civilians, with the choice of weaponry possibly indicating an intent to deliberately attack the civilian population. This illustrates how customary IHL and international criminal law can serve to strengthen protection under the Refugee Convention by adapting it to the specific circumstances of victims of armed conflict. It also shows how the above analysis contributed to an understanding of international refugee law, international human rights law,

IHL and international criminal law not as compartmentalised elements of a fragmented international legal order, but as interrelated components of the international framework for the protection of the individual in armed conflict that may well be developing towards an international law for humankind.

As regards the Refugee Convention grounds, customary IHL offers little interpretative guidance, though civilians might constitute a particular social group in exceptional circumstances such as a highly militarised society in which non-membership in armed forces is cognisable and with the group likely being defined by additional criteria.

Historically, international refugee law evolved against the backdrop of conflict-induced forced displacement and other contextual factors. In today's world, forced displacement caused by armed conflict continues to pose major challenges to international refugee protection. This book has focussed on the Refugee Convention as the bedrock of the international system for refugee protection, addressing the challenges pertaining to the interpretation and application of the refugee definition in Article 1A(2) Refugee Convention in light of international human rights law, customary IHL and international criminal law. There are, of course, a number of other challenges posed by conflict-induced forced displacement, some of which are briefly outlined in this section.

Effective refugee protection for individuals compelled to flee from armed conflict also comprises measures that go beyond the design and implementation of refugee status determination procedures. Many asylum-seekers from war-torn countries in the Middle East and Africa reach Europe by crossing the Mediterranean. The resultant challenges were highlighted, for example, by the European Commissioner for Home Affairs and the UN High Commissioner for Refugees with reference to the Libyan conflict:

> "[W]e have seen more than a million people leave everything behind and flee the war in Libya. … Men, women and children putting their lives at risk in often unseaworthy boats, trying to cross the Mediterranean in rapidly variable weather – an unknown but large number drowning in the attempt."[1066]

Such perilous journeys by sea raise a number of concerns which must be addressed when seeking a comprehensive solution to the protection of refugees who fled from armed conflict in their country of origin. A comprehensive international response must include the provision of the necessary assistance to boats in distress and compliance with the obligation of *non-refoulement*, in particular as regards the adoption of interception measures at sea.[1067] The

1066 Cecilia Malmström and Antonio Gutierrez, "60 Years of the Geneva Refugee Convention: Europe Must Uphold Its Values" (2011), available at http://ec.europa.eu/commission_2010-2014/malmstrom/news/what-written/archives/2011/07/20110728_en.htm#, accessed 10.03.2015.

1067 See generally Guy S. Goodwin-Gill, "The Right to Seek Asylum: Interception at Sea and the Principle of Non-Refoulement", *International Journal of Refugee Law* 23, no. 3

same applies to interception measures on land. For instance, Iraqi, Jordanian and Turkish border guards were reported to have pushed Syrians fleeing the armed conflict back into Syria, to have closed border checkpoints and to have severely restricted border crossings.[1068] Access to safety is an indispensable element of effective refugee protection for individuals forced to flee from armed conflict.

Furthermore, having escaped the perils of armed conflict in their country of origin and having obtained refugee protection in the receiving country is essential, but for many refugees it is not necessarily the end of their ordeal. Living conditions in receiving countries can be dire, as the UN Secretary-General emphasised:

> "Displacement ... continues to be one of the principal features of contemporary conflict and arguably the most significant humanitarian challenge that we face. But often it is only the beginning of an ordeal that may last for years or even decades, marked by suffering, deprivation and a daily fight for survival."[1069]

Thus, ensuring adequate standards of living and finding durable solutions to "war refugees" is of pivotal importance.[1070] Another crucial element of

---

(2011): 443–457. The judgment of the European Court of Human Rights in the case *Hrsi Jamaa v. Italy* shows that there has been some progress in curtailing the interception of asylum-seekers at sea. The court held that Italy's "push-back" operations interdicting migrants and asylum-seekers at sea and returning them to Libya amounted to a violation of Article 3 of the European Convention on the Protection of Human Rights and Fundamental Freedoms (adopted 4 November 1950, entered into force 3 September 1953, 213 UNTS 222) (ECHR). See *Hrsi Jamaa v. Italy*, Application No. 27765/09, Merits, 23 February 2012, paras. 122–138.

1068 See Human Rights Watch, "Iraq/Jordan/Turkey: Syrians Blocked from Fleeing War" (2013), available at www.hrw.org/news/2013/07/01/iraqjordanturkey-syrians-blocked-fleeing-war, accessed 10.03.2015. Of these three States, only Turkey is a party to the Refugee Convention and its Protocol, having maintained the original geographical limitation of the refugee definition to refugees from Europe. See UNHCR, "States Parties to the 1951 Convention relating to the Status of Refugees and the 1967 Protocol" (2011), available at www.unhcr.org/3b73b0d63.html, accessed 10.03.2015. Promotion of accession to the Refugee Convention and/or its Protocol and the lifting of the geographic limitation to the refugee definition could thus be considered further steps towards ensuring effective protection of individuals displaced by armed conflict as refugees.

1069 UN Secretary-General, *Report of the Secretary-General on the Protection of Civilians in Armed Conflict*, UN Doc. S/2007/643 (28 October 2007), para. 5.

1070 The judgment of the European Court of Human Rights in the case *M.S.S. v. Belgium and Greece* underscores the obligation of receiving States to ensure adequate living conditions for asylum-seekers. The court held that the general living conditions endured by an Afghan asylum-seeker in Greece (and thousands of other asylum-seekers in the country) amounted to inhuman and degrading treatment in violation of Article 3 ECHR. See *M.S.S. v. Belgium and Greece*, Application No. 30696/09, Merits, 21 January 2011, paras. 249–263. On reception conditions and inhuman or degrading treatment, see also the judgment of the Courtf Justice of the European Union, Joined Cases C-411/10 and C-49 3-/10, *N.S. v. Secretary of State for the Home Department and M.E. and others v. Refugee Commissioner and Minister for Justice,*

international refugee protection is burden-sharing. After all, about 80% of the world's refugees live in developing countries.[1071] Indeed, the Refugee Convention emphasises in its preamble that

> "the grant of asylum may place unduly heavy burdens on certain countries, and that a satisfactory solution of a problem of which the United Nations has recognised the international scope and nature cannot therefore be achieved without international co-operation."[1072]

Only if all challenges are met will refugee protection for individuals forcefully displaced by armed conflict truly be achieved.

Equality and Law Reform, Judgment of 21 December 2011, OJ C274/21 and OJ C13/18, para. 86.

1071 See UNHCR, "Global Report 2013", 84.

1072 Fourth preambular recital of the Refugee Convention.

BIBLIOGRAPHY

Dapo Akande, "Classification of Armed Conflicts: Relevant Legal Concepts", in *International Law and the Classification of Conflicts*, edited by Elizabeth Wilmshurst, 32–79, Oxford: Oxford University Press, 2012 (Akande, "Classification of Armed Conflicts").

T. Alexander Aleinikoff, "The Mandate of the Office of the United Nations High Commissioner for Refugees", in *Research Handbook on International Law and Migration*, edited by Vincent Chetail and Céline Bauloz, 389–416, Cheltenham/Northampton: Edward Elgar, 2014.

Deborah Anker, *Law of Asylum in the United States*, Thomson West, 2011.

Deborah E. Anker, "Refugee Law, Gender, and the Human Rights Paradigm", *Harvard Human Rights Journal* 15, (2002): 133–154 (Anker, *Refugee Law*).

Kelly D. Askin, "Prosecuting Wartime Rape and other Gender-Related Crimes under International Law: Extraordinary Advances, Enduring Obstacles", *Berkeley Journal of International Law* 21 (2003): 288–349.

Cecilia M. Baillet, "Assessing *Jus Ad Bellum* and *Jus in Bello* within the Refugee Status Determination Process: Contemplations on Conscientious Objectors Seeking Asylum", *Georgetown Immigration Law Journal* 20 (2006): 337–384.

M. Cherif Bassiouni, *International Criminal Law*, Vol. III International Enforcement, Leiden: Martinus Nijhoff, 2008.

Céline Bauloz, "The (Mis)Use of International Humanitarian Law under Article 15(c) of the EU Qualification Directive", in *Refuge from Inhumanity? War Refugees and International Humanitarian Law*, edited by David James Cantor and Jean-François Durieux, 247–569, Leiden: Koninklijke Brill, 2014.

John B. II Bellinger and William J. II Haynes, "A US Government Response to the International Committee of the Red Cross Study Customary International Humanitarian Law", *International Review of the Red Cross* 89, no. 866 (2007): 443–471 (Bellinger and Haynes, "A US Government Response").

Kazimierz Bem, "The Coming of a 'Blank Cheque' – Europe, the 1951 Convention, and the 1967 Protocol", *International Journal of Refugee Law* 16, no. 4 (2004): 609–627.

Kazimierz Bem, "Defining the Refugee. American and Dutch Asylum Case-Law 1975–2005", Vrije Universiteit Amsterdam, 2007.

Orna Ben-Naftali, *International Humanitarian Law and International Human Rights Law*, Oxford: Oxford University Press, 2011 (Ben-Naftali, *International Humanitarian Law*).

Chaloka Beyani, "International Legal Criteria for the Separation of Members of Armed Forces, Armed Bands and Militia from Refugees in the Territories of Host States", *International Journal of Refugee Law* 12 (2000): 251–271.

Andrea Binder, *Frauenspezifische Verfolgung vor dem Hintergrund einer menschenrechtlichen Auslegung des Flüchtlingsbegriffs unter besonderer Berücksichtigung der schweizerischen, deutschen, kanadischen und amerikanischen Flüchtlings- und Asylpraxis*, Basel et al.: Helbing & Lichtenhahn, 2001 (Binder, *Frauenspezifische Verfolgung*).

Erik Bjorge, "Human Rights, Treaties, Third-Party Effect", in *Max Planck Encyclopedia of Public International Law*, edited by Rüdiger Wolfrum, Oxford: Oxford University Press, 2011, available at www.mpepil.com, accessed 10.03.2015.

Maarten Bos, "Theory and Practice of Treaty Interpretation", *Netherlands International Law Review* 27, no. 2 (1980): 135–170 (Bos, "Theory and Practice of Treaty Interpretation").

Michael Bossin and Laila Demirdache, "A Canadian Perspective on the Subjective Component of the Bipartite Test for 'Persecution': Time for Re-evaluation", *Refuge* 22, no. 1 (2005): 108–118 (Bossin and Demirdache, "A Canadian Perspective").

Michael Bothe, "Customary International Humanitarian Law: Some Reflections on the ICRC Study", *Yearbook of International Humanitarian Law* 8 (2005): 143–178.

Michael Bothe, "Direct Participation in Hostilities in Non-International Armed Conflict", *Expert Paper for the Second Expert Meeting on the Notion of Direct Participation in Hostilities, The Hague, 25–26 October 2004* (2004), available at www.icrc.org/eng/assets/files/other/2004-05-expert-paper-dph-icrc.pdf, accessed 10.03.2015.

Michael Bothe, "Friedenssicherungsrecht und Kriegsrecht", in *Völkerrecht*, edited by Wolfgang Graf Vitzthum, 639–740, Berlin: De Gruyter, 2010.

Michael Bothe, "The Historical Evolution of International Humanitarian Law, International Human Rights Law, Refugee Law and International Criminal Law", in *Krisensicherung und Humanitärer Schutz - Crisis Management and Humanitarian Protection. Festschrift für Dieter Fleck*, edited by Horst Fischer, Ulrike Froissart, Wolff Heintschel von Heinegg and Christian Raap, 37–45, Berlin: Berliner Wissenschaftsverlag, 2004 (Bothe, "The Historical Evolution").

Michael Bothe, "Humanitäres Völkerrecht und Menschenrechte", *Humanitäres Völkerrecht Informationsschriften* 1 (2008): 4–8.

Michael Bothe, "Humanitäres Völkerrecht und Menschenrechte: Auf der Suche nach Synergien und Schutzlücken", in *Völkerrecht als Wertordnung. Common Values in International Law. Festschrift für? Essays in Honour of Christian Tomuschat*, edited by Pierre-Marie Dupuy, Bardo Fassbender, Malcolm N. Shaw and Karl-Peter Sommermann, 63–90, Kehl: N.P. Engel, 2006.

Michael Bothe, "War Crimes", in *The Rome Statute of the International Criminal Court: A Commentary*, edited by Antonio Cassese, Paola Gaeta and John R.W.D. Jones, 379–426, Oxford: Oxford University Press, 2002 (Bothe, "War Crimes").

Michael Bothe, Karl Josef Partsch and Waldemar A. Solf, *New Rules for Victims of Armed Conflicts: Commentary on the two 1977 Protocols Additional to the Geneva Conventions of 1949*, The Hague/Boston: Martinus Nijhoff, 1982 (Bothe, Partsch and Solf, *New Rules for Victims of Armed Conflicts*).

Bill Bowring, "Fragmentation, *Lex Specialis* and the Tension in the Jurisprudence of the European Court of Human Rights", *Journal of Conflict & Security Law* 2009, no. 14 (2009): 3.

Ulrike Brandl, "Die Anwendbarkeit des Flüchtlingsbegriffs der Genfer Flüchtlingskonvention auf Bürgerkriegsflüchtlinge", in *Temporary Protection für Flüchtlinge in Europa. Analysen und Schlussfolgerungen*, edited by Hannes Tretter, 179–219, Vienna: Verlag Österreich, 2005 (Brandl, "Die Anwendbarkeit des Flüchtlingsbegriffs").

Susan Breau, "Protected Persons and Objects", in *Perspectives on the ICRC Study on Customary International Humanitarian Law*, edited by Elizabeth Wilmshurst and Susan Breau, 169–203, Cambridge: Cambridge University Press, 2007 (Breau, "Protected Persons and Objects").

Anne-Marie L.M. Brouwer, *Supranational Criminal Prosecution of Sexual Violence. The ICC and the Practice of the ICTY and the ICTR*, Antwerp/Oxford: Intersentia, 2005.

Thomas Buergenthal, *International Human Rights in a Nutshell*, St. Paul: West, 1988.

François Bugnion, "Droit de Genève et Droit de La Haye", *International Review of the Red Cross* 83, no. 844 (2001): 901–922.

François Bugnion, *The International Committee of the Red Cross and the Protection of War Victims*, Oxford: Macmillan, 2003.

Peter Butcher, "Assessing Fear of Persecution in a War Zone", *Georgetown Immigration Law Journal* 5, (1991): 435–473 (Butcher, "Assessing Fear of Persecution").

Antônio Augusto Cançado Trindade, *International Law for Humankind: Towards a New Jus Gentium (I). General Course on Public International Law*, The Hague Academy of International Law, Recueil des Cours/Collected Courses, Leiden/Boston: Martinus Nijhoff, 2005 (Cançado Trindade, *International Law for Humankind*).

Antônio Augusto Cançado Trindade, *International Law for Humankind: Towards a New Jus Gentium (II). General Course on Public International Law*, The Hague Academy of International Law, Recueil des Cours/Collected Courses, Leiden/Boston: Martinus Nijhoff, 2005.

Nergis Canefe, "The Fragmented Nature of the International Refugee Regime and Its Consequences: A Comparative Analysis of the Applications of the 1951 Convention", in *Critical Issues in International Refugee Law: Strategies toward Interpretative Harmony*, edited by James C. Simeon, 174–210, Cambridge: Cambridge University Press, 2010.

Enzo Cannizzaro, "Proportionality in the Law of Armed Conflict", in *The Oxford Handbook of International Law in Armed Conflict*, edited by Andrew Clapham, Paola Gaeta (editors), Tom Haeck and Alice Priddy (assistant editors), 332–352, Oxford: Oxford University Press: 2014.

Jean-Yves Carlier, *Droit d'asile et des réfugiés. De la protection aux droits*, Hague Academy of International Law, Recueil des Cours/Collected Courses, Vol. 332, The Hague et al.: Martinus Nijhoff, 2008.

Jean-Yves Carlier, "The Geneva Refugee Definition and the 'Theory of the Three Scales'", in *Refugee Rights and Realities. Evolving International Concepts and Regimes*, edited by Frances Nicholson and Patrick Twomey, 37–105, Cambridge: Cambridge University Press 1999 (Carlier, "The Geneva Refugee Definition").

Jean-Yves Carlier, Dirk Vanheule, Klaus Hullmann and Carlos Peña Galiano, eds., *Who Is a Refugee? A Comparative Case Law Study*, The Hague: Kluwer Law International, 1997.

Burrus M. Carnahan, "Lincoln, Lieber and the Laws of War: The Origins and Limits of the Principle of Military Necessity", *The American Journal of International Law* 92, no. 2 (1998): 213–231 (Carnahan, "Lincoln, Lieber and the Laws of War").

Bridgette A. Carr, "We Don't Need to See Them Cry: Eliminating the Subjective Apprehension Element of the Well-Founded Fear Analysis for Child Refugee Applicants", *Pepperdine Law Review* 33 (2005–2006): 535–573.

Antonio Cassese, *International Criminal Law*, 2nd ed., Oxford: Oxford University Press, 2008.

Vincent Chetail, "Are Refugee Rights Human Rights? An Unorthodox Questioning of the Relations between Refugee Law and Human Rights Law" (2012), available at http://papers.ssrn.com/sol3/papers.cfm?abstract_id=2147763, accessed 10.03.2015.

Vincent Chetail, "Armed Conflict and Forced Migration. A Systematic Approach to International Humanitarian Law, Refugee Law, and International Human Rights Law", in *The Oxford Handbook of International Law in Armed Conflict*, edited by Andrew Clapham, Paola Gaeta (editors), Tom Haeck and Alice Pritty (assistant editors), 700–736, Oxford: Oxford University Press, 2014 (Chetail, "Armed Conflict and Forced Migration").

Christine Chinkin, "Gender and Armed Conflict", in *The Oxford Handbook of International Law in Armed Conflict*, edited by Andrew Clapham, Paola Gaeta (editors), Tom Haeck and Alice Pritty (assistant editors), 675–699, Oxford: Oxford University Press, 2014 (Christine Chinkin, "Gender and Armed Conflict").

Andrew Clapham, *Human Rights Obligations of Non-State Actors*, Oxford: Oxford University Press, 2006 (Andrew Clapham, *Human Rights Obligations*).

Coalition to Stop the Use of Child Soldiers, *Child Soldiers Global Report*, 2008, available at www.hrw.org/sites/default/files/reports/Child_Soldiers_Global_Report_Summary.pdf, accessed 10.03.2015.

Commission on Human Rights, *Contemporary Forms of Slavery. Systematic rape, sexual slavery and slavery-like practices during armed conflict*, UN Doc. E/CN.4/Sub.2/2000/21 (6 June 2000).

Committee Against Torture, *Conclusions and Recommendations on the Second Periodic Report of the United States of America*, UN Doc. CAT/C/USA/CO/2 (25 July 2006).

Committee on Economic, Social and Cultural Rights, *General Comment 3*, UN Doc. E/1991/23 (14 December 1990) (Committee on Economic, Social and Cultural Rights, *General Comment 3*).

Committee on Economic, Social and Cultural Rights, *General Comment No. 7. The Right to Adequate Housing (Art. 11.1 of the Covenant): Forced Evictions*, UN Doc. E/1998/22 (20 May 1997) (Committee on Economic, Social and Cultural Rights, *General Comment No. 7*).

Committee on Economic, Social and Cultural Rights, *General Comment No. 15*, UN Doc. E/C.12/2002/11 (20 January 2002).

Committee on the Elimination of Discrimination against Women, *General Recommendation No. 28 on the Core Obligations of States Parties under Article 2 of the Convention on the Elimination of All Forms of Discrimination against Women*, UN Doc. CEDAW/C/GC/28 (16 December 2010).

Rosa da Costa, "Maintaining the Civilian and Humanitarian Character of Asylum", *Legal and Protection Policy Research Series* (2004), available at www.unhcr.org/protect/PROTECTION/40ebf51b4.pdf, accessed 10.03.2015.

Council of the European Union, "Joint Position Defined by the Council on the basis of Article K.3 of the Treaty on European Union on the Harmonized Application of the Definition of the Term 'Refugee' in Article 1 of the Geneva Convention of 28 July 1951 Relating to the Status of Refugees (Annex 1)" (1996), available at www.refworld.org/docid/3ae6b37f44.html, accessed 10.03.2015 (Council of the European Union, "Joint Position").

James Crawford and Patricia Hyndman, "Three Heresies in the Application of the Refugee Convention", *International Journal of Refugee Law* 1, no. 2 (1989): 155–179.

Anthony Cullen, *The Concept of Non-International Armed Conflict in International Humanitarian Law*, Cambridge: Cambridge University Press, 2010 (Cullen, *The Concept of Non-International Armed Conflict in International Humanitarian Law*).

Karen da Costa, *The Extraterritorial Application of Selected Human Rights Treaties*, Leiden: Martinus Nijhoff Publishers, 2012.

Vahakn N. Dadrian, "The Historical and Legal Interconnections Between the Armenian Genocide and the Jewish Holocaust: From Impunity to Retributive Justice", *Yale Journal of International Law* 23, (1998): 503–559.

Sara E. Davies, "Redundant or Essential? How Politics Shaped the Outcome of the 1967 Protocol", *International Journal of Refugee Law* 19, no. 4 (2007): 703–727.

Els Debuf, "Expert Meeting on Procedural Safeguards for Security Detention in Non-International Armed Conflict. Chatham House and International Committee of the Red Cross, 22–23 September 2008", *International Review of the Red Cross* 91, no. 876 (2009): 859–881.

Bryan Deschamp and Rebecca Dowd, "Review of the Use of UNHCR Executive Committee Conclusions on International Protection" (2008), available at www.unhcr.org/483d701f2.html, accessed 10.03.2015 (Deschamp and Dowd, "Review of the Use of UNHCR Executive Committee Conclusions").

Yoram Dinstein, *The Conduct of Hostilities under the Law of International Armed Conflict*, 2nd ed., Cambridge: Cambridge University Press, 2010 (Dinstein, *The Conduct of Hostilities*).

Yoram Dinstein, "Military Necessity", in *Max Planck Encyclopedia of Public International Law*, edited by Rüdiger Wolfrum, Oxford: Oxford University Press, 2009, available at www.mpepil.com, accessed 10.03.2015 (Dinstein, "Military Necessity").

Committee on the Elimination of Racial Discrimination, *General Recommendation 25. Gender Related Dimensions of Racial Discrimination*, UN Doc. A/55/18 (20 March 2003).

Shane Darcy, *Judges, War and Law. The Judicial Development of International Humanitarian Law*, Cambridge: Cambridge University Press, 2014 (Darcy, *Judges, War and Law*).

Knut Dörmann, "Detention in Non-International Armed Conflict", in *Non-International Armed Conflict in the Twenty-first Century*, edited by Kenneth Watkin and Andrew J. Norris, 347–366, Newport: US Naval War College, 2012 (Dörmann, "Detention").

Knut Dörmann, "The Legal Situation of 'Unlawful/Unprivileged Combatants'", *International Review of the Red Cross* 85, no. 849 (2003): 45–74.

Oliver Dörr, "Interpretation of Treaties", in *Vienna Convention on the Law of Treaties. A Commentary*, edited by Oliver Dörr and Kirsten Schmalenback, 520–570, Heidelberg et al.: Springer, 2012 (Dörr, "Interpretation").

Louise Doswald-Beck and Sylvain Vité, "International Humanitarian Law and Human Rights Law", *International Review of the Red Cross* no. 293 (1993): 94–119.

William Gerald Downey, Jr, "The Law of War and Military Necessity", *The American Journal of International Law* 47, no. 2 (1953): 251–262 (Downey, "The Law of War").

Cordula Droege, "Elective affinities? Human Rights and Humanitarian Law", *International Review of the Red Cross* 90, no. 871 (2003): 501–548 (Droege, "Elective affinities?").

Cordula Droege, "Transfer of Detainees – Legal Framework, Non-refoulement and Contemporary Challenges", *International Review of the Red Cross* 90, no. 871 (2008): 669–701.

Jean-François Durieux, "Of War, Flows, Laws and Flaws: A Reply to Hugo Storey", *Refugee Survey Quarterly* 31, no. 3 (2012): 161–176 (Durieux, "Of War, Flows, Laws and Flaws").

Jean-François Durieux and Agnès Hurwitz, "How Many is too Many? African and European Responses to Mass Influxes of Refugees", *German Yearbook of International Law* 47 (2004): 105–159.

Jean-François Durieux and David James Cantor, "Refuge from Inhumanity? Canvassing the Issues", in *Refuge from Inhumanity? War Refugees and International Humanitarian Law*, edited by David James Cantor and Jean-François Durieux, 3–38, Leiden: Koninklijke Brill, 2014 (Durieux and Cantor, "Refuge from Inhumanity? Canvassing the Issues").

Jonah Eaton, "The Internal Protection Alternative Under European Union Law: Examining the Recast Qualification Directive", *International Journal of Refugee Law* 24, no. 4 (2012): 765–792 (Eaton, "The Internal Protection Alternative").

Alice Edwards, "Crossing Legal Borders: The Interface Between Refugee Law, Human Rights Law and Humanitarian Law in the 'International Protection' of Refugees", in *International Humanitarian Law and Human Rights Law. Towards a New Merger in International Law*, edited by Roberta Arnold and Noëlle Quénivet, 421–446, Boston et al.: Martinus Nijhoff Publishers, 2008 (Edwards, "Crossing Legal Borders").

Alice Edwards and Agnes Hurwitz, "Introductory Note to the Arusha Summary Conclusions on Complementarities between International Refugee Law, International Human Rights Law", *International Journal of Refugee Law* 23, no. 4 (2011): 856–859 (Edwards and Hurwitz, "Introductory Note").

Terje Einarsen, "Drafting History of the 1951 Convention and the 1967 Protocol", in *The 1951 Convention relating to the Status of Refugees and its 1967 Protocol*, edited by Andreas Zimmermann (editor), Jonas Dörschner and Felix Machts (assistant editors), 39–73, Oxford: Oxford University Press, 2011 (Einarsen, "Drafting History").

European Legal Network on Asylum, "Information Note on Syrian Asylum Seekers and Refugees in Europe" (2013), available at www.ecre.org/component/content/article/70-weekly-bulletin-articles/506-ecreelena-publishes-information-note-on-syrians-seeking-protection-in-europe.html, accessed 10.03.2015.

European Migration Network, "EU and Non-EU Harmonised Protection Statuses in Belgium" (2011), available at www.emnbelgium.be/sites/default/files/publications/

eu_and_non-eu_harmonised_protection_statuses_in_belgium_0.pdf, accessed 10.03.2015.

Hilary Evans Cameron, "Risk Theory and 'Subjective Fear': The Role of Risk Perception, Assessment, and Management in Refugee Status Determinations", *International Journal of Refugee Law* 20, no. 4 (2008): 567–585.

Expert Meeting on Complementarities between International Refugee, Law International Criminal Law and International Human Rights Law, Arusha, 11–13 April 2011, "Summary Conclusions" (2011), available at www.refworld.org/docid/4e1729d52.html, accessed 10.03.2015 (Expert Meeting on Complementarities between International Refugee Law, International Criminal Law and International Refugee Law, "Arusha Summary Conclusions").

Expert Roundtable, "Summary Conclusions on International Protection of Persons Fleeing Armed Conflict and Other Situations of Violence" (2012), available at www.unhcr.org/refworld/docid/50d32e5e2.html, accessed 10.03.2015.

Expert Roundtable Organized by the United Nations High Commissioner for Refugees and the International Institute of Humanitarian Law, "Summary Conclusions: Internal Protection / Relocation / Flight Alternative", in *Refugee Protection in International Law. UNHCR's Global Consultations on International Protection*, edited by Erika Feller, Volker Türk, and Frances Nicholson, 418–421, Cambridge: Cambridge University Press, 2001 (Expert Roundtable Organized by the United Nations High Commissioner for Refugees and the International Institute of Humanitarian Law, "Summary Conclusions: Internal Protection").

Expert Roundtable Organized by the United Nations High Commissioner for Refugees and the International Institute of Humanitarian Law, "Summary Conclusions: membership of a particular social group", in *Refugee Protection in International Law. UNHCR's Global Consultations on International Protection*, edited by Erika Feller, Volker Türk, and Frances Nicholson, 312–313, Cambridge: Cambridge University Press, 2001.

Theo Farrell and Olivier Schmitt, "The Causes, Character and Conduct of Armed Conflict, and the Effects of on Civilian Populations, 1990–2010" (2012), available at www.unhcr.org/4f8d606d9.html, accessed 10.03.2015 (Farrell and Schmitt, "The Causes, Character and Conduct of Armed Conflict, and the Effects of on Civilian Populations, 1990–2010").

Federal Department of Foreign Affairs, "Protecting the Civilian Population in Armed Conflict" (2011), available at www.eda.admin.ch/eda/en/home/topics/human/hum/proci.html, accessed 10.03.2015.

Erika Feller, "Refugee Protection 50 Years On", *International Review of the Red Cross* 843, (2001): 581–606.

Erika Feller and Anja Klug, "Refugees, United Nations High Commissioner (UNHCR)", in *Max Planck Encyclopedia of Public International Law*, edited by Rüdiger Wolfrum, Oxford: Oxford University Press, 2007, available at www.mpepil.com, accessed 10.03.2015.

William J. Fenrick, "The Rule of Proportionality and Protocol I in Conventional Warfare", *Military Law Review* 98 (1982): 91–127 (Fenrick, "The Rule of Proportionality").

First Colloquium on Challenges in International Refugee Law convened by the Program in Refugee and Asylum Law of the University of Michigan Law School, "The

Michigan Guidelines on the Internal Protection Alternative", *Michigan Journal of International Law* 21 (1999–2000): 133–140 (First Colloquium on Challenges in International Refugee Law. Convened by the Program in Refugee and Asylum Law of the University of Michigan Law School, "The Michigan Guidelines on the Internal Protection Alternative").

Dieter Fleck. "Die IKRK-Gewohnheitsstudie: polarisierend oder konsensbildend?", *Humanitäres Völkerrecht Informationsschriften* 22, no. 3 (2009): 120–124.

Dieter Fleck, "The Law of Non-International Armed Conflicts", in *The Handbook of International Humanitarian Law*, edited by Dieter Fleck, 605–635, Cambridge: Cambridge University Press, 2008.

Antonio Fortin, "The Meaning of 'Protection' in the Refugee Definition", *International Journal of Refugee Law* 12, no. 4 (2001): 548–576.

Michelle Foster, "Causation in Context: Interpreting the Nexus Clause in the Refugee Convention", *Michigan Journal of International Law* 23 (2001–2002) (Foster, "Causation in Context").

Michelle Foster, "The 'Ground with the Least Clarity': A Comparative Study of Jurisprudential Developments relating to 'Membership of a Particular Social Group'", *UNHCR Legal and Protection Policy Research Series* 25 (2012), available at www.unhcr.org/4f7d8d189.html, accessed 10.03.2015 (Foster, "The 'Ground with the Least Clarity'").

Michelle Foster, *International Refugee Law and Socio-Economic Rights. Refuge from Deprivation*, Cambridge: Cambridge University Press, 2007 (Foster, *International Refugee Law*).

Duncan French, "Treaty Interpretation and the Incorporation of Extraneous Legal Rules", *International and Comparative Law Quarterly* 55, no. 2 (2006): 281–314.

Eric Fripp, "Inclusion of Refugees from Armed Conflict. Combatants and Ex-combatants", in *Refuge from Inhumanity? War Refugees and International Humanitarian Law*, edited by David James Cantor and Jean-François Durieux, 128–154, Leiden: Koninklijke Brill, 2014.

Eric Fripp, "International Humanitarian Law and the Interpretation of 'Persecution' in Article 1A(2) CSR51", *International Journal of Refugee* Law 26, no. 3 (2014): 382–403 (Eric Fripp, "International Humanitarian Law").

Jochen Frowein, "United Nations (UN)", in *Max Planck Encyclopedia of Public International Law*, edited by Rüdiger Wolfrum, Oxford: Oxford University Press, 2009, available at www.mpepil.com, accessed 10.03.2015.

Richard K. Gardiner, *Treaty Interpretation*, Oxford: Oxford University Press, 2010.

Madeleine Garlick, "UNHCR and the Implementation of Council Directive 2004/83/EC on Minimum Standards for the Qualification and Status of Third Country Nations or Stateless Persons as Refugees or as Persons who Otherwise Need International Protection and the Content of the Protection Granted (The EC 'Qualification Directive')", in *The Qualification Directive: Central Themes, Problem Issues, and implementation in Selected Member States*, edited by Karin Zwaan, 59–69, Nijmegen: Wolf Legal Publishers, 2007.

Hans-Peter Gasser, "International Committee of the Red Cross (ICRC)", in *Max Planck Encyclopedia of Public International Law*, edited by Rüdiger Wolfrum, Oxford: Oxford University Press, 2009, available at www.mpepil.com, accessed 10.03.2015.

Hans-Peter Gasser, "International Humanitarian Law and Human Rights Law in Non-International Armed Conflicts: Joint Venture or Mutual Exclusion?", *German Yearbook of International Law* 45 (2002): 149–162.

Hans-Peter Gasser, "Protection of the Civilian Population", in *The Handbook of International Humanitarian Law*, edited by Dieter Fleck, 237–324, Cambridge: Cambridge University Press, 2008.

Hans-Peter Gasser and Nils Melzer, *Humanitäres Völkerrecht*, Zürich: Schluthess Juristische Medien, 2012.

Emanuela-Chiara Gillard, "Humanitarian Law, Human Rights and Refugee Law – Three Pillars", *Statement at the International Association of Refugee Law Judges World Conference 21–23 April 2005* (2005), accessed 13.10.2013.

Waltraud von Glahn, *Der Kompetenzwandel internationaler Flüchtlingsorganisationen – vom Völkerbund bis zu den Vereinten Nationen*, Baden-Baden: Nomos, 1992 (Glahn, *Kompetenzwandel*).

Michal Gondek, *The Reach of Human Rights in a Globalizing World: Extraterritorial Application of Human Rights Treaties*, Antwerp: Intersentia, 2009.

Guy S. Goodwin-Gill, "The Dynamic of International Refugee Law", *International Journal of Refugee Law* 25, no. 4, 631–666.

Guy S. Goodwin-Gill, "The International Law of Refugee Protection", in *The Oxford Handbook of Refugee and Forced Migration Studies*, edited by Elena Fiddian-Qasmiyeh, Gil Loescher, Katy Long and Nando Sigona, 36–47, Oxford: Oxford University Press, 2014.

Guy S. Goodwin-Gill, "The Right to Seek Asylum: Interception at Sea and the Principle of Non-Refoulement", *International Journal of Refugee Law* 23, no. 3 (2011): 443–457.

Guy S. Goodwin-Gill, "The search for the one, true meaning…", in *The Limits of Transnational Law. Refugee Law, Policy Harmonization and Judicial Dialogue in the European Union*, edited by Guy S. Goodwin-Gill and Hélène Lambert, 2004–2241, Cambridge: Cambridge University Press, 2010 (Goodwin-Gill, "The search for the one, true meaning").

Guy S. Goodwin-Gill and Jane McAdam, *The Refugee in International Law*, 3rd ed., Oxford: Oxford University Press, 2007 (Goodwin-Gill and McAdam, *The Refugee in International Law*).

Brian Gorlick, "Common Burdens and Standards: Legal Elements in Assessing Claims to Refugee Status", *International Journal of Refugee Law* 15, no. 3 (2003): 357–376.

David E. Graham, "Defining Non-International Armed Conflict: A Historically Difficult Task", in *Non-International Armed Conflict in the Twenty-first Century*, edited by Kenneth Watkin and Andrew J. Norris, 43–55, Newport, RI: US Naval War College, 2012.

Atle Grahl-Madsen, *The Status of Refugees in International Law*, Vol. I, Leiden: A.W. Sijthoff, 1966 (Grahl-Madsen, *Status of Refugees*).

Christopher Greenwood, "Historical Development and Legal Basis", in *The Handbook of International Humanitarian Law*, edited by Dieter Fleck, 1–44, Oxford: Oxford University Press, 2008.

Christopher Greenwood, "The relationship between *ius ad bellum* and *ius in bello*", *Review of International Studies* 9 (1983): 221–234 (Greenwood, "Historical Development and Legal Basis").

Kay Hailbronner, *Asyl- und Ausländerrecht*, 2nd ed., Stuttgart: W. Kohlhammer, 2008 (Hailbronner, *Asyl- und Ausländerrecht*).

Rodger Haines, "Gender-related Persecution (Article 1A(2))", in *Refugee Protection in International Law. UNHCR's Global Consultations on International Protection*, edited by Erika Feller, Volker Türk, and Frances Nicholson, 319–350, Cambridge: Cambridge University Press, 2003 (Haines, "Gender-related Persecution").

Matthew Happold, "Excluding Children from Refugee Status: Child Soldiers and Article 1F of the Refugee Convention", *American University International Law Review* 17 (2002): 1131–1176.

Lotta Harbom and Peter Wallensteen, "Armed Conflicts, 1946–2009", *Journal of Peace Research* 47, no. 4 (2010): 501–509.

James C. Hathaway, "The Evolution of Refugee Status in International Law: 1920–1950", *International and Comparative Law Quarterly* 33 (1984): 348–380 (Hathaway, "Evolution of Refugee Status").

James C. Hathaway, "International Refugee Law: The Michigan Guidelines on the Internal Protection Alternative", *Michigan Journal of International Law* 21 (1999–2000): 131–133.

James C. Hathaway, "Is Refugee Status Really Elitist? An Answer to the Ethical Challenge", in *Europe and Refugees: A Challenge? L'Europe et les Refugiés: Un Défi?*, edited by Jean-Yves Carlier and Dirk Vanheule, 79–88, The Hague et al.: Kluwer Law International, 1997.

James C. Hathaway, *The Law of Refugee Status*, Toronto: Butterworths, 1991.

James C. Hathaway, "New Directions to Avoid Hard Problems: The Distortion of the Palliative Role of Refugee Protection", *Journal of Refugee Studies* 8, no. 3 (1995): 288–294.

James C. Hathaway, "The Relationship Between Human Rights and Refugee Law: What Refugee Law Judges Can Contribute", in *Realities of Refugee Determination on the Eve of a New Millennium: The Role of the Judiciary. 3rd Conference of the International Association of Refugee Law Judges. October 1998 Ottawa*, edited by International Association of Refugee Law Judges, 80–90, Haarlem, 1998.

James C. Hathaway, *The Rights of Refugees Under International Law*, Cambridge: Cambridge University Press, 2005 (Hathaway, *The Rights of Refugees*).

James C. Hathaway and Michelle Foster, "The Causal Connection ("Nexus") to a Convention Ground", *International Journal of Refugee Law* 15, no. 3 (2003): 461–476 (Hathaway and Foster, "The Causal Connection").

James C. Hathaway and Michelle Foster, "Internal Protection/Relocation/Flight Alternative as an Aspect of Refugee Status Determination", in *Refugee Protection in International Law. UNHCR's Global Consultations on International Protection*, edited by Erika Feller, Volker Türk, and Frances Nicholson, 357, Cambridge: Cambridge University Press, 2003.

James C. Hathaway and Michelle Foster, *The Law of Refugee Status*, 2nd ed., Cambridge: Cambridge University Press, 2014.

James C. Hathaway and William S. Hicks, "Is There a Subjective Element in the Refugee Convention's Requirement of 'Well-Founded Fear'?", *Michigan Journal of International Law* 26 (2004–2005): 505–562 (Hathaway and Hicks, "Is There a Subjective Element").

W. Hays Parks, "The ICRC Study on Customary IHL: A Preliminary Assessment", *American Society of International Law Proceedings* 99 (2005): 208–212.

Hans-Joachim Heintze, "On the Relationship between Human Rights Law Protection and International Humanitarian Law", *International Review of the Red Cross* 85, no. 856 (2004): 789–814.

Jean-Marie Henckaerts, "Customary International Humanitarian Law: A Response to US Comments", *International Review of the Red Cross* 89, no. 866 (2007): 473–488 (Henckaerts, "Customary International Humanitarian Law: A Response to US Comments").

Jean-Marie Henckaerts, "Deportation and Transfer of Civilians in Time of War", *Vanderbilt Journal of Transnational Law* 26 (1993–1994).

Jean-Marie Henckaerts, "The Grave Breaches as Customary International Law", *Journal of International Criminal Justice* 7, no. 4 (2009): 683–701.

Jean-Marie Henckaerts, "Proportionality", in *The Oxford Companion to International Criminal Justice*, edited by Antonio Cassese, 469–470, Oxford: Oxford University Press, 2009.

Jean-Marie Henckaerts, "Study on Customary International Humanitarian Law: A Contribution to the Understanding and Respect for the Rule of Law in Armed Conflict", *International Review of the Red Cross* 87, no. 857 (2005): 175–212.

Jean-Marie Henckaerts and Louise Doswald-Beck, *Customary International Humanitarian Law, Vol. I: Rules*, Cambridge: Cambridge University Press, 2005 (Henckaerts and Doswald-Beck, *Customary International Humanitarian Law*).

Jean-Marie Henckaerts and Louise Doswald-Beck, *Customary International Humanitarian Law, Vol. II: Practice*, Cambridge: Cambridge University Press, 2005.

Ian Henderson, *The Contemporary Law of Targeting. Military Objectives, Proportionality and Precautions in Attack under Additional Protocol I*, Leiden/Boston: Martinus Nijhoff, 2009 (Henderson, *The Contemporary Law of Targeting*).

Joachim Henkel, "Who Is a Refugee? Refugees from Civil War and Other Internal Armed Conflicts", paper presented at the First International Judicial Conference, Inner Temple, London, 1–2 December 1995 (Henkel, "Who Is a Refugee? Refugees from Civil War and Other Internal Armed Conflicts").

Matthias Herdegen, "Interpretation in International Law", in *Max Planck Encyclopedia of Public International Law*, edited by Rüdiger Wolfrum, Oxford: Oxford University Press, 2013, available at www.mpepil.com, accessed 10.03.2015 (Herdegen, *Interpretation*).

Monika Heupel and Bernhard Zangl, "Von 'alten' und 'neuen' Kriegen – Zum Gegenstand kriegerischer Gewalt", *Politische Vierteljahresschrift* 45, no. 3 (2004): 346–369.

Rainer Hofmann, "Die Rechtskontrolle von Organen der Staatengemeinschaft", in *Die Rechtskontrolle von Organen der Staatengemeinschaft. Vielfalt der Gerichte – Einheit des Prozessrechts?*, edited by Rainer Hofmann, August Reinisch, Thomas Pfeiffer, Stefan Oeter, and Astrid Stadler, 1–42, Heidelberg: C.F. Müller Verlag, 2007.

Rainer Hofmann, "Nachfluchtgründe und Flüchtlingsvölkerrecht", *Neue Verwaltungszeitschrift* 6, no. 4 (1987): 299–301.

Louise W. Holborn, *The International Refugee Organization. A Specialized Agency of the United Nations. Its History and Work 1946–1952*, London et al.: Oxford University Press, 1956 (Holborn, *The International Refugee Organization*).

Louise W. Holborn, "The Legal Status of Political Refugees, 1920–1938", *American Journal of International Law* 32 (1938): 680–703.

Louise W. Holborn, *Refugees: A Problem of Our Time. The Work of the United Nations High Commissioner for Refugees, 1951–1972*, Vol. I, Metuchen, NJ: The Scarecrow Press, 1975 (Holborn, *Refugees*).

Vanessa Holzer, "The 1951 Refugee Convention and the Protection of People Fleeing Armed Conflict and Other Situations of Violence", *Legal and Protection Policy Research Series* (2012), available at www.unhcr.org/refworld/docid/50474f062.html, accessed 10.03.2015.

Vanessa Holzer, "Persecution and the Nexus to a Refugee Convention Ground in Non-International Armed Conflict: Insights from Customary International Humanitarian Law", in *Refuge from Inhumanity? War Refugees and International Humanitarian Law*, edited by David James Cantor and Jean-François Durieux, 101–127, Leiden: Brill, 2014 (Holzer, "Persecution").

Human Rights Committee, *Concluding Observations*, UN Doc. CCPR/C/79/Add.93 (18 August 1998).

Human Rights Committee, *Concluding Observations*, UN Doc. CCPR/CO/78/ISR (5 August 2003).

Human Rights Committee, *Concluding Observations*, UN Doc. CCPR/C/USA/CO/3 (15 September 2006).

Human Rights Committee, *General Comment 29: States of Emergency (Article 4)*, UN Doc. CCPR/C/21/Rev.1/Add.11 (31 August 2001) (Human Rights Committee, *General Comment 29: States of Emergency (Article 4)*).

Human Rights Committee, *General Comment 31: Nature of the General Legal Obligation on States Parties to the Covenant*, UN Doc. CCPR/C/21/Rev. 1/Add. 13 (26 May 2004) (Human Rights Committee, *General Comment 31: Nature of the General Legal Obligation on States Parties to the Covenant*).

Human Rights Committee, *General Comment No. 08: Right to Liberty and Security of the Persons (Art. 9)*, UN Doc. HRI/GEN/1/Rev.9 (30 June 1982).

Human Rights Watch, "Iraq/Jordan/Turkey: Syrians Blocked from Fleeing War" (2013), available at www.hrw.org/news/2013/07/01/iraqjordanturkey-syrians-blocked-fleeing-war, accessed 10.03.2015.

ICRC, "Annual Report" (2011), available at www.icrc.org/eng/resources/documents/annual-report/icrc-annual-report-2011.htm, accessed 10.03.2015.

ICRC, "How is the Term 'Armed Conflict' Defined in International Humanitarian Law? Opinion Paper" (2008), available at www.icrc.org/eng/resources/documents/article/other/armed-conflict-article-170308.htm, accessed 10.03.2015 (ICRC, "How is the Term 'Armed Conflict' Defined").

ICRC, "International Humanitarian Law and the Challenges of Contemporary Armed Conflict", *30th International Conference of the Red Cross and Red Crescent, Geneva, 26–30 November 2007* (2007), available at www.icrc.org/eng/assets/files/other/ihl-challenges-30th-international-conference-eng.pdf, accessed 10.03.2015.

ICRC, "International Humanitarian Law and the Challenges of Contemporary Armed Conflicts", *31st International Conference of the Red Cross and Red Crescent, Geneva, 28 November – 1 December 2011* (2011), available at www.icrc.org/eng/assets/files/red-cross-crescent-movement/31st-international-conference/31-int-conference-ihl-challenges-report-11-5-1-2-en.pdf, accessed 10.03.2015.

ICRC, "Interpretative Guidance on the Notion of Direct Participation in Hostilities under International Humanitarian Law" (2009), available at https://www.icrc.org/eng/resources/documents/article/review/review-872-p991.htm, accessed 10.03.2015 (ICRC, "Interpretative Guidance on Direct Participation").

ICRC, "Press Release No. 1567, Iran-Iraq conflict: The ICRC condemns the use of chemical weapons" (1988), available at www.icrc.org/customary-ihl/eng/docs/v2_rul_rule74, accessed 10.03.2015.

ICRC, "Strengthening Legal Protection for Victims of Armed Conflict. Draft Resolution and Report prepared for the 31st International Conference of the Red Cross and Red Crescent", 31IC/11/5.1.1 (2011), available at www.icrc.org/eng/assets/files/red-cross-crescent-movement/31st-international-conference/31-int-conference-strengthening-legal-protection-11-5-1-1-en.pdf, accessed 10.03.2015.

ICRC, "Syria: ICRC and Syrian Arab Crescent Maintain Aid Effort Amid Increased Fighting" (2012), available at www.icrc.org/eng/resources/documents/update/2012/syria-update-2012-07-17.htm, accessed 10.03.2015.

ICRC, "What is International Humanitarian Law?" (2004), available at www.icrc.org/eng/resources/documents/legal-fact-sheet/humanitarian-law-factsheet.htm, accessed 10.03.2015.

ICTY, "Final Report to the Prosecutor by the Committee Established to Review the NATO Bombing Campaign Against the Federal Republic of Yugoslavia", *International Legal Materials* 39 (2000): 1257–1283.

Immigration and Refugee Board of Canada, "Civilian Non-Combatants Fearing Persecution in Civil War Situations. Guidelines Issued by the Chairperson Pursuant to Section s65(3) of the Immigration Act" (1996), available at www.irb-cisr.gc.ca/Eng/BoaCom/references/pol/GuiDir/Pages/GuideDir01.aspx, accessed 10.03.2015 (Immigration and Refugee Board of Canada, "Civilian Non-Combatants Fearing Persecution in Civil War Situations").

Internal Displacement Monitoring Centre, "Global Overview 2011. People Internally Displaced by Conflict and Violence" (2012), available at www.unhcr.org/50f95f7a9.html, accessed 10.03.2015.

International Conference of the Red Cross and Red Crescent, "Resolution 1. Strengthening Legal Protection for Victims of Armed Conflict" (2011), available at www.icrc.org/eng/resources/documents/resolution/31-international-conference-resolution-1-2011.htm, accessed 10.03.2015.

International Law Association, "Final Report on the Meaning of Armed Conflict in International Law" (2010), available at www.ila-hq.org/en/committees/index.cfm/cid/1022, accessed 10.03.2015.

Knut Ipsen, "Combatants and Non-Combatants", in *Handbook of International Humanitarian Law*, edited by Dieter Fleck, 79–118, Oxford: Oxford University Press, 2008.

Ivor C. Jackson, *The Refugee Concept in Group Situations*, The Hague et al.: Martinus Nijhoff Publishers, 1999 (Jackson, *The Refugee Concept*).

Richard B. Jackson, "Perfidy in Non-International Armed Conflicts", in *International Law Studies*, edited by Kenneth Watkin and Andrew J. Norris, 237–259, Newport, RI: US Naval War College, 2012.

Stéphane Jaquemet, "The Cross-Fertilization of International Humanitarian Law and International Refugee Law", *International Review of the Red Cross* 83, no. 843 (2001): 651–674 (Jaquemet, "Cross-Fertilization").

Stéphane Jaquemet, "Under What Circumstances Can a Person Who Has Taken an Active Part in the Hostilities of an International or a Non-International Armed Conflict become an Asylum Seeker?", *UNHCR Legal and Protection Policy Research Series* (2004), available at www.unhcr.org/protect/PROTECTION/40ebf49a4.pdf, accessed 10.03.2015.

Mélanie Jaques, *Armed Conflict and Displacement. The Protection of Refugees and Displaced Persons under International Humanitarian Law*, Cambridge: Cambridge University Press, 2012 (Jaques, *Armed Conflict and Displacement*).

Kate Jastram, "Economic Harm as a Basis for Refugee Status and the Application of Human Rights Law to the Interpretation of Economic Persecution", in *Critical Issues in International Refugee Law. Strategies toward Interpretative Harmony*, edited by James C. Simeon, 143–173, Cambridge: Cambridge University Press, 2010.

Chris af Jochnick and Roger Normand, "The Legitimation of Violence: A Critical History of the Laws of War", *Harvard International Law Journal* 35, no. 1 (1994): 49–95.

Martin Jones, "The Refusal to Bear Arms as Grounds for Refugee Protection in the Canadian Jurisprudence", *International Journal of Refugee Law* 20, no. 1 (2008): 123–165.

Michael Kagan and William P. Johnson, "Persecution in the Fog of War: The House of Lords' Decision in Adan", *Michigan Journal of International Law* 23 (2001–2002): 247–264.

Mary Kaldor, *New & Old Wars*, 2nd ed., Cambridge: Polity Press, 2006.

Walter Kälin, "Flight in Times of War", *International Review of the Red Cross* 843 (2001): 629–650 (Kälin, "Flight in Times of War").

Walter Kälin, "Refugees and Civil Wars: Only a Matter of Interpretation?", *International Journal of Refugee Law* 3, no. 3 (1991): 435–451 (Kälin, "Refugees and Civil Wars").

Walter Kälin, "Supervising the 1951 Convention Relating to the Status of Refugees: Article 35 and beyond", in *Refugee Protection in International Law*, edited by Erika Feller, Volker Türk, and Frances Nicholson, 613–666, Cambridge: Cambridge University Press, 2003 (Kälin, "Supervising the 1951 Convention).

Frits Karlshoven and Liesbeth Zegveld, *Constraints on the Waging of War. An Introduction to International Humanitarian Law*, 4th ed., Cambridge: Cambridge University Press, 2011.

Frits Karlshoven and Liesbeth Zegveld, *Constraints on Waging War. An Introduction to International Humanitarian Law*, 3rd ed., Geneva: International Committee of the Red Cross, 2001.

David Keen, *The Economic Functions of Violence in Civil Wars*, Oxford: Oxford University Press, 1998.

Ninette Kelley, "Internal Flight / Relocation / Protection Alternative: Is It Reasonable?", *International Journal of Refugee Law* 14, (2002): 4–43 (Kelley, "Internal Flight / Relocation / Protection Alternative: Is It Reasonable?).

Karoline Kerber, "International Humanitarian Law as a Source of Protection for Refugees from Areas of Armed Conflict", *Refuge* 16, no. 6 (1997): 6–8.

Timo Koivurova, "Due Diligence", in *Max Planck Encyclopedia of Public International Law*, edited by Rüdiger Wolfrum, Oxford: Oxford University Press, 2007, available at www.mpepil.com, accessed 10.03.2015.

Robert Kolb, "Human Rights and Humanitarian Law", in *Max Planck Encyclopedia of Public International Law*, edited by Rüdiger Wolfrum, Oxford: Oxford University Press, 2009, available at www.mpepil.com, accessed 10.03.2015 (Kolb, "Human Rights and Humanitarian Law").

Martti Koskenniemi and Päivi Leino, "Fragmentation of International Law? Postmodern Anxieties", *Leiden Journal of International Law* 15, no. 3 (2002): 553–579.

Pirkko Kourula, *Broadening the Edges. Refugee Definition and International Protection Revisited*, The Hague/Boston/London: Martinus Nijhoff Publishers, 1997.

David Kretzmer, "Targeted Killing of Suspected Terrorists: Extra-Judicial Executions or Legitimate Means of Defence?", *European Journal of International Law* 16, no. 2 (2005): 171–212.

David Kretzmer, Rotem Giladi and Yuval Shany, "International Humanitarian Law and International Human Rights Law: Exploring Parallel Application", *Israel Law Review* 40 (2007): 306–309.

Heike Krieger, "A Conflict of Norms: The Relationship between Humanitarian Law and Human Rights Law in the ICRC Customary Law Study", *Journal of Conflict & Security Law* 11 (2006): 265–291.

Hélène Lambert, "Transnational Judicial Dialogue, Harmonization and the Common European Asylum System", *International & Comparative Law Quarterly* 58, no. 3 (2009): 519–543.

Hélène Lambert and Theo Farrell, "The Changing Character of Armed Conflict and the Implications for Refugee Protection Jurisprudence", *International Journal of Refugee Law* 22, no. 2 (2010): 237–273.

Elihu Lauterpacht and Daniel Bethlehem, "The Scope and Content of the Principle of *Non-Refoulement*: Opinion", in *Refugee Protection in International Law. UNHCR's Global Consultations on International Protection*, edited by Erika Feller, Volker Türk and Francis Nicholson, 89–177, Cambridge: Cambridge University Press, 2001.

Kathleen Lawand, "Internal Conflicts or other Situations of Violence – What is the Difference for Victims?" (2012), available at www.icrc.org/eng/resources/documents/interview/2012/12-10-niac-non-international-armed-conflict.htm, accessed 10.03.2015 (Lawand, "Internal Conflicts").

Corinne Lewis, "UNHCR's Contribution to the Development of International Refugee Law: Its Foundations and Evolution", *International Journal of Refugee Law* 17 (2005): 76–90.

Corinne Lewis, *UNHCR and International Refugee* Law, Abingdon/New York: Routledge, 2012.

Anja Lindroos, "Addressing Norm Conflicts in a Fragmented Legal System: The Doctrine of *Lex Specialis*", *Nordic Journal of International Law* 74 (2005): 27–66 (Lindroos, "Addressing Norm Conflicts").

Gil Loescher, Alexander Betts, and James Milner. *The United Nations High Commissioner for Refugees (UNHCR). The politics and practice of refugee protection into the twenty-first century*, London/New York: Routledge, 2008.

Tillmann Löhr, *Die kinderspezifische Auslegung des völkerrechtlichen Flüchtlingsbegriffs*, Baden-Baden: Nomos, 2009 (Löhr, *Die kinderspezifische Auslegung*).

Cátia Lopes and Noëlle Quénivet, "Individuals as Subjects of Humanitarian Law and Human Rights Law", in *International Humanitarian Law and Human Rights Law. Towards a Merger in International Law*, edited by Roberta Arnold and Noëlle Quénivet, 199–236, Leiden/Boston: Martinus Nijhoff, 2008.

Graça Machel, *Impact of Armed Conflict on Children. Report of the Expert of the Secretary-General submitted pursuant to Resolution 48/157*, UN Doc. A/51/306 (26 August 1996).

Tara Magner, "Does a Failed State Country of Origin Result in a Failure of International Protection? A Review of Policies Toward Asylum-Seekers in Leading Asylum Nations", *Georgetown Immigration Law Journal* 15 (2001): 703–726.

Cecilia Malmström and Antonio Gutierrez, "60 Years of the Geneva Refugee Convention: Europe Must Uphold Its Values" (2011), available at http://ec.europa.eu/commission_2010-2014/malmstrom/news/what-written/archives/2011/07/20110728_en.htm#, accessed 10.03.2015.

Nora Markard, *Kriegsflüchtlinge. Gewalt gegen Zivilpersonen in bewaffneten Konflikten als Herausforderung für das Flüchtlingsrecht und den subsidiären Schutz*, Tübingen: Mohr Siebeck, 2012 (Markard, *Kriegsflüchtlinge*).

Anne-Charlotte Martineau, "The Rhetoric of Fragmentation: Fear and Faith in International Law", *Leiden Journal of International Law* 22 (2009): 1–28.

Reinhard Marx, "The Criteria of Applying the 'Internal Flight Alternative' Test in National Refugee Status Determination Procedures", *International Journal of Refugee Law* 14 (2002): 179–218 (Reinhard Marx, "The Criteria of Applying the 'Internal Flight Alternative' Test").

Reinhard Marx, "The Notion of Persecution by Non-State Agents in German Jurisprudence", *Georgetown Immigration Law Journal* 15 (2000–2001): 447–461.

Reinhard Marx, "Völkervertragsrechtliche Abschiebungshindernisse für Flüchtlinge", in *Aktuelle asylrechtliche Probleme der gerichtlichen Entscheidungspraxis in Deutschland, Österreich und der Schweiz*, edited by Klaus Barwig and Walter Brill, 103–140, Baden-Baden: Nomos, 1996.

David Matas, "Armed Opposition Groups", *Manitoba Law Journal* 24 (1996–1997): 621–664.

Penelope Mathew, James C. Hathaway, and Michelle Foster, "The Role of State Protection in Refugee Analysis. Discussion Paper No. 2, Advanced Refugee Law Workshop, International Association of Refugee Law Judges, Auckland, New Zealand, October 2002", *International Journal of Refugee Law* 15 (2003): 444–460 (Mathew, Hathaway, and Foster, "The Role of State Protection in Refugee Analysis").

Nele Matz-Lück, "Harmonization, Systemic Integration, and 'Mutual Suportiveness' as Conflict-Solution Techniques: Different Modes of Interpretation as a Challenge to

Negative Effects of Fragmentation?", *Finnish Yearbook of International Law* XVII, (2006): 39–52.

Jane McAdam, "Interpretation of the 1951 Convention", in *The 1951 Convention relating to the Status of Refugees and its 1967 Protocol: A Commentary*, edited by Andreas Zimmermann (editor), Jonas Dörschner and Felix Machts (assistant editors), 75–115, Oxford: Oxford University Press, 2011.

Jane McAdam, "Rethinking the Origins of 'Persecution' in Refugee Law", in *International Journal of Refugee Law* 25, no. 4 (2014): 667–692 (McAdam, "Rethinking the Origins").

Robert McCorquodale, "Non-State Actors and International Human Rights Law", in *Research Handbook on International Human Rights Law*, edited by Sarah Joseph and Adam McBeth, 97–114, Cheltenham/Northampton, MA: Edward Elgar, 2010.

Campbell McLachlan, "The Principle of Systemic Integration and Article 31(3)(c) of the Vienna Convention", *International and Comparative Law Quarterly* 54 (2005): 279–320.

Robert McLaughlin, "Legal-Policy Considerations and Conflict Characterisation at the Threshold between Law Enforcement and Non-International Armed Conflict", *Melbourne Journal of International Law* 13, no. 1 (2012): 1–28.

Frédéric Mégret and Florian Hoffmann, "The UN as a Human Rights Violator? Some Reflections on the United Nations Changing Human Rights Responsibilities", *Human Rights Quarterly* 25, no. 2 (2003): 314–342.

Nils Melzer, *Targeted Killing in International Law*, Oxford: Oxford University Press, 2008 (Melzer, *Targeted Killing*).

Theodor Meron, "The Geneva Conventions as Customary Law", *American Journal of International Law* 81, no. 2 (1987): 348–370.

Theodor Meron, "The Humanization of Humanitarian Law", *American Journal of International Law* 94 (2000): 239–278.

Theodor Meron, "The Martens Clause, Principles of Humanity, and Dictates of Public Conscience", *American Journal of International Law* 94 (2000): 239–278.

Theodor Meron, "Rape as a Crime under International Humanitarian Law", *American Journal of International Law* 87 (1993).

Theordor Meron, *The Humanization of International Law*, Leiden/Boston: Martinus Nijhoff, 2006.

Guénaël Mettraux, *International Crimes and the Ad Hoc Tribunals*, Oxford: Oxford University Press, 2006 (Mettraux, *International Crimes*).

Henri Meyrowitz, "Le droit de guerre et les droit de l'homme", *Revue de Droit Militaire et Droit de la Guerre* 88 (1972): 1095–1105.

Marco Milanović, *Extraterritorial Application of Human Rights Treaties: Law, Principles, and Policy*, Oxford: Oxford University Press, 2011.

Marco Milanović, "Norm Conflicts, International Humanitarian Law, and Human Rights Law", in *International Humanitarian Law and International Human Rights Law*, edited by Orna Ben-Naftali, 95–128, Oxford: Oxford University Press, 2011.

Erik Møse, "The Criminality Perspective", *Georgetown Immigration Law Journal* 15, no. 3 (2000–2001): 463–478.

Elizabeth Mottershaw, "Economic, Social and Cultural Rights in Armed Conflict: International Human Rights Law and International Humanitarian Law", *The International Journal of Human Rights* 12, no. 3 (2008): 449–470.

Amrei Müller, *The Relationship between Economic, Social and Cultural Rights and International Humanitarian Law. An Analysis of Health-Related Issues in Non-International Armed Conflicts*, Leiden/Boston: Martinus Nijhoff, 2013 (Müller, *The Relationship between Economic, Social and Cultural Rights and International Humanitarian Law*).

Iris Müller, "Follow-up der IKRK-Gewohnheitsrechtsstudie", *Humanitäres Völkerrecht Informationsschriften* 22, no. 3 (2009): 131–136.

Niraj Nathwani, *Rethinking Refugee Law*, The Hague et al.: Martinus Nijhoff, 2003.

Eloisa Newalsing, "Jean-Marie Henckaerts and Louise Doswald-Beck (eds.), Customary International Humanitarian Law, Geneva and Cambridge, International Committee of the Red Cross and Cambridge University Press (2005)", *Leiden Journal of International Law* 21, no. 1 (2008): 255–279.

Leah M. Nicholls, "The Humanitarian Monarchy Legislates: The International Committee of the Red Cross and the Rules of Customary International Humanitarian Law", *Duke Journal of Comparative and International Law* 17 (2006): 223–252.

Gregror Noll, *Proof, Evidentiary Assessment and Credibility in Asylum Procedures*, Leiden/Boston: Martinus Nijhoff, 2005.

Manfred Nowak, "Torture and Other Cruel, Inhuman, or Degrading Treatment or Punishment", in *The Oxford Handbook of International Law in Armed Conflict*, edited by Andrew Clapham, Paola Gaeta (editors), Tom Haeck and Alice Priddy (assistant editors), 387–409, Oxford: Oxford University Press, 2014.

Roger O'Keefe, "State Immunity and Human Rights: Heads and Walls, Hearts and Minds", *Vanderbilt Journal of Transnational Law* 44 (2011): 999–1045.

Maria O'Sullivan, "Acting the Part: Can Non-State Entities Provide Protection Under International Refugee Law?", *International Journal of Refugee Law* 24, no. 1 (2012): 85–110 (O'Sullivan, "Acting the Part").

Office of the United Nations High Commissioner for Human Rights, "Enforced or Involuntary Disappearance. Fact Sheet No. 6/Rev. 3" (2009), available at www.ohchr.org/Documents/Publications/FactSheet6Rev3.pdf, accessed 10.03.2015.

Valerie Oosterveld, "Women and Girls Fleeing Conflict: Gender and the Interpretation and Application of the 1951 Refugee Convention", *UNHCR Legal and Protection Policy Research Series* (2012), available at www.unhcr.org/refworld/docid/504dcb172.html, accessed 10.03.2015 (Oosterveld, "Women and Girls").

Alexander Orakhelashvili, "The Interaction between Human Rights and Humanitarian Law: Fragmentation, Conflict, Parallelism, or Convergence?", *European Journal of International Law* 19, no. 1 (2008): 161–182.

Organization for Security and Co-operation in Europe, "Kosovo/Kosova. As Seen, As Told. An Analysis of the Human Rights Findings of the OSCE Kosovo Verification Mission October 1998 to 1999" (1999), available at www.osce.org/odihr/17772, accessed 10.03.2015.

Kate Parlett, *The Individual in the International Legal System. Continuity and Change in International Law*, Cambridge: Cambridge University Press, 2011 (Parlett, *The Individual in the International Legal System*).

Joost Pauwelyn, *Conflict of Norms in Public International Law: How WTO Law Relates to other Rules of International Law*, Cambridge: Cambridge University Press, 2009.

Joost Pauwelyn, "Fragmentation of International Law", in *Max Planck Encyclopedia of Public International Law*, edited by Rüdiger Wolfrum, Oxford: Oxford University Press, 2006, available at www.mpepil.com, accessed 10.03.2015.

Jelena Pejic, "Conflict Classification and the Law Applicable to Detention and the Use of Force", in *International Law and the Classification of Conflicts*, edited by Elizabeth Wilmshurst, 80–116, Oxford: Oxford University Press, 2012.

Jelena Pejic, "Procedural Principles and Safeguards for Internment/Administrative Detention in Armed Conflict and Other Situations of Violence", *International Review of the Red Cross* 87, no. 858 (2005): 375–391 (Pejic, "Procedural Principles").

Jelena Pejic, "The Right to Food in Situations of Armed Conflict: The Legal Framework", *International Review of the Red Cross* 83, no. 844 (2001): 1097–1109 (Pejic, "The Right to Food").

Jelena Pejić, "Status of Armed Conflicts", in *Perspectives on the ICRC Study on Customary International Humanitarian Law*, edited by Elizabeth Wilmshurst and Susan Breau, 77–100, Cambridge: Cambridge University Press, 2007.

Jean Pictet, ed., *Commentary on the Fourth Geneva Convention Relative to the Protection of Civilian Persons in Times of Armed Conflict*, Geneva: International Committee of the Red Cross, 1958.

Jean Pictet, ed., *Commentary on the Geneva Convention for the Amelioration of the Condition of the Wounded and Sick in Armed Forces in the Field*, Geneva: International Committee of the Red Cross, 1952.

Jean Pictet, ed., *Commentary on the Second Geneva Convention for the Amelioration of the Condition of the Wounded, Sick and Shipwrecked Members of Armed Forces at Sea of 12 August, 1949*, Geneva: International Committee of the Red Cross, 1960.

Jean Pictet, ed., *Commentary on the Third Geneva Convention Relative to the Treatment of Prisoners of War*, Geneva: International Committee of the Red Cross, 1960.

Jean Pictet, *Development and Principles of International Humanitarian Law*, Dordrecht: Martinus Nijhoff, 1985.

Ryszard Piotrowicz, "Displacement and Displaced Persons", in *Perspectives on the ICRC Study on Customary International Humanitarian Law*, edited by Elizabeth Wilmshurst and Susan Breau, 337–353, Cambridge: Cambridge University Press, 2007 (Piotrowicz, "Displacement").

Matthew E. Price, *Rethinking Asylum. History, Purpose, and Limits*, Cambridge: Cambridge University Press, 2009.

René Provost, *International Human Rights and Humanitarian Law*, Cambridge: Cambridge University Press, 2002.

Nancie Prud'homme, "*Lex Specialis*: Oversimplifying a More Complex and Multifaceted Relationship", *Israel Law Review* 40 (2007): 356–395.

Jean-François Quéguiner, "Dix ans après la création du Tribunal pénal international pour l'ex-Yougoslavie: évaluation de l'apport de sa jurisprudence au droit international humanitaire", *International Review of the Red Cross* 85, no. 850 (2003): 271–311.

Jean-François Quéguiner, "The Principle of Distinction: Beyond an Obligation of Customary International Humanitarian Law", in *The Legitimate Use of Military*

Force. The Just War Tradition and the Customary Law of Armed Conflict, edited by Howard M. Hensel, 161–188, Aldershot: Ashgate, 2008.

Jaya Ramji-Nogales, Andrew I. Schoenholtz and Philip G. Schrag, *Refugee Roulette: Disparities in Asylum Adjudication and Proposals for Reform*, New York: New York University Press, 2009.

Eibe Riedel, "Economic, Social, and Cultural Rights in Armed Conflict", *The Oxford Handbook of International Law in Armed Conflict*, edited by Andrew Clapham, Paola Gaeta (editors), Tom Haeck and Alice Priddy (assistant editors), 441–468, Oxford: Oxford University Press: 2014.

A.P.V. Rogers, *Law on the Battlefield*, 3rd ed., Manchester: Manchester University Press, 2012.

A.P.V. Rogers, "The Principle of Proportionality", in *The Legitimate Use of Military Force. The Just War Tradition and the Customary Law of Armed Conflict*, edited by Howard M. Hensel, 189–218, Aldershot: Ashgate, 2007.

Cape Town Roundtable on International Protection of Persons Fleeing Armed Conflict and Other Situations of Violence, 13–14 September 2012, "Summary Conclusions" (2012), available at www.refworld.org/docid/50d32e5e2.html, accessed 10.03.2015.

Roundtable on the Future of Refugee Convention Supervision, "Summary Conclusions", *Journal of Refugee Studies* 26, no. 3 (2013): 327–330.

Bonaventure Rutinwa, "Refugee Claims Based On Violation of International Humanitarian Law: The 'Victim's' Perspective", *Georgetown Immigration Law Journal* 15 (2000–2001).

Yves Sandoz, Christophe Swinarski and Bruno Zimmermann, eds., *Commentary on the Additional Protocols of 8 June 1977 to the Geneva Conventions of 12 August 1949*, Geneva: Martinus Nijhoff, 1987 (Sandoz, Swinarski, and Zimmermann, eds., *Commentary on the Additional Protocols of 8 June 1977 to the Geneva Conventions of 12 August 1949)*.

Marco Sassòli, "Internment", in *Max Planck Encyclopedia of Public International Law*, edited by Rüdiger Wolfrum, Oxford: Oxford University Press, available at www.mpepil.com, accessed 10.03.2015.

Marco Sassòli, "The Role of Human Rights and International Humanitarian Law in New Types of Armed Conflicts", in *International Humanitarian Law and International Human Rights Law*, edited by Orna Ben-Naftali, 34–94, Oxford: Oxford University Press, 2011.

Marco Sassòli, Anotine A. Bouvier and Anne Quintin, *How does Law Protect in War? Cases, Documents and Teaching Materials on Contemporary Practice in International Humanitarian Law*, vol. I, 2011, available at www.icrc.org/eng/assets/files/publications/icrc-0739-part-i.pdf, accessed 10.03.2015.

Marco Sassòli and Laura M. Olson, "The Judgment of the ICTY Appeals Chamber on the Merits in the Tadic Case", *International Review of the Red Cross* 82, no. 839 (2000): 733–769 (Sassòli and Laura M. Olson, "The Judgment of the ICTY").

Marco Sassòli and Laura M. Olson, "The Relationship between Humanitarian Law and Human Rights Law where It Matters: Admissible Killing and Internment of Fighters in Non-International Armed Conflict", *International Review of the Red Cross* 90, no. 871 (2008): 599–627.

William A. Schabas, "*Lex Specialis*? Belt and Suspenders? The Parallel Operation of Human Rights Law and the Law of Armed Conflict, and the Conundrum of *Jus Ad Bellum*", *Israel Law Review* 40, no. 2 (2007): 592–613 (Schabas, "*Lex Specialis*? Belt and Suspenders?").

Dietrich Schindler and Jiri Toman, *The Laws of Armed Conflicts*, The Hague: Martinus Nijhoff, 1988.

Michael N. Schmitt, "The Interpretative Guidance on the Notion of Direct Participation in Hostilities: A Critical Analysis", *Harvard National Security Journal* 1, no. 1 (2010): 5–44.

Michael N. Schmitt, "Military Necessity and Humanity in International Humanitarian Law: Preserving the Delicate Balance", *Virginia Journal of International Law* (2010): 795–838 (Schmitt, "Military Necessity").

Second Colloquium on Challenges to International Refugee Law, "The Michigan Guidelines on Nexus to a Convention Ground", *Michigan Journal of International Law* 23 (2001–2002): 211–221 (Second Colloquium on Challenges to International Refugee Law, "The Michigan Guidelines on Nexus").

Security Council, *Resolution 582*, UN Doc. S/RES/582 (24 February 1986).

Security Council, *Resolution 827*, UN Doc. S/RES/827 (25 May 1993).

Marina Sharpe, "The 1969 OAU Convention and the Protection of People fleeing Armed Conflict and Other Situations of Violence in the Context of Individual Refugee Status Determination" (2011), available at www.refworld.org/docid/50fd3edb2.html, accessed 10.03.2015.

Annette Simon, *UN-Schutzzonen – Ein Schutzinstrument für verfolgte Personen? Eine Analyse anhand der internationalen Schutzzonen im Irak, in Ruanda und Bosnien-Herzegowina mit besonderem Blick auf die schweren Menschenrechtsverletzungen in der safe area Srebrenica*, Berlin et al.: Springer, 2005.

John Hope Simpson, *The Refugee Problem. Report of a Survey*, London/New York/Toronto: Oxford University Press, 1939 (Simpson, *The Refugee Problem)*.

Nicholas Sitaropoulos, *Judicial Interpretation of Refugee Status: In Search of a Principled Methodology Based on a Critical Comparative Analysis, with Special Reference to Contemporary British, French, and German Jurisprudence*, Baden-Baden: Nomos, 1999.

Sandesh Sivakumaran, "Re-envisaging the International Law of Internal Armed Conflict", *European Journal of International Law* 22, no. 1 (2011): 219–254.

Sandesh Sivakumaran, "Sexual Violence against Men in Armed Conflict", *European Journal of International Law* 18, no. 2 (2007): 253–277.

Claudena M. Skran, "Historical Development of International Refugee Law", in *The 1951 Convention relating to the Status of Refugees and its 1967 Protocol*, edited by Andreas Zimmermann (editor), Jonas Dörschner and Felix Machts (assistant editors), 3–36, Oxford: Oxford University Press, 2011 (Skran, "Historical Development").

Waldemar A. Solf, "Protection of Civilians Against the Effects of Hostilities Under Customary International Law and Under Protocol I", *American University International Law Review* 1, no. 1 (1986): 117–135.

Special Rapporteur on the Right to Food, *The Right to Food. Preliminary Report of the Special Rapporteur of the Commission on Human Rights on the Right to Food*, UN Doc. A/56/210 (23 July 2001).

Special Representative of the Secretary-General on Sexual Violence in Conflict, *Statement before the Security Council*, UN Doc. S/PV.6722 (23 February 2012).

Daniel J. Steinbock, "Interpreting the Refugee Definition", *UCLA Law Review* 45 (1998): 733–815.

Henry J. Steiner, Philip Alston and Ryan Goodman, *International Human Rights in Context. Law, Politics, Morals*, Oxford: Oxford University Press, 2008.

Naomi S. Stern, "Evian's Legacy: The Holocaust, the United Nations Refugee Convention, and Post-War Refugee Legislation in the United States", *Georgetown Immigration Law Journal* 19 (2004–2005): 313–331.

Mark R. von Sternberg, *The Grounds of Refugee Protection in the Context of International Human Rights and Humanitarian Law. Canadian and United States Case Law Compared*, The Hague/London/New York: Martinus Nijhoff, 2002 (Sternberg, *The Grounds of Refugee Protection*).

Mark R. von Sternberg, "Outline of United States Asylum Law: Substantive Criteria and Procedural Concerns", *Defending Immigration Removal Proceedings* (2011): 31–76.

Mark R. von Sternberg, "The Plight of the Non-Combatant in Civil War and the New Criteria for Refugee Status", *International Journal of Refugee Law* 9, no. 2 (1997): 169–195.

Mark R. von Sternberg, "Political Asylum and the Law of Internal Armed Conflict: Refugee Status, Human Rights and Humanitarian Concerns", *International Journal of Refugee Law* 5, no. 2 (1993): 153–185.

Hugo Storey, "Armed Conflict in Asylum Law: The 'War-Flaw'", *Refugee Survey Quarterly* 31, no. 2 (2012): 1–32 (Storey, "Armed Conflict in Asylum Law").

Hugo Storey, "The Internal Flight Alternative Test: The Jurisprudence Re-examined", *International Journal of Refugee Law* 10, no. 3 (1998): 499–532 (Storey, "The Internal Flight Alternative Test").

Hugo Storey, "Persecution: Towards a Working Definition", in *Research Handbook on International Law and Migration*, edited by Vincent Chetail and Céline Bauloz, 459–518, Cheltenham/Northampton: Edward Elgar, 2014 (Storey, "Persecution").

Hugo Storey, "The 'War Flaw' and Why it Matters", in, *Refuge from Inhumanity? War Refugees and International Humanitarian Law*, edited by David James Cantor and Jean-François Durieux, 39–56, Leiden: Koninklijke Brill, 2014 (Storey, "The 'War Flaw' and Why it Matters").

Hugo Storey and Rebecca Wallace, "War and Peace in Refugee Law Jurisprudence", *American Journal of International Law* 95 (2001): 349–366 (Storey and Rebecca Wallace, "War and Peace in Refugee Law").

Study Group of the International Law Commission, *Fragmentation of International Law: Difficulties Arising from the Diversification and Expansion of International Law. Report of the Study Group of the International Law Commission Finalized by Martti Koskenniemi*, UN Doc. A/CN.4/L.682 (13 April 2006) (Study Group of the International Law Commission, *Fragmentation of International Law*).

Sub-Commission on Prevention of Discrimination and Protection of Minorities, *The Right to Freedom of Movement. Sub-Commission Resolution 1996/9*, UN Doc. E/CN.4/SUB.2/RES/1996/9 (28 August 1997).

Mark Symes and Peter Jorro, *Asylum Law and Practice*, 2nd ed., Haywards Heath: Bloomsbury Professional, 2010.

Jerzy Sztucki, "The Conclusions on the International Protection of Refugees Adopted by the Executive Committee of the UNHCR Programme", *International Journal of Refugee Law* 1, no. 3 (1989): 285–318 (Sztucki, "The Conclusions on International Protection").

Jerzy Sztucki, "Who Is a Refugee? The Convention Definition: Universal or Obsolete?", in *Refugee Rights and Realities. Evolving International Concepts and Regimes*, edited by Frances Nicholson and Patrick Twomey, 55–80, Cambridge: Cambridge University Press, 1999.

Blanche Tax, "Refugee by Association", in *Forced Migration Review* 47 (2014): 26–27.

Ruti Teitel, *Humanity's Law*, Oxford: Oxford University Press, 2011.

Lotta Themnér and Peter Wallensteen, "Armed Conflicts, 1946–2011", *Journal of Peace Research* 49, no. 4 (2012): 565–575.

Lotta Themnér and Peter Wallensteen, "Armed Conflicts, 1946–2012", *Journal of Peace Research* 50, no. 4 (2013): 509–521.

Daniel Thürer, *International Humanitarian Law: Theory, Practice, Context*, The Hague Academy of International Law, Recueil des Cours/Collected Courses, Vol. 338, Leiden: Martinus Nijhoff, 2011 (Thürer, *International Humanitarian Law*).

Tullio Treves, "Customary International Law", in *Max Planck Encyclopedia of Public International Law*, edited by Rüdiger Wolfrum, Oxford: Oxford University Press, 2009, available at www.mpepil.com, accessed 10.03.2015.

Otto Triffterer, "The Preventive and the Repressive Function of the International Criminal Court", in *The Rome Statute of the International Criminal Court. A Challenge to Immunity*, edited by Mauro Politi and Giuseppe Nesi, 137–175, Dartmouth: Ashgate, 2001.

Volker Türk, *Das Flüchtlingshochkommissariat der Vereinten Nationen (UNHCR)*, Berlin: Duncker & Humblot, 1992 (Türk, *Flüchtlingshochkommissariat*).

Volker Türk, "Introductory Statement at the 54th Meeting of the Standing Committee of the Executive Committee of the High Commissioner's Programme" (2012), available at www.unhcr.org/4fedc0609.html, accessed 10.03.2015 (Türk, "Introductory Statement").

Volker Türk and Rebecca Dowd, "Protection Gaps", *in The Oxford Handbook of Refugee and Forced Migration Studies*, edited by Elena Fiddian-Qasmiyeh, Gil Loescher, Katy Long, and Nando Sigona, 278–289, 2014.

Volker Türk, "UNHCR's Supervisory Responsibility", *Revue Québécoise de Droit International* 14, no. 1 (2001): 135–158 (Türk, "UNHCR's Supervisory Responsibility").

UK Border Agency, *Considering the Protection (Asylum) Claim and Assessing Credibility* (2011).

UN Commission of Experts, *Final Report of the United Nations Commission of Experts Established pursuant to Security Council Resolution 780 (1992)*, UN Doc. S/1994/674 (27 May 1994).

UN Commission on Human Rights, *Periodic Report by the Special Rapporteur on the Situation of Human Rights in the Former Yugoslavia*, UN Doc. S/1995/933-A/50/727 (4 October 1995).

UN General Assembly, *Declaration on Territorial Asylum. Resolution 2312 (XXII)*, UN Doc. A/6716 (14 December 1967).

UN General Assembly, *Questions of Atrocities Committed by the North Korean and Chinese Communist Forces against United Nations Prisoners of War in Korea. Resolution 804 (VII)*, UN Doc. A/804/VIII (3 December 1953).
UN General Assembly, *Resolution 40/33*, UN Doc. A/RES/40/33 (29 November 1985).
UN General Assembly, *Resolution 45/113*, UN Doc. A/RES/45/113 (14 December 1990).
UN General Assembly, *Resolution 61/177*, UN Doc. A/61/488 (20 December 2008).
UN General Assembly, *Resolution 61/177*, UN Doc. A/RES/61/177 (20 December 2006).
UN General Assembly, *Resolution 133*, UN Doc. A/47/133 (18 December 1992).
UN General Assembly, *Resolution 271A (III)*, UN Doc. 10 December 1948.
UN General Assembly, *Resolution 428 (V)*, UN Doc. 14 December 1959.
UN General Assembly, *Resolution 1166(XII)*, UN Doc. 26 November 1957.
UN General Assembly, *Resolution 1672 (XVI)*, UN Doc. 18 December 1961.
UN General Assembly, *Resolution 1783 (XVII)*, UN Doc. 7 December 1962.
UN General Assembly, *Resolution 2444*, UN Doc. 19 December 1968.
UN Mission to Investigate Allegations of the Use of Chemical Weapons in the Syrian Arab Republic, "Report on the Alleged Use of Chemical Weapons in the Ghouta Area of Damascus on 21 August 2013" (2013), available at www.un.org/disarmament/content/slideshow/Secretary_General_Report_of_CW_Investigation.pdf, accessed 10.03.2015.
UN Secretary-General, *Report of the Secretary-General on the Protection of Civilians in Armed Conflict*, UN Doc. S/2001/331 (30 March 2001).
UN Secretary-General, *Report of the Secretary-General on the Protection of Civilians in Armed Conflict*, UN Doc. S/2007/643 (28 October 2007).
UN Secretary-General, *Report of the Secretary-General on the Protection of Civilians in Armed Conflict*, UN Doc. S/2009/277 (29 May 2009).
UN Secretary-General, *Report of the Secretary-General on the Protection of Civilians in Armed Conflict*, UN Doc. S/2005/740 (28 November 2005).
UN Secretary-General, *Report of the Secretary-General on the Protection of Civilians in Armed Conflict*, UN Doc. S/1999/957 (8 September 1999).
UN Secretary-General, *Report of the Secretary-General on Children and Armed Conflict*, UN Doc. A/68/878-S/2014/339 (15 May 2014).
UN Security Council, *Resolution 237*, UN Doc. A/237/1967 (1967).
UN Special Rapporteur on Violence against Women, *Report on violence against women perpetrated and/or condoned by the State during times of armed conflict (1997–2000)*, UN Doc. E/CN.4/2001/73 (23 January 2001).
UNHCR, "Agents of Persecution – UNHCR Position" (1995), available at www.refworld.org/docid/3ae6b31da3.html, accessed 10.03.2015.
UNHCR, "Annotated Comments on the EC Council Directive 2004/83/EC of 29 April 2004 on Minimum Standards for the Qualification and Status of Third Country Nationals or Stateless Persons as Refugees or as Persons Who Otherwise Need International Protection and the Content of the Protection Granted (OJ L 204/12 of 20.9.2004)" (2005), available at www.refworld.org/docid/4200d8354.html, accessed 10.03.2015 (UNHCR, "Annotated Comments on the EC Council Directive").
UNHCR, "Asylum in the European Union. A Study of the Implementation of the Qualification Directive" (2007), available at www.refworld.org/docid/473050632.html, accessed 10.03.2015 (UNHCR, "Asylum in the European Union").

UNHCR, "Asylum Trends, First half of 2014. Levels and Trends in Industrialized Countries", available at www.unhcr.org/5423f9699.html, accessed 10.03.2015.
UNHCR, "Asylum Trends 2013. Levels and Trends in Industrialized Countries" (2014), available at www.unhcr.org/5329b15a9.html, accessed 10.03.2015;
UNHCR, "Asylum Levels and Trends in Industrialized Countries" (2010), available at www.unhcr.org/4d8c5b109.html, accessed 10.03.2015.
UNHCR, "Background Paper on Refugees and Asylum-Seekers from Sri Lanka" (2004), available at www.unhcr.org/refworld/docid/40d837f42.html, accessed 10.03.2015.
UNHCR, "Background Paper on Refugees and Asylum Seekers from the Democratic Republic of Congo" (2000), available at www.unhcr.org/refworld/docid/3ae6a6574.html, accessed 10.03.2015.
UNHCR, "Eligibility Guidelines for Assessing the International Protection Needs of Afghan Asylum-Seekers" (2007), available at www.refworld.org/docid/477ce70a2.html, accessed 10.03.2015 (UNHCR, "Eligibility Guidelines for Assessing the International Protection Needs of Afghan Asylum-Seekers 2007").
UNHCR, "Eligibility Guidelines for Assessing the International Protection Needs of Asylum-Seekers from Afghanistan" (2009), available at www.unhcr.org/refworld/docid/4a6477ef2.html, accessed 10.03.2015 (UNHCR, "Eligibility Guidelines for Assessing the International Protection Needs of Asylum-Seekers from Afghanistan 2009").
UNHCR, "Eligibility Guidelines for Assessing the International Protection Needs of Asylum-Seekers from Afghanistan" (2010), available at www.refworld.org/docid/4d0b55c92.html, accessed 10.03.2015 (UNHCR, "Eligibility Guidelines for Assessing the International Protection Needs of Asylum-Seekers from Afghanistan 2010").
UNHCR, "Eligibility Guidelines for Assessing the International Protection Needs of Asylum-Seekers from Afghanistan" (2013), available at www.refworld.org/docid/51ffdca34.html, accessed 10.03.2015 (UNHCR, "Eligibility Guidelines for Asylum-Seekers from Afghanistan 2013").
UNHCR, "Eligibility Guidelines for Assessing the International Protection Needs of Asylum-Seekers from Colombia" (2010), available at www.refworld.org/docid/4bfe3d712.html, accessed 10.03.2015 (UNHCR, "Eligibility Guidelines for Assessing the International Protection Needs of Asylum-Seekers from Colombia 2010").
UNHCR, "Eligibility Guidelines for Assessing the International Protection Needs of Asylum-Seekers from Iraq" (2012), available at www.unhcr.org/refworld/docid/4fc77d522.html, accessed 10.03.2015 (UNHCR, "Eligibility Guidelines for Assessing the International Protection Needs of Asylum-Seekers from Iraq 2012").
UNHCR, "Eligibility Guidelines for Assessing the International Protection Needs of Asylum-Seekers from Somalia" (2010), available at www.refworld.org/docid/4be3b9142.html, accessed 10.03.2015 (UNHCR, "Eligibility Guidelines for Assessing the International Protection Needs of Asylum-Seekers from Somalia 2010").
UNHCR, "Eligibility Guidelines for Assessing the International Protection Needs of Asylum-Seekers from Sri Lanka" (2009), available at www.unhcr.org/refworld/docid/49de0b6b2.html, accessed 10.03.2015 (UNHCR, "Eligibility Guidelines for

Assessing the International Protection Needs of Asylum-Seekers from Sri Lanka 2009").

UNHCR, "Eligibility Guidelines for Assessing the International Protection Needs of Asylum-Seekers from Sri Lanka" (2010), available at www.unhcr.org/refworld/docid/4c31a5b82.html, accessed 10.03.2015 (UNHCR, "Eligibility Guidelines for Assessing the International Protection Needs of Asylum-Seekers from Sri Lanka 2010").

UNHCR, "Eligibility Guidelines for Assessing the International Protection Needs of Iraqi Asylum-Seekers" (2009), available at www.refworld.org/docid/49f569cf2.html accessed 10.03.2015 (UNHCR, "Eligibility Guidelines for Assessing the International Protection Needs of Iraqi Asylum-Seekers 2009").

UNHCR, "Eligibility Guidelines for Assessing the International Protection Needs of Iraqi Asylum-Seekers" (August 2007), available at www.unhcr.org/refworld/docid/46deb05557.html, accessed 10.03.2015 (UNHCR, "Eligibility Guidelines for Assessing the International Protection Needs of Iraqi Asylum-Seekers August 2007").

UNHCR, "ExCom Members and How to Apply" (2012), available at www.unhcr.org/pages/49c3646c89.html, accessed 10.03.2015.

UNHCR, "The Executive Committee's Origins and Mandate", available at www.unhcr.org/pages/49c3646c86.html, accessed 10.03.2015.

UNHCR, "Executive Committee of the High Commissioner's Programme (ExCom)", available at www.unhcr.org/pages/49c3646c83.html, accessed 10.03.2015.

UNHCR, "Global Report 2012" (2012), available at www.unhcr.org/gr12/index.xml, accessed 10.03.2015.

UNHCR, "Guidance Note on Refugee Claims Relating to Sexual Orientation and Gender Identity" (2008), available at www.refworld.org/docid/48abd5660.html, accessed 10.03.2015.

UNHCR, "Guidance Note on Refugee Claims relating to Victims of Organized Gangs" (2010), available at www.refworld.org/docid/4bb21fa02.html, accessed 10.03.2015.

UNHCR, *Guidelines on International Protection No. 1: Gender-Related Persecution within the Context of Article 1A(2) of the 1951 Refugee Convention and/or its 1967 Protocol relating to the Status of Refugees*, UN Doc. HCR/GIP/02/01 (7 May 2002) (UNHCR, *Guidelines on International Protection No. 1*).

UNHCR, *Guidelines on International Protection No. 2: "Membership of a Particular Social Group" within the Context of Article 1A(2) of the 1951 Refugee Convention and/or its 1967 Protocol relating to the Status of Refugees*, UN Doc. HRC/GIP/02/02 (7 May 2002) (UNHCR, *Guidelines on International Protection No. 2*).

UNHCR, *Guidelines on International Protection No. 3: Cessation of Refugee Status under Article 1C(5) and (6) of the 1951 Convention relating to the Status of Refugees (the "Ceased Circumstances" Clauses)*, UN Doc. HRC/GIP/03/03 (23 February 2003) (UNHCR, *Guidelines on International Protection No. 3*).

UNHCR, *Guidelines on International Protection No. 4: "Internal Flight or Relocation Alternative" within the Context of Article 1A(2) of the 1951 Convention and/or 1967 Protocol relating to the Status of Refugees*, UN Doc. HRC/GIP/03/04 (23 July 2003) (UNHCR, *Guidelines on International Protection No. 4*).

UNHCR, *Guidelines on International Protection No. 5: Application of the Exclusion Clauses: Article 1F of the 1951 Convention relating to the Status of Refugees*, UN Doc. HRC/GIP/03/05 (4 September 2003) (UNHCR, *Guidelines on International Protection No. 5*).

UNHCR, *Guidelines on International Protection No. 6. Religion-Based Refugee Claims under Article 1A(2) of the 1951 Convention and/or the 1967 Protocol relating to the Status of Refugees*, UN Doc. HRC/GIP/04/06 (28 April 2004) (UNHCR, *Guidelines on International Protection No. 6*).

UNHCR, *Guidelines on International Protection No. 7: The application of Article 1A(2) of the 1951 Convention and/or 1967 Protocol relating to the Status of Refugees to Victims of Trafficking and Persons at Risk of Being Trafficked*, UN Doc. HCR/GIP/06/07 (7 April 2006) (UNHCR, *Guidelines on International Protection No. 7*).

UNHCR, *Guidelines on International Protection No. 8: Child Asylum Claims under Articles 1(A)2 and 1(F) of the 1951 Convention and/or 1967 Protocol relating to the Status of Refugees*, UN Doc. HCR/GIP/09/08 (22 December 2009) (UNHCR, *Guidelines on International Protection No. 8*).

UNHCR, *Guidelines on International Protection No. 10: Claims to Refugee Status related to Military Service within the context of Article 1A(2) of the 1951 Convention and/or the 1967 Protocol relating to the Status of Refugees*, UN Doc. HCR/GIP/13/10 (3 December 2013) (UNHCR, *Guidelines on International Protection No. 10*).

UNHCR, *Handbook on Procedures and Criteria for Determining Refugee Status under the 1951 Convention and the 1967 Protocol relating to the Status of Refugees*, UN Doc. HCR/IP/4/Eng/REV.1 (1992) (UNHCR, *Handbook*).

UNHCR, "Information Note on Article 1 of the 1951 Convention" (1995), available at www.refworld.org/docid/3ae6b32c8.html, accessed 10.03.2015.

UNHCR, "International Protection Considerations Regarding Colombian Asylum-Seekers and Refugees" (2005), available at www.unhcr.org/refworld/docid/422c832e4.html, accessed 10.03.2015 (UNHCR, "International Protection Considerations Regarding Colombian Asylum-Seekers and Refugees 2005").

UNHCR, "International Protection Considerations regarding Colombian Asylum-Seekers and Refugees" (2002), available at www.unhcr.org/refworld/docid/3d92d4204.html, accessed 10.03.2015 (UNHCR, "International Protection Considerations regarding Colombian Asylum-Seekers and Refugees 2002).

UNHCR, "International Protection Considerations with Regard to People Fleeing Southern and Central Somalia" (2014), available at www.refworld.org/docid/52d7fc5f4.html, accessed 10.03.2015.

UNHCR, "Interpreting Article 1 of the 1951 Convention relating to the Status of Refugees" (2001), available at www.refworld.org/docid/3b20a3914.html, accessed 10.03.2015.

UNHCR, "Note on Burden and Standard of Proof in Refugee Claims" (1998), available at www.unhcr.org/refworld/docid/3ae6b3338.html, accessed 10.03.2015.

UNHCR, *Note on International Protection*, UN Doc. A/AC.96/975 (2 July 2003) (UNHCR, *Note on International Protection* (2003)).

UNHCR, *Note on International Protection*, UN Doc. A/AC.96/1053 (30 June 2008) (UNHCR, *Note on International Protection* (2008)).

UNHCR, *Note on International Protection*, UN Doc. A/AC.86/930 (7 July 2000) (UNHCR, *Note on International Protection* (2000)).
UNHCR, *Note on International Protection*, UN Doc. A/AC.96/1098 (2011) (UNHCR, *Note on International Protection* (2011)).
UNHCR, *Note on International Protection*, UN Doc. A/AC.96/882 (2 July 1997) (UNHCR, *Note on International Protection* (1997)).
UNHCR, *Note on International Protection*, UN Doc. A/AC.96/850 (1 September 1995) (UNHCR, *Note on International Protection* (1995)).
UNHCR, *Note on International Protection*, UN Doc. A/AC.96/898 (3 July 1998) (UNHCR, *Note on International Protection* (1998)).
UNHCR, "Note on Issues related to Eligibility for International Protection in the Context of Fumigations" (2007), available at www.unhcr.org/refworld/pdfid/46b6d62f2.pdf, accessed 10.03.2015.
UNHCR, "Number of Forcibly Displaced Rises to 43.3 Million Last Year, The Highest Level Since Mid-1990s" (2010), available at www.unhcr.org/4c176c969.html, accessed 10.03.2015.
UNHCR, "Opinion of UNHCR regarding the Question of Non-State Persecution, as Discussed with the Committee on Human Rights and Humanitarian Aid of the German Parliament (Lower House)" (1999), available at www.unhcr.org/refworld/docid/3df755477.html, accessed 10.03.2015 (UNHCR, "Opinion of UNHCR regarding the Question of Non-State Persecution").
UNHCR, "Position on Returns to North Kivu, South Kivu and Adjacent Areas in the Democratic Republic of Congo Affected by On-going Conflict and Violence in the Region" (2012), available at www.refworld.org/docid/50a369022.html, accessed 10.03.2015 (UNHCR, "Position on the Kivus").
UNHCR, "Position on the International Protection Needs of Asylum-Seekers from Sri Lanka" (2006), available at www.refworld.org/docid/459a1fcb2.html, accessed 10.03.2015 (UNHCR, "Position on the International Protection Needs of Asylum-Seekers from Sri Lanka 2006").
UNHCR, "Refugee Status Determination. Identifying Who Is a Refugee. Self-Study Module 2" (2005), available at www.refworld.org/docid/43141f5d4.html, accessed 10.03.2015.
UNHCR, "Safe at Last? Law and Practice in Selected EU Member States with Respect to Asylum-Seekers Fleeing Indiscriminate Violence" (2011), available at www.unhcr.org/refworld/docid/4e2ee0022.html, accessed 10.03.2015.
UNHCR, "Statement on Subsidiary Protection under the EC Qualification Directive for People Threatened by Indiscriminate Violence" (2008), available at www.refworld.org/docid/479df7472.html, accessed 10.03.2015.
UNHCR, "States Parties to the 1951 Convention relating to the Status of Refugees and the 1967 Protocol" (2011), available at www.unhcr.org/3b73b0d63.html, accessed 10.03.2015.
UNHCR, "Syria Conflict Contributing to Rising Asylum Claims in Industrialized Countries" (2013), available at www.unhcr.org/5149c6f46.html, accessed 10.03.2015 (UNHCR, "Syria Conflict").
UNHCR, "Trends in Asylum Applications Lodged in Europe, North-America, Australia and New Zealand, 2001: Updated Tables" (2002), available at www.unhcr.org/3c887b9d4.html, accessed 10.03.2015.

UNHCR, "UNHCR and Human Rights. A Policy Paper Resulting from Deliberations in the Policy Committee on the Basis of a Paper Prepared by the Division of International Protection" (1997), available at www.unhcr.org/refworld/docid/3ae6b332c.html, accessed 10.03.2015.

UNHCR, "UNHCR Observations on the Commission's Proposal for a Joint Action Concerning Temporary Protection of Displaced Persons" (1997), available at www.unhcr.org/43662e3a2.html, accessed 10.03.2015.

UNHCR, "UNHCR Position on Claims for Refugee Status Under the 1951 Convention relating to the Status of Refugees Based on a Fear of Persecution Due to an Individual's Membership of a Family or Clan Engaged in a Blood Feud" (2006), available at www.unhcr.org/refworld/docid/44201a574.html accessed 10.03.2015.

UNHCR, "UNHCR Position on Returns to Southern and Central Somalia" (2014), available at www.refworld.org/docid/53a04d044.html, accessed 10.03.2015.

UNHCR Executive Committee, *Conclusion No. 48 (XXXXVIII) Military or Armed Attacks on Refugee Camps and Settlements* (1987).

UNHCR Executive Committee, *Conclusion No. 71 (XLIV)* (1993).

UNHCR Executive Committee, *Conclusion No. 73 (XLIV) Refugee Protection and Sexual Violence* (1993).

UNHCR Executive Committee, *Conclusion No. 80 (XLVII) Comprehensive and Regional Approaches Within a Protection Framework* (1996).

UNHCR Executive Committee, *Conclusion No. 81 (XLCIII)* (1997).

UNHCR Executive Committee, *Conclusion No. 83 (XLVIII)* (1997).

UNHCR Executive Committee, *Conclusion No. 84 (XLVIII) on Refugee Children and Adolescents* (1997).

UNHCR Executive Committee, *Conclusion No. 85 (XLIX)* (1998).

UNHCR Executive Committee, *Conclusion No. 87 (L)* (1999).

UNHCR Executive Committee, *Conclusion No. 93 (LIII). Conclusion on reception of asylum-seekers in the context of individual asylum systems* (8 October 2002).

UNHCR Executive Committee, *Conclusion No. 94 (LIII) on the Civilian and Humanitarian Character of Asylum* (2002).

UNHCR Executive Committee, *Conclusion No. 95 (LIV)* (2003).

UNHCR Executive Committee, *Conclusion No. 98 (XIV)* (2003).

UNHCR Executive Committee, *Conclusion on the Provision of International Protection Including Through Complementary Forms of Protection (Conclusion No. No. 103 [LVI])*, UN Doc. A/AC.96/1021 (7 October 2005).

US Citizenship and Immigration Services, "Asylum Officer Basic Training Course, Asylum Eligibility Part III: Nexus and the Five Protected Characteristics" (2009), available at www.uscis.gov/portal/site/uscis/menuitem.5af9bb95919f35e66f61417-6543f6d1a/?vgnextoid=2a1d1a877b4bc110VgnVCM1000004718190aRCRD&vgnextchannel=3a82ef4c766fd010VgnVCM1000000ecd190aRCRD, accessed 10.03.2015.

US Citizenship and Immigration Services, "Refugee, Asylum and International Operations Directorate, Officer Training: Definition of Persecution and Eligibility based on Past Persecution" (2012), available at www.uscis.gov/portal/site/uscis/menuitem.5af9bb95919f35e66f614176543f6d1a/?vgnextoid=17412765b826f310VgnVCM100000082ca60aRCRD&vgnextchannel=e88514c0cee47210VgnVCM100000

082ca60aRCRD, accessed 10.03.2015 (US Citizenship and Immigration Services, "Asylum Officer Basic Training").

Jacques Vernant, *The Refugee in the Post-War World*, London: George Allen & Unwin, 1953.

Mark E. Villiger, "The Rules on Interpretation: Misgivings, Misunderstandings, Miscarriage? The 'Crucible' Intended by the International Law Commission", in *The Law of Treaties Beyond the Vienna Convention*, edited by Enzo Canniyyaro, 105–122, Oxford: Oxford University Press, 2011 (Villiger, "The Rules on Interpretation").

Sylvain Vité, "Typology of Armed Conflicts in International Humanitarian Law: Legal Concepts and Actual Situations", *International Review of the Red Cross* 91, no. 873 (2009): 69–94.

Wolfgang Graf Vitzthum, "Begriff, Geschichte und Rechtsquellen des Völkerrechts", in *Völkerrecht*, edited by Wolfgang Graf Vitzthum, 6–71, Berlin: De Gruyter, 2010.

Erich Vranes. "*Lex Superior, Lex Specialis, Lex Posterior* – Zur Rechtsnatur der 'Konfliktlösungsregeln'", *Zeitschrift für ausländisches öffentliches Recht und Völkerrecht* 65 (2005): 391–405.

Kenneth Watkin, "Assessing Proportionality: Moral Complexity and Legal Rules", *Yearbook of International Humanitarian Law* 8 (2005): 3–53.

Paul Weis, "The 1967 Protocol relating to the Status of Refugees and Some Questions of the Law of Treaties", *British Yearbook of International Law* 42 (1967): 39–70.

Paul Weis, "Legal Aspects of the Convention of 21 July 1951 relating to the Status of Refugees", *British Yearbook of International Law* 30 (1953): 478–488.

David Weissbrodt and Clay Collins, "The Human Rights of Stateless Persons", *Human Rights Quarterly* 28 (2006): 245–276.

Gerhard Werle, *Völkerstrafrecht*, Tübingen: Mohr Siebeck, 2012.

Jan Willms, "Without Order, Anything Goes? The Prohibition of Forced Displacement in Non-international Armed Conflict", *International Review of the Red Cross* 91, no. 875 (2009): 547–565.

Elizabeth Wilmshurst, "Conclusions", in *International Law and the Classification of Conflicts*, edited by Elizabeth Wilmshurst, 478–502, Oxford: Oxford University Press, 2012.

Elizabeth Wilmshurst, "Conclusions", in *Perspectives on the ICRC Study on Customary International Humanitarian Law*, edited by Elizabeth Wilmshurst and Susan Breau, 401–414, Cambridge: Cambridge University Press, 2007.

Daniel Wilsher, "Non-State Actors and the Definition of a Refugee in the United Kingdom: Protection, Accountability or Culpability?", *International Journal of Refugee Law* 15, no. 1 (2003): 68–112.

Rüdiger Wolfrum and Dieter Fleck, "Enforcement of International Humanitarian Law", in *The Handbook of International Humanitarian Law*, edited by Dieter Fleck, Oxford: Oxford University Press, 2008.

Cornelis Wouters, "Protecting People fleeing Conflict and Generalized Violence. UNHCR's Perspective", paper presented at the Joint Council of Europe/UNHCR Colloquium of Regional Human Rights Courts in Interpreting and Enforcing Legal Standards for the Protection of Forcibly Displaced Persons, Strasbourg, 15–16 June 2011.

Cornelis Wolfram Wouters, *International Legal Standards for the Protection from Refoulement*, Antwerp: Intersentia, 2009.

Jason D. Wright, "'Excessive' Ambiguity: Analysing and Refining the Proportionality Standard", *International Review of the Red Cross* 94, no. 775 (2012): 819–854.

Alfred M. Zayas, "International Law and Mass Population Transfers", *Harvard International Law Journal* 16 (1975): 207–258.

Liesbeth Zegveld, *Accountability of Armed Opposition Groups in International Law*, Cambridge: Cambridge University Press, 2002.

Marjoleine Zieck, "Article 35 of the 1951 Convention/Article II of the 1967 Protocol", in *The 1951 Convention relating to the Status of Refugees. A Commentary*, edited by Andreas Zimmermann (editor), Jonas Dörschner and Felix Machts (assistant editors), 1459–1510, Oxford: Oxford University Press, 2011.

Andreas Zimmermann, "Preface", in *The 1951 Convention relating to the Status of Refugees and its 1967 Protocol*, edited by Andreas Zimmermann (editor), Jonas Dörschner and Felix Machts (assistant editors), v–vi, Oxford: Oxford University Press, 2011.

Andreas Zimmermann and Rainer Hofmann, eds., *Unity and Diversity in International Law. Proceedings of an International Symposium of the Kiel Walther Schücking Institute of International Law (November 4–7, 2004)*, Berlin: Duncker & Humblot, 2006.

Andreas Zimmermann and Claudia Mahler, "Article 1A, para. 2", in *The 1951 Convention relating to the Status of Refugees and its 1967 Protocol*, edited by Andreas Zimmermann (editor), Jonas Dörschner and Felix Machts (assistant editors), Oxford: Oxford University Press, 2011 (Zimmermann and Claudia Mahler, "Article 1A, para. 2").

Aristide R. Zolberg, Astri Suhrke and Sergio Aguayo, *Escape from Violence. Conflict and the Refugee Crisis in the Developing World*, Oxford/New York: Oxford University Press, 1989.

www.ingramcontent.com/pod-product-compliance
Ingram Content Group UK Ltd.
Pitfield, Milton Keynes, MK11 3LW, UK
UKHW051921100926
8556IPUK00021B/1312